NEW MANA

TRANSFORMATIONS OF A CLASSIC CONCEPT
IN PACIFIC LANGUAGES AND CULTURES

NEW MANA

TRANSFORMATIONS OF A CLASSIC CONCEPT IN PACIFIC LANGUAGES AND CULTURES

Edited by Matt Tomlinson
and Ty P. Kāwika Tengan

MONOGRAPHS IN
ANTHROPOLOGY SERIES

PRESS

Published by ANU Press
The Australian National University
Acton ACT 2601, Australia
Email: anupress@anu.edu.au
This title is also available online at press.anu.edu.au

National Library of Australia Cataloguing-in-Publication entry

Title: New mana : transformations of a classic concept in Pacific languages and cultures / editors: Matt Tomlinson, Ty P. Kāwika Tengan.

ISBN: 9781760460075 (paperback) 9781760460082 (ebook)

Series: Monographs in anthropology series.

Subjects: Language and culture--Pacific Area.
Languages in contact--Pacific Area.
Sociolinguistics--Pacific Area.

Other Creators/Contributors:
Tomlinson, Matt, 1970- editor.
Tengan, Ty P. Kāwika, 1975- editor.

Dewey Number: 306.442096

Cover design and layout by ANU Press.
Cover Art: *Ki'i Kupuna: Maka*, by Carl Franklin Ka'ailā'au Pao. 2013. Acrylic, graphite, and shellac on canvas, 74 inches x 56 inches.

Contents

List of Figures

List of Tables

Acknowledgements

Many people have participated in, helped with and contributed to this project in diverse ways over the years. Here we would especially like to acknowledge Aunty Agnes Shea, who provided the Welcome to Country at the 'New Mana' workshop in Canberra in September 2013, Ping-Ann Addo, Mitiana Arbon, Carolyn Brewer, Karen Brison, James Flexner, Chris Fung, Paul Geraghty, Tēvita O. Ka'ili, Ana Kitolelei, the Reverend Latu Latai, 'Okusitino Māhina, Gwendoline Malogne-Fer, Areti Metuamate, Carlos Mondragón, Nick Mortimer, Michelle O'Toole, Andrew Pawley, Malcolm Ross, Albert J. Schütz, Bradd Shore, Ross Smith, Marata Tamaira, Jack Taylor and Geoffrey White. This volume was developed as part of Matt Tomlinson's Future Fellowship project (#FT110100524) with the Australian Research Council, 'Divine Power in Indigenous Christianity: Translation, Theology, and Pacific Politics'. Funding for the 'New Mana' workshop was provided by three organisations at The Australian National University: the Research School of Asia and the Pacific and the Departments of Anthropology and Pacific Studies, the latter two in the School of Culture, History and Language. Subsidies for the publication of this book were granted by the ANU Publication Subsidy Committee, the ANU Pacific Institute Publications Subsidy, and the Department of Anthropology at the University of Hawai'i at Mānoa. We are grateful to all of these people and organisations for their generous, collective mana in bringing the book together.

Matt Tomlinson and Ty P. Kāwika Tengan
November 2015

About the Cover Art

Located within the collections storage facility of the National Museum of Scotland is a box that contains a relic of Hawaiian antiquity—an akua kāʻai or 'god stick'. The object is anthropomorphic in appearance, its facial characteristics comprising a furrowed brow, slanted hollowed-out eyes, and a mouth pulled back in a grimace of truculent defiance. In the ancestral past, this portable wood sculpture functioned as a physical manifestation of divine mana and potency—it was the dwelling place of a god. But an examination of the figure's lower torso reveals a sight that mars its otherwise commanding presence. The phallus has been crudely cut away and reduced to a mess of chaotic striations. Its mutilation articulates with a broader historical context—which began around the early nineteenth century—wherein male and female genitalia on kiʻi kūpuna (carved images of Hawaiian gods and ancestors) were summarily excised by European missionaries, traders and, in some cases, Hawaiians themselves as Christian values and beliefs gradually seeped into the bedrock of indigenous society.

Carl Franklin Kaʻailāʻau Pao, the artist whose work, *Kiʻi Kupuna: Maka,* features on the cover of this publication, argues that the emasculation of kiʻi kūpuna, like the castrated akua kāʻai in the National Museum of Scotland, was not merely limited to the physical objects but it also had an adverse effect on the collective mana of the Hawaiian people. In response to what he believes has been a 'symbolic-spiritual stripping', Pao actively seeks to restore Hawaiian mana, in part by recuperating the iconography of the ule and kohe—male and female reproductive organs, respectively—through his art.

In *Kiʻi Kupuna: Maka* (2013), Pao invokes male and female streams of procreative power through his abstract profile portrait of an ancestral carved image. The face of the kiʻi is depicted in detail with flared nostrils and, more significantly, a gaping mouth that contains the maka or centre of a flower. This is represented as a solid orange form comprising eight nodes, the largest symbolising the pistil or female sex organ of the plant and the smaller ones constituting the stamen or male sex organ. At the centre of the maka is a single sphere, the embryonic seed of the next generation (or perhaps, as Tengan writes in chapter two, 'an eye peering out'). The mouth of the kiʻi functions as a sacred, protective space, safeguarding the maka—a metaphor for the Hawaiian people—as it regenerates itself in a perpetual cycle of growth and renewal. In this work, Pao uses a visual language informed by the past and the present to envision and instantiate a new Hawaiian mana. One that is revitalised, re-sexed and restored to pono (balance).

A. Marata Tamaira

A Note on the Typesetting

In preparing this volume, the editors asked contributors to make their own decisions about whether or not to italicise 'mana' and whether or not to indicate macrons in Oceanic language terms. On italicisation, some authors have preferred not to italicise the term 'mana', indicating its non-marginality within the encompassing English-language text; others have preferred to keep the term italicised in order to highlight its distinction and focus as the subject of analysis. Some contributors, such as Besnier and Jolly in their afterword, use different typography when talking about a general concept (mana), a metalinguistic label in scholarship (*mana*), and the specific word in a specific language (*'mana'*). On macrons, contributors have followed regional conventions. For example, those writing about Hawai'i include them, whereas those writing about Fiji do not. When quoting other published authors, we retain their typography within the quote. We also retain macrons in the names of authors who designate themselves that way.

Introduction: Mana Anew

Matt Tomlinson and Ty P. Kāwika Tengan

Mana, like *culture*, is a term that once inspired anthropological theory but now lives an ambiguous half-life in scholarly discourse. The goal of this book is to refocus attention on mana for three reasons. First is the simple fact that many people in Oceania and elsewhere use the term prominently in political, religious, and artistic projects as well as everyday discourse. Although mainstream anthropological attention to mana waned at the end of the twentieth century, discourse about mana thrives in many Oceanic societies. It also circulates outside of traditional Oceanic contexts—sometimes far outside, as in New Age movements, fantasy fiction and online gaming. The second reason to focus on mana anew is that it can offer scholars fresh insights about relationships between aesthetics, ethics, and power and authority. Third, a new focus on mana has the potential to generate new forms of anthropological practice. By engaging collaboratively with Indigenous communities on this specific topic, anthropologists, Indigenous and otherwise, can actively take part in developing new understandings of mana that have practical consequences—the production of new mana, in effect. The authors of the following chapters examine mana from multiple angles that converge on a single point: the contention that thinking about mana at this historical moment is ethnographically vital and theoretically promising in new ways.

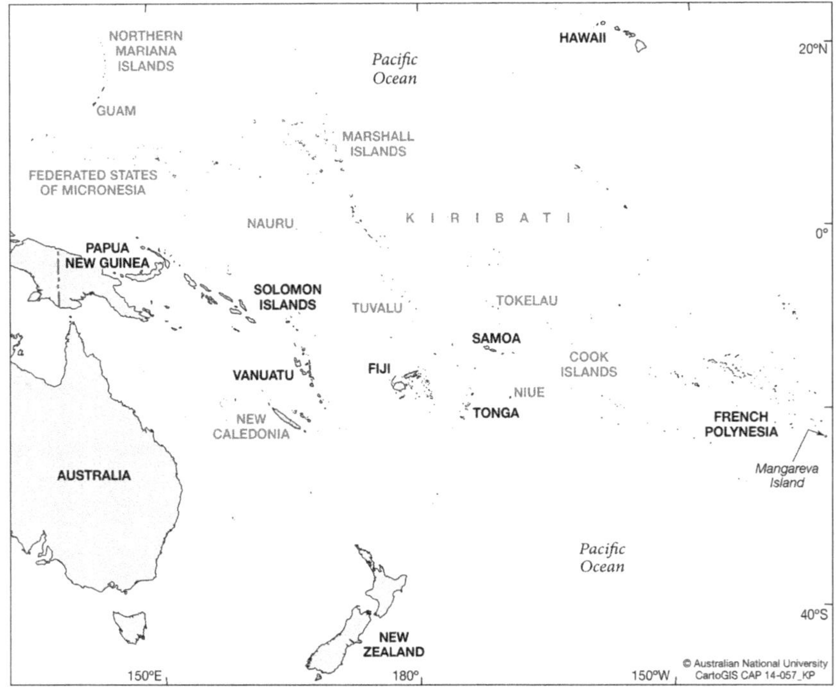

Figure 1. Map of Oceania.

Source © The Australian National University, CAP CartoGIS.

Anthropological articulations

The conventional history of western scholarship on mana begins with the Anglican missionary-anthropologist R.H. Codrington's *The Melanesians*, published in 1891. Other missionaries had paid close attention to mana decades before this, however, as they tried to understand Oceanic ideologies of human and spiritual power. For example, Lorrin Andrews published a Hawaiian-language vocabulary in 1836 that included, among its definitions of mana, 'power, might, supernatural power, divine power', 'powerful, strong', and as the verb *ho'omana*, 'to ascribe power, to worship, to render homage' (Andrews 1836: 98). John Davies' Tahitian dictionary of 1851 defined the term as 'power, might, influence', 'powerful, mighty, affluent', and 'to be in power, possess influence' (Davies 1991

[1851]: 129).[1] A dictionary of Samoan by George Pratt, from 1862, translated mana succinctly as 'supernatural power' and 'to exert supernatural power' (Pratt 1862: 146). Many more examples could be listed; our point is simply that mana was squarely in missionaries' fields of view before it gained widespread scholarly visibility, and it played a vital but complex role in Bible translations in many Oceanic languages.[2]

Codrington wrote a letter in 1877 to Max Müller in which he first defined mana in the way that would become classic in anthropology. Müller quoted Codrington's letter in his second Hibbert Lecture of 1878, and it is worth quoting the quotation in turn:

> Mr. R.H. Codrington, an experienced missionary and a thoughtful theologian, says in a letter, dated July 7, 1877, from Norfolk Island: 'The religion of the Melanesians consists, as far as belief goes, in the persuasion that there is a supernatural power about, belonging to the region of the unseen; and, as far as practice goes, in the use of means of getting this power turned to their own benefit. The notion of a Supreme Being is altogether foreign to them, or indeed of any Being occupying a very elevated place in their world.'
>
> ...
>
> And again: 'There is a belief in a force altogether distinct from physical power, which acts in all kinds of ways for good and evil, and which it is of the greatest advantage to possess or control. This is Mana. The word is common, I believe, to the whole Pacific, and people have tried very hard to describe what it is in different regions. I think I know what our people mean by it, and that meaning seems to me to cover all that I hear about it elsewhere. It is a power or influence, not physical, and in a way, supernatural; but it shows itself in physical force, or in any kind of power or excellence which a man possesses. This Mana is not fixed in anything, and can be conveyed in almost anything; but spirits, whether disembodied souls or supernatural beings, have it, and can impart it; and it essentially belongs to personal beings to originate it, though it may act through the medium of water, or a stone, or a bone. All Melanesian

1 Note the switch from 'influence' to 'affluence' in Davies' translation, which could indicate a link of mana with prosperity—or could simply be a printer's error.

2 Tregear's *Maori-Polynesian Comparative Dictionary*, published in the same year as Codrington's classic work and drawing on many previously published sources, lists definitions of mana in Māori, Samoan, Tahitian, Hawaiian, Tongan, Rarotongan, Marquesan, Mangarevan and Paumotan, with comparative references to mana in Fijian, Malagasy, Malay and Sikayana (Tregear 1891: 203).

> religion, in fact, consists in getting this Mana for one's self, or getting it used for one's benefit—all religion, that is, as far as religious practices go, prayers and sacrifices.' (Müller 1910 [1878]: 55–56)

After this lengthy quotation, Müller adds a brief summary of his own, describing mana as 'one of the early, helpless expressions of what the apprehension of the infinite would be in its incipient stages, though even the Melanesian Mana shows ample traces both of development and corruption' (Müller 1910 [1878]: 56). Thus mana, in Müller's use of Codrington, is an index pointing toward infinity: a name for a force that transcends all names and exceeds all forces. In this paradoxical position it might seem like a mystical concept, but note how Müller attempts to historicise mana by slotting it into an evolutionary progression (it belongs to the 'incipient stages' of religious understanding) while commenting on the fact that it has undergone both 'development' and 'corruption'. Codrington himself, in his famous 1891 publication, emphasised the fact that mana was not taken for granted, but subject to testing: 'the presence of it is ascertained by proof … all conspicuous success is a proof that a man has *mana*' (Codrington 1957 [1891]: 119–20).

Mana became an object of widespread scholarly interest because of this Codrington- and Müller-derived understanding of it as an elementary religious concept, people's foundational attempt to understand the limits and mechanisms of power for effective action in the world (see also Golub and Peterson, this volume). The core of Codrington's definition, still quoted often, is that mana 'is what works to effect everything which is beyond the ordinary power of men, outside the common processes of nature' (Codrington 1957 [1891]: 118–19). Seen in this way, it has strong associations with divinity, magic and charisma, and it is no wonder that nineteenth- and early twentieth-century missionaries and anthropologists focused on it so intensely.

Focusing on mana, for that era's anthropology, largely meant identifying its role in the evolution of religious thought and practice. Émile Durkheim, for example, identified mana as the 'totemic principle', the foundational concept (found under many names) through which the collective consciousness symbolises itself to itself. Describing totemism as 'the religion … of an anonymous and impersonal force', he wrote that mana was one name for this force, and thus the same elementary idea denoted by Australian Aboriginal totems, Algonquin *manitou*, Siouan *wakan*, Iroquois *orenda*, and so forth (1965 [1915]: 217, 222–223; after making these comparisons, he duly quotes Codrington). Durkheim's nephew, Marcel Mauss, credited Codrington's work as 'admirably observed and described', then followed his uncle in comparing mana with analogous terms from different languages, and defined mana in part as 'power, *par excellence*, the genuine effectiveness of things which corroborates their practical actions without annihilating them ... It is the spirit which contains all efficacy and all life' (Mauss 1972 [1950]: 109, 111). R.R. Marett paired mana with *tabu* (taboo), proposing that the former was 'the positive aspect of the supernatural' and the latter was the negative one: 'negatively, the supernatural is *tabu*, not to be lightly approached, because, positively, it is *mana*, instinct with a power above the ordinary' (Marett 1929: 99). Taken together as 'the *tabu-mana* formula', Marett suggested, they offered a better minimal definition of religion than E.B. Tylor's 'animism' did.[3]

A critical backlash against these universalist and evolutionary tendencies began to develop before long. Ian Hogbin compared Guadalcanal, Malaita and Ontong Java (in the Solomon Islands) and Wogeo (in Papua New Guinea) and concluded that mana was an Indigenous concept in the first two places but not in the latter two; thus mana cannot be considered a universal concept, and any attempt to theorise 'primitive' religion in terms of mana is inherently flawed (Hogbin 1936: 274; see also Eliade 1958: 21; Smith 2002). Raymond Firth noted that in the hands of scholars such as Durkheim, Mauss, and Marett, 'the word *mana* becomes something of a technical term describing a specialized abstraction of the theoretical anthropologist and, as such, may have little in common with the same term as used in native phraseology' (Firth 1940: 487; see also Evans-Pritchard 1965). In pointed contrast, Firth went on to provide a densely detailed description of what mana and the partly synonymous *manu* meant in Tikopia.[4]

3 When Sigmund Freud drew on the term 'taboo' to theorise the repression of desire, he adopted the understanding of mana as a kind of contagious force, or '[a] peculiar power inherent in persons and ghosts, which can be transmitted from them to inanimate objects, [and] is regarded as a source of the taboo' (Freud 1918 [1913]: 29). He also quoted Northcote W. Thomas' article on taboo from the eleventh edition of the *Encyclopædia Britannica*, which characterised *mana* as electricity which charges people and things: 'They are the seat of tremendous power which is transmissible by contact, and may be liberated with destructive effect if the organisms which provoke its discharge are too weak to resist it' (quoted in Freud 1918 [1913]: 29).

4 R.R. Marett, however, had explicitly dismissed this kind of criticism decades earlier, writing that '[w]hen the science of Comparative Religion employs a native expression such as *mana*, or *tabu*, as a general category, it is obliged to disregard to some extent its original or local meaning' (Marett 1929: 99).

It was Claude Lévi-Strauss who pushed the anthropological critique furthest when he argued that mana serves as a 'floating signifier', a sign that arises from a gap between knowledge and symbolism. Concepts like mana, he wrote, are 'somewhat like algebraic symbols, [and] occur to represent an indeterminate value of signification, in itself devoid of meaning and thus susceptible of receiving any meaning at all' (1987 [1950]: 55, 63). Agreeing with Mauss that mana is a universal type, but developing the analysis according to his own structuralist model, Lévi-Strauss wrote that 'conceptions of the *mana* type' are likely 'a universal and permanent form of thought':

> I see in *mana*, *wakan*, *orenda*, and other notions of the same type, the conscious expression of a *semantic function*, whose role is to enable symbolic thinking to operate despite the contradiction inherent in it. That explains the apparently insoluble antinomies attaching to the notion of mana, which struck ethnographers so forcibly, and on which Mauss shed light: force and action; quality and state; substantive, adjective and verb all at once; abstract and concrete; omnipresent and localised. And, indeed, *mana* is all those things together; but is that not precisely because it is none of those things, but a simple form, or to be more accurate, a symbol in its pure state, therefore liable to take on any symbolic content whatever? (Lévi-Strauss 1987 [1950]: 53, 63–64; emphasis in original)

Mana means diverse things, according to Lévi-Strauss, because it floats in a sea of semiotic overload. He slyly placed mana alongside the divine at the limits of signification, writing that mana's mediation of knowledge and symbolism always involves 'a non-fit and overspill which divine understanding alone can soak up' (Lévi-Strauss 1987 [1950]: 62). In this way, mana keeps structures coherent partly by exceeding them.[5]

5 See also James Faubion (2010: 93), who notes that floating signifiers are 'especially effective carrier[s] of conceptions of the transcendent and the absolute' but also, in their proliferation of possibilities—their 'omnipotentiality', as Faubion puts it—they are 'also auratic, atmospheric, ineffable, beyond articulation. The floating signifier is thus made for the mystic as the semiotic abyss that is also a plenitude and thus a topos of the excess that can only be experienced, never pinned down or spelled out.' A resonant instance of this gesturing toward ineffability and transcendence comes in the work of the Samoan theologian Ama'amalele Tofaeono, who writes that *mana* 'cannot be clearly explained in words, but must be experienced' (Tofaeono 2000: 169; see also Oroi, this volume).

Christopher Bracken presents the Lévi-Strauss moment as a definitive ending: 'From 1891, when Codrington started the craze, until 1950, when Lévi-Strauss brought it abruptly to a close, the discourse of anthropology could not stop speaking of mana' (Bracken 2007: 134). Indeed, since Lévi-Strauss' critique, it is difficult to think of mana without thinking of anthropological projects that assign meaning presumptively rather than trace articulations carefully. And yet, *pace* Bracken, mainstream anthropology (crazed or otherwise) continued to attend to mana in the late twentieth century, although not with the same field-defining prominence as before. Three notable examples are found in the work of Roger Keesing, Valerio Valeri, and Bradd Shore.

Keesing decried Codrington's influence on studies of mana and followed Firth in criticising scholars who turned mana into a thing onto which they could project their own metaphysical ideas. He tried to identify shared characteristics of mana across Oceania, and wrote that the term 'in Oceanic languages [is] canonically a stative verb, not a noun: things and human enterprises and efforts *are* mana' (Keesing 1984: 138; see also Keesing 1985, 1988, 1992). Valeri, examining the use of mana in nineteenth-century Hawaiian texts, noted that the term does not appear especially often but that the concept of mana was evidently central to traditional religious practices. It was based on 'fellowship', or reciprocal relations in which gods, the source of mana, are made mana by human worship (Valeri 1985: 103; see also Valeri 1990). Shore (1989) has offered the most recent comprehensive overview of mana, focusing on Polynesia, and concludes that it is always associated with 'generative potency' and vitality which comes from the gods. He also argues persuasively for a distinction between western Polynesian conceptions of power keyed to sacred but 'desexualized' relationships between brothers and sisters and eastern Polynesian conceptions of power keyed to sexual relationships between husbands and wives.[6]

6 Other notable recent studies situate mana in relation to headhunting and the nurturance of blessing-bestowing ancestors (Dureau 2000) and ecology, seasonality and production (Mondragón 2004). Outside of anthropology, however, social-evolutionary presuppositions live on in the work of scholars who treat mana as an ur-power, a label for spiritual efficacy that is not only (ab)original but is also prototypical. For example, in her *History of God*, Karen Armstrong initially identifies mana as a Pacific Islands concept, but then goes on to apply the term to the religious understandings of the Babylonians, Israelites and 'the ancient Middle East' in general (see Armstrong 1993: 4, 7, 13, 15).

Indigenous scholars, artists, and activists have expressed and taken up concepts of mana in ways that sometimes resonate with classical anthropological representations and sometimes do not. Meanwhile, mana has become a feature of various forms of deterritorialised global culture including the New Age movement and the virtual worlds of gaming. We now turn to new uses of mana in order to ground ourselves ethnographically as we ask: what is going on with mana right now?

Now in effect

One of the main reasons to refocus on mana, as mentioned above, is its prominence outside of academic anthropology. In Oceania, discourse about mana has flourished in political, religious and artistic fields, with especially strong contributions from activists, theologians, poets and novelists.

In places like Aotearoa New Zealand and Hawai'i, connections between mana and political power are frequently made explicit. Indeed, several scholars have characterised the acquisition of mana as historically the major aim of Māori politics (e.g. Bowden 1979; Parsonson 1981; Salmond 1975; see also Lian 1987). The Māori Declaration of Independence, from 1835, invoked both mana and the neologism *Kingitanga* (from 'king') in referring to 'sovereign power and authority', prompting Māori author Sir Mason Durie to write that 'Mana has both worldly and ethereal meanings, but ... as used in the Declaration of Independence it spells out authority and control' (Durie 1998: 2, 247, 248). Critics of the translation of the Treaty of Waitangi from 1840 have noted that the neologism *kawanatanga* was used in translating 'sovereignty', whereas 'had the word *mana* been used, then the purpose of the treaty as an instrument ceding sovereignty would have been absolutely clear' (Walker 1984: 268). In the past few decades, several political parties have given themselves names that draw on mana as an emblem, including Mana Motuhake (translated as 'separate sovereignty' by Walker 1984: 280) in the late 1970s, the evanescent Mana Wahine Te Ira Tangata in the late 1990s, and the Mana Party, created by Hone Harawira in April 2011 (see, respectively, Walker 1984: 278–80; Catt 2000; *New Zealand Herald* 2011). Beyond political parties, the terms *mana motuhake* and *mana wahine* are in wider circulation as labels for movements and approaches focused on Māori interests (see e.g. Pihama 2001; Smith 1992).

Figure 2. March of MANA (Movement for Aloha No ka 'Āina), Honolulu, January 2013.

Source: Photograph by Kai Markell, used with permission.

Valeri, writing of the eighteenth-century Hawaiian chiefly class, described 'god-given mana' as 'the true source of legitimacy' in claiming rank (1990: 168). Lilikalā Kame'eleihiwa (1992: 49) characterised Kauikeaouli Kamehameha III, who authored the Hawaiian Kingdom's first set of modern laws beginning in 1839, as a king 'in a constant ... search of the *mana* that protects and empowers'. Contemporary Kanaka 'Ōiwi (Indigenous Hawaiians) continue to articulate mana with sovereignty projects and aspirations in numerous ways (Trask 1999: 91–92; Tengan 2008: 158–59). Efforts to reclaim individual and collective mana, believed to reside in bones (*iwi*), have been mapped onto struggles to protect burial sites from developments and to repatriate Native Hawaiian ancestral remains from museums over the past 25 years; these experiences have also, in part, led to the reclaiming of the term Kanaka 'Ōiwi (literally 'People of the Bone') as an identity marker (Ayau and Tengan 2002: 177–79). Since 2007–08, the organisation Movement for Aloha No ka ʻĀina (MANA) has been advocating a platform of independence and social justice that includes the protection of burials 'in hopes to increase the reciprocal flow of mana within relationships spiritual and physical' (MANA 2013). At the same time, the Office of Hawaiian Affairs (OHA), a state agency established in 1978 to administer funds and programs for Native Hawaiians, has recently unveiled as their new slogan 'Mana is our Legacy' (Crabbe 2013). In short, mana is used as an emblem, a defining element which activists and officials use to both represent and generate a sense of political effectiveness.

In modern Oceania, mana is often linked to Christianity. The historian Malama Meleisea, observing how Christianity 'transformed the nature of chiefly authority' in Samoa, writes that missionaries and Samoan church leaders who replaced traditional priests were characterised as bearers of a new kind of mana: 'Their *mana* was God's "grace", which is the contemporary meaning of *mana* in the Samoan language' (Meleisea 1987: 13; see also Hardin this volume; Shore 1982: 248). Theologians have drawn upon mana to articulate their visions of modern Oceania and the relationship between divine power and human agency in Indigenous Christianity.[7] For example, the Methodist theologian Ilaitia Tuwere, writing from an explicitly Fijian cultural context, argues that mana 'bridges the gulf' between land and people (called the *vanua*) and the church (Tuwere 2002: 136). This makes it central to Indigenous Fijian social relations, uniting markedly political and religious realms of authority, especially the chiefly system and the Methodist Church. But Tuwere, with admirable scholarly caution, writes that 'The concept of *mana* poses an immediate problem for a sustained theological reflection because of its ambiguity' (2002: 135).

7 Keesing, curiously, had invoked theology to explain why mana is often characterised as a substance in eastern Polynesia—the kind of characterisation he accused anthropologists of making so recklessly elsewhere. Whereas anthropologists had turned mana into a substance because of 'their own folk metaphors of power and the theories of nineteenth-century physics', according to Keesing, eastern Polynesians did so because their societies developed aristocracies who depended on 'a class of theologians' to validate and celebrate their sacred power (Keesing 1984: 148, 152; emphasis removed). Regarding Christian influence on conceptions of mana, however, Keesing had no interest. Indeed, he analytically separated (real, true, pre-Christian) mana from whatever modern Oceanic Christians might say about it, writing that 'despite the wholesale destruction of Oceania religions by Christianity, we have … ethnographic evidence on mana' (Keesing 1984: 138). This kind of analysis misses the point that Oceanic Christianities incorporated and transformed other religious beliefs and practices and vice versa.

Rather than fight this ambiguity by offering a new definition, he uses this ambiguity as a theological tool, writing that mana 'does not exhaust the nature of God but … is the only meaningful way of describing God and what his power may mean in the Fijian context' (165).

Mana has also received vigorous attention in the arts. At the bare level of titles, several periodicals have taken *Mana* as their name, including a literary journal published in Suva, Fiji, beginning in the mid-1970s; a multicultural and multilingual newspaper in Auckland in the late 1970s; and two glossy popular magazines, one Māori-oriented and one Hawaiian-oriented.[8] For that matter, *Mana* has also been the title of a historical novel (Jackson 1969), an illustrated inspirational booklet (Zambucka 1974), a Hawaiian slack-key guitar album (Pahinui 1997), and the evening show performed for several years at the Polynesian Cultural Center (PCC), the Mormon theme park in La'ie, Hawai'i.[9] But beyond mere titles, mana has been the theme and subject matter for novels and poems. A key theme of Alan Duff's controversial *Once Were Warriors* is the loss and recovery of mana, with the brawling, alcoholic Jake Heke able to demonstrate his strength only by annihilating himself and his family while his wife, Beth, turns to Māori tradition for new hope. In a key passage, Beth imagines herself addressing a large audience, lamenting:

> And we used to war all the time, us Maoris. Against each other. True. It's true, honest to God, audience. Hated each other. Tribe against tribe. Savages. We were savages. But warriors, eh. It's very important to remember that. Warriors. Because, you see, it was what we lost when you, the white audience out there, defeated us. Conquered us. Took our land, our *mana*, left us with nothing. But the warriors thing got handed down, see. Well, sort of handed down; in a mixed-up sense it did. (Duff 1990: 41)

8 The Suva-based journal, published by the Creative Arts Society, began as *The Mana Annual of Creative Writing* in 1973. Its second volume came out in 1974, but its third and final volume did not appear until 1977. By then, the Society had already published a more academic journal called *Mana Review* in 1976, which became *Mana: A South Pacific Journal of Language and Literature* from 1977 onward.

9 The current show at the PCC is titled 'Hā: Breath of Life', and its main character is named Mana (Polynesian Cultural Center 2013).

Beth's lament, in the novel, becomes a defiantly triumphant speech in the film version, where she tells Jake, 'Our people once were warriors. But not like you, Jake. They were people with mana, pride. People with spirit. If my spirit can survive living with you for eighteen years, then I can survive anything' (Tamahori 1994).

Figure 3. *MANA: The Hawaiian Magazine*, January/February 2013.

Source: Courtesy *MANA Magazine*.

Figure 4. *Mana: The Māori Magazine for Everyone*, Issue 108, October/November 2012.

Source: *Mana: The Māori Magazine for Everyone*.

The double movement of mana's loss and recuperation, seen so starkly in *Once Were Warriors*, was characterised by Albert Wendt as integral to emerging creative arts in Oceania. Wendt wrote that colonialism had destroyed sources of mana (which he equated with 'artistic and imaginative energy') but also created the possibility of a new kind of artist, free to explore his or her 'own mana unfettered by accepted conventions' (1980a: xiv, xvi; see also Pao 2014). Mana is said to be manifest in diverse types of performance, such as music, dance and oratory. The revitalisation of the Hawaiian language has been simultaneously framed as a revival of the mana of words, which find their fullest expression and effectiveness when spoken, sung or chanted. In the case of the Hawaiian/R&B/Reggae artist Mana Kaleilani Caceres, the combination of musical genres and the English and Hawaiian languages in his widely popular song allowed him to assert that the US 'couldn't take the mana' of the Hawaiian people (Caceres 2001). The 2010 Hawai'i International Film Festival's 'Audience Favorite' was *Mana i ka Leo: Power of the Voice* (Carrillo et al. 2010), a 30-minute documentary on Hawaiian chant (*oli*) that successfully aimed to immerse the audience in an experience of power, beauty and emotion of the art. In her poem 'He Mana Kō ka Leo', national slam poet champion Jamaica Osorio reflects on the multiple ways that this generation of artists has given voice to the Hawaiian Nation and 'made mana a tangible performance to be called upon' (2013).

In the newest of mana's new iterations, the term has become detached from Oceania in deterritorialised global culture, as described by the concluding chapters in this volume: Rachel Morgain's on New Age mana and Alex Golub's and Jon Peterson's on mana in fantasy fiction and games such as *World of Warcraft*. In such locations, mana's potential universalism is pushed to its furthest limit as a thing detachable from place, not dependent on ethnic, political or religious identity, and able to be gathered up and spent in new ways.

The New Age case is an especially vivid example of mana's transformation in appropriation. New Age beliefs about mana were developed prominently in the work of Max Freedom Long, a mid-twentieth-century American author who claimed to have rediscovered ancient Hawaiian religious principles. Long claimed that the former curator of Honolulu's Bishop Museum, William Tufts Brigham, had spent decades collecting information from Hawaiian experts (*kāhuna*). Brigham then supposedly passed this knowledge onto Long: 'Dr. Brigham, knowing that the end of his life was approaching, and having found a young man with a consuming interest and desire to dig deeper into the mystery, made ready to lay his robe on my shoulders. He trained me in the proper approach, and gave me all the information he had gathered over the long period' (Long 1953: 7). Long established a group called Huna Research (the Hawaiian term *huna* connotes secrecy, and Long used it as a label for his own metaphysical system) and spent the next several decades publishing his 'discoveries' in books and bulletins. A posthumously published collection of some of his short writings was devoted specifically to mana (Long 1981).[10]

In Long's pseudo-Hawaiian framework, mana is a universal life force and can be used to heal. It can also be used for more mundane tasks like sharpening razor blades. One of Long's followers, Serge King, claimed to have invented several mana-generating and channelling machines, including the Manaplate—'a sheet of metal between two sheets of plastic'—and the Manabox—'a small, copper-lined plastic box 3" x 3" x ½" [7.62cm x 7.62cm x 1.27cm] … A razor blade can be sharpened by merely aligning it properly and laying it on top of the cover. Twenty-five to fifty shaves with a [Gillette] Blue Blade are common, and over one hundred shaves have been reported' (King 1978: 59, 60). King referred to the well-known works of Wilhelm Reich and Franz Mesmer in justifying his claims about harnessing vital energy, and he experimented with razor blades (among other things) because other advocates of psychic power had already argued that placing them inside pyramid-shaped containers would keep them sharp.

New Age understandings of mana veer sharply from traditional Oceanic ones, to say the least. To many readers, King's Manaplates and Manaboxes will seem like comical hybrids of spirit and science, distant cousins of Victorian parlour photographs showing ghostly faces hovering above the faces of the living. But to dismiss New Age understandings as false and fanciful would be to miss the key point that uptake creates its own meanings in new contexts. Long's and King's mana is not, ultimately, the mana described by Hawaiian *kāhuna*, and it is vulnerable to the charge of being a form of 'disrespect, exploitation, and cultural distortion and appropriation', as Lisa Kahaleole Hall (2005: 412) characterises Huna work. But this take on mana has now been around for decades, both shaping and fitting into a global philosophy of the power of positive thinking and the cultivation of individual spirituality. And this global philosophy continues to manifest itself in unexpected places: divinatory 'mana cards', for example, or the ingredients list for a plastic container of shredded pork.

10 The author of a recent article on the relationship between William Tufts Brigham and Max Freedom Long argues that the men could not have known each other well and might not even have met (Chai 2011).

Figure 5. 'Mana card' from Becker (1998).

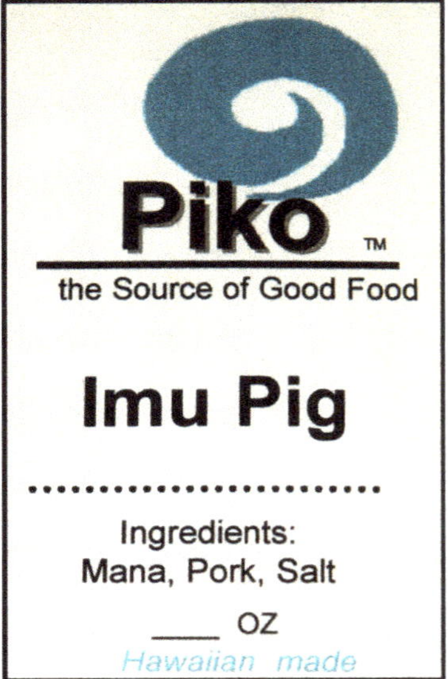

Figure 6. Label on a container of shredded roast pork, purchased in Honolulu, mid-2000s.

In considering treatments of mana in such contexts as New Age discourse and fantasy games, scholars must be careful not to critique them by homogenising Oceanic mana in order to use it as a foil. If a single fact was well established by the mid and late twentieth-century critiques in anthropology, it is that mana has diverse meanings across the cultural, historical, religious, and political contexts spanning the Pacific. Understanding the divergent uses of the term 'mana' does not require endorsing any of them; rather, it demands close attention to the chains of transmission and transformation that have shaped and reshaped what mana signifies and the values it both absorbs and manifests, including silence as well as speech, loss as well as gain, novelty as well as tradition.

Aesthetics and ethics

In this volume, we argue that the analysis of mana, which is typically framed in terms of power, authority and efficacy, can benefit by breaking this frame to ask first about aesthetic and ethical dimensions, letting questions of power emerge as they are relevant. This is a tactic on our part, a strategy for developing new insights. We acknowledge that in order to understand the pragmatics of mana, one needs to understand ideologies of power. But if one begins with power, it is too easy to relegate aesthetics and ethics to secondary importance, whereas the latter may decisively shape the possible expressions of the former.

In writing about the aesthetics of mana, we are referring to the ways in which mana is understood in terms like repetition, balance and complementarity. For example, writing of Hawai'i, Herman Pi'ikea Clark explains that 'the repetitive features carved onto a temple idol … contribut[ed] to the aesthetic quality and appearance [and] also served as a mnemonic feature to aid in the recall of information to those who had the capacity to read its design' (2006: 12). As these images were among the most important vessels for channelling the mana of the divine into the world of the living, such patterns established and maintained the genealogical linkages between gods and people. Adrienne Kaeppler makes a similar argument for tattoo designs when she writes that the 'primarily linear … rows of triangles, chevrons, and crescents/arches', the last of which are also found on drums, 'may be symbolic of human beings joined together as lineal and collateral descendants who trace their relationships back to the gods' (1988: 168). Chants, which Valeri calls 'total works of art', similarly use repetition to symbolise and effect relations of mana (Valeri 1990: 177). As Stokes (1930: 12–13) puts it:

> The mere recitation of names forms a chain along which the accumulated *mana* of ages untold may be moved into the recipient shell … The chain then becomes a verbal tube, the leaks of which are closed by the repetition of the innumerable name variations. (Cited in Valeri 1990: 178)

Significantly, contemporary Kanaka 'Ōiwi artists and performers continue to draw on these ancestral patterns in projects meant to channel mana to future generations (Clark 2011; Goodyear-Ka'ōpua 2013; see also Tamaira 2015).

Another way to analyse mana through aesthetics is to take a linguistic approach focused on poetics in performance. Such an approach can draw on, among other resources, Roman Jakobson's description of the 'poetic function' of language. Jakobson argued that language has several basic functions, each keyed to an element in a speech event. One of these is the poetic function, manifest in a 'focus on the message for its own sake' (Jakobson 1960: 356). With the poetic function, a message's meaning or force depends less on speakers' intentions and the context of speaking than on features inherent to the message itself. Jakobson argued that the standard structural-linguistic model of meaning as the intersection of selection and combination is skewed for poetic purposes. In structural linguistics, following Ferdinand de Saussure, a phrase such as 'mana deserves attention' is meaningful because of (1) the selection of these particular terms from a universe of alternatives (one could replace 'mana' in this phrase with *tabu*, or culture, or power, or discourse, etc.), and (2) the grammatical combination of selected terms. Jakobson argues that the poetic function, in contrast, 'projects the principle of equivalence from the axis of selection into the axis of combination' (Jakobson 1960: 358). That is, the axis of equivalence is mapped onto the syntagmatic connections between terms. In Tomlinson's (2006) argument about mana in Fijian ceremonial language, mana is analysed in this way as it serves poetically to make a ritual effective by drawing out relationships of equivalence into formulaic ritual sequences.

We hasten to add that we do not see structural linguistics as the only, or even the most useful, way to rethink mana—and not only because it was the matrix within which Lévi-Strauss developed his argument about mana being 'liable to take on any symbolic content whatever'. The main problem is that the explanatory power of structural linguistics has been surpassed by that of Peircean semiotics; it is more useful to examine mana's iconic, indexical and symbolic significance than to get caught up in contrasts between selection and combination, or, for that matter, to place too much emphasis on whether mana is a verb or a noun, *à la* Keesing. In referring to Jakobson, we simply mean to emphasise that it is possible to analyse mana primarily in terms of poetics just as it can be analysed fruitfully in terms of aesthetics more broadly.

Ethics is another key area in which anthropologists can develop and sharpen analyses of mana. In a recent volume on ethics in everyday speech and action, Michael Lambek writes that attention to the ethical can help anthropologists avoid falling into the trap of reducing everything to the self-interested pursuit of power. 'Ethnographers commonly find that the people they encounter are trying to do what they consider right or good, are being evaluated according to criteria of what is right and good, or are in some debate about what constitutes the human good', he writes. 'Yet anthropological theory tends to overlook all this in favor of analyses that emphasize structure, power, and interest' (2010a: 1). Although mana is typically associated in the scholarly literature with power—and power, aesthetics and ethics are not neatly separated domains—we want to ground the analysis of mana in aesthetics and ethics so that power emerges as an object of investigation when relevant but does not shape investigations through presupposition.

Classic scholarship on mana did in fact pose the question of whether mana was ethically marked. In identifying mana as the totemic principle, Durkheim linked it firmly with moral responsibility: 'while the totemic principle is a totemic force, it is also a moral power' (Durkheim 1965 [1915]: 219). Indeed, for Durkheim, the morality of mana is grounded in a way that power and effectiveness are not. Members of a clan, including the totemic figure itself, 'are morally bound to one another; they have definite duties of assistance, vendetta, etc., towards each other; and it is these duties which constitute kinship', whereas in terms of power, mana 'is located nowhere definitely and it is everywhere' (Durkheim 1965 [1915]: 219, 223). Other scholars, including Codrington, explicitly denied any moral or ethical dimension to mana (see Kolshus, this volume). Marett, for example, wrote that mana and taboo are existential concepts with an 'absence of moral significance. The mystic potentiality is alike for good and evil' (Marett 1929: 113).[11]

Without endorsing an encompassing Durkheimian model of collective consciousness, we suggest that Durkheim's insight about the fundamentally social nature of mana—a point emphasised by later scholars such as Valeri (1985, 1990) and Wende Elizabeth Marshall (2011)—makes more sense of much Oceanic mana than Codrington's and Marett's models of mana as amoral power. As a scholar of Māori philosophy puts it, 'an important element of *mana* is the ethical element. In many contexts, when the word *mana* is used there is not only a claim about what is going on in the world but also some value

11 See also Aletta Biersack (1996: 90–91) for an analysis of mana as knowledge for the Paiela of Papua New Guinea, with the observation that purposeful action, good and bad alike, conjoins bodies with mana-in-minds.

judgment' (Patterson 2000: 232). There is a value judgment because mana is not a disembodied term but an ethical mediation. Whether it is a mediation between the divine and the human, the demonic and the human, good humans and bad ones, or signs and referents is a dynamic that many Oceanic citizens continue to explore in belief and practice.[12]

Mary Kawena Pukui, E.W. Haertig and Catherine A. Lee (1972: 152) note that Kanaka 'Ōiwi believe that '*mana*, abused or misused, could be diminished or even lost'. Thus the proper management of mana entails *kuleana*—responsibilities and rights defined in relation to others. Goodyear-Ka'ōpua characterises the anticolonial 'cultural/political work' of the Native Hawaiian Charter School Hālau Kū Māna as a process of *ho'omana* ('creating mana'), which she suggests 'communicate[s] the idea of practices that open the mutual flow of mana within a relationship—cultural practices that work toward pono (justice/balance)' (2013: 207–08). Speaking with students who walked barefoot and chanted in protest marches in the mid-2000s, she relates how they 'talked about the importance of being able to see, hear, and feel the mana of a living nation' and arrived at a 'sense of kuleana to add their leo [voice] and mana to that collective Hawaiian voice' (2013: 209). Goodyear-Ka'ōpua's *kuleana* as an educator and activist extends to her scholarship, which she uses to further *ho'omana* the voices and the people with whom she has worked collaboratively.[13]

Following the lead of Indigenous and other scholars whose research emerges from and contributes to processes of *ho'omana*, we suggest that mana offers our field a new way of imagining the aesthetics, ethics and power of anthropological analysis and practice. A reorientation might begin with a genealogical exploration of mana's transformations in particular locales. Understanding the conditions for the generation of mana would suggest avenues for investigating and theorising the potency of differently mediated relations. One crucial set of anthropological relations to remediate would be with the Indigenous communities whose day-to-day struggles over mana necessitate a stance of engaged collaboration. The implications for this range from

12 For a critique of the view that *mana* can be equated with truth, put forth most notably by A.M. Hocart (1914) and Marshall Sahlins (1985), see Matt Tomlinson (2009).

13 Goodyear-Ka'ōpua is a co-founder of both the Hālau Kū Māna Charter School and the MANA (Movement for Aloha No ka 'Āina) political organisation.

research design to dissemination. The first collaborative publication of Indigenous anthropologists in Oceania, which came from a set of redefined meeting spaces, was explicit on this: 'The most important goal of our sessions and this collection has been the making and maintaining of relationships that create the context for sharing *aloha* (affection and empathy) and producing mana, a spiritual power and potency that has marked our interactions' (Tengan, Ka'ili and Fonotī 2010: 161). So too might this volume, and the dialogues it is meant to engender, find mana anew.

Plan of the book

The volume begins with Noenoe K. Silva's chapter on transformations in the use of 'mana' as a term in Hawaiian political discourse. Drawing on nineteenth-century Hawaiian-language sources, Silva shows that mana was mentioned in early newspapers for purposes of Christian evangelism: it denoted God's power manifest in performative speech. The Hawaiian kingdom's first Constitution (1840) did not use the term 'mana', but instead used 'ōlelo' (meaning 'speech, language, word, statement, as well as to say, to tell, etc.') in discussing governmental power(s). However, the Constitution of 1852 did employ mana, bringing together its meaning as power/authority and another meaning, 'branch' (here, for branches of government). 'Hawaiian speakers, readers, and listeners', Silva argues, 'would … expect such language play and ambiguity'. Next, she examines the writings of the historian Samuel Mānaiakalani Kamakau on the Hawaiian ali'i (rulers), including his analysis of the mana of Kamehameha I and the famous Law of the Splintered Paddle. Silva observes how 'Kamehameha's pronouncement of the law, or his performance of it, constitutes his mana'. She concludes her chapter by turning to the situation of contemporary Kanaka Hawai'i/Kanaka 'Ōiwi (Native Hawaiians), urging that 'mana should be revived as a keyword' for the collective good.

In the following chapter, Ty P. Kāwika Tengan's examination of 'the mana of Kū' remains in Hawai'i and moves the focus to a museum exhibition. The event, held at the Bishop Museum in 2010, reunited three carved figures of Kū for the first time in almost 200 years. (One of the figures is permanently at the Bishop, but the others are at the Peabody Essex Museum in Salem and the British Museum.) Kū is the short-form name of the Hawaiian god who embodies masculine generative power and is often referred to (reductively, Tengan points out) as 'the god of war'. Tengan worked with the museum as a consultant and scholar, and thus had direct experience of how people thought and talked about the mana of Kū on this historic occasion. Discussing the exhibition, and people's experiences of seeing the three figures reunited, he observes how ethical and aesthetic criteria informed people's expectations of the potential for Kū's masculine power to be made manifest. Ethically speaking, was it safe to bring the three figures together? After all, the project director, Noelle Kahanu, observed that some older Hawaiians were anxious about 'the mana … that might be *re*-animated'. A different perspective was offered by Keone Nunes, a tattoo and hula master, who described the mana as 'very welcoming … very heartfelt'. In terms of aesthetics, modern-day Hawaiians worked 'to "read" the designs that were unfamiliar to many', realising that patterns and motifs were not just decorative but spiritually potent and practically useful. Tengan writes that the creative work of attempting to understand the mana of Kū aesthetically can be 'viewed as an opportunity for reconnection and recreation of culture and mana', and he proposes that close engagement of the sort seen at the exhibition can, in the future, foster more productive and trusting ties between Indigenous communities, museums and anthropologists.

Following Tengan's contribution, Andy Mills turns to pre-Christian Tonga to examine mana's relationship to *tapu* (tabu) and chiefliness. Mills develops his argument by focusing on what he calls the '*manava* system', a complex of bodily relationships based on processes of intake (such as inhaling, drinking, eating and insemination) and outflow (such as exhaling, eliminating, menstruating and giving birth). Although mana and *manava* are not related linguistically, Mills describes how they seem to intersect conceptually because 'the performative qualities of mana and chiefliness were also those of great *manava*'. He examines pre-Christian practices related to different kinds of tabu, which he categorises as 'episodic' (a tabu state, eventually fatal, caused by transgression), 'relational' (an intrinsically tabu state, such as a commoner's relationship to a chief), and 'regulatory' (the restriction of activities or the consumption of particular foods). Mills presents historical accounts of ritual practices such as genital bloodletting, tattooing and mass ceremonial defecation on the Tu'i Tonga's tomb as material enactments of metaphysical transformations, part of a religious system in which articulations of divinity, society and the body ultimately depended on mana's articulation with tabu in the hierarchy of chiefliness.

Next, Katerina Martina Teaiwa reflects on the possibilities of generating new mana in diaspora, focusing on the situation of Pacific Islanders living in Australia. She observes that those Islanders who achieve social prominence in Australia often do so either as athletes or popular artists, setting up a dynamic in which they may come to be seen as responsible for their communities' collective mana. This creates significant pressure, but Teaiwa notes that there are also significant opportunities: 'When Pacific players don't just play as brown bodies, when they draw media attention to their Pacific heritage and the centrality of "family, faith and culture" … the effect can be powerful.' She describes her experiences working with the National Rugby League's Education and Welfare Office as well as its Pacific Council, contributing to projects such as the exhibitions, performances and displays at the celebrated 'Body Pacifica' event in western Sydney in 2010 and a leadership camp meant to educate professional rugby players more deeply about their heritage.

The following three chapters explore the history of anthropological scholarship on mana. Alan Rumsey begins his contribution by discussing work on mana from Codrington to Firth and Keesing, and then critiques a recent argument by the linguist Juliette Blevins in which she attempts to trace the term 'mana' back to Proto Malayo-Polynesian as well as to locate forms of it in non-Austronesian languages within New Guinea. Next, Rumsey turns to his fieldsite in the Western Highlands of Papua New Guinea and describes how the Tok Pisin loanword *pawa* (power) is used in ways similar to Firth's and Keesing's portrayals of mana. He concludes his chapter with a useful comparison of methods of comparison ('a meta-level comparison'), focusing on the work of Raymond Williams and Marilyn Strathern. Rumsey observes that this volume's attention to new mana is close to Williams' 'key words' treatment, and he urges readers to approach 'the comparative exercise … as one that takes place within a single intercultural field within which terms and multiple forms of understanding circulate and interact with each other'.

Thorgeir Kolshus directly addresses Codrington's legacy and argues that, despite Keesing's criticism of his influence, Codrington was well-informed and accurate in his observations and descriptions of mana gleaned from his two years' experience on Mota Island in northern Vanuatu. Kolshus recognises Codrington's model of mana in present-day Motese discourse and practice, including its lack of intrinsic moral evaluation. He adds a crucial historical dimension by noting that Motese concepts of mana are shaped by Polynesian influences and have, in turn, affected much of Melanesia due to Motese serving as the *lingua franca* of the Melanesian Mission. Mana, as Kolshus shows, is 'on the move', not only within Melanesia and Oceania more widely but also across church denominations in present-day Mota: when the Assemblies of God arrived on the island around a decade earlier, he observes, they did not speak of mana; but now, likely influenced by the Anglicans and more general understandings of power's operation, they speak of mana in reference to the Holy Spirit. Kolshus concludes that mana 'bridges central Melanesian notions of agency and efficacy—not as a substitute for pre-Christian versions, but rather as an extension of the old principles, introducing a common cosmological theme that provides a comparative axis through an otherwise culturally and linguistically diverse area'. A close ethnographic and historical focus is necessary for any comparison of mana and similar concepts, Kolshus argues, and he is critical of recent anthropological writing on ontology which (counterintuitively, considering the ontologists' stated aims) generalises mana to the point where it loses all social grounding and analytic sharpness, mashed 'into ethnographic pulp'.

The following chapter, by Anglican priest and theologian Aram Oroi analyses anthropological scholarship in light of Oroi's personal experiences as a clergyman whom people ask to 'press the button' to activate mana in the world. As Oroi explains, for Arosi speakers of Makira, Solomon Islands, mana is part of God's Christian creation. It is used in linguistically versatile ways and is manifest in its effects—it is lived and engaged, rather than extensively theorised. And, crucially, it 'is associated with relationships and connections'. He reviews the anthropological scholarship on mana and, while revisiting the criticisms of Codrington, observes that Codrington's scholarship resonates with that of the Solomon Islands theologian Esau Tuza, who writes that a person can 'direct' mana through 'a living relationship'. The activation of mana, expressed metaphorically as pressing a button, is something in which a priest such as Oroi plays a crucial role. As he describes in several vivid stories, Anglican priests are asked both to hurt people and heal them by activating mana. A key theological voice in this volume, Oroi points out that 'it is one thing to observe mana at work. It is another thing to actually become an instrument of mana to direct and manifest mana.'

The book's eighth chapter, by Alexander Mawyer, resonates with Oroi's discussion of the mana of institutions but moves from the church to the state. At the heart of Mawyer's discussion is the remarkable story of Warren, a man born on Pitcairn Island and living on Mangareva, who asks Mawyer to get an official birth certificate made for him so that he will legally exist as a citizen. In making his request, Warren uses forms of the term 'mana' several times, referring to the action of 'stamping' his identity and authorising and empowering his citizenship. Discussing the case, Mawyer draws on Agamben's writings on *homo sacer* to observe the tensions between expressions of power at different levels, from the state to the individual struggling for recognition, and he argues that mana 'might be seen to be a culturally specific working out of issues of authority, power, and social force elsewhere worked out in terms of *imperium* and *auctoritas* (the authority of sovereigns, states, political regimes, collectives, or their agents)'. Mana is therefore central to political subjectivity—but, Mawyer notes, it is not always the object of great discursive attention. In older Mangarevan texts and in his own fieldwork experience on Mangareva, mana was not often mentioned; in older Tahitian texts it was not often mentioned either. Mawyer notes, however, that there is now a popular commercial efflorescence of the term in Tahiti. Indeed, he writes of 'mana-saturated shopping' and similar contexts of use which complexly complement potent political uses of the term in the region.

Matt Tomlinson and Sekove Bigitibau then offer a close reading of new Indigenous Fijian theologies of mana and its local counterpart, *sau*. They observe that in older Fijian language texts, mana is often associated with the act of speaking, but that in Methodist missionaries' translations of the Bible mana became readily conceptualisable as an object—a thing, detachable from contexts of use and hence useful as an emblem of Indigenous spirituality, an object of philosophical analysis, and something whose aesthetic and ethical qualities can matter in new ways. Although many Fijians continue to use the term 'mana' in performative ritual speech to make the words spoken earlier effective and truthful, Tomlinson and Bigitibau note that not all Indigenous Fijians have considered 'mana' to be a genuinely local term. One group that does focus strongly on mana and its implications for understanding Fijian society and spirituality, however, is Methodist theologians, who attend to mana in order to negotiate a careful balance between honouring chiefly authority and displacing it in the name of divine authority.

In the following chapter, Jessica Hardin describes the 'ordinary ethics' by which Pentecostals in Samoa seek to channel divine mana. Like Tomlinson and Bigitibau, she analyses the relationship between a pair of terms, here, *mana* and *pule* (authority). Hardin observes that prayer and fasting are two techniques by which Samoan Pentecostals attempt to 'establish a connection to the divine', serving as conduits for God's mana while deemphasising their own individual agency. Analysing the discourse of mana and *pule* that she recorded in church sermons and prayers at a hospital and a diabetes clinic, Hardin argues that healing is thought to be made possible through performative language that invokes God's ultimate power. In this way, humans cannot act effectively themselves, but can have God act effectively on their behalf: 'Speaking of [human] ineffectiveness', she observes, 'is essential to bringing about effective action.'

The volume then offers chapters by Rachel Morgain and Alex Golub and Jon Peterson that examine deterritorialised, global mana. Morgain examines the history of New Age movements' use of mana as a term and concept and situates this uptake in the context of alternative metaphysical philosophies of the nineteenth and early twentieth centuries, such as Madame Blavatsky's Theosophy and Franz Mesmer's theory of universal 'animal magnetism'. The system of spiritual teachings and practices known as Huna, created by Max Freedom Long and developed further by his student Serge King, drew on Hawaiian terminology to articulate an understanding of humans' power to tap into cosmic forces for healing and wholeness. Huna-esque mana filters into modern New Age movements like Feri and Reclaiming, whose practitioners, Morgain writes, understand mana as 'a key component of a cosmic system to which all people potentially have access as individuals, regardless of their social context'. Criticisms of New Age mana as inauthentic, Morgain argues, correctly note the ways global spiritual practices are radically decontextualised in New Age borrowing, but they also run the risk of misinterpreting New Age practitioners' motives and sincerity. Huna's mana, she observes, may not really be Hawaiian, but this does not mean that those who embrace it are faking their commitment.

Golub and Peterson, in their contribution, trace the complex history of 'how mana left the Pacific' to become widely known in the contemporary world through fantasy games. As they observe, more people have encountered mana through fantasy games than through Pacific Islands history or ethnography, and '[i]f there is a hegemonic definition of mana today, it is that used in [the videogame] World of Warcraft'. Golub and Peterson begin by relating how mana was discussed in the massively influential works of Carl Jung (and, following him, Joseph Campbell) and Mircea Eliade. Popular interest in these authors meshed with American baby boomers' desires for new kinds of liberation, which also motivated interest in the literature on millennialism; Larry Niven, a renowned science fiction writer, first heard of mana when he read Peter Worsley's *The Trumpet Shall Sound* (1968). Mana then metamorphosed into something new when it became a 'game mechanic' (part of a game's structure) in fantasy games on the model of 'spell points', or quanta of expendable energy. Golub and Peterson suggest that understanding mana's diffusion in gaming is a key task, even—or especially—for those interested in the Pacific who are keen in participating in a 'global conversation'.

The volume concludes with an epilogue by Niko Besnier and Margaret Jolly in which they consider mana in terms of its 'shape-shifting' qualities interwoven with its regional spread and historical durability. They address the themes of the preceding chapters and emphasise the need to go beyond false ideals of translation for a fuller engagement with the practices that shape the concept of mana. As part of this engagement, they urge scholars to consider mana's semiotic properties and performative aspects, and to look to moments such as Christianity's arrival and local uptake as 'contexts in which to explore the interdigitation of *mana* with changing ideologies of language, the truth, and humans' relationships to it'.

* * *

In encouraging fresh attention to mana, this volume will hopefully encourage both new thinking and new engagement: mana matters, in Oceania and beyond, to a wide range of people in a dazzling constellation of projects that invite anthropological attention and commitment. To conclude this introduction in an appropriate way, we would like to pair statements by two former scholarly antagonists whose views on mana, we submit, might be reconciled in the chapters that follow. Roger Keesing, in an archived set of handwritten notes on mana prepared for a conference at King's College in Cambridge, pleaded with his audience 'to set aside everything you know about the Oceanic concept of mana … imagine, if you can, that the concept I'm talking about is not mana, but one you never heard of' (1988: 4a).[14] His text reads like a call to intellectual salvation: escape the (linguistic, historical) bonds that drag down understandings of mana, forgetting mana in order to learn about it anew. We agree with his impulse to approach mana in new ways, although whereas Keesing hoped to go back to an origin point—the goal of his talk was to reconstruct mana's meanings in Proto-Oceanic, 4,000 years ago—in this volume we attend to more recent pasts as well as unfolding presents and imagined futures. In this spirit, we turn to Haunani-Kay Trask, who concludes her poetry collection *Night Is a Sharkskin Drum* with the work 'Into Our Light I Will Go Forever'. In chantlike verse, Trask moves through the Hawaiian landscape in an eroticised celebration of its beauty, life, pungency and power. Into the great canoe of Kanaloa, the Hawaiian deity, she takes readers onto the open ocean and then concludes the poem's journey: 'Into our sovereign suns, / drunk on the *mana* / of Hawai'i' (Trask 2002: 62). Although our consideration of mana in this book is not limited to Hawai'i, nor even limited to Oceania, who can resist Trask's urgent call to launch ourselves outward and look for mana in the future?

14 Material from these notes was later published in Keesing (1992).

References

Archival Repository

Keesing Roger M. 1988. Handwritten notes on *mana* for a conference at King's College, Cambridge. MSS 0427, Box 18, Mandeville Special Collections Library, University of California at San Diego.

Books, journal articles and chapters

Andrews, Lorrin. 1836. *A Vocabulary of Words in the Hawaiian Language*. Lahainaluna: Press of the High School.

Armstrong, Karen. 1993. *A History of God: The 4,000-Year Quest of Judaism, Christianity and Islam*. New York: Ballantine Books.

Ayau, Edward Halealoha and Ty Kāwika Tengan. 2002. Ka Huaka'i O Nā 'Ōiwi: The journey home. In *The Dead and Their Possessions: Repatriation in Principle, Policy and Practice*, ed. Cressida Fforde, Jane Hubert and Paul Turnbull, pp. 171–89. New York: Routledge.

Becker, Catherine Kalama. 1998. *Mana Cards: The Power of Hawaiian Wisdom* [divination cards]. Hilo: Radiance Network.

Biersack, Aletta. 1996. Word made flesh: Religion, the economy, and the body in the Papua New Guinea Highlands. *History of Religions* 36(2): 85–111.

Bloch, Maurice (ed.). 1975. *Political Language and Oratory in Traditional Society*. London: Academic Press.

Bowden, Ross. 1979. *Tapu* and *Mana:* ritual authority and political power in traditional Maori society. *Journal of Pacific History* 14(1–2): 50–61.

Bracken, Christopher. 2007. *Magical Criticism: The Recourse of Savage Philosophy*. Chicago: University of Chicago Press.

Caceres, Mana Kaleilani. 2001. Couldn't take the Mana. *Who I Am…* [CD]. Dallas: Catapult.

Carrillo, Ruben (Director, Producer), Dawn Kaniaupio and Scott Culbertson (Producers). 2010. *Mana i ka Leo: Power of the Voice*. [DVD]. Honolulu: 4 Miles LLC.

Catt, Helena. 2000. The New Zealand Election of 27 November 1999. *Australian Journal of Political Science* 35(2): 299–304.

Chai, Makana Risser. 2011. Huna, Max Freedom Long, and the idealization of William Brigham. *Hawaiian Journal of History* 45: 101–21.

Clark, Herman Pi'ikea. 2006. Kūkulu Kauhale o Limaloa: A Kanaka Maoli culture based approach to education through visual studies. Doctor of Education dissertation, College of Education, Massey University.

——. 2011. Ka Muhe'e, He I'a Hololua: Kanaka Maoli art and the challenge of the global market. In *Globalization and Contemporary Art*, ed. Jonathan Harris, pp. 137–46. West Sussex: Wiley-Blackwell.

Codrington, R.H. 1957 [1891]. *The Melanesians: Studies in Their Anthropology and Folk-Lore*. New Haven: Human Relations Area Files Press.

Crabbe, Kamana'opono. 2013 (May). Mana is our legacy. *Ka Wai Ola o OHA: The Living Water of OHA* 30(5): 3.

Davies, John. 1991 [1851]. *A Tahitian and English Dictionary with Introductory Remarks on the Polynesian Language and a Short Grammar of the Tahitian Dialect*. Papeete: Editions Haere Po no Tahiti.

Duff, Alan. 1990. *Once Were Warriors*. New York: Vintage International.

Dureau, Christine. 2000. Skulls, *Mana* and causality. *Journal of the Polynesian Society* 109(1): 71–97.

Durie, Mason H. 1998. *Te Mana, Te Kāwanatanga: The Politics of Māori Self-Determination*. Auckland: Oxford University Press.

Durkheim, Emile. 1965 [1915]. *The Elementary Forms of the Religious Life*, trans. Joseph Ward Swain. New York: Free Press.

Eliade, Mircea. 1958. *Patterns in Comparative Religion*, trans. Rosemary Sheed. London: Sheed and Ward.

Evans-Pritchard, E.E. 1965. *Theories of Primitive Religion*. Oxford: Clarendon Press.

Faubion, James. 2010. From the ethical to the themitical (and back): Groundwork for an anthropology of ethics. In *Ordinary Ethics: Anthropology, Language, and Action*, ed. Michael Lambek, pp. 84–101. New York: Fordham University Press.

Fforde, Cressida, Jane Hubert and Paul Turnbull (eds). 2002. *The Dead and Their Possessions: Repatriation in Principle, Policy and Practice*. New York: Routledge.

Firth, Raymond. 1940. The analysis of *Mana*: An empirical approach. *Journal of the Polynesian Society* 49: 483–510.

Frankenberry, Nancy K. (ed.). 2002. *Radical Interpretation in Religion*. Cambridge: Cambridge University Press.

Freud, Sigmund. 1918 [1913]. *Totem and Taboo: Resemblances between the Psychic Lives of Savages and Neurotics*, trans. A.A. Brill. New York: Vintage.

Goodyear-Ka'ōpua, Noelani. 2013. *The Seeds We Planted: Portraits of a Native Hawaiian Charter School*. Minneapolis, MN: University of Minnesota Press.

Gunn, Michael (ed.). 2014. *Atua: Sacred Gods from Polynesia*. Canberra: National Gallery of Australia.

Hall, Lisa Kahaleole. 2005. 'Hawaiian at heart' and other fictions. *The Contemporary Pacific* 17(2): 404–13.

Harris, Jonathan (ed.). 2011. *Globalization and Contemporary Art*. West Sussex: Wiley-Blackwell.

Henare, Amiria, Martin Holbraad and Sari Wastell (eds). 2007. *Thinking through Things: Theorising Artefacts Ethnographically*. London: Routledge.

Hocart, A.M. 1914. Mana. *Man* 14: 97–101.

Hogbin, H. Ian. 1936. Mana. *Oceania* 6: 241–74.

Holbraad, Martin. 2007. The power of powder: Multiplicity and motion in the divinatory cosmology of Cuban Ifá (or *Mana*, again). In *Thinking through Things: Theorising Artefacts Ethnographically*, ed. Amiria Henare, Martin Holbraad and Sari Wastell, pp. 189–225. London: Routledge.

Howard, Alan and Robert Borofsky (eds). 1989. *Developments in Polynesian Ethnology*. Honolulu: University of Hawai'i Press.

Jackson, Laurence. 1969. *Mana*. London: Stanmore Press.

Jakobson, Roman. 1960. Closing statement: Linguistics and poetics. In *Style in Language*, ed. T.A. Sebeok, pp. 350–77. Cambridge, MA: M.I.T. Press.

Kaeppler, Adrienne. 1988. Hawaiian tattoo: A conjunction of genealogy and aesthetics. In *Marks of Civilization: Artistic Transformations of the Human Body*, ed. Arnold Rubin, pp. 157–70. Los Angeles: Museum of Cultural History, University of California, Los Angeles.

Kaho'ohanohano, Moana. 1998. Mana wahine/Mana kāne. *'Ōiwi: A Native Hawaiian Journal* 1: 110.

Kame'eleihiwa, Lilikalā. 1992. *Native Lands and Foreign Desires—Pehea Lā e Pono Ai?* Honolulu: Bishop Museum Press.

Keesing, Roger M. 1984. Rethinking *Mana*. *Journal of Anthropological Research* 40(1): 137–56.

——. 1985. Conventional metaphors and anthropological metaphysics. *Journal of Anthropological Research* 41(2): 201–217.

——. 1992. Some problems in the study of Oceanic religion. *Anthropologica* 34(2): 231–46.

King, Serge. 1978. *Mana Physics: The Study of Paraphysical Energy*. New York: Baraka Books.

Lambek, Michael. 2010a. Introduction. In *Ordinary Ethics: Anthropology, Language, and Action*, ed. M. Lambek, pp. 1–36. New York: Fordham University Press.

—— (ed.). 2010b. *Ordinary Ethics: Anthropology, Language, and Action*. New York: Fordham University Press.

Lévi-Strauss, Claude. 1987 [1950]. *Introduction to the Work of Marcel Mauss*, trans. Felicity Baker. London: Routledge & Kegan Paul.

Lian, Kwen Fee. 1987. Interpreting Maori history: A case for a historical sociology. *Journal of the Polynesian Society* 96(4): 445–71.

Long, Max Freedom. 1953. *The Secret Science at Work: The Huna Method as a Way of Life*. Marina del Rey, CA: DeVorss Publications.

——. 1981. *Mana, or Vital Force: Selections from* Huna Research Bulletins. Cape Girardeau, MO: Huna Research.

MANA (Movement for Aloha No ka 'Āina). 2013. About. Online: www.facebook.com/movementforalohanokaaina/info (accessed 10 June 2013).

Marett, R.R. 1929 (4th ed.). *The Threshold of Religion*, London: Methuen and Co.

Marshall, Wende Elizabeth. 2011. *Potent Mana: Lessons in Power and Healing*. Albany: SUNY Press.

Mauss, Marcel. 1972 [1950]. *A General Theory of Magic*, trans. Robert Brain. London: Routledge and Kegan Paul.

Meleisea, Malama. 1987. *The Making of Modern Samoa: Traditional Authority and Colonial Administration in the Modern History of Western Samoa*. Suva: Institute of Pacific Studies, University of the South Pacific.

Middleton, Sue and Alison Jones (eds). 1992. *Women and Education in Aotearoa 2*. Wellington: Bridget Williams Books.

Mondragón, Carlos. 2004. Of winds, worms and *mana:* The traditional calendar of the Torres Islands, Vanuatu. *Oceania* 74(4): 289–308.

Müller, F. Max. 1910 [1878]. *Lectures on the Origin and Growth of Religion as Illustrated by the Religions of India: The Hibbert Lectures, Delivered in the Chapter House, Westminster Abbey, in April, May and June, 1878*. London: Longmans, Green, and Co.

New Zealand Herald. 2011. Harawira targets 'intelligent Maori votes', 1 May. Online: www.nzherald.co.nz/nz/news/article.cfm?c_id=1&objectid=10722717 (accessed 7 January 2013).

Ohnuki-Tierney, Emiko (ed.). 1990. *Culture through Time: Anthropological Approaches*. Stanford: Stanford University Press.

Oliver, W.H. and B.R. Williams (eds). 1981. *The Oxford History of New Zealand*. Oxford: Clarendon Press.

Osorio, Jamaica. 2013 (May/June). He Mana Kō ka Leo. *Mana: The Hawaiian Magazine* 2(1): 56.

Pahinui, James 'Bla'. 1997. *Mana* [CD] Santa Cruz, CA: Dancing Cat Records.

Pao, Carl Franklin Ka'ailā'au. 2014. Ākua. In *Atua: Sacred Gods from Polynesia*, ed. Michael Gunn, p. 167. Canberra: National Gallery of Australia.

Parsonson, Ann. 1981. The pursuit of Mana. In *The Oxford History of New Zealand*, ed. W.H. Oliver and B.R. Williams, pp. 140–67. Oxford: Clarendon Press.

Patterson, John. 2000. Mana: Yin and yang. *Philosophy East and West* 50(2): 229–41.

Pihama, Leonie E. 2001. Tīhei Mauri Ora / Honouring our voices: Mana Wahine as a Kaupapa Māori theoretical framework, 2 vols. PhD dissertation, University of Auckland.

Polynesian Cultural Center (PCC). 2013. Hā: Breath of life. Online: www.polynesia.com/evening-show.html (accessed 10 June 2013).

Pratt, George. 1862. *A Samoan Dictionary: English and Samoan, and Samoan and English; with a Short Grammar of the Samoan Dialect*. Malua, Samoa: London Missionary Society Press.

Pukui, Mary Kawena, E.W. Haertig and Catherine A. Lee. 1972. *Nānā i ke Kumu (Look to the Source)*. Honolulu: Hui Hānai.

Rubin, Arnold (ed.). 1988. *Marks of Civilization: Artistic Transformations of the Human Body*. Los Angeles: Museum of Cultural History, University of California.

Sahlins, Marshall. 1985. *Islands of History*. Chicago: University of Chicago Press.

Salmond, Anne. 1975. Mana makes the man: A look at Maori oratory and politics. In *Political Language and Oratory in Traditional Society*, ed. Maurice Bloch, pp. 45–63. London: Academic Press.

Sebeok, T.A. (ed.). 1960. *Style in Language*. Cambridge, MA: M.I.T. Press.

Shore, Bradd. 1982. *Sala'ilua: A Samoan Mystery*. New York: Columbia University Press.

——. 1989. *Mana* and *Tapu*. In *Developments in Polynesian Ethnology*, ed. Alan Howard and Robert Borofsky, pp. 137–73. Honolulu: University of Hawai'i Press.

Smith, Jonathan Z. 2002. Manna, Mana everywhere and /˘/˘/. In *Radical Interpretation in Religion*, ed. Nancy K. Frankenberry, pp. 188–212. Cambridge: Cambridge University Press.

Smith, Linda Tuhiwai. 1992. Maori women: Discourses, projects and Mana wahine. In *Women and Education in Aotearoa 2*, ed. Sue Middleton and Alison Jones, pp. 33–51. Wellington: Bridget Williams Books.

Stokes, John F.G. 1930. An evaluation of early genealogies used for Polynesian history. *Journal of the Polynesian Society* 39: 1–42.

Tamahori, Lee (Director). 1994. *Once Were Warriors* [film]. Auckland: Communicado.

Tamaira, Andrea Marata. 2015. Frames and counterframes: Envisioning contemporary Kanaka Maoli art in Hawai'i. PhD dissertation, The Australian National University.

Tengan, Ty P. Kāwika. 2008. *Native Men Remade: Gender and Nation in Contemporary Hawai'i*. Durham: Duke University Press.

Tengan, Ty P. Kāwika, Tēvita O. Ka'ili and Rochelle Tuitagava'a Fonotī. 2010. Genealogies: Articulating indigenous anthropology in/of Oceania. *Pacific Studies* 33(2–3): 139–67.

Tofaeono, Ama'amalele. 2000. *Eco-Theology: Aiga–The Household of Life, A Perspective from Living Myths and Traditions of Samoa*. Erlangen: Erlanger Verlag für Mission und Ökumene.

Tomlinson, Matt. 2006. Retheorizing Mana: Bible translation and discourse of loss in Fiji. *Oceania* 76(2): 173–85.

——. 2009. Efficacy, truth, and silence: Language ideologies in Fijian Christian conversions. *Comparative Studies in Society and History* 51(1): 64–90.

Trask, Haunani-Kay. 1999. *From a Native Daughter: Colonialism and Sovereignty in Hawai'i*. Revised Edition. Honolulu: University of Hawai'i Press.

——. 2002. *Night Is a Sharkskin Drum*. Honolulu: University of Hawai'i Press.

Tregear, Edward. 1891. *The Maori-Polynesian Comparative Dictionary*. Wellington: Lyon and Blair.

Tuwere, Ilaitia S. 2002. *Vanua: Towards a Fijian Theology of Place*. Suva and Auckland: Institute of Pacific Studies at the University of the South Pacific and College of St John the Evangelist.

Valeri, Valerio. 1985. *Kingship and Sacrifice: Ritual and Society in Ancient Hawaii*, trans. Paula Wissing. Chicago: University of Chicago Press.

——. 1990. Constitutive history: Genealogy and narrative in the legitimation of Hawaiian kingship. In *Culture through Time: Anthropological Approaches*, ed. Emiko Ohnuki-Tierney, pp. 154–92. Stanford: Stanford University Press.

Walker, R.J. 1984. The genesis of Maori activism. *Journal of the Polynesian Society* 93(3): 267–81.

Wendt, Albert. 1980a. Introduction. In *Lali: A Pacific Anthropology*, ed. Albert Wendt, pp. xiii–xix. Auckland: Longman Paul.

—— (ed.). 1980b. *Lali: A Pacific Anthropology*. Auckland: Longman Paul.

Worsley, Peter. 1968. *The Trumpet Shall Sound: A Study of 'Cargo' Cults in Melanesia*. New York: Schocken Books.

Zambucka, Kristin. 1974. *Mana*. Auckland: self-published.

1

Mana Hawai'i: An Examination of Political Uses of the Word Mana in Hawaiian

Noenoe K. Silva

I want to begin by acknowledging that I am not in the field of anthropology, nor have I made a long study of the concept of mana. I am entering into this conversation from my standpoint as Kanaka Hawai'i, or Native Hawaiian, as a scholar whose focus is on Hawaiian-language historical and literary texts, and whose PhD is from and whose location is in a political studies department. Matt Tomlinson and Ty Kāwika Tengan, in their introduction, suggest that 'a reorientation [to mana as a concept] might begin with a genealogical exploration of mana's transformations in particular locales'. As a scholar outside of the discipline of anthropology, this is perhaps where I can make a contribution.

What I will talk about here is how the word and concept 'mana' has been used in select Hawaiian texts historically, and I will touch briefly on the contemporary uses and appropriations of the term. What I have to say is confined to specifically Hawaiian uses of the term and, as Tomlinson and Tengan point out in their chapter, 'mana has diverse meanings across the cultural, historical, religious, and political contexts spanning the Pacific'.

What I have found in my research is how the word mana appears in constitutions and laws as well as in some religious essays. It is performative—it takes speech in order to produce action, and that action constitutes and/or creates, increases or decreases mana. The word is used often to describe a *collective* rather than individual good. 'Mana' emerges in various political contexts, for example in the conversion to Christianity, in constitutional crises, and in comparisons of Hawaiian practice with the US Civil War. Its significations occur at different levels and the word is often ambiguous, as Hawaiian is characterised by its frequent language play. Good writers in Hawaiian seek out ambiguity for punning, allusions, metaphors, and so forth.

Let me preface my discussion with a short history of Hawaiian-language newspapers because they are crucial to any research into Hawaiian historical, cultural or linguistic topics. Newspapers in our native language began in 1834 with the paper of the secondary school Lahainaluna Seminary, established by Congregationalist missionaries sent to Hawai'i by the American Board of Commissioners for Foreign Missions. By the 1840s, the Hawaiian Kingdom was sponsoring a newspaper in Hawaiian. Until 1861, all Hawaiian-language papers were controlled by Congregational missionaries or ex-missionaries (Silva 2008). From 1861 on, Kanaka Hawai'i produced their own independent papers, and served as writers and editors of papers of various churches. In the 1880s and 1890s, there were five or more different Hawaiian-language papers in publication at any given moment (Silva 2004). After the US took over Hawai'i and imposed English in more domains, the newspapers dwindled, but the last did not go out of business until 1948 (Chapin 1984; Mookini 1974).

Kanaka 'Ōiwi were literate in great numbers. Newspapers were very popular as sources of entertainment and news, but also for political organising. All issues of the day were thoroughly debated in the papers. Histories were published and critiqued, as were genealogies, geographies, songs, and the merits of this or that religion. Well-educated readers posed difficult puzzles for each other, some requiring knowledge of several languages to solve. These included discussions and questions about specific words in Hawaiian. In these thousands of pages, we can read and formulate some questions and do some analyses of what our ancestors thought about almost any topic or word. Because of digitising projects, it has recently become easier to access much of this archive; in addition to the microfilm rolls in use since the 1970s, we now have the Papakilo Database as well as the Hawaiian Nūpepa Collection. These newspapers are the main sources of my research for this chapter.

As Tomlinson and Tengan point out, Claude Lévi-Strauss identified mana as a 'floating signifier', one that may have attached to it any number of ideas. They critique misuses of Lévi-Strauss' point because, in reality, it should not mean that mana can mean simply anything. My point is to anchor some of those meanings in actual documents and essays in Hawaiian and to show how the uses of the word significantly shifted in Hawaiian-language political discourse in the mid-nineteenth century. In the early newspapers, which were highly focused on converting Kanaka to Christianity, mana was almost exclusively used in conjunction with Jehovah. Missionaries appropriated Hawaiian words to convey their religious concepts, so mana was used for the various powers of God.

Here are some examples. This first one was written by a missionary, a teacher of Lahainaluna in the school paper.

No ka mana o ke Akua.	Concerning the mana of God.
Eia kona mana, i ka hana ana i ka lani a me ka honua, i ka hana ana i ka mea o ka lani, o ka la a me ka mahina, o ka hoku a me ke ao; i ka hana ana i na mea a pau o ka honua, i na laau a pau, i ka wai, i ka ai, i ke kapa, i ka holoholona, i ke kanaka, i ke kai a me ka ia. No kona mana, ua malama ia mai kakou a hiki ia nei. Nolaila, e huli ae kakou ma kona mana. Malaila kakou e pakele ai i ka inaina o ke Akua e kau mai nei. (*Ka Lama Hawaii* 28 February 1834: 3)	This is his mana, the creation of the heavens and the earth, making the things of the sky, the sun and the moon, the stars and the earth/light; making everything of the earth, all the plants, water, food, coverings, animals, people, the sea, and the fish. Because of his mana, we have been cared for until now. Therefore, let us turn (convert) to his mana. It is there we shall escape the wrath of God that is coming to pass (or is coming down).[1]

1 All translations are my own unless specified otherwise.

Page four of that paper was reserved for student contributions, and here is an excerpt. The students at Lahainaluna included adults and young adults, like Davida Malo and Samuel Mānaiakalani Kamakau, both of whom became important figures in Hawaiian government, politics and other arenas.[2] Many of the student essays concerned the changing nature of 'pono', or what was right, good, ethical. This is an excerpt from one of those essays.

... he **mana** ko ke Akua nui o ka lani, no ka mea, lohe no ia ia ka pohaku ke olelo aku, a me ka wai, a me ka Moana, a me na kuahiwi, a me na puu, a me ka lani, a me ka honua, a me na mea a pau loa. Lohe no ia ia na mea pepeiao ole, a me na mea uhane ole, aka o ke kanaka, aole hoolohe i ka ke Akua olelo; hoopaakiki ka naau. (*Ka Lama Hawaii* 14 March 1834: 4)	... The great God of heaven has **mana**, because these listen to him when he speaks: the rock, the water, the Ocean, the mountains, and the hills, and the heavens, and the earth, and everything. Things without ears listen to him, and things without spirits, but people do not listen to what God says, the na'au (mind/feelings) is stubborn.

The contrast between how the haole (white American) missionary uses the word mana and how the Kanaka student uses it is striking. For the missionary, God's mana exists regardless of whether or not anyone believes in him; we understand him as powerful because he created the heavens and earth. People should be fearful of God, and only turning to his mana will allow anyone to escape his wrath. For the Hawaiian student, in contrast, God has mana because a variety of sentient beings, whom we would classify as inanimate, *listen to him when he speaks*. God's mana is conceptualised as performed in speech, and is dependent on someone listening. This idea is related to the Hawaiian word for religion: ho'omana. Ho'o- is a causative prefix, so in some sense the word means to give mana. Deities do not have mana unless some being(s) interact with them in some way. In Hawaiian thought, these other beings that the student mentions—the ocean, waters, hills, etc.—are our relatives. It seems to me that this Kanaka convert has brought that sensibility into his understanding of the mana of God.

2 Malo was important to the Christian mission, having assisted in translation of the Bible. Kamakau, in addition to prolific history writing, served as a judge as well as legislator.

In this same era, mana is used to describe weapons and the power of the ali'i (rulers). This example is from a news report about a dispute between some sailors from Borabora (a.k.a. Bora Bora, currently part of the Society Islands) and their captain, concerning their pay. The sailors took a small boat and carried it onto shore. Another person went to tell Hoapili, the ali'i nui (ruler), about the theft. Hoapili ordered them to return the boat. They didn't, and Hoapili then pronounced them in violation of the law and sentenced them to hard labour at road repair. The person reporting the incident wrote this:

Eia kekahi manao. He hoailona keia, he mea e hoike ai i ka **mana** o na alii. Ina haalele ia mau Borabora i ka Hoapili olelo a hoopai ole oia ia lakou, malaila paha e akaka ai ka hemahema o ke kanawai (*Ke Kumu Hawaii* 24 December 1834: 2).	Here is another thought. This is a sign that demonstrates the **mana** of the ali'i [plural]. If the Borabora men rejected Hoapili's word and he did not punish them, the weakness of the law would be seen there perhaps.

Here again we see that the mana of the ali'i—which is performed in speech—is being discussed as requiring practice and a certain kind of follow-up with action. If Hoapili failed to follow through with punishment for a violation, then his original speech would lack mana. This took place at a time prior to written laws.

Mana in Hawaiian Constitutions

I note here that in the first Constitution of Hawai'i in 1840, the word mana was never used. That document set out the structure of the government, including the roles of the Ali'i Nui (King), his/her executive called the Kuhina Nui, an upper house of a legislature called the 'aha'ōlelo o nā ali'i, a lower house of representatives elected by the populace, island governors, judges, and Supreme Court judges. In all of this, the word used to denote power/s is *'ōlelo* rather than mana. The word 'ōlelo signifies speech, language, word, statement, as well as to say, to tell, etc. (Pukui and Elbert 1986: 284). Probably the most often quoted proverb in Hawaiian is this one: I ka 'ōlelo nō ke ola, i ka 'ōlelo nō ka make (In 'ōlelo is life, in 'ōlelo is also death). This proverb expresses how seriously verbal pronouncements were taken by our people—they literally could mean that a person would live or die, as we shall see later.

In the 1840 Constitution, the section detailing the upper house names the ali'i who are appointed, and says 'Na lakou nei kekahi olelo o ke aupuni. … O keia poe nae ka poe hooholo i ka olelo. Aole e hana ia kekahi kanawai no ka aina me ko lakou lohe ole' (Some 'ōlelo of the government belongs to them. However, these are the people who decide on the 'ōlelo. No law can be made for the land without their hearing it) (*Ke Kumu Kanawai a Me Na Kanawai O Ko Hawaii Pae Aina* 1994: 5). Wherever authority or decision-making is indicated, the word 'ōlelo seems to be used, never mana.

By the 1850s, however, we begin to see the word mana used for governmental powers. In the 1852 Kumukānāwai (Constitution), the word is used to delineate the powers of the three branches of government. For the first time now we are seeing the government using language very reminiscent of the US and less like the native language. Why does the word mana emerge at this time? Perhaps the reason is because they are translating from English.

NO NA **MANA**. Pauku 23. E maheleia ka **mana** o ke Aupuni i ekolu Apana okoa, oia hoi ka **Mana** Hooko, ka **Mana** Kau Kanawai a me ka **Mana** Hookolokolo; e ku kaawale ia mau **mana** ekolu; aole hoi e huiia na **mana** hope elua iloko o ke kanaka hookahi, a iloko o ka Aha hookahi paha. (Kumukanawai 1852)	OF **POWERS**. Art. 23. The Supreme **power** of the Kingdom, in its exercise, is divided into the Executive, Legislative and Judicial **branches**; these are to be preserved distinct; the two last **powers/branches** cannot be united in any one individual or body.

Coincidentally, one of the words for branch is mana, so the word used for the three branches of government is also mana. In Hawaiian, the other sense of the word mana as power and authority would be heard along with the sense of branch. There would be no separating it, as Hawaiian listeners at that time would not have been accustomed to the English-language phrase, branches of government. Hawaiian speakers, readers, and listeners would also expect such language play and ambiguity as I explained earlier.

The years between the 1840 and 1852 constitutions saw a significant shift in the balance of power among the mō'ī, the ali'i, and haole—missionaries and colonialist career-seekers like William Little Lee. The mō'ī's control over all the land was divided in a māhele with the other ali'i, which was followed by the Kuleana Act of 1850 that attempted to fairly distribute some of the land to maka'āinana (Kame'eleihiwa 1992; Perkins 2013). The intent was to allow private ownership of land as was the custom in Europe and the US. This change in land tenure reflected the attempts of the ali'i to prevent colonisation by any of the Mana Nui, or Great Powers, such as Great Britain, France, or the USA. The 1852 Constitution continued this trend, borrowing language and philosophy more from Great Britain and the US than the 1840 Constitution did. The excerpt above shows how explicitly the concept of the tripartite division of powers of government was adopted from the US, whereas the 1840 Constitution simply laid out the new structure of government (Osorio 2002: 87). The most major change was the curtailing of the power of the mō'ī: in the 1840 structure the mō'ī 'was at once the executive, a member of the House of Nobles, and chief judge of the Supreme Court ... The [1852 Constitution] consigned the king ... to a more limited role as the kingdom's chief executive' (Osorio 2002: 87). This came about because changes in the law allowed both naturalised male citizens and male denizens of age to vote for the House of Representatives in 1851. According to Jonathan Kay Kamakawiwo'ole Osorio's history, seven of the 24 representatives elected were haole (Osorio 2002: 67–69). Kamehameha IV, Alexander Liholiho, educated in English at the Royal Chiefs' Children's School, governed with this Constitution from 1854 until his death in 1863.

When Kamehameha IV died and Lota Kapuāiwa took the throne as Kamehameha V in 1864, however, a constitutional crisis ensued. Kamehameha V wanted a new constitution and instead of convening the legislature that had just been elected, he had new elections held for delegates to a convention ('Aha 'Elele). This precipitated a 'ninau mana' or a 'mana question' in the newspapers. Did this 'Aha 'Elele have the mana, or legitimate authority, to create a new constitution?

After several delegates to the convention produced resolutions questioning the mana of the 'Aha, on July 14, 1864, the sixth day of the convention, the Mō'ī (King) reiterated his belief in this process, using the word mana. Here is an excerpt from his speech:

> Ua hoakakaia mai ka manao ma keia olelo hooholo, aohe **mana** o keia Ahaolelo [n]ui e hoololi i ke Kumukanawai. [O] Ko'u manao … eia na **mana** ekolu o Ko'u Aupuni iloko o keia Keena. Mai na **mana** hea la i loaa mai ai ke Kumukanawai o ka A. D. 1852 ? Ke olelo nei Au a me Ko'u mau Kuhina, na Kamehameha III.
>
> Ina he mea **mana** kekahi e hana i ke Kumukanawai i ka A. D. 1852, alaila, aia no ia **mana** iloko o na palena o keia Aupuni mai Hawaii a Niihau. A ina aole ia **mana** iloko o keia Keena, alaila, aia la i hea. Ke manao nei Au, eia no ia ia nei. He Moi no o Kamehameha III ma Kona ano Alii mai o ka wa Kahiko, aole ma ka **mana** i haawiia iaia ma ke Kumukanawai. (Ka Nupepa Kuokoa, 16 July 1864: 2)

> The opinion explained in this resolution is that this 'Aha'ōlelo has no **mana** to change the Constitution … my opinion … is that the three **mana** (branches) of my Government are here in this Office. From which **mana** was the 1852 Constitution obtained? I and my cabinet are saying, it was Kamehameha III.
>
> If there were some other **mana** to make the 1852 Constitution, then, that **mana** would have been inside the boundaries of this Government, between Hawai'i and Ni'ihau. If that **mana** is not in this Office, then where is it? I think it is here. Kamehameha III was a Mō'ī in his position as an Ali'i from ancient times, not through any **mana** given to him in the Constitution.

As it turned out, Kamehameha V's convention did not exercise the mana the Mō'ī believed it to have. The Mō'ī eventually cancelled it and he and his cabinet wrote the new constitution. According to Osorio, one of the points of disagreement that caused the convention to stall was the disenfranchisement of the poor and landless. Osorio says, 'That meant that Hawaiians' disposition toward sharing and charity … had to be actively discouraged' (Osorio 2002: 120). I bring this up because our most eminent historian and genealogist of the nineteenth century, Samuel Mānaiakalani Kamakau, began writing his important historical work just two years after these political struggles. He had always been concerned about how Kanaka 'Ōiwi were being represented in histories, especially those written by foreigners, and he had been trained in historiography and oral history gathering by the missionary Sheldon Dibble at Lahainaluna. He was concerned about the changes in the economic system that pitted people against each other and resulted in poverty and homelessness.

His series on Kamehameha I ran for about one year in *Ka Nupepa Kuokoa* (until September 1867), after which he continued it to cover the reigns of Kamehameha II and III, for the following two years, until October 1869. At the end, Kamakau dwells upon how our kūpuna (ancestors) made peace after battles, and were concerned for the welfare of people. For example, in a war, if one side is winning and the other is being utterly destroyed:

... ina i ka wa kaua nui ... make ka Moi o kekahi aoao, a luku wale aku ka aoao lanakila i ka aoao pio, alaila, kukala mai la ka Moi o ka aoao lanakila i ke kanawai o ke ola, a ua ola ka aoao pio, ua pau ka luku (Kamakau 7 October 1869: 1).	If in the time of a great war, the Mō'ī of one side died, and the winning side was destroying the losing side, then the Mō'ī of the winning side would declare the law of life, and the losing side would live, and the destruction would be stopped.

Prisoners would be released and could not be detained, and no prisoners could be made into slaves, or condemned to the group known as kauā. Kamakau then gives specific examples of when such a law was used, such as at the battle over the 'ai noa (end of the kapu system). Kamakau writes:

O keia mau hana naauao a ka lahui Hawaii i ka wa kahiko a hiki i ke au o Kamehameha I ame Kamehameha II ame Kamehameha III.... Na wai i ao mai i keia lahui i keia mau hana naauao aloha i ka wa kahiko, na ka baibala anei? (Kamakau 7 October 1869: 1).	These were wise actions of the lāhui Hawai'i in ancient times until the eras of Kamehameha I, II, and III. Who taught this lāhui these wise merciful actions in the ancient times, was it the Bible?

He answers the last question no, since in the Bible prisoners are kept as slaves. He goes on to say that only in Hawai'i did a King willingly implement a constitution. He further asserts, 'O ke aloha o na alii i na makaainana, a o ke aloha o na makaainana i na alii, oia ke kumu i kukulu ia ai ke kumukanawai Hawaii' (The aloha of the ali'i for the maka'āinana [people], and the aloha of the maka'āinana for the ali'i was the reason or foundation upon which the Hawaiian constitution was built (Kamakau 7 October, 1869: 1)). This is a continuation of Kamakau's critique of western governance and religion, and advocacy of the value of Hawaiian practices.

Kamakau goes on to say that each mō'ī has had a kumukānāwai (constitution); Kamehameha I's kumukānāwai was the kānāwai Māmalahoa (Law of the Splintered Paddle). He says it consists of just one sentence, 'however, its nature was multiple, and the most important characteristic of it was life' (Kamakau 7 October 1869: 1). Several months later, in a new history of Hawai'i that Kamakau was writing, he meditated on the nature of Kamehameha's mana. This section was never put into the 'history' translation called *Ruling Chiefs of Hawaii*, but instead went into the book called *The People of Old*, which focuses on religion and other works of kāhuna (ritual specialists) (Kamakau 1992; Kamakau 1991).[3] It appears under the heading of 'He Kanawai Mamalahoa'. Here Kamakau tells the story of how Kamehameha had been beaten with a club or paddle by some fishermen, and afterwards proclaimed the law: 'E hele ka elemakule a moe i ke ala, e hele ka luahine a moe i ke ala, e hele ke keiki a moe i ke ala' (Kamakau 24 March 1870: 1), 'Let the old men, the old women and the children sleep [in safety] on the highway' (Kamakau 1991 (trans.): 15). Because of this story, the law came to be known in English as the Law of the Splintered Paddle. Kamakau then asks how the Māmalahoa law became a law with mana. He answers:

> Ua ae like na Kuhina na 'lii a me na kahuna, a me na mea **mana** a pau, a ua ae like lakou a pau e lilo ke kanawai Mamalahoa he kanawai kuakoko no ko Kamehameha la hanau ana mai ka opu mai o kona makuahine. (Kamakau 24 March 1870: 1)

> It was because the counselors, the chiefs, the kahunas, and all the **powerful** persons had agreed that the Mamalahoa law was Kamehameha's birthright, from the time he came from his mother's womb. (Kamakau 1991 (trans.): 15)

And he explains that similar laws existed before Kamehameha and such laws of life were well-known to our people. What is important in this passage is the collective decision-making about this law. No ali'i

3 In other contexts, kāhuna also includes experts in any profession, male or female, including house locating and building, ocean vessel construction, medicine, etc. (Pukui and Elbert 1986).

is a dictator; he or she is surrounded by these 'powerful persons' or people with mana. Without them, Kamehameha would not have had this law ascribed to him.

Kamakau further explains:

> O ke kanawai Mamalahoa, oia kona **mana** p[a] lena ole ma kona Nohoalii Moi ma kona aupuni, aole kekahi mea poino a pilikia a pio, a luku, a hookahe koko, a ua kau ia ke kanawai Mamalahoa, ua laa ia no ke ola a no ka pomaikai. (Kamakau 24 March 1870, *Ke Au Okoa*: 1)

> The Māmalahoa law was his boundless **mana** in his rule as Mō'ī over his aupuni: no one was [to be] abused, oppressed, imprisoned, destroyed or have blood shed, and when the Māmalahoa law was invoked, it was dedicated to life and good fortune/ blessings/ prosperity. (my translation)

> The *kanawai* Mamalahoa gave him unlimited **power** while ruler of his kingdom. Anyone so unfortunate as to be taken captive and about to be killed could be saved by Kamehameha pronouncing the Mamalahoa law; it was consecrated to the saving of lives and fortunes. (Kamakau 1991 (trans.): 15)

Here Kamakau says that the Māmalahoa law constituted Kamehameha's mana. Pukui translates the sentence as the law giving Kamehameha unlimited power, but the sentence is not actually constructed using any of the words for 'give', rather it is an existential structure, an equational sentence in Hawaiian grammar. Part A, the kānāwai Māmalahoa, 'equals' or actually *is* Part B, Kamehameha's mana.

Kamakau illustrates this with the story of the decisive battle for the island of Hawai'i between Kamehameha and his rival Keōua. Keōua had been lured to a supposed meeting for a truce, but was killed instead, and offered as a sacrifice at Kamehameha's new heiau, Pu'ukoholā. Among Keōua's followers was a son of Kamehameha himself, Ka'ōleiokū. The 'ohana of the ali'i were completely intertwined and close relatives often found themselves on opposite sides in battle. Kamehameha's circle of ali'i and advisors strongly suggested killing all of Keōua's people, but Kamehameha instead insisted on proclaiming the kānāwai Māmalahoa, which saved them all, including his son.

Thus Kamakau seems to be saying that the power to grant life, to refrain from killing, was Kamehameha's kumukānāwai, and was the basis for his boundless mana. Kamehameha's pronouncement of the law, or his performance of it, constitutes his mana. Kamakau is reinforcing that this was a kumukānāwai, a foundation for laws that protected lives.

While mana ali'i is undoubtedly bound up with genealogy and hierarchy—the higher the rank the closer to divine status and thus the greater an ali'i's initial mana—this explanation or theory of Kamakau's complicates matters (in a good way) for us. Kamakau explains elsewhere that rank alone does not make an ali'i successful, and we have many stories of ali'i who behaved poorly or weakly and lost their lives because of it (see Pukui 1995: 74–77, 131–33).

Because the US Civil War was still very fresh in Hawaiians' minds—they received weekly news reports and some of the missionary sons and a few Kānaka had fought on the side of the Union[4]—Kamakau was also making a point about mana and pono. He wrote a few paragraphs at this time explaining that while the ali'i did war against each other, peacemaking always followed, and never were people imprisoned afterwards, nor were they ever made into slaves, bought, sold, or traded. It is evident to me that Kamakau is making a statement about the value of the old ali'i system and the dangers of following western models of governance, war and even religion.

I think what Kamakau was most concerned about was the welfare of his people and he used this point about the Māmalahoa law to illustrate that it was peacemaking as much as winning battles that made Kamehameha Ka Na'i Aupuni, or the one who created one government over the whole archipelago.

The original Congregational missionaries also waged discursive battles against Catholicism (to which Kamakau converted) and Anglicanism, and Kamakau rages against this senseless warring. He writes, for example:

4 For more on Hawai'i individuals involved in the US Civil War, see *Hawai'i Sons of the Civil War*, a planned documentary film. Online: hawaiisonsofthecivilwar.com/ (accessed 5 October 2015).

A o ka hoolilo ana o na aoao hoomana Akua ia Hawaii nei i kahua hoouka kaua no ka lakou mau olelo, i lilo na keiki a ka lahui Hawaii, i lahui akamai i ka hoopaapaa, e haalele ana i ka **mana** o ka olelo a ke Akua. Ka inoa o ka **mana** o ka olelo a ke Akua ka mea nana e hoohuli i ka naau o ka lehulehu, eia ka! o ka hookolekole waha—ea. (Kamakau 7 October 1869: 1)	And the different Christian denominations converting/ transforming Hawai'i into a battlefield over their dogma, caused the children of the Hawaiian people to change into people skilled in argument, abandoning the **mana** of the word of God. I thought the **mana** of the word of God was the thing to convert the hearts of the people, but! it is rude talk.

Kamakau was also a great critic of how capitalism creates poverty, and holds up the old Hawaiian system as one in which no one goes hungry. That is another obvious meaning of the Māmalahoa law for us today, as we watch our brothers, sisters, kūpuna and keiki (children) try to survive on beaches and sidewalks.

Fast forward: Mana in the present day

Between Kamakau's time and ours, American culture has become hegemonic in Hawai'i nei. Hawaiians have become a minority in our own land, and almost all media is now in English rather than Hawaiian. No newspapers in Hawaiian are sold on the streets of Honolulu. As Haunani-Kay Trask trenchantly observes, Hawaiian culture is prostituted for tourist dollars. This is reflected in some contemporary appropriations of the word mana (Trask 1999: 136–47). The *Huffington Post,* for example, recently ran an essay called '5 Hawaiian Words to Redefine Health, Happiness and Power in your Life' (5 September 2013), which assumes that Hawaiian words and values can be appropriated for the already privileged. The article seems aimed at the wealthy who live part-time or vacation regularly in Hawai'i. While all of their short paragraphs describing each word are worth ignoring, the last one, 'mana', draws on one of the multitude of books on the fake Hawaiian religion, huna (see Hall 2005: 411). They say, 'Mana is a life energy that flows through all things and is highly individual', which I would contrast with the collective, reciprocal and performative nature of mana described in the Kanaka Maoli writings I have discussed. Then the *Huffington Post* illustrates this with a rather lecherous photo of a young Senator Daniel Inouye, calling him 'one of the best examples of mana' (5 September 2013).

In the Hawaiian community, movements for sovereignty and social justice have been continuous since they first arose in the 1970s (Goodyear-Ka'ōpua, Hussey and Wright 2014). The concept and word mana is gaining new favour: we have a new political organisation called MANA (Movement for Aloha no ka 'Āina), and a glossy magazine called *Mana*. I do not think, however, that mana has really been a keyword for us as we continue to face challenges to maintaining or creating a resurgence of Hawaiian life in our islands. Having done this research on how this word mana was used by our kūpuna, I now think that mana should be revived as a keyword. Its connection to the Māmalahoa law could be made more well-known among all our people. Perhaps we should endeavour to build mana collectively, based upon the life-affirming principle of Māmalahoa. Some activists are using the kānāwai Māmalahoa in their calls for justice now. The photo below shows Hawaiian activists deploying the kānāwai Māmalahoa when the City and County of Honolulu was evicting (De)occupy Honolulu from a public sidewalk. (Occupy Honolulu was inspired by Occupy Wall Street, and its name was changed to (De)occupy Honolulu after Hawaiian activists became involved.)

Further, outside of movement politics, I see Kānaka everywhere engaged in positive projects for our people, in education, voyaging, language revitalisation, hula, etc. Is this mana we are already building together?

Figure 7. De-occupy Honolulu, 2012.

Source: Photograph by H. Doug Matsuoka, used with permission.

In 1905, Joseph Moku'ōhai Poepoe published a history of Kamehameha I in his newspaper called 'Ka Na'i Aupuni'. In the introduction these words appear in capital letters: UA PAU NA LANI MOI, AKA, KE OLA NEI NO NA HULU MAKAAINANA, A O [LA]KOU NA KOO O KA NA'I AUPUNI (The monarchial ali'i are gone, but the precious remnants of Maka'āinana still live, and they are the supports of Ka Na'i Aupuni) (Hooulumahiehie 1905: 1). It seems to me that 'the supports of Ka Na'i Aupuni' means two things: one is that Ka Na'i Aupuni—Kamehameha's government—metaphorically is the Hawaiian islands and the Hawaiian people. More mundanely, it is the name of the newspaper and Poepoe wanted people to support it. He was, however, a huge supporter of Hawaiian language and lifeways. The important part is that even though the native government has been gone for some time now, we, the common people, can still support each other and the life of the lāhui.

Conclusion

In this chapter, I have reviewed some instances of the word and concept mana in a selection of Hawaiian-language contexts. The word was most commonly used in early Hawaiian writing in conjunction with Jehovah as Congregationalist missionaries converted the first generation of Hawaiians. In the first written Hawaiian Constitution, where we might have expected the word mana, we see instead the word ʻōlelo to express the exercise of power. ʻŌlelo, the spoken word, implied action would follow; for an ali'i to say something was enough to make it so. In such contexts, mana is seen to be performative and collective, and not to signify individuals amassing and exercising power. In later constitutions, we do see the word mana where we expect it, likely because of translation from English, which was becoming increasingly dominant. The ali'i nui were all being educated in English in the Royal Chiefs' Children's School, and English-language speaking advisors to the Mō'ī were common. In the writings of Samuel Mānaiakalani Kamakau in the 1860s and 1870s, it appears that he was more concerned with the concept of pono than with mana. Today, the word mana has been (mis)appropriated in touristic and New Age rhetoric.

We are seeing a rise, however, in the use of the word mana among sovereignty and self-determination activism. This is cause for optimism as we work to bring our lives into a state of pono through collective action. My hope is that this chapter might contribute in some small way towards that cause.

References

Digital repositories

Hawaiian Nūpepa Collection. *Ulukau: Hawaiian Electronic Library*. Online: nupepa.org/ (accessed 5 October 2015).

Papakilo Database. Online: papakilodatabase.com/main/main.php (accessed 5 October 2015).

Books, journal articles, and chapters

Chapin, Helen Geracimos. 1984. Newspapers of Hawaii 1834 to 1903: From 'He Liona' to the Pacific Cable. *Hawaiian Journal of History* 18: 47–86.

Goodyear-Ka'ōpua, Noelani, Ikaika Hussey and Erin Kahunawaika'ala Wright (eds). 2014. *A Nation Rising: Hawaiian Movements for Life, Land, and Sovereignty*. Narrating Native Histories. Durham: Duke University Press.

Hall, Lisa Kahaleole. 2005. 'Hawaiian at heart' and other fictions. *The Contemporary Pacific* 17(2): 404–13.

Hawai'i Sons of the Civil War. n.d. Planned documentary film. Online: hawaiisonsofthecivilwar.com/ (accessed 8 October 2015).

Hooulumahiehie. 1905. 'Kamehameha I.: Ka Na'i Aupuni O Hawaii'. *Ka Na'i Aupuni*, 27 November.

Huffington Post. 2013. 5 Hawaiian words to redefine health, happiness and power in your life. 5 September. Online: www.huffingtonpost.com/2013/09/03/hawaiian-health-and-happiness_n_3854391.html?ir=Australia (accessed 8 October 2015).

Kamakau, S.M. 1869–1870. 'Ka Moolelo Hawaii'. *Ke Au Okoa*.

Kamakau, Samuel Manaiakalani. 1991. *Ka Po'e Kahiko = the People of Old*, ed. Dorothy B. Barrère, trans. Mary Kawena Pukui. Bernice P. Bishop Museum Special Publication 51. Honolulu, HI: Bishop Museum Press.

Kamakau, Samuel Manaiakalani. 1992 [revised ed.]. *Ruling Chiefs of Hawaii*. Honolulu, HI: Kamehameha Schools Press.

Kame'eleihiwa, Lilikalā. 1992. *Native Land and Foreign Desires: How Shall We Live in Harmony (Ko Hawai'i 'Āina a Me Nā Koi Pu'umake a Ka Po'e Haole: Pehea Lā E Pono Ai?)*. Honolulu, HI: Bishop Museum Press.

Ke Kumu Kanawai a Me Na Kanawai O Ko Hawaii Pae Aina. 1994 [reprint]. Green Valley, NV: Ted Adameck.

Mookini, Esther. 1974. *The Hawaiian Newspapers*. Honolulu: Topgallant Publishing Co.

Osorio, Jonathan Kay Kamakawiwoole. 2002. *Dismembering Lāhui: A History of the Hawaiian Nation to 1887*. Honolulu: University of Hawai'i Press.

Perkins, Mark Umi. 2013. Kuleana: A genealogy of native tenant rights. PhD dissertation. University of Hawai'i at Mānoa. Online: search.proquest.com.eres.library.manoa.hawaii.edu/pqdtft/docview/1430295574/abstract/EE935508F7964E90PQ/1?accountid=27140 (accessed 8 October 2015).

Pukui, Mary Kawena. 1995. *Folktales of Hawai'i He Mau Ka'ao Hawai'i*. Bishop Museum Special Publication 87. Honolulu, HI: Bishop Museum Press.

Pukui, Mary Kawena and Samuel H. Elbert. 1986 [revised and enlarged edition]. *Hawaiian Dictionary: Hawaiian-English, English-Hawaiian*. Honolulu: University of Hawaii Press.

Silva, Noenoe K. 2004. *Aloha Betrayed: Native Hawaiian Resistance to American Colonialism*. Durham, NC: Duke University Press.

Silva, Noenoe K. and Iokepa Badis. 2008. Early Hawaiian newspapers and Kanaka Maoli intellectual history, 1834–1855. *Hawaiian Journal of History* 42: 105–34.

Trask, Haunani-Kay. 1999 [revised ed.]. *From a Native Daughter: Colonialism and Sovereignty in Hawai'i*. Honolulu: University of Hawai'i Press.

2

The Mana of Kū: Indigenous Nationhood, Masculinity and Authority in Hawai'i

Ty P. Kāwika Tengan

A long time ago, the god Kū lived in Hawai'i as a human. When a famine brought his family to the brink of starvation, he told his wife that he could save them only if he went on a journey from which he could not return. At first she refused but then finally consented when she heard the cries of their hungry children. Kū then stood on his head and disappeared into the earth. The woman's tears watered that spot, and from it grew the 'ulu (breadfruit) tree whose fruits saved all the people (Pukui with Green 1995: 8).

In 2008, Bernice Pauahi Bishop Museum (Bishop Museum) project director Noelle Kahanu wept as she stood before a seven-and-a-half-foot tall carved wooden ki'i (image) of Kū that was a part of a Polynesian exhibit at the Musée du Quai Branly in Paris, France (Jolly 2011: 125; White 2010). This ki'i, on loan from the British Museum in London, was one of only three temple images of Kū (all carved from breadfruit) that survived the 1819 dismantling of the Hawaiian precolonial state religion known as the 'aikapu; the other two images resided at the Bishop Museum in Honolulu and the Peabody Essex Museum (PEM) in Salem, Massachusetts. Speaking at the 'Exhibiting Polynesia: Past, Present, and Future' symposium at Quai Branly, Kahanu pondered the significance of reuniting the three Kū images: 'We dream that they will once again stand together and that which is separated by oceans shall be united' (Kahanu 2012).

In 2010, on the bicentennial of Kamehameha's unification of the Hawaiian Kingdom, the three Kū stood together for four months at the Bishop Museum in a historic exhibit entitled *E Kū Ana Ka Paia: Unification, Responsibility, and the Kū Images*. The Hawaiian title, which translates to 'The Wall Will Stand', came from a prophecy chant dating to the time of Kamehameha. Kahanu, who organised and curated the exhibit, had spoken of this prophecy when she was at Quai Branly two years prior. Speaking in 2010 on a Native Hawaiian radio talk show, she explained:

> It's said that [the prophet Kapihe] predicted this overturning, the ending of the 'aikapu and the coming of a new religious system … In today's context, it really represents a kind of an overturning of social and political order and a reemergence of Hawaiian nationhood and solidarity. And it's really I think in that context that this exhibit fits … for what it means to come together as a people. (Kahanu 2010)

Indeed, over 71,300 visitors (65 per cent of whom were residents) came together at the museum between June and October, including numerous Hawaiian cultural organisations that gave offerings of chants, dances and the fruits of the land (Bishop Museum 2010: 2). The second 'Aha Kāne Native Hawaiian Men's Health Conference held its opening ceremonies in the presence of the Kū, seeking to draw inspiration from the deity of male generative power. In their end of the year report, the Bishop Museum featured an anonymous comment left in the guest book that read, 'That may be the true *mana* of *Kū*, to bring together from there, to bridge differences, to impress, to educate, to inspire, to unite us all!' (Bishop Museum 2010: 2).

As a member of the community consultant team and as the humanities scholar for the exhibit, I was both participant in and witness to the cultural, social and political workings of calling forth the 'mana of Kū' (or 'mana Kū', as it was sometimes referred to). Not surprisingly, these towering 800-pound wood carvings became focal points for talking about mana, a term that people defined in a variety of ways that included 'spiritual power' (Enomoto 2010), 'belonging' (Grace 2010), and 'status' (Nākānelua 2010). Even when people were not using the term directly, talk of supernatural agency, spectacular accomplishment, and Indigenous empowerment all highlighted the continued significance of mana in contemporary Hawaiian society.

For the remainder of this chapter, I will reflect on the experiences and conversations I was involved in to explore the ways that mana figured into discourses of and struggles over Native Hawaiian nationhood, masculinity and authority. I argue that invocations of mana as both essence and practice reflect strategies for asserting Indigenous continuity despite and through historical, political and cultural transformations. Here I highlight the ethical, aesthetic and political dimensions of remaking Indigenous masculinities as a form of mana Kū. The exhibit and related events also offer insights into the possibilities and limitations of thinking about the role of mana in the reshaping of relationships between Native peoples, anthropologists and museums (Clifford 2013).

The departure of Kū

Kū, one of the four major male deities (along with Lono, Kāne and Kanaloa) in the Hawaiian pantheon, is most famously (and reductively) known as 'the god of war'. In actuality, the martial aspect was only one of many attributed to this deity. Broadly speaking, Kū is the deity of male generative power who is frequently paired with his female counterpart Hina. The most famous manifestation of Kū is Kūkā'ilimoku, the island-snatching Kū that Kamehameha inherited from his uncle and used to legitimate his campaign of conquest in the late eighteenth and early nineteenth century.

The precise origin of these three images in particular, and how they ended up leaving Hawai'i, is somewhat unclear. The English missionary William Ellis who was touring the islands in 1823 observed three ki'i still standing at Ahu'ena, a temple Kamehameha restored and rededicated to Lono at his final residence and first Capital of Kamakahonu in Kona (Tengan and Roy 2014). At the time Ellis was making his tour of Hawai'i Island, Governor Kuakini had converted the heiau into a fort, where the ki'i stood 'like sentinels amidst the guns' (Ellis 1825: 323). As Kahanu stated on an interview for a local television station, 'That gathering of *three* images has not been seen by human eyes since that time' (Hyden 2010).

And indeed, up until the last few months before the exhibit was held, it was unknown whether or not they *would* be seen together. Recalling her talk at Quai Branly in 2008, Kahanu described a 'miracle of miracles' when Lissant Bolton, who was curator of the Pacific Collection of the British Museum and in the audience, told her an international loan was possible (Kahanu 2012). Yet concerns among the loaning institutions remained, in part due to the fact that PEM's director Dan Monroe had been a member of the NAGPRA (Native American Graves Protection and Repatriation Act) Review Committee that handled the Kawaihae (a.k.a. Forbes Cave) case that divided the Hawaiian community deeply (and publicly) in a dispute over ki'i that came from a burial cave on Hawai'i Island (Johnson 2011). There were fears that the Kū images would become the focus of a new and pitched repatriation battle over the authority of museums to own and control Hawaiian culture.

Within the Hawaiian community, important ethical concerns arose. In order to ensure that the proper cultural and social protocols were followed, Kahanu gathered a team of community consultants comprised of cultural experts. Kahanu's memory of these discussions matches mine: 'You have an older, more conservative Hawaiian group that were *fearful*. So, what happens when the three come together? What about the mana, or energy that might be *re*-animated? ... Who's responsible if you *awaken* something? ... These are really, really *big* concerns' (Kahanu 2012). Men in the consultant group who were versed in rituals related to Kū agreed to take on the kuleana (responsibility) of developing the proper protocols and procedures for bringing the ki'i to Hawai'i, receiving the offerings during the exhibit, and returning the ki'i back. Indeed, most of the consultants were anticipating that Kū *would* awaken, and with him the Hawaiian people.

Less than six months before the exhibit was to open, all of the museums were finally on board. However, now the primary obstacle was the lack of funds. At the last minute, the Office of Hawaiian Affairs came through with a $US100,000 grant. Kahanu recalled:

> So, you know, to me, it's sort of like, um, *they* [the Kū images] chose to come. In other words, there's only so much people can do to make something happen. And at some point there is a higher plane of involvement ... [Y]ou put your words out there ... and at some point they're engaged, they hear the call, *they* decide that *they* want to be here, and then they facilitate the process of ultimately getting here. That's my only explanation. (Kahanu 2012)

It is hard to describe this as anything less than a manifestation of mana. As Sahlins has put it (1981: 31):

> Yet, again, one is in the presence of something familiarly Hawaiian: a structure of the long run—*mana*. Perhaps most essentially, *mana* is the creative power Hawaiians describe as making visible what is invisible, causing things to be seen, which is the same as making them known or giving them form.

The return of Kū

Two weeks before the exhibit, a team made up of Bishop Museum staff and members of the Hale Mua Native Hawaiian Men's group embarked on a journey to Salem and London to ensure that the Kū images were properly and ceremoniously readied for their return to Hawai'i. As I have written elsewhere (Tengan 2008), the Hale Mua was formed as an organisation for Hawaiian men to reconnect with their history and culture, primarily through the practice of warrior art forms and ceremonies, and to forge bonds of communion and support that would enable them to be leaders in their families and communities. In particular, this responded to a pervasive discourse of Hawaiian emasculation—the perception that Hawaiian men had become ineffectual as women came to take on the dominant roles in the home and the nation. This process has also been understood metaphorically and literally as the loss of Kū and his mana; the return of Kū would likewise symbolise the restoration of 'Ōiwi men's identities and kuleana. As Kyle Nākānelua, head of the Hale Mua, explained to me in 1999:

> Because we're a male, masculine oriented group, our 'imi 'ana (searching) is towards the masculinity of the culture because there's been so much femininity ... [I]f you believe, everything has its place and time, then it should hold true to da fact that there should be a place and a time for the mana Kū. There's a time for healing, there's a time for building mana. (Tengan 2008: 144)

Yet since, as Jolly notes, 'male potency emerges in relation—and sometimes in resistance—to the hegemonic forces of colonialism and contending imperial models of masculinity' (Jolly 2008: 1), invocations of mana Kū can potentially reinforce structures of settler heteropatriarchy (Morgensen 2011). Thus the selection of the consultant group and the delegation was also scrutinised, to which Kahanu responded by citing the significance of returning the kuleana of Kū to the men who had trained for it.

The 'search' for the mana of Kū—here indexing Hawaiian male potency and generative power—came full circle for Nākānelua when he was selected to be a part of the Bishop Museum delegation in 2010. He kept a journal of the trip, detailing the signs in the heavens and challenges on earth they encountered. At a particularly trying time in London, he wrote about the need to continue with his daily 'ho'omana' (prayer, ritual, worship; literally 'to create mana'):

> Must go through the rituals anyway. It is about affirming who we are and the conduct that is necessary for us to perpetuate our duties and responsibilities. … This whole journey is about affirming ourselves as a people in relationship to our ancestors that have gone before us. The ritual allows us to commune with that way of being. (Nākānelua 2010: 3)

Indeed, much the same could be said about the journeys of all Hawaiians who have sought to revitalise mana as a central component of healing, decolonising, and rebuilding nation (Marshall 2011).

Despite all of the hardships and challenges, the exhibition *E Kū Ana Ka Paia* was successfully opened on 4 June 2010. Speaking on a panel discussion after he officiated at the opening ceremonies, tattoo and hula master and community consultant Keone Nunes addressed any of the lingering fears that some might have in the Hawaiian community:

> When you go in there, you don't feel that you're fearful for your life, but you can feel the mana of these images in a very welcoming way, in a very heartfelt way … There's a lot of things that it can represent for each and every one of us … who come and see these images for something that is beyond the carved image, beyond the wood. But you see the mana of these images. (Nunes 2010)

Aesthetics of mana

As Nunes' comment suggests, the exhibit led to an intense meditation on and redefinition of the aesthetics of mana. The *Honolulu Star-Bulletin* quoted Peabody Essex Museum director and CEO Dan Monroe stating that 'the statues are "masterpieces which reflect the artistic genius of native Hawaiians''' (Gee 2010). While such praise is certainly deserved, it is also limiting in its focus on 'masterpieces' and 'artistic genius'. As Herman Pi'ikea Clark explains:

> In contrast to European art, which evolved to become an autonomous and socially detached class of objects and images produced principally for aesthetic engagement … the objects and images created in a Kanaka Maoli cultural context were designed to function as components within an integrated social, religious, governmental and economic system … In this setting, Kanaka Maoli visual culture served as visual signifiers, utilitarian tools and repositories of genealogical narrative and cultural knowledge. (Clark 2011: 139)

In specific relation to ki'i, he comments:

> the repetitive features carved onto a temple idol, though contributing to the object's aesthetic quality and appearance, also served as a mnemonic feature to aid in the recall of information to those who had the capacity to read its design. (Clark 2006: 12)

Much of the challenge for the contemporary Kanaka 'Ōiwi community was in fact how to 'read' the designs that were unfamiliar to many. One of the unique features of the ki'i from the British Museum was the presence of what appeared to be dozens of tiny faces carved into the long headdress (or hair) that extends down to the base. Various interpretations were put out, including the thought that it might be the face of a dog (which was a body form of Kū).

Rather than see this lack of knowledge as a shortcoming, it might instead be viewed as an opportunity for reconnection and recreation of culture and mana. The Kanaka Maoli artist Kalamakūloa (David He'akoelekauaikalani Kalama Jr), whose work was featured in the exhibit's brochure next to my essay, spent 54 days at the museum drawing charcoal sketches of the ki'i from various angles (Figure 8) (Dawrs 2011). In the process, he witnessed large and small ceremonies that were conducted as community members laid offerings before Kū, and he himself came to be an individual/activity to be viewed and interacted with by visitors and news crews. On his website *moku mana*, which he translates as 'power island' (Kalama Productions Inc. 2010–11), he created a page entitled 'Makakū' as an online space for communing with the ki'i and others who forged meaningful connections to Kū.[1] On it was

1 More recent work can also be found on David He'akoelekauaikalani Kalama Jr n.d. *Kalamakūloa*. Online: www.kalamakuloa.com/Aloha.html (accessed 7 October 2015).

a slideshow of his sketches, a YouTube video he created entitled 'Ki'i Akua – 54 Nights with Kū' (Kalamakūloa 2011b), and a link to purchase his ebook of the same name (Kalamakūloa 2011a). In the book *Ki'i Akua – 54 Nights with Kū*, Kalamakūloa provides an analysis of the 'Kona Style' that the ki'i were carved in:

> What also makes the 'Kona Style' significant is the '*waha*' complex—the jaw, mouth, tongue.
>
> Words are alive in our tradition. They can bring and take away. Words have *mana*.
>
> What if the *waha*, the mouth, is the central motive of the entire sculpture? As the focus point it accepts the counter-point of the arching headdress complex, with the nose as leading focus, and repeated with the pectoral chest. Metaphors, symbolism, animism ... These structural themes are rendered with meticulous and often symmetrical precision. (Kalamakūloa 2011a, Locations 235–36)

Figure 8. *Kūkolu Aka Mahina* by Kalamakūloa.

Source: Used with permission of artist.

Kalamakūloa's analysis calls up the explicit linkages between speech, voice and power that Noenoe K. Silva notes in her readings of the shifting meanings of 'mana' in the nineteenth-century Hawaiian Kingdom (see Silva, this volume). Like Silva, Kalamakūloa underlines the contemporary significance of renewed understandings: 'The return of these *Ki'i Akua* of *Kū*, can be seen as an *ho'ailona*—an omen, a message from the ancestors. The *Ki'i* are portals to connect to the Life Force, where we can commune with the Divine Energy, our ancestors, our past and the future' (Kalamakūloa 2011a, Location 321). As with other Kanaka 'Ōiwi artists, performers, scholars and educators, his work draws on ancestral patterns to channel new mana to future generations (Clark 2011).

Two weeks after the exhibit opened, the 'Aha Kāne Native Hawaiian Men's Health conference held its opening ceremonies at the Bishop Museum. The second such conference since 2006, the 'Aha Kāne was in many ways an extension of the project of the Hale Mua out to a broader constituency of Hawaiian men. Billy Kahalepuna Richards, board member of the 'Aha Kāne as well as communications director at the Partners in Development Foundations, a Vietnam Veteran (Marine), lua master, and community consultant for the Kū Exhibit, recalled, 'I think the *combined* mana of those who participated in the opening *lifted* that particular 'Aha Kāne to another level' (Richards 2012). Thomas Ka'auwai Kaulukukui Jr, a keynote speaker at the 'Aha Kāne, board chairman of the Queen Lili'uokalani Trust, a former judge, Vietnam Veteran (Army paratrooper), lua master, and consultant, spelled out the ways in which veterans who had gone through the lua martial arts training or participated in the 'Aha Kāne came to a deeper understanding of their Hawaiian warrior identity:

> For me and for most who have had military training, lua training is an affirmation that warriorhood, which we experience in the American military, is part of our DNA ... For *most* of us, it transforms our lives ... *Enormously* powerful. The 'Aha Kāne is another means of doing that, for males looking into male responsibility ... And maybe that aspect of the Kū personality, if you want to call it, for those of us who are veterans illustrates most clearly than anything else you could learn, about the *tie* between your Hawaiianness, and your DNA, and that aspect of your *mana*, and your skill. (Kaulukukui 2012)

For Richards, who had consciously adopted Kū as his god when he went to Vietnam, the Kū exhibit and the 'Aha Kāne was a reconnection in a different way. When it was time for the two Kū images to go back, his brother-in-law Kyle Nākānelua was unable to make the return trip. At first Richards did not feel it was right for him to take Nākānelua's place, but his wife Debbie Nākānelua Richards told him, 'Kū took you through war. Maybe it's time to thank him' (Peabody Essex Museum 2010). It was thus that Richards closed the circle with ceremony (see also Tengan 2015).

The art of re-membering

Did I forget to mention that the Kū image is literally dis-membered? Speaking at the opening panel named 'Nā Maka o Kū' ('The Many Faces of Ku'),[2] Nunes explained to the audience that sometime after the end of the 'aikapu in 1819 when the temple images were being torn down and burned, someone (perhaps Hawaiian, perhaps not) broke off the ule (penis) of the ki'i that now resided at the Bishop Museum (see also Ganaden 2014). While this was a pattern found among other male images, the ule of the other two ki'i from London and Salem were still intact. The occasion of bringing all three ki'i together renewed ongoing discussions and negotiations that Nunes had been having for years with the Bishop Museum regarding the restoration of Kū. Comparing it with Michelangelo's sculpture of David, which was repaired after a man vandalised it in 1991, Nunes asked the audience if our artwork and artist was any less important. If not, he asked, 'why is it that we allow … the only one we have in Hawai'i to be incomplete, to be emasculated?' The question was as much of a challenge to the museum, whose concerns had to do with curatorial conservation, as it was to the broader Hawaiian community

2 The other panelist was Sam Kaha'i Ka'ai, a kālai ki'i (carver of images), orator, and co-founder with Kyle Nākānelua of the Hale Mua men's group. For more on Ka'ai's important contributions to rethinking aspects of Kū in the Hawaiian movement, as well as his comments at the panel, see Tengan (2014a; 2014b). As I relate elsewhere (Tengan 2008: 83), Sam also discussed another famous dis-membering in Hawaiian history when the high chief Keōuakū'ahu'ula ceremonially cut off the tip of his penis before Kamehameha slew and sacrificed him to Kū at Pu'ukoholā Heiau in 1791. In the context of contemporary efforts to build mana that would bring Hawaiians together and reclaim sovereignty, Keōuakū'ahu'ula was re-membered as leader who sacrificed all in order that his descendants and people may live on into the future, not unlike the story of Kū the breadfruit tree.

still fearful of the potency of Kū. For Nunes, the castration of the image was a powerful metaphor and metonym for the emasculation of Hawaiian men. The association between image and man was quite literal for him as he argued that the desecration of the kiʻi was one of the main reasons that Hawaiian men had 'been floundering for years and years, because we are not intact' (Nunes 2010). But now with all three kiʻi reunited, Nunes found another meaning of the term 'maka' that named his panel: 'a beginning'.[3] Writing of a similarly powerful exhibition in Kodiak Island (Alaska) that saw the return of ancestral Suqpiaq masks held in France, James Clifford writes of it as 'a restorative connection across time and space. A homecoming and a beginning' (2013: 309). So too did the arrival of Kū herald a renewal of mana for Hawaiian men, who were claiming new agency and authority in matters of cultural representation. Nunes pushed to assert that 'it's a community thing', and that 'if the community says it's necessary to restore Kū to his fullness', it should happen. While Hawaiian men may not have had much of a say in the past, which he related directly to the emasculation of the kiʻi, today, as Nunes playfully put it, 'we're starting to grow another pair!' (Nunes 2010).

Four years after the other two Kū returned to the British Museum and the Peabody Essex, the Bishop Museum's kiʻi remained incomplete. This, however, did not stop ʻŌiwi artists from finding new and creative ways of 'manning up'. In 2014, Carl F.K. Pao and Solomon Enos collaborated with Drew Broderick to put on a show entitled *Pewa II: Remasculation and Human Seed Ships* (8 May – 8 June) at the contemporary art space of SPF Projects in Honolulu. Pao is known for his larger-than-life carvings of wooden ule. In his 'Artist Statement' (Pao 2014a), which I quote at length here, Pao explains that the emasculation of kiʻi with the advent of Christianity:

> was performed as a way to remove the mana from these kiʻi (actually, most kiʻi did not even survive this period, as the majority were destroyed by fire). Another possible reason for the emasculation could have taken place as these kiʻi made their way to other shores. Historical accounts reveal the disfiguring of kiʻi to make them more appropriate to their new owners by way of trade or purchase.

3 Recall that Makakū is also the name of the page dedicated to Kū on Kalamakūloa's Mokumana site. Online: mokumana.com/MANA/Makaku/Makaku.html (accessed 7 October 2015).

Understanding all of this got me to wonder if this act of emasculation had any sort of affect on our Hawaiian psyche. Especially, if when you look around at all of the commercial mainstream images appropriating ki'i kupuna [ancestral images], none have ule or penises. And what of all of the cheap or even expensive reproductions? No ule. If ki'i kupuna are to be portraits of our kupuna [ancestors], then what message is this sending? No ule, then no future?

Figure 9. *Ki'i Kupuna: Maka.*

Source: By Carl F. K. Pao, used with permission of artist.

Thus his work seeks to restore mana through 'remasculation', which he defines as '[a] process of decolonising, de-indoctrinating, and remembering the importance of the male role in our Hawaiian societal structure and systems. To not re-member and to continue to emasculate the images of our kupuna is only to reassure an imbalance of our people and lāhui [nation] and a continued emasculation of ourselves' (Pao 2014a).

The two-storey space of SPF Projects, formerly a taxi cab garage, featured Pao's *Remasculation* pieces on the bottom floor.[4] Walking in from the open garage doorway, one's eyes were drawn immediately to the centre of the room, where stood a 40-inch tall, 12-inch diameter (101.6 cm tall, 30 cm diameter), black wooden ule with lines and arches of pewa, bow tie-shaped patches of wood inserted along fissures to repair cracks. On the wall in the back of the ule hung a painting entitled *Ki'i Kupuna: Maka* (see Figure 9). The image depicts a close-up of the face of a ki'i, in particular, half of its nostril and mouth (part of the 'waha complex' that Kalamakūloa mentions above). Yet the focal point is not the mouth itself, but what is in it—an eye peering out, taking the form of the 'masculine element of the flower', especially its 'stamens' (Pao 2014a). On the left wall was a large, brown felt cutout panel of a ki'i of Kū that visitors were invited to approach, blindfolded, and rub on it a red felt ule (like pin the tail on the donkey, but not). Three ule carved from niu (coconut tree wood) between 10–12 inches (25.4 cm – 30 cm) were displayed next to this. Chiselled into the floor were well-endowed petroglyphs 'presented by the Post-Historic Museum of the Possible Aboriginal Hawaiian', whose other artefact was a grill upon which wooden ule of both Indigenous and foreign woods were barbecued. And on the right wall appeared excerpts of text taken (quite improbably) from my research, including the following quote:

4 Enos' *Human Seed Ships* on the top floor, a continuation of his *Polyfantastica* work, was comprised of dozens of digital drawings painted on 9" x 12" (22.9 cm x 30 cm) mailing envelopes that represented a future for Hawaiian productivity and generation as the 'seed' of Hawaiiankind was to be spread across the universe to inseminate new lands. The text on the wall beneath the stairs that went to the second floor was meant to connect the two spaces, as was the smoke from the burnt ule on the grill.

> Bodies figure centrally in the gendered work of decolonization, for it is there that alternative forms of being and acting—in the Hawaiian case, those based in ea (sovereignty, life, breath), mo'okū'auhau (genealogy), and mana (spiritual power and authority)—are re-membered.[5]

In an interview, Pao (2014b) described his aesthetic, which works with complementary colours (usually bright) and surfaces (frequently large), as a 'search for being pono', which is 'to be in balance'. There is also a significant play on kaona (layered meanings), often to humorous effect. His discussion of 'maka'—which means eye, face and stamen all at once (in addition to much more, including the 'beginning' described by Nunes above)—exemplifies what Brandy Nālani McDougall (2014: 1) has called 'kaona as a decolonial aesthetic practice'. Pao (2014b) explained:

> Some might argue that politically charged or driven artwork is not necessarily for aesthetic purposes … and that political art is usually just message driven, and it's not about pretty flowers and trying to capture a moment or anything of beauty; it's more or less just driving a point. But then I guess that's also, for a lack of better word, 'the beauty of art', is that within a political work, you can disguise it as something beautiful. Maybe that's, when we get into the discussion of mana and kaona, I was just thinking about it, the work that I do with the maka is taking the stamen of the flower as the ule, as the male essence, but disguising it in a flower. So I have these compositions that are just full of ule, but then how many people are going to recognize that? They're just going to see it as a flower. But if I was to just make it very blatantly obvious that these components of the flower were actual penises, then are they gonna be turned off by it, or are they going to see it as something other? So [laughing], to each his own! [More laughter.]
>
> But I like to think that following in the, I guess the whole [pause] 'tradition', or the 'aha—that lineage, link, that cord—back to our ancestors and to the future, that having art that's purposeful is part of our traditions of the things that we made were of purpose.

5 Slightly modified from its original form, which appears in Tengan (2014b).

ʻAha moments and open-endings

I end with a final note on the significance of the term ʻaha that Pao spoke of, and some of its kaona. Describing the Kū image from the British Museum, Kalamakūloa (2011a) writes, 'The hair echoes the fruit spray of young coconut, and descend into *ʻaha*, knotted cords, an allusion to prayers and numbering in fours and tens' (Location 247). As given in the Hawaiian Dictionary, some of the broader definitions of ʻaha include:

> 1. n. Meeting, assembly, gathering, convention ... 2. nvi. Sennit; cord braided of coconut husk, human hair, intestines of animals; string for a musical instrument; to stretch the *ʻaha* cord for the outline of a house so that the posts may be properly placed; measurement of an edge or border ... 3. n. A prayer or service whose efficacy depended upon recitation under taboo and without interruption. The priest was said to carry a cord (*ʻaha*) ... 4. n. Millipede, so called because it coils itself up like a string. 5. n. Any of the needlefishes of the family Belonidae ... 6. n. Design supposed to resemble the continuing track of a duck, carved on tapa beaters. (Pukui and Elbert 1986: 5)

Its first set of meanings includes conferences, such as in ʻAha Kāne Men's Conference; the second and third entries have received the most anthropological attention, especially in reference to ceremonies that were done on temples with Kū images during the ʻaikapu period. Shore (1989: 152–53) and Valeri (1985: 295–308) have noted the significance of the ʻaha as both symbol and container of divine mana, organising and binding the generative power of the gods to chiefs who are genealogically descended from them. Tēvita Kaʻili, Rochelle Fonotī and I have argued for a renewed attention to the role that ʻaha, with all of its kaona, could play in forging new genealogies for Indigenous anthropology in Oceania, including the debates over and production of mana in anthropological gatherings (Tengan, Kaʻili and Fonoti 2010), such as the two that produced this volume (see Introduction). Drawing from my experiences with *E Kū Ana Ka Paia* and *Remasculation*, I suggest that some of the strained relations between Indigenous communities, anthropologists and museums might be overcome by establishing a shared commitment to building mana through an emphasis on ceremonial practice, genealogical reckoning, and creating new gathering spaces for the community.

I do this, though, with hesitant and cautious hope. As Clifford notes: 'A symptomatic critique of heritage work may see it as occupying a comfortable niche in postmodern "multicultural" hegemonies: every identity gets its exhibition, website, coffee-table book, or film' (2013: 259). He responds:

> The old/new articulations, performances, and translations of identity are not enough to bring about structural socioeconomic change. But they reflect and to a real extent create new conditions for indigenous solidarity, activism, and participation in diverse public spheres. When they are understood as part of a wider politics of self-determination, heritage projects are open ended in their significance. (Clifford 2013: 259)

Taking this approach, I would explore the suggestive aspects of Mary Kawena Pukui and Samuel H. Elbert's definition of ʻaha as 'to stretch the *ʻaha* cord for the outline of a house so that the posts may be properly placed', and their example of '*E kiʻi i ke kaula e ʻaha ai*, get a cord to stake out the house with' (1986: 5). Here we might think of ʻaha as the practice of actively retrieving (kiʻi), stretching, and loosening the bounds of tradition and heritage in a process of gauging connections, negotiating relationships, and resetting borders in the present so that structures in, of, and on our future homes will be pono—proper and in balance. Such an approach is even more important when addressing the challenges that arise when Indigenous genealogical lines clash and compete over the mana of anthropology or the museum, which was clearly the case in the Kawaihae struggle. While time and space do not permit me to explore the implications of ʻaha praxis much further, I would suggest that in order for it to be effective—to have mana—it must articulate (Clifford 2013: 60–62) powerful linkages that allow people to see what was once unseen and imagine new possibilities and potential ways of being. These would be instantiated in what Carl F.K. Pao calls ʻaha moments:

> Like they say, you know, one of the recent expressions or whatevers is 'aha moments.' Well, I think of it as ʻaha, not 'aha!' It's not, you're going, 'Ah, I turned the light on.' It's 'Ah, I made that link. I reconnected.' That's how I see it. And now I can, yeah, that link will continue. (Pao 2014b)

For veterans like Thomas Kaulukukui and Billy Richards, the ʻaha moment came when they realised the mana of Kū was in their 'DNA'. While the future of Kānaka ʻŌiwi men and women may be open-ended, Kū has empowered a sense of agency and continuity in those who have engaged him. As one anonymous comment left at the Bishop Museum proclaimed: 'PAST, PRESENT + FUTURE ... KŪ IS A PART OF HAWAI'I, ITS PEOPLE AND OUR MANA!'

Acknowledgements

I would like to thank Noelle Kahanu, Carl F.K. Pao, Kalamakūloa and Matt Tomlinson for their comments on and assistance with this chapter. All mistakes are mine.

References

Bishop Museum. 2010. Annual Report. Online: www.bishopmuseum.org/images/pdf/annual_report.pdf, (accessed 2 November 2010).

Clark, Herman Pi'ikea. 2006. Kūkulu Kauhale o Limaloa: A Kanaka Maoli Culture Based Approach to Education through Visual Studies. D.Ed. dissertation, College of Education, Massey University.

——. 2011. Ka Muhe'e, He I'a Hololua: Kanaka Maoli Art and the challenge of the global market. In *Globalization and Contemporary Art*, ed. Jonathan Harris, pp.137–46. West Sussex: Wiley-Blackwell.

Clifford, James. 2013. *Returns: Becoming Indigenous in the Twenty-First Century*. Cambridge, MA: Harvard University Press.

Dawrs, Stu. 2011. Regarding Ku. *Hana Hou! The Magazine of Hawaiian Airlines* 14(1) (February–March). Online: www.hanahou.com/pages/Magazine.asp?Action=DrawArticle&ArticleID=945&MagazineID=60 (accessed 7 October 2015).

Ellis, William. 1825. *A Journal of a Tour around Hawaii, the Largest of the Sandwich Islands*. New York: Crocker and Brewster.

Enomoto, Kekoa. 2010. Hawaiian homecoming. 'Unprecedented' exhibit reunites trio of ancient Hawaiian artifacts. *The Maui News*. 27 June. Online: www.mauinews.com/page/content.detail/id/532814.html?nav=12 (accessed 7 October 2015).

Ganaden, Sonny. 2014. The Last Statues of Kū. *Flux Hawaii* (Winter). Online: fluxhawaii.com/the-last-statues-of-ku/ (accessed 25 March 2016).

Gee, Pat. 2010. Gathering of the Gods. *Honolulu Star-Bulletin*. 4 June. Online: archives.starbulletin.com/content/20100604_Gathering_of_the_gods (accessed 9 October 2015).

Goodyear-Kaopua, Noelani, Ikaika Hussey and Erin Kahunawaika'ala Wright (eds). 2014. *A Nation Rising: Hawaiian Movements for Life, Land, and Sovereignty*. Durham: Duke University Press.

Grace, Shantelle. 2010. Farewell, for now. *Honolulu Weekly*. 22 September. Online: honoluluweekly.com/cover/2010/09/farewell-for-now/ (accessed 7 October 2015).

Graham, Laura R. and H. Glenn Penny (eds). 2014. *Performing Indigeneity: Global Histories and Contemporary Experiences*. Lincoln: University of Nebraska Press.

Harris, Jonathan (ed.). 2011. *Globalization and Contemporary Art*. West Sussex: Wiley-Blackwell.

Howard, Alan and Robert Borofsky (eds). 1989. *Developments in Polynesian Ethnology*. Honolulu: University of Hawai'i Press.

Hyden, Amber-Lynn. 2010. Ku images come home. *KITV News*, 21 May. Online: www.youtube.com/watch?v=T27mhe0Sxz8 (accessed 2 November 2010).

Innes, Robert Alexander and Kim Anderson (eds). 2015. *Indigenous Men and Masculinities: Legacies, Identities, Regeneration*. Winnipeg: University of Manitoba Press.

Jolly, Margaret. 2008. Moving masculinities: Memories and bodies across Oceania. *The Contemporary Pacific* 20(1): 1–24.

——. 2011. Becoming a 'new' museum? Contesting Oceanic visions at Musée du Quai Branly. *The Contemporary Pacific* 23(1): 108–39.

Johnson, Greg. 2011. Courting culture: Unexpected relationships between religion and law in contemporary Hawai'i. In *After Secular Law*, ed. Winnifred Fallers Sullivan, Robert A. Yelle and Mateo Taussig-Rubbo, pp. 282–301. Stanford, CA: Stanford University Press.

Kahanu, Noelle. 2010. Interview on 'Bishop Museum' program of Nā 'Ōiwi 'Ōlino Radio Program. Office of Hawaiian Affairs. Online: www.naoiwiolino.com/?p=330 (accessed 2 November 2012).

——. 2012. Lecture in ANTH/ES 486 Peoples of Hawai'i class, University of Hawai'i at Mānoa. 6 March.

Kalama Productions Inc. 2010–11. *moku mana*. Website. Online: www.mokumana.com/MANA/Aloha.html (accessed 6 October 2015).

Kalamakūloa (David H. Kalama Jr). 2011a. *Ki'i Akua – 54 Nights with Kū*. Kindle Ebook. Online: www.amazon.com/Kii-Akua-Nights-KÃ%C2%BC-Noeau-ebook/dp/B004INHXEQ/ref=sr_1_1?ie=UTF8&qid=1444305387&sr=8-1&keywords=54+nights+ku (accessed 9 October 2015).

——. 2011b. Ki'i Akua – 54 Nights with Kū. Online: www.youtube.com/watch?v=CmopShftl28 (accessed 13 October 2014).

Kaulukukui, Thomas Ka'auwai Jr. 2012. Interview with author, Honolulu. 24 September.

Marshall, Wende Elizabeth. 2011. *Potent Mana: Lessons in Power and Healing*. Albany, NY: SUNY Press.

McDougall, Brandy Nālani. 2014. Putting feathers on our words: Kaona as a decolonial aesthetic practice in Hawaiian literature. *Decolonization: Indigeneity, Education & Society* 3(1): 1–22.

Morgensen, Scott Lauria. 2011. Review: *Making Space for Indigenous Feminism*, J. Green (Zed Books, 2007); *Native Americans and the Christian Right*, A. Smith (Duke University Press, 2008); *Native Men Remade*, T. Tengan (Duke University Press, 2008); *Mapping the Americas*, S. Huhndorf (Cornell University Press, 2009). *Signs: Journal of Women in Culture and Society* 36(3): 766–76.

Nunes, Keone. 2010. Remarks at 'Nā Maka o Kū' Panel Discussion. Audio recording made by Geoffrey White. 4 June.

Nākānelua, Kyle. 2010. Moʻolelo Huakaʻi o Ku Kiʻi. Unpublished manuscript.

Pao, Carl F.K. 2014a. Artist Statement. Posted at *Pewa II: Remasculation and Human Seed Ships* show at SPF Projects, Honolulu, 8 May – 8 June.

——. 2014b. Interview by author in Honolulu. 9 October.

Peabody Essex Museum (PEM). 2010. He's back! Kū returns amid honors from Hawaiian delegation. Online: www.pem.org/aux/pdf/collection/KuSmall.pdf (accessed 2 November 2012).

Pukui, Mary Kawena and Samuel H. Elbert. 1986. *Hawaiian Dictionary*, revised and enlarged. Honolulu: University of Hawaiʻi Press.

Pukui, Mary Kawena with Laura C.S. Green. 1995. *Folktales of Hawaiʻi: He Mau Kaʻao Hawaiʻi*. Honolulu: Bishop Museum Press.

Richards, William Kahalepuna. 2012. Interview by author in Honolulu. 21 September.

Sahlins, Marshall. 1981. *Historical Metaphors and Mythical Realities: Structure in the Early History of the Sandwich Islands Kingdom*. Ann Arbor: University of Michigan Press.

Shore, Bradd. 1989. *Mana* and *Tapu*. In *Developments in Polynesian Ethnology*, ed. Alan Howard and Robert Borofsky, pp. 137–73. Honolulu: University of Hawaiʻi Press.

Sullivan, Winnifred Fallers, Robert A. Yelle and Mateo Taussig-Rubbo (eds). 2011. *After Secular Law*. Stanford, CA: Stanford University Press.

Tengan, Ty P. Kāwika. 2008. *Native Men Remade: Gender and Nation in Contemporary Hawaiʻi*. Durham: Duke University Press.

——. 2014a. Portrait: Sam Kahaʻi Kaʻai. In *A Nation Rising: Hawaiian Movements for Life, Land, and Sovereignty*, ed. Noelani Goodyear-Kaopua, Ikaika Hussey and Erin Kahunawaikaʻala Wright, pp. 115–23. Durham: Duke University Press.

——. 2014b. The return of Kū? Re-membering Hawaiian masculinity, warriorhood, and nation. In *Performing Indigeneity: Global Histories and Contemporary Experiences*, ed. Laura R. Graham and H. Glenn Penny, pp. 206–46. Lincoln: University of Nebraska Press.

——. 2015. The face of Kū: A dialogue on Hawaiian warriorhood with Thomas Ka'auwai Kaulukukui Jr and William Kahalepuna Richards Jr. In *Indigenous Men and Masculinities: Legacies, Identities, Regeneration*, ed. Robert Alexander Innes and Kim Anderson, pp. 231–44. Winnipeg: University of Manitoba Press.

Tengan, Ty P. Kāwika and Lamakū Mikahala Roy. 2014. 'I search for the channel made fragrant by the Maile': Genealogies of discontent and hope. *Oceania* 84(3): 315–30.

Tengan, Ty P. Kāwika, Tēvita O. Ka'ili and Rochelle Tuitagava'a Fonoti. 2010. Genealogies: Articulating Indigenous anthropology in/of Oceania. *Pacific Studies* 33(2/3): 139–67.

Valeri, Valerio. 1985. *Kingship and Sacrifice: Ritual and Society in Ancient Hawai'i*, trans. Paula Wissing. Chicago: University of Chicago Press.

Villanueva, Zach. 2010. Kū exhibit inspires tears, smiles, awe. *Ka Wai Ola: The Living Water* 27(12): 13.

White, Geoffrey. 2010. Museum mediations: Reflections on cultural politics at the Bishop Museum and the Musée du Quai Branly. Paper prepared for conference on 'Framing Cultures' Marseille: Centre de Recherche et de Documentation sur l'Océanie, Université de Provence, 5–6 November.

3

Bodies Permeable and Divine: Tapu, Mana and the Embodiment of Hegemony in Pre-Christian Tonga

Andy Mills

This ethnohistorical essay explores the body's metaphysical conceptualisation in pre-Christian Tonga to explain the former relationship between the concepts of *mana* (metaphysical efficacy), *tapu* (ritual prohibition or closure) and *'eiki* (chiefliness). These concepts have often been discussed as interrelated in historical Polynesia—chiefly persons and things being considered mana and therefore sources of tapu. The precise theological basis of their relationship, however, has not been adequately addressed. Here I explore the nature of mana and tapu in pre-Christian Tonga up to the early nineteenth century. It is well documented that Christian conversion in Tonga triggered the breakdown of what Methodist missionaries called the 'tapu system', a complex of hierarchical principles, avoidance relationships, economic controls, ritual prohibitions and ceremonial practices explored centrally here. Practically speaking, this historical process of cosmological transformation spanned the period 1820–75, and permanently changed the ontological realities of kin and gender relations, class identities and political legitimacy in Tonga (Lawry 1850; West 1865: 126).

I argue that a sophisticated metaphysical system existed in Tonga during the late eighteenth and early nineteenth centuries which conceptually articulated the phenomenological perception of mana through tapu, and tapu through bodily experience. Historical evidence presented here shows that mana and chiefliness had complex relationships with tapu and one another precisely because their interaction was physiologically mediated. I reconstruct the anatomical concept of *manava* to interpret the phenomenology of tapu; the interpersonal dynamics of the *'api* (territorially restricted household of co-resident siblings and their conjugal units) and *kainga* (extended kin group of several *'api*); the ritual transformations of the life cycle and the articulation of social class (Tupouniua 1977: 13–14). By this route, I will explore how mana, tapu and *'eiki* interacted through embodied experience. Derived from the perceptual phenomenology of Maurice Merleau-Ponty (1962), the anthropology of embodiment takes the view that the body is what Thomas J. Csordas (1990: 39–40) defined as 'the existential ground of culture', calling for us 'to investigate how cultural objects (including selves) are constituted … in the ongoing indeterminacy and flux of adult cultural lives'. Viewed thus, enculturated human interactions, and particularly ritual practices, become embodied texts of legible *action signs*, subject to parsing for the deduction of phenomenological realities informing them (Bargatzky 1996; Farnell 1999: 358ff).

Mana's analysis has been consistently concerned with embodiment and materiality. Although the mana Robert H. Codrington (1891: 118–19) encountered in Melanesia was a supernatural, non-physical influence through which things were achieved, early anthropologists modelled it as a hydraulic metaphysical life force that persons or objects contained—akin to the Greek humours, Chinese *qi* or Hindu *prana* (Handy 1927; Marett 1929). Raymond Firth's (1940: 490–92) discussion of mana and *manu* on Tikopia rejected simplistic hydraulic interpretations, but his belief in mana's immateriality led him to discount Tikopian statements that mana resided in the hands or lips of a chief as metaphorical, despite observing that his informants only identified mana through the material evidence of its effects. He also overlooked the possibility that mana might have both material and immaterial manifestations. Most subsequent works have read mana as an adjectival or adverbial quality of immaterial efficacy that persons, objects and acts *are* (Keesing 1984; Sahlins 1985: 37–38;

Shore 1989: 137–39). Claude Lévi-Strauss (1987: 63–64) took mana's immateriality further, deeming it a 'floating signifier' lacking any stable meaning: a classic case of what scholars don't understand being minimised as meaningless.

The debate over mana has clearly been motivated by western philosophical preoccupations with dualisms of mind and body, idealism and materialism, rather than the characteristics of Polynesian religious systems; anything which manifests the efficacy of both gods and human beings is self-evidently material, immaterial and polysemic. Bradd Shore's (1989: 163) regional analysis of mana and tapu in Polynesia recognised this, modelling a 'complex economy of powers' through which the benevolence and fertility of deities and ancestors, the ritual and secular leadership of chiefs, the reproductive and productive labour of men and women, and the lives of animals and sacrificial victims became commodities circulating in a unified system. Mana consequently becomes fluid cultural capital commensurating these commodities by their common manifestation of it—a currency of sociality specifically transcending false distinctions between materiality and immateriality to articulate the relationships of the divine and mortal, living and dead, chiefly and common.

Mana and tapu were understood differently in each Austronesian society because their meanings diverged over four millennia of migration into Remote Oceania (Kirch and Green 2000: 239–41). Robert Blust (2007) supports such a view in deducing that mana primarily signified 'thunder' in the Proto-Oceanic (POC) language spoken by the makers of Lapita-style ceramics in the Bismarck Archipelago four millennia ago. Thunder is one of its modern Tongan meanings (Churchward 1959: 329–30). We must seriously consider the possibility that (circa 1100 BC) Tonga's original settlers may still have primarily viewed mana as a meteorological phenomenon rather than metaphysical efficacy. This alterity of ancient mana has wider significance, because Patrick V. Kirch and Roger C. Green (2000: 201–36 *passim*) have reconstructed the 'Ancestral Polynesian Society' (circa 500 BC – 500 AD) in Western Polynesia as a classless kinship-based society of small autonomous communities. This suggests that the eighteenth-century understanding of the Tongan chiefly class (*hou'eiki*) as intrinsically mana and tapu developed as an aspect of those crystallising class identities during the later first millennium AD, because oral histories begin shortly afterwards which strongly associate the *hou'eiki* with divinely derived mana (Campbell 2001; Mahina 1990). While archaeological lexicostatistics can illuminate these major processes of Tongan prehistory, it implies that the relationship between mana, tapu and *'eiki* has undergone complex transformations. I contend that, to understand this relationship, we must reconstruct how tapu was physiologically experienced, and a precondition of that is an understanding of *manava*.

The *manava* system as embodied vitality

Considering how few discussions of *manava* have been published, it is notable that all assert an etymological origin in mana (Collocott 1921: 433–34; Refiti 2008, 2009; Wendt 1996: 42). According to historical comparative linguistics, however, *manava* is one of two modern Tongan reflexes of the Proto-Malayo-Polynesian (PMP) word *ma-ñawa* (literally 'breath'), which signifies the heart, lungs, stomach, intestines, womb and bowels. The other reflex, *mānava*, still signifies the breath (Robert Blust, personal communication, 2014; *Polynesian Lexicon Project Online* 2015; *Austronesian Comparative Dictionary* 2015); neither word originated in mana. As E.E.V. Collocott (1921: 433–34) observed, it is clear that *manava* and *mānava* encompassed the body's organs and processes of animation. Evidencing that the psyche was equally implicated, John Martin (1818: 312) recorded that the *fotomanava* (tailbone of the *manava*, the heart's right auricle) was the bodily location of a person's consciousness. The term *loto* (inside) has largely replaced *manava* in modern Tongan, but still preserves its conflation of the viscera into a unified meta-organ and the affective core. Notably, those organs subsumed into the *manava* perform the body's processes of exchange: taking in air, water, food and sperm; expelling carbon dioxide, urine, faeces, menstrual blood and neonates—*manava* and *mānava* mediate the physical boundary between an organism and its environment. These animation processes are also subject to rhythmic muscular contractions and convulsions, and this link is explicitly retained by *manava*'s two recombinant nouns: *manamanava* and *manavanava*, which both signify throbbing sensations (Churchward 1959: 331).

Manava's historical significance as the primary Tongan concept of bodily animation led it to develop several dependent constructions, such as the verbs *manava'aki* (literally 'about *manava*', meaning 'to eat') and *mānava'aki* (about *mānava*, meaning to breathe). These terms generalised *manava-mānava* into a conceptual cluster that encompassed respiratory, digestive and reproductive animation. Similarly, *manava-fasi* (literally 'broken *manava*') signifies under-nourishment in Tongan, and illustrates that the conversion of food into observable health was (logically) contingent upon the proper functioning of *manava*. Further affective complexity emerges when we consider another branch of dependent constructions which indicate a strong connection between *manava*, courage and fear (see Table 1).

Table 1. Dependent Tongan constructions of emotion from *manava*.

Tongan	English	English Gloss
Manava-hoko	articulated *manava*	courageous
Manava-lahi	big *manava*	courage
Manava-si'i	little *manava*	nervousness
Manava-fo'i	defeated *manava*	fear
Manava-he	*manava*-less	abject terror
Fakatau-manava	test *manava*	to pluck up courage

Source: C. Maxwell Churchward, 1959. *Tongan Dictionary*. Nuku'alofa: Government Printing Press, pp. 106, 330–31.

Evidently, larger or smaller *manava* enabled more or less courage. *Manava* was tested in some way by fearful situations, and either withstood them or was overpowered and diminished. By interconnecting the breath and courage, *manava-mānava* explains why sneezing was considered a terrible omen when early nineteenth-century warriors set out to war; an involuntary expulsion of breath suggested an incontinence of *manava* that warriors wanted to avoid (Martin 1818: 249–50). Connecting *manava* with courage sheds further light, because historical sources for both early nineteenth-century Tonga and Fiji record that the liver (Tongan *'ate*, Fijian *yate*) was the body's repository of courage (Im Thurn 1922a: cviii–cix; Martin 1818: 312). To summarise: respiration, digestion, reproduction, consciousness and courage were unified by a single bodily *manava* system. The *manava* was a meta-organ, and we can reconstruct that the right auricle of the heart and the liver were its sub-loci of consciousness and courage respectively. Variable quantities or sizes of *manava* resided within the body, reflecting variable quantities of embodied vitality, being and will for the Tongans of 200 years ago. Let us next address tapu, as it was through the *manava* system that tapu manifested its detrimental effect.

The phenomenology of tapu in pre-Christian Tonga

I now begin a substantial discussion of the phenomenological realities and ritual management of tapu. I make a heuristic (if artificial) distinction here between three different senses of tapu in historical Tonga, signifying the different contexts in which it was used. I define *episodic tapu* as a potentially fatal episode of metaphysically induced sickness; *relational tapu* as a prohibitive relationship between two persons or things which engendered an episodic tapu in the inferior; and *regulatory tapu* as a prohibition imposed by chiefly authorities on specific food resources or activities for political, religious or economic reasons. I will address each here. Tongan tapu translates into English as 'sacred', 'forbidden' and 'closed', and although it was regrettably omitted from Shore's regional synthesis (1989: 143–48), this third quality of closure is integral. Closure is a quality repeated by the term *malu*, a verb indicating the act of observing a tapu and a noun indicating a strict physical closure (such as constipation or inability to urinate). Several terms connote the release or absence of tapu, but the most common was *ngofua*, meaning 'not tapu', 'permissible' or 'easy' (Churchward 1959: 13, 26, 390); tapu was therefore a problematic affliction described in terms of a physical closure.

One acquired an episodic tapu state by accidentally or unavoidably performing certain transgressions, which caused sickness and ultimately death unless it was released (Beaglehole 1988, II: 176–77; Martin 1818: 353–55). The known causes of episodic tapu in pre-Christian Tonga included touching the head, corpse, personal effects or food leftovers of a person more chiefly than oneself, eating in their sight-line, and eating a meat species or using a bathing place reserved for a higher social class (Collocott 1921: 420; Gifford 1929: 124).

As well as touching sources of tapu with the hands, eating was a metaphysically dangerous activity fundamental to episodic tapu development, and so the digestive processes of the *manava* system were closely involved. Importantly, an episodic tapu created by touch was not life-threatening to the transgressor unless they touched their hands to their mouth. Early observer William Mariner (Martin 1818: 104) explained:

> [H]e must not feed himself with his own hands, but must be fed by somebody. He must not even use a toothpick himself, but must guide another person's hand holding the toothpick. If he is hungry, and there is no-one to feed him, he must go down upon his hands and knees, and pick up his victuals with his mouth. And if he infringes upon any of these rules, it is firmly expected that he will swell up and die.

Mariner's description conveys several facts: in order to threaten life, an episodic tapu needed to be physically ingested to enter the *manava* system; although the hands became episodically tapu, they were not *internally* connected with the *manava* system of the torso, but could only transmit the episodic tapu to it at its own opening. Nonetheless, the belief that handedness was determined by liver position in the abdomen shows that *manava* strongly influenced manual agency, although the relationship was one-way (Martin 1818: 312–13). That the victim could not use a toothpick indicates that normal material objects offered no barrier to the tapu. However, that the victim might hold another's hand and use a toothpick shows that the episodic tapu state was not physically contagious between people. Finally, that the victim 'will swell up and die' indicates a powerful visceral reaction to the tapu entering the *manava* system of the torso.

Adult men were key sources of tapu; it was dangerous for a man's child or wife to ever touch his head, touch any part of him while he was eating, consume his food or drink, or touch his bed, headrest, staff, weapons, fly-whisk or fan (Collocott 1921: 418; Gifford 1929: 18). If the man gave his permission for these acts, however, no episodic tapu ensued. As well as a concern for his head, we can recognise the preoccupation with eating and food outlined above, and those personal artefacts which he held in his hands. Prohibitions on the touching or consumption of an individual's food or personal possessions reflect the contagious distribution of personhood into artefacts (Frazer 1925: 11; Gell 1998: 96–104). Breaking the rules controlling contact with his private property, food and body caused the transgressor sickness, swelling and eventual death unless the man performed *amohi* (relational stroking) of their head, throat or belly. The location depended on how the tapu was contracted, how much time had elapsed, and how far into the body the swelling phenomenon had penetrated. The hands were a primary source, and the alleviation, of episodic tapu within the household.

Further insights emerge concerning the emotion of *manahi* ('relational mana', a superior's anger). If a child, younger sibling or wife defied a senior man, his *manahi* had the power to cause them to sicken, swell up at the throat or abdomen and eventually die from asphyxiation or abdominal rupture—that is, develop an episodic tapu at any distance. This was only averted by submitting to his will and receiving *amohi* (Gifford 1929: 326–27). *Manahi* (a relational function of the superior's mana) ideologically enforced status asymmetry in the household by remotely engendering an episodic tapu which attacked the transgressor's *manava* system.

Episodic tapu was embodied, ingested and travelled downwards through the throat to the liver and other internal organs, causing an increasingly life-threatening swelling as it descended. Episodic tapu was indexed by those symptoms that western medicine classifies as scrofula, goitres, lymphatic and abdominal cysts, cirrhosis, tumours and similar disorders. Swellings (*kahi*) in the abdomen and neck are still frequently treated by traditional Tongan medicine, and attributed to internal blockages (George 1995; McGrath 1999: 493). Around 1800, postmortem eviscerations were frequently performed to assess a person's moral conduct by inspecting the size, shape, colour and markings on the liver, which was disfigured by tapu infractions (Martin 1818: 128n*). Episodic tapu in Tonga was materially embodied by engendering *kahi* swellings through the flow of vitality within the *manava* system.

Releasing episodic tapu

Episodic tapu was released by several methods. We have already encountered the *amohi* stroking of the head, throat or belly between a man and his subordinate family. If an unrelated victim knew that they had not eaten or touched their mouth since contracting the episodic tapu, they performed *moemoe'i*: pressing their palms, backhands and forehead successively onto the sole of the foot of the more chiefly person from whom they had contracted the tapu, or (failing that) any high chief. Beyond the ritual's physical submission, *moemoe'i* describes the act of searching for something with the foot (as when gathering shellfish in the sea); the superior was seeking out and removing the episodic tapu (Beaglehole 1988, III: 116–17, 952–54; Labillardiere 1800, II: 144–46).[1] Discussing *moemoe'i,* Mariner observed that '[The Tongans] are very subject to indurations of the liver, and certain forms of scrofula … which, as they conceive, frequently happen from a neglect of this ceremony' (Martin 1818: 128, 247). *Fota* (to massage by squeezing) was a more intensive form of *moemoe'i* required if the episodic tapu had been ingested; the superior pressed the sole of their foot on the victim's belly to neutralise the episodic tapu and prevent an abdominal *kahi* (Martin 1818: 355). Other common methods of releasing uningested episodic tapu were *veipa* and *fanofano,* which involved washing the hands in the sap of an immature banana tree (Collocott 1921: 436; Churchward 1959: 537).

The life-threatening swellings at the liver and throat caused by episodic tapu resulted from their being major nodes of the *manava* system. The largest of the viscera, the liver's susceptibility to episodic tapu arose from its function as the central organ of the *manava* system. The throat's susceptibility reflected it being the route by which breath and food pass from the head into the body. I discussed above that the terms tapu and *malu* signify tight closure, and the neck (as a physical narrowing) is partially 'closed' to begin with and logically prone to complete closure. The relationship between tapu and asphyxiation demands that we reconsider the pre-Christian practice of *naukia*—ritual killing by strangulation when making human sacrifices, executing the wives of dead chiefs to accompany them in the afterlife, and performing euthanasia. Those condemned to sacrifice were termed *tangata tapu* (tapu men), and their heads were shaved and painted with turmeric prior to killing. Two men throttled them with a barkcloth rope (Martin 1818: 348–49), which can be seen as a mechanical *malu* (closure) rendering the offering tapu before presentation. Thus, what

1 Tonga's paramount sacred king, the Tu'i Tonga, was almost constantly beset by the people to perform *moemoe'i* for them, as immortalised by the artist John Webber in his 1777 watercolour *Poulaho, King of the Friendly Isles, Drinking Kava* (Joppien and Smith 1988, III: 318, image 3.55).

amohi and *moemoe'i* prevented, *naukia* achieved. In neighbouring Fiji, such strangling was termed *yateba* and retained an etymological reference to the liver (*yate*) as its locus of effect (Im Thurn 1922a: cix).

Relational tapu and the ʻeiki-tuʻa dichotomy

I will now consider relational tapu in order to reconstruct the sociological basis of episodic tapu. Relational tapu identifies those situations where one individual was intrinsically tapu to another. The causes of relational tapu were primarily a complex set of kin relations and simpler social class identities. Several animal foods were prohibited for commoners, and the animal species that could serve as a manifestation vehicle for each individual's ancestral deity was equally tapu. Relational tapu emerged from the interaction between the social or species identities of two persons or animals, and episodic tapu was the sickening effect of exposure to relational tapu's defining conditions. In Piercean semiotic terms, a relational tapu was the *legisign* or systemic law, of which episodic tapu were the *sinsigns* or cases. In most cases, relational tapu was therefore an immutable condition which could not be released or rendered *ngofua*. As we shall see below, however, this was not always the case.

The category of *'eiki* (chief or chiefly) and its antonym *tu'a* (commoner or common) were the articulating principles of relational tapu. Between any two Tongans, one is always *'eiki* to the other, who is correspondingly *tu'a*. Within the traditional *'api* household or the wider *kainga* kin group, everyone was asymmetrically ranked relative to the others, and relative *'eiki-tu'a* statuses were determined by four fundamental rules of kinship. First, between *tokoua* (same-sex siblings)[2] the social rank of the father, mother and primogeniture successively defined relative *'eiki* and *tu'a* statuses; this was equally true for males and females. Second, sisters (*tuofefine*) were invariably *'eiki* to their brothers (*tuonga'ane*; see James 1995). Third, husbands were *'eiki* to their wives. Fourth, immediately superior generations were *'eiki* to immediately inferior ones (Bott 1982: 57; Tupouniua 1977: 22–25; Van der Grijp 1993: 131–33). The foregoing examples of episodic tapu and *manahi* show that it was these four hierarchical

2 As in all variants of the 'Hawaiian' kinship system, Tongan kinship makes no classificatory distinction between genetic siblings and cousins (Tupouniua 1977: 22–25).

principles which created relational tapu; all episodic tapu contractors share the *tu'a* position within these dyads. Those who were relatively *'eiki* within the household were relationally tapu to those who were *tu'a* in relation to them. Thus, male (*tuonga'ane*) and female (*tuofefine*) siblings had a strong avoidance relationship because sisters were tapu to brothers (Aoyagi 1966: 162; Gifford 1929: 21–22). The father's sister (*mehekitanga*), as well as having particular rights and privileges in relation to her brother's children, was tapu to them (Douaire-Marsaudon 1996; Taumoefolau 1991). In contrast, the mother's brother (*tuasina*) was the focus of the *fahu* relationship through which his sororal nephew or niece had remarkable freedom to consume his food, claim his possessions and touch his head without incurring the episodic tapu that would debilitate his own children (Gifford 1929: 22–26). The grandfather (*kui tangata*) was similarly free to interact with his grandchildren (Völkel 2010: 183), and these double-articulated relationships illustrate the parallel redoubling and cancelling-out of tapu or *ngofua* statuses. Perhaps most compelling, foreign *matāpule* heralds were impervious to all causes of episodic tapu; lacking local kin relations and incapable of genealogical location, they were neither *'eiki* nor *tu'a* to any Tongan, and sat outside the laws of relational tapu altogether (Gifford 1929: 141).

To summarise, the recorded principles of relational tapu organising episodic tapu's occurrence were a direct transformation of the *'eiki-tu'a* (chiefly-common) dichotomy as it articulated interpersonal hierarchy within the household. Domestically, the 'tapu system' was a rational and sophisticated one that articulated status asymmetry, and *manava* was the physiological concept which embodied it. As to why genealogical rank engendered tapu, we can make an etic interpretation that the *'eiki-tu'a* dimension collapsed filial piety, primogeniture, the marital subordination of women and the junior status of in-marrying sisters-in-law into a single operant principle. Tapu can therefore be construed as an ideological construct articulating (through *manava*) what we might call a *kainga mode of production* (cf. Godelier 1986: 232–36; Sahlins 1972). However, this view fails to account for the individual, relationship-specific, and longitudinally increasing nature of rank, which rendered everyone both inferior and superior in different relationships and life stages (Biersack 1982). In this way, the domestic *'eiki*-tapu-*manava* interaction amounted to a truly hegemonic system in the Gramscian sense (1992: 155).

The ageing process changed one's *'eiki* and *tu'a* statuses, because every birth or marriage created new asymmetrical relationships, and every death (excepting religious interactions) eliminated a set. Consequently, individuals became progressively *'eiki* to more of their living kin over time. Seniority was therefore proximity to death and deceased or divine sources of mana. *'Eiki* was (paradoxically) both deathliness and the ancestral source of life, as shown by the origin myth of the first Tu'i Tonga Aho'eitu, apical ancestor of the most chiefly lineage in Tonga. His divine father Tangaloa 'Eitumatupu'a descended from the sky to impregnate the mortal woman Ilaheva Va'epopua, who was descended (like all *tu'a* commoners) from worms (Gifford 1929: 49; Helu 1999; Mahina 1990). Reaching his majority, her demigod son Aho'eitu ascended into the sky to claim his inheritance; his four divine half-brothers, however, jealously killed him and ate his body. Discovering this, Tangaloa forced the brothers to regurgitate Aho'eitu's remains into a kava bowl, in which Tangaloa magically resurrected him. Thereafter both dead and alive concurrently, Tangaloa sent Aho'eitu back to earth to rule Tonga as the origin of the state's mana.

Manava and the ritual dynamics of the pre-Christian life cycle

Because a person's mana, and the number of persons to whom they were relationally tapu, grew over their lifetime, the pre-Christian ritual practices of the life cycle are replete with references to embodied *manava* processes. Rites of passage marking maternity and birth, puberty, adulthood and death physically engaged with the *manava* system in managing diachronically increasing seniority, deathliness, mana and relational tapu. Indeed, only contextualisation in terms of the *manava* system renders such ritual actions readable.

Maternity and the birth rite

Shore (1989: 144–48) discussed womanhood as intrinsically *noa* in Central Polynesia (a term equivalent, though not cognate, to *ngofua*), in opposition to the categorically tapu status of masculinity. F. Allan Hanson (1982), however, provides a very thorough refutation of the misogynistic earlier twentieth-century academic notion of the vulva, menstrual blood and womanhood itself as intrinsically polluting in

Polynesia, and demonstrates that Polynesian women could be just as tapu as men, as well as possessing a distinct power to release tapu states. Cosmological differences between pre-Christian Tonga and Aotearoa New Zealand suggest little applicability to Tonga of Hanson's affinity thesis that the vulva served as a gateway to the *po* and the power of the *atua*; my view is rather that the state-changing power of the vulva was the woman's own *manava*.

In Tonga, the radiant influence of the vulva meant that women were forbidden to step over categorically male products such as weapons, fishing canoes and equipment, or growing yam vines, for fear that their efficacy would be weakened (Gifford 1929: 344); the vulva's power as a conduit of the woman's *manava* was antagonistic to the efficacy of categorically male activities. Men were equally prohibited from interfering in women's work, and the clear inference is that (like familial interactions) gendered activities were rendered vulnerable by cross-gender interactions, not the intrinsic tapu state of one gender or another.

As a consequence of these considerations, childbirth was marked with considerable ritual. As soon as a woman delivered, she and the baby were painted all over with turmeric (*enga*). Repeatedly encountered in life crises, turmeric warmed and enlivened mother and child, and increased the mother's milk (Gifford 1929: 185). Turmeric's yellow-orange colour formerly belonged to the red colour classification (*kulokula*), the mana colour, and painting the skin red reflected a desire to imbue the body with mana. The postnatal rite consisted of the *'ulumotu'a* (senior head of the *'api* household) cutting the umbilicus with a woodworking adze (*toki*), and offering up a prayer that a boy might become a great warrior or fisherman, a girl a beautiful mother (Collocott 1921: 419–20). Ritual cutting with an adze (rather than the bamboo knife normally used for surgery) was symbolically charged: the *toki* was a significant object in Tonga, and the cosmogonic myth describes the god Tangaloa creating the archipelago by scattering woodchips from his workshop into the ocean (Ve'ehala and Fanua 1977). Cutting was primordial creativity. The umbilicus was the conduit by which antenatal vitality was imparted, and its severance began the baby's reliance on its own breath (*mānava*). As in other Polynesian cultures, the umbilicus was buried in a little tumulus outside the house (Gifford 1929: 185–86). Mother and child were secluded for five days and prohibited from bathing. For the first 10 days, the mother ate only yams and hot coconut milk. Daily washing and repainting with turmeric continued for two months, until the baby was considered strong enough to be moved (Gifford 1929: 185–86, 191).

Puberty rites

Although celebrated, the first menstruation rendered a girl relationally tapu to those around her, and her mother secluded her in bed until the period ended, painting her daily with turmeric and forbidding her to bathe lest the flow cease. Bathing in a chiefly pool was also a common source of episodic tapu, and therefore the body's lower orifices must have been permeable to episodic tapu like the mouth. At the end of the treatment, a postmenopausal relative took the girl to bathe with aromatic herbs, which released her tapu state (Gifford 1929: 186–87). First menstruation therefore required similar treatments of seclusion, painting and no bathing as childbirth, and we can hypothesise that expulsions from the vulva drained the *manava* system. That said, avoiding bathing to prevent the period stopping prematurely shows that the blood flow was an integral part of her tapu seclusion, and must be fully completed.

When boys first showed pubic hair, the rite of supercision was organised for a cohort of similar age. All males except the Tu'i Tonga underwent supercision, and boys who refused were no longer permitted to eat with the household or touch anyone's food—a clear indication that they also became relationally tapu at puberty. Supercision was performed by cutting the foreskin longitudinally along the top of the glans, opening it with an action sign readable as a release of the penis' tapu closure. Afterwards, the boys were bandaged and secluded together in a house for five days under strict tapu conditions against bathing, eating anything sweet or red, drinking more than one cup of water a day, walking or working. On the sixth day, the boys similarly took a tapu-releasing bath (*kaukautapu*) in the sea (Gifford 1929: 187–89). Against a view of the genders or genitals as either categorically *ngofua* or tapu, puberty rites show that adolescence rendered boys and girls temporarily relationally tapu until the completion of genital bleeding, food observances and the tapu-releasing bath. Perhaps modelled on the rite of first menstruation, supercision constituted what Bloch (1992: 4) defined as a sublimated act of rebounding violence against the initiand; a cosmologically necessary trauma which reasserted the normative system of relational tapu based on genealogical location (Hanson 1982: 335).

Otherwise short-haired, pre-Christian Tongan children wore a long lock of hair (*fangafanga* for girls, *tope* for boys) on one temple. For girls, this indexed hymen integrity, and was cut off at marriage unless they had had sex beforehand. For boys, the *tope* was cut off after the *kaukautapu* to indicate their classificatory adulthood. The maternity, birth and puberty rites consequently demonstrate a structuralist scheme-transfer, wherein ritual action signs of bleeding and cutting created a symbolic equivalence between the navel's umbilicus, the head's lock, the penis' foreskin, the vulva's menstrual blood and hymen as a class of parallel bodily exuviae on the vertical plane of bodily symmetry. These analogous transformational bleeds and cuts reveal the systemic interconnection of the head, navel and genitals as the upper, central and lower orifices of the *manava* system. Naturally or artificially induced bleeds and cutting, seclusion and bathing transformed the classification of individuals and released them from relationally tapu states (Gell 1993: 82–95; Turner 1974). Only at life crises, in fact, could relational tapu could be altered.

Tatatau and tokolosi

Another rite of passage featuring extensive bloodletting was the tattooing (*tatatau*) of young men, which began shortly after puberty. Missionary activity suppressed Tongan *tatatau* in the mid-nineteenth century, although it was universally practiced on men beforehand. Men were not deemed fully adult, and were spurned by women, until their *tatatau* was complete (Vason 1840: 179–80). Like the Samoan *pe'a*, *tatatau* covered the hips, lower belly, buttocks, thighs and (sometimes) the genitals (Labillardiere 1800; Mallon 2010). Alfred Gell (1993: 87–95) argued that Samoan *tatau* wrapped the young man's increasingly mana and tapu genitals, and subordinated his will to the kin group. Because the Tongan puberty rites discussed above indicate temporary relational tapu developing at puberty, and then being released, we can infer that male genitalia were not generally considered tapu, and therefore *tatatau* cannot readily be explained on this basis. As in weapon engraving and barkcloth painting, the iconography of Tongan *tatatau* predominantly replicated abstracted weaving motifs (Mills 2008: 301–306). Like the fine waist-mats worn over the same body area on formal occasions, *tatatau* can therefore be read as expressing the wearer's respectful location of themselves within the social network (Herda 1999; Sahlins 1985: 85–87). Furthermore, the wrapping of people and objects in textiles historically instantiated and insulated divine or chiefly presences throughout Oceania (Hooper 2002; Kuechler 1999). I therefore view *tatatau* as an art that insulated and energised the wearer's abdominal *manava* system through textile replication and transformative tapu-releasing bloodletting.

The male genital bloodletting technique of *tokolosi* is also illuminating. *Tokolosi* was practiced in Tonga and Fiji to cure tetanus, internal bleeding caused by abdominal wounds, and (in a lesser form) 'general languor and inactivity of the system' (Martin 1818: 392–94). These three conditions have seemingly unrelated symptoms unless considered with reference to the *manava* system. The shaking, lockjaw and spasms of tetanus, abdominal wounds near the liver and a general lack of vitality can all be viewed as dysfunctions in the *manava* system. In its minor form, the procedure involved the insertion of a reed catheter into the penile urethra as far as the perineum, causing pain and profuse bleeding. In more serious cases of tetanus and abdominal wounds, a doubled-over cord was then inserted into the urethra through this reed, the perineum and urethra pierced with a knife and the end of the cord drawn out through the incision. The reed was removed, and the cord periodically drawn back and forth to reinitiate the bleeding. Penile-perineal bloodletting aimed to regulate dysfunctions in the *manava* system, and presumably because the penis possessed a categorical expelling association. Although mana's redness throughout Polynesia surely derives from blood, the ritual significance of bloodletting in pre-Christian Tonga has been underemphasised. For example, many ailments are still treated herbally in traditional Tongan medicine as accumulations of 'bad blood' (*fakatoto kovi*) resulting from the displeasure of deceased ancestors (George 1995: 30)—interpretable as a latter-day variation of post-mortem *manahi*. Bleeding, therefore, although synonymous with relational tapu events of the life cycle, was specifically a mechanism of their resolution and passage. By rebalancing the *manava*, it reasserted the *ngofua* conditions of ordinary life and structural relations.

Death rites

The *hou'eiki* (chiefly class) were widely thought to possess immortal souls whereas *tu'a* (commoners) did not (Collocott 1921). Commoners were buried in the bush with little ceremony and funerary rites were largely concerned with the relational tapu of chiefs. In death as in eating, the entire body of a more *'eiki* person became relationally tapu (Gifford 1929: 196). Touching a corpse produced an episodic tapu in the hands, but an un-releasable 10-month episodic tapu resulted from handling the corpse of a high chief. To avoid this contagion, those attending the body were forbidden from approaching the head and sat facing the deceased's feet (Gifford 1929: 199). High chiefs appointed specialist *matāpule* heralds as undertakers (*ha'atufunga*) to oversee their funerals; even for them, handling the corpse occasioned their contracting the *nima tapu* (hand tapu), which prevented them from feeding themselves for five, 10 or 15 days, depending on the deceased's rank (Gifford 1929: 197).

When a man died, his children's heads were shaved. When a chief died, all those he governed singed off their hair. When the Tu'i Tonga died, all Tongans shaved their heads (Gifford 1929: 199). These acts of haircutting also coincided with ritual bloodletting. An almost universal feature of high chiefly funerals was *foa'ulu*, mass self-mutilation of the head: men beat their scalps with clubs or cut them with knives, pierced their cheeks with spears, or scoured them with abrasives until they bled (Martin 1818: 349–50; Valeri 1989). In the puberty rites and *tatatau*, bleeding released relational tapu associated with an individual's classificatory maturation and haircutting marked that maturation's attainment. Logically, therefore, the haircutting and head-wounding of chiefly funerals equally released the relational tapu incumbent upon men due to their classificatory elevation through the superior's death.

Foa'ulu was never performed at the funeral of the Tu'i Tonga, which suggests that he possessed a different ontological status to all other *hou'eiki*. One might suggest that, like his apical ancestor Aho'eitu, he was not viewed as categorically alive or dying in the normal sense, and therefore his inferiors did not undergo the same hierarchical elevation. Replacing this bloodletting in the funerary rites of the Tu'i Tonga, a remarkable ritual phase occurred immediately after interment. For 15 nights, more than 60 male mourners defecated on the royal tomb. At sunrise each morning, female mourners approached the burial mound with baskets and shells, and removed the faeces. Martin wrote: 'to demonstrate their great veneration for the high character of Tooitonga … it was the duty of the most exalted nobles … to perform [these] … offices, rather than the sacred ground, in which he was buried should remain polluted' (1818: 352–53). The Tu'i Tonga's interment rendered the burial mound itself tapu, and only an act of mass ritual defecation could achieve its release. Faeces became a powerfully *ngofua* ritual substance by emerging exhausted from the *manava* system.[3]

The foregoing data reveal a set of ritual action signs materially instantiating ontological change through interaction with the *manava* system: bloodletting, haircutting, painting with turmeric, the proscription and prescription of bathing, and seclusion in multiples of five days. These practices transformed categorical identities, ranks and relational tapu statuses, and stand in a higher scalar relationship to the phenomena and treatment of everyday episodic tapu. They also show that the crown, mouth, throat, heart, liver, navel, genitals and anus shared nodal functions within a substantially tubular anatomical model, with which all states of episodic and relational tapu, and all activities of their release, were directly concerned.

Mana, class identity and chiefly interaction

Bridging the ontological gap between divine and human status, incumbent Tongan chiefs were ideologically positioned as the conduit of divine mana and fertility for the district and population they governed (Biersack 1990: 48; Kaeppler 1999: 36; Latukefu 1974: 1–3; Sahlins 1985: 78–103). Both mana and *'eiki* were inferred by historical Tongans from the vitality, good nourishment and sexual potency, courage, agency and authority of individuals. Although mana and *manava* are not linguistically related, therefore, the performative qualities of *'eiki* strongly correlate with both mana *and* great, resilient *manava* (Bott 1982; Gifford 1929: 124; Marcus 1980: 18, 1989; Sahlins 1985: 47, 50).

3 Similar ritual practices occurred elsewhere in Polynesia: at the conclusion of the investiture rite of an *ari'i rahi* in the Society Islands, for example, members of the Arioi society performed ritual urination and defecation on his body to release his extremely tapu status (Claessen 2000: 723).

The entanglement of tapu with ingestion and digestive processes through *manava* made foodways central to the performance of class identity, and determined both commensality and food tapu. There was a relational tapu on anyone eating in the sight of superiors (or watching them eat). In the 1770s, James Cook observed that seldom were more than two or three Tongans of any class found eating together; on one occasion, Cook invited two high-ranking chiefs aboard HMS *Resolution* for lunch. In his superior's presence, the lesser chief 'would not sit down and eat before him, but ... got to the other end of the table and sat and ate with his back towards him' (Beaglehole 1988, II: 253; Collocott 1921: 423). Termed *kaitafoki*, this technique shielded the inferior's open mouth from the superior's gaze and prevented an episodic tapu from entering his *manava* system. Relatedly, when the Tu'i Tonga ate, only his tapu-immune foreign *matāpule* could serve him, while all Tongans had to face the opposite direction or contract an episodic tapu (Beaglehole 1988, III: 880). Like the radiant influence of the vulva discussed above, the Tu'i Tonga's open mouth exposed any viewer to the dangerous *manava* inside him. Evidently, the mouth and eye both disseminated episodic tapu states to less chiefly individuals and contracted them from more chiefly individuals. The belief that the chiefly mouth and gaze had a radiant debilitating capacity at distance closely paralleled *manahi*, if they were not the same phenomenon. The body's susceptibility to this broadcast relational tapu also explains the requirement that commoners strip down to the waist and expose their belly to any chief as they passed (Vason 1840: 162): exposure of the abdomen invited an episodic tapu if any cause existed, and can be read as public submission to the embodied ideological mechanism.

Elite commensality became most socially charged through the royal kava ceremony, Tonga's highest political rite. In this enduring ceremony, the seating position and drinking order of chiefly titleholders in the circle above the kava bowl directly reflects their relative rank. Traditionally, people of intermediate *mua* class sat below the bowl, while *tu'a* commoners merely looked on from outside the building, behind the *mua*. It is a powerful indication of the cultural legacy of the *manava* system that the Tongan nation's highest political ceremony still inscribes the hierarchical organisation of the nobility through a succession of public consumption acts. Given the historical danger of mutually observed chiefly consumption, the ceremony's performative representation of the aristocratic hierarchy is made possible only by the uniquely *ngofua* quality of kava, which could never be rendered tapu (Biersack 1991; Martin 1818: 355).

The consumption of meat was rigidly controlled by species as an expression of class hierarchy. The domesticated meat species (pig, dog, chicken) were relationally tapu to Tongan commoners, who acquired animal protein from rats, fish and shellfish (Beaglehole 1988, III: 169). The most prestigious marine prey (bonito, shark and turtle) were also relationally tapu to commoners, and many minor chiefs did not consider themselves *'eiki* enough to consume turtle (Bataille-Benguigui 1988; Martin 1818: 312). Among the *hou'eiki* themselves, hierarchical size preference also existed, so that larger pigs, bonito or sharks were passed upwards for consumption at an appropriate rank (Gifford 1929: 102–108).[4]

Unlike the genealogically articulated episodic-relational tapu system discussed above, (class: species) relational food tapu restrictions appropriated resources cultivated and husbanded by commoners for elite consumption, and were profoundly ideological. Superficially *appearing* to be the same phenomena because their episodic outcomes were the same, class-based relational tapu differed significantly from those of the *kainga*, and those between members of the *hou'eiki*. While kinship-based relational tapu were relationship-specific and (over a lifetime) zero-sum, class-based prohibitions alienated *tu'a* labour power to privilege the *hou'eiki*.

Class identities universalised and mapped the *'eiki–tu'a* dimension onto society, rendering the *hou'eiki* relationally tapu to all lower classes and necessitating complex genealogical calculations of relative rank within their own interactions too (Korn 1978). As Phyllis Herda (1987) discusses, these genealogical calculations were driven by the cosmological concept of relative *sino'i'eiki* (chiefliness in body) between chiefly individuals, a value of proximal descent from the god Tangaloa. Herda therefore characterises two opposed rank constructions: *kainga rank* (those asymmetries articulating relational tapu) and *sino'i'eiki rank*. Framed in terms of the archaeology of cosmology, *'eiki* anciently

4 In war, human meat was occasionally consumed, but only from those of lower rank than the consumer (Lawry 1850). Where individuals of lower classificatory rank did kill and consume higher-status enemies without seeming consequences, this was read as an indicator of the victor's previously unrecognised mana.

amounted to Herda's *kainga rank*. Due to a woman's superiority to her brothers and inferiority to her husband, the *'eiki-tu'a* dichotomy which rendered individuals within the *'api* relationally tapu to one another, and dated back to the Ancestral Polynesian Period, also ranked *'api* within each *kainga* asymmetrically. Over many generations, this inevitably generated complex chains of pyramidal hierarchy between *kainga*, articulated by relational tapu at every link. The crystallisation of that pyramid into a set of stratified and ontologically distinct classes was not inevitable, however, and beliefs that the *hou'eiki* alone possessed immortal souls due to Tangaloan ancestry, relational tapu on animal foods, and class endogamy, were key ideological components instantiating those differences.

During the sixteenth century, instabilities in the Tu'i Tonga succession led to the rise of *hingoa fakanofo* (invested name) titles that recognised authority (*pule*) and great capability (*ivilahi*) as the primary traits of *'eiki* (Campbell 2001; Marcus 1980: 15–19). This decreasing significance of *sino'i'eiki* as a source of authority is relevant here. Because class-based relational tapu applied equally to all members of the *hou'eiki*, many of them occasioned relational tapu in other classes without the underpinning cosmological legitimacy of divine ancestry. By eliding *sino'i'eiki*, the causal interconnection of classificatory *'eiki* with relational tapu and *manava*'s vulnerability formed a compelling, embodied class system well into the early nineteenth century, despite fundamental changes in the genealogy of kingship. Indeed, this elision created further opportunities for ideological redeployment.

Regulatory tapu

A key example of this is regulatory tapu, the third heuristic subtype discussed here. Although they were class-based relational tapu phenomena in their influence and episodic outcomes, regulatory tapu were not universal legisigns emerging from the interaction of immutable class identities. Instead, they operationalised relational tapu conditions as manipulable sinsigns of their own distinct law. Regulatory tapu encompasses cases where the *hou'eiki* could (at will) impose relational tapu states on activities or food resources as a means of social control. For example, to avoid famine resulting from food presentations associated with public events such as the *Inasi*

(New Yam Harvest Ceremony), chiefly marriages, funerals or diplomatic visits, a chief's *matāpule* or priest would place regulatory tapu on the slaughter of certain animals, the crops of certain plantations, or fishing in certain bays. They were generally marked by the suspension of a woven pandanus shark-effigy from a prominent tree (the *taungatapu* or tapu anchor) with the implication that any transgressor would be eaten the next time they bathed (Gifford 1929: 343–44; Martin 1818: 353–54). Although regulatory tapu was often good local governance, it fundamentally departed from the genealogically articulated rationality of domestic relational tapu, and the universality of influence demonstrated by class-based relational tapu.

Discussion

The *manava* system was an embodying cornerstone of pre-Christian cosmology in Tonga, and greatly facilitates explanations of traditional medicine, interpersonal interaction and ritual practice. Through the body's permeability and exchange processes, the *manava* system provided the physiological mechanism of episodic tapu, which was articulated by relational tapu conditions arising from asymmetrical rank between individuals in a kin group, between individuals of different classes, and between individuals and resources over which the elite exerted ideological control. Tapu therefore emerges as an operant principle that articulated status asymmetry through the bodily vulnerability of *manava*'s downwards flow through a tubular torso. In the case of senior kin, and the *hou'eiki*, the danger of higher status was not limited to touch or ingestion, but radiated out from their gaze, open mouth or simple displeasure.

Mana had a complex relationship with tapu and chiefliness in historical Tonga because the nature of *'eiki* itself has undergone radical transformations over the last 3,000 years; because the cosmological properties, physical impact and ritual management of tapu conditions have adapted in different ways as a response to those transformations; because mana and chiefliness were distinct but mutually influencing personal qualities; and because the sociocultural system documented in the eighteenth century was an uneven accretion of these transforming traditions. Mediated by its complex relationship with *'eiki*, mana became a somatic reality for pre-Christian Tongans through the embodying mechanism of relational tapu's influence on the *manava*. This mana-*'eiki*-tapu-*manava* triple-articulation physicalised the metaphysical and conjugated the sociostructural with the divine. In turn, the bodily interconnection of mana and tapu rendered them both susceptible to the ritual action signs enumerated here.

Within the *'api* and wider *kainga*, the ancient hegemonic principles of the classless Ancestral Polynesian kin group achieved historical stability through the ephemeral and zero-sum nature of its subordination. The *hou'eiki* class-alterity construct of divine descent from Tangaloa (which defined *sino'i'eiki*) abstracted and reified the domestic construct of relative and ephemeral *'eiki* (before the twelfth century CE) into an effective ideological superstructure underpinning a stable class system (Korn 1978; Mahina 1990). Dominant for several centuries, this tapu-embodied stratification itself went through further transformations between the sixteenth and eighteenth centuries, which diminished the role of divine descent in the mediation of mana's equivalence to chiefliness and relational tapu, and rendered the tapu system a subtle and effective mechanism of socioeconomic regulation. Chiefly persons and things were not simply mana and therefore tapu in pre-Christian Tonga; rather, tapu emerged from a historical succession of dependently abstracted chiefliness constructs, each possessing a distinct and indirect relationship with mana.

References

Aoyagi, Machiko. 1966. Kinship organisation and behaviour in a contemporary Tongan village. *Journal of the Polynesian Society* 75(2): 141–76.

Austronesian Comparative Dictionary. Online: www.trussel2.com/ACD (accessed 15 September 2015).

Bargatzky, Thomas. 1996. Embodied ideas: An essay on ritual and politics in pre-capitalist society. In *Ideology and the Formation of Early States*, ed. Henri J.M. Claessen and Jarich G. Oosten, pp. 298–320. Leiden: E.J. Brill.

Bataille-Benguigui, Marie-Claire. 1988. The fish of Tonga: Prey or social partners? *Journal of the Polynesian Society* 97(2): 185–98.

Beaglehole, John C. (ed.). 1988. *The Journals of Captain James Cook on his Voyages of Discovery*. 3 volumes. Millwood, NY: Kraus Reprint.

Biersack, Aletta. 1982. Tongan exchange structures: Beyond descent and alliance. *Journal of the Polynesian Society* 91(2): 181–212.

——. 1990. Blood and garland: Duality in Tongan history. In *Tongan Culture and History*, ed. Phyllis Herda, Jennifer Terrell and Niel Gunson, pp. 46–58. Canberra: The Australian National University.

——. 1991. Kava'onau and the Tongan chiefs. *Journal of the Polynesian Society* 100(3): 231–68.

Bloch, Maurice. 1992. *Prey into Hunter: The Politics of Religious Experience*. Cambridge: Cambridge University Press.

Blust, Robert. 2007. Proto-Oceanic *mana revisited. *Oceanic Linguistics* 46(2): 404–23.

Bott, Elizabeth. 1982. *Tongan Society at the Time of Captain Cook's Visits: Discussions with Her Majesty Queen Salote Tupou*. Wellington: The Polynesian Society.

Buttigieg, Joseph A. (ed.). 1992. *Prison Notebooks, vol. 1*. New York: Columbia University Press.

Campbell, Iain Christopher. 2001. *Island Kingdom: Tonga Ancient and Modern*. Christchurch: Canterbury University Press.

Churchward, C. Maxwell. 1959. *Tongan Dictionary*. Nuku'alofa: Government Printing Press.

Claessen, Henri J.M. 2000. Ideology, leadership and fertility: Evaluating a model of Polynesian chiefship. *Bijdragen tot de Taal-, Land- en Volkenkunde* 156(4): 707–35.

Claessen, Henri J.M. and Jarich G. Oosten (eds). 1996. *Ideology and the Formation of Early States*. Leiden: E.J. Brill.

Codrington, Robert H. 1891. *The Melanesians: Studies in their Anthropology and Folk-lore*. Oxford: Clarendon Press.

Collocott, E.E.V. 1921. The supernatural in Tonga. *American Anthropologist* 23(4): 415–44.

Csordas, Thomas J. 1990. Embodiment as a paradigm for anthropology. *Ethos* 18(1): 5–47.

Douaire-Marsaudon, Françoise. 1996. Neither black nor white: The father's sister In Tonga. *Journal of the Polynesian Society* 105(2): 139–64.

Farnell, Brenda. 1999. Moving bodies, acting selves. *Annual Review of Anthropology* 28: 341–73.

Firth, Raymond. 1940. The analysis of mana: An empirical approach. *Journal of the Polynesian Society* 49(4): 483–510.

Frazer, James G. 1925. *The Golden Bough: A Study in Magic & Religion*. New York: Macmillan.

Gell, Alfred. 1993. *Wrapping in Images: Tattooing in Polynesia*. Oxford: Clarendon Press.

——. 1998. *Art and Agency: An Anthropological Theory*. Oxford: Oxford University Press.

George, Lisa O. 1995. Ethnomedicine in the Tongan Islands. *Harvard Papers in Botany* 1(6): 1–36.

Gifford, Edwin W. 1929. *Tongan Society*. Honolulu: Bernice P. Bishop Museum.

Godelier, Maurice. 1986. *The Making of Great Men*. Cambridge: Cambridge University Press.

Gramsci, Antonio. 1992. *Prison Notebooks, vol. 1*, ed. Joseph A. Buttigieg. New York: Columbia University Press.

Handy, E.S.C. 1927. *Polynesian Religion*. Honolulu: Bernice P. Bishop Museum.

Hanson, F. Allan. 1982. Female pollution in Polynesia? *Journal of the Polynesian Society* 91(3): 335–81.

Helu, 'I. Futa. 1999. *Critical Essays: Cultural Perspectives from the South Seas*. Canberra: Journal of Pacific History.

Herda, Phyllis. 1987. Gender, rank and power in 18th century Tonga: The case of Tupoumoheofo. *Journal of Pacific History* 22(4): 195–208.

——. 1999. The changing texture of textiles in Tonga. *Journal of the Polynesian Society* 108(2): 149–67.

Herda, Phyllis, Jennifer Terrell and Niel Gunson (eds). 1990. *Tongan Culture and History: Papers from the 1st Tongan History Conference held in Canberra, 14–17 January 1987*. Canberra: Dept. of Pacific and Southeast Asian History, The Australian National University.

Herle, Anita, Nick Stanley, Karen Stevenson and Robert L. Welsch (eds). 2002. *Pacific Art: Persistence, Change, Meaning*. Honolulu: University of Hawaii Press.

Hooper, Steven. 2002. Memorial images of Eastern Fiji: Materials, metaphors and meanings. In *Pacific Art: Persistence, Change, Meaning*, ed. Anita Herle, Nick Stanley, Karen Stevenson and Robert L. Welsch, pp. 309–23. Honolulu: University of Hawaii Press.

Howard, Alan and Robert Borofsky (eds). 1989. *Developments in Polynesian Ethnology*. Honolulu: University of Hawaii Press.

Huntsman, J. (ed.). 1995. *Tonga and Samoa: Images of Gender and Polity*. Christchurch: Macmillan Brown Centre for Pacific Studies.

Im Thurn, Everard. 1922a. Introduction. In *The Journal of William Lockerby, Sandalwood Trader in the Fijian Islands During the Years 1808–1809*, ed. Everard Im Thurn. London: The Hakluyt Society.

—— (ed.). 1922b. *The Journal of William Lockerby, Sandalwood Trader in the Fijian Islands During the Years 1808–1809*, London: The Hakluyt Society.

James, Kerry E. 1995. 'Rank overrules everything': Hierarchy, social stratification and gender in Tonga. In *Tonga and Samoa: Images of Gender and Polity*, ed. J. Huntsman, pp. 59–83. Christchurch: Macmillan Brown Centre for Pacific Studies.

Joppien, Rudiger and Bernard Smith. 1985, 1985a, 1988. *The Art of Captain Cook's Voyages*. 3 volumes. New Haven, CT: Yale University Press.

Kaeppler, Adrienne L. 1999. *From the Stone Age to the Space Age in 200 Years: Tongan Art and Society on the Eve of the Millennium*. Tofoa, Kingdom of Tonga: The Tongan National Museum.

Keesing, Roger M. 1984. Rethinking 'mana'. *Journal of Anthropological Research* 40(1): 137–56.

Kirch, Patrick V. and Roger C. Green. 2001. *Hawaiki, Ancestral Polynesia: An Essay in Historical Anthropology*. Cambridge: Cambridge University Press.

Korn, Shulamit R.D. 1978. Hunting the ramage: Kinship and the organisation of political authority in Aboriginal Tonga. *Journal of Pacific History* 13(1/2): 107–13.

Kuechler, Susanne. 1999. Binding in the Pacific: Between loops and knots. *Oceania* 69(3): 145–57.

Labillardiere, Jacques-Julien. H. 1800. *Voyage in Search of La Perouse ... During the Years 1791, 1792, 1793 & 1794*. 2 volumes. London: John Stockdale.

Latukefu, Sione. 1974. *Church and State in Tonga: The Wesleyan Methodist Missionaries and Political Development, 1822–1875*. Canberra: Australian National University Press.

Lawry, Walter. 1850. *Friendly and Feejee Islands: A Missionary Visit to Various Stations in the South Seas, in the Year 1847 by the Reverend Walter Lawry, General Superintendent of the Wesleyan Missions in New Zealand, etc*. London: Charles Gilpin.

Lévi-Strauss, Claude. 1987 [1950]. *Introduction to the Work of Marcel Mauss*, trans. Felicity Baker. London: Routledge & Kegan Paul.

Mahina, 'Okusitino. 1990. Myths and history: Some aspects of history in the Tu'i Tonga myths. In *Papers from the First Tongan History Conference*, ed. Phyllis Herda, Jennifer Terrell and Niel Gunson, pp. 1–11, 30–45. Canberra: Australian National University Press.

Mallon, Sean. 2010. Samoan Tattooing, Cosmopolitans, Global Culture. In Adams, Mark, Sean Mallon, Peter W. Brunt and Nicholas Thomas (ed.), *Tatau: Samoan Tattoo, New Zealand Art, Global Culture*, pp. 15–32. Wellington: Te Papa Press.

Marcus, George E. 1980. *The Nobility and the Chiefly Tradition in the Modern Kingdom of Tonga*. Wellington: The Polynesian Society.

——. 1989. Chieftainship. In *Developments in Polynesian Ethnology*, ed. Alan Howard and Robert Borofsky, pp. 175–209. Honolulu: University of Hawaii Press.

Marett, R.R. 1929 (7th ed.). s.v. Mana. *Encyclopaedia Britannica* 14: 770–71.

Martin, John. 1818. *An Account of the Natives of the Tonga Islands in the South Pacific Ocean: With an Original Grammar and Vocabulary of their Language. Compiled and Arranged from the Extensive Communications of William Mariner, Several Years Resident in Those Islands*. London: John Murray.

McGrath, Barbara B. 1999. Swimming from island to island: Healing practice in Tonga. *Medical Anthropology Quarterly* (n.s.) 13(4): 483–505.

Merleau-Ponty, Maurice. 1962. *Phenomenology of Perception*. London: Routledge & Kegan Paul.

Mills, Andy. 2008. Tufunga Tongi 'Akau: Tongan club carvers & their arts. PhD dissertation, University of East Anglia.

Polynesian Lexicon Project Online. Online: pollex.org.nz/ (accessed 1 August 2015).

Refiti, Albert L. 2008. The forked centre: Duality and privacy in Polynesian spaces and architecture. In *Alternative: Special Edition: Critiquing Pasifika Education*. Auckland: Nga Pae o te Maramatanga.

——. 2009. Whiteness, smoothness and the origin of Samoan architecture. *Interstices* 10: 9–19.

Rutherford, Noel (ed.). 1977. *Friendly Islands: A History of Tonga*. Melbourne: Oxford University Press

Sahlins, Marshall D. 1972. *Stone Age Economics*. Oxford: Routledge.

——. 1985. *Islands of History*. Chicago: University of Chicago Press.

Shore, Bradd. 1989. Mana and tapu. In *Developments in Polynesian Ethnology*, ed. Alan Howard and Robert Borofsky, pp. 137–73. Honolulu: University of Hawaii Press.

Taumoefolau, Melenaite. 1991. Is the father's sister really black? *Journal of the Polynesian Society* 100(1): 91–98.

Tupouniua, Penisimani. 1977. *A Polynesian Village: The Process of Change*. Suva: South Pacific Social Sciences Association.

Turner, Victor Witter. 1974. *Dramas, Fields, and Metaphors: Symbolic Action in Human Society*. New York: Cornell University Press.

Valeri, Valerio. 1989. Death in heaven: Myths and rites of kinship in Tongan kingship. *History & Anthropology* 4: 209–47.

Van der Grijp, Paul. 1993. *Islanders of the South: Production, Kinship and Ideology in the Polynesian Kingdom of Tonga*. Leiden: Koninklijk Instituut voor Taal-, Land- en Volkenkunde Press.

Vason, George. 1840. *Life of the Late George Vason of Nottingham, One of the Troop of Missionaries First Sent to the South Sea Islands by the London Missionary Society in the Ship Duff, Captain Wilson, 1796*. London: John Snow.

Ve'ehala and Tupou P. Fanua. 1977. Oral tradition and prehistory. In *Friendly Islands: A History of Tonga*, ed. Noel Rutherford, pp. 27–39. Melbourne: Oxford University Press.

Völkel, Svenja. 2010. *Social Structure, Space and Possession in Tongan Culture and Language*. Amsterdam: Benjamins.

Wendt, Albert. 1996. Tatauing the Post-Colonial Body. *Span* 42–43: 15–29.

West, Thomas. 1865. *Ten Years in South-Central Polynesia: Being Reminiscences of a Personal Mission to the Friendly Islands and their Dependencies*. London: James Nisbet & Co.

4

Niu Mana, Sport, Media and the Australian Diaspora

Katerina Martina Teaiwa

Prelude

In the trailer for *In Football We Trust*, a documentary directed by Tony Vainuku and produced by Erika Cohn of Idle Wild films, several young Polynesian men identify themselves as playing high school football. An inter title appears stating that approximately 150,000 Samoans and Tongans now live in the United States and are 56 times more likely to make it into the National Football League (NFL) than any other 'race' despite one in four of the same group living in poverty. And why is their success rate so high? Words like 'faith', 'talent', 'culture', 'warrior' and 'family' flash across the screen, followed by: 'it's the only option' (IFWT Productions and ITVS 2014).

Former running back Vai Sikahema appears, stating that it is unfair for kids growing up to be told they will make it into the NFL. But then a series of players and a mother make it clear that football is seen as a 'door', a pathway to major success, not just for the individual but for the whole family. A young man says that all his mother's brothers are in prison, and all his father's brothers are in prison as well. The soundtrack for the trailer is a bombastic chorus that increases in tempo as the final words proclaim the film title encapsulating a spirit of American patriotism, faith, even blind faith, and also a worrying edge. What if you don't make it? Or what if you do make it and life just gets more challenging? The suicide of Samoan All-Pro NFL player Junior Seau by gunshot in 2012 hangs like a spectre over this trailer. His autopsy showed he had suffered from numerous head injuries. He left no suicide note but a page was found handwritten with the lyrics of his favourite country song, 'Who I Ain't'. Co-written by his friend, Jamie Paulin, it describes a man who regrets the person he has become (Steeg 2012).

Introduction

In this chapter I present some preliminary thoughts on 'new mana' and a discussion of how globalisation and the Pacific diaspora might compel us to reimagine key Pan-Pacific concepts such as mana, tapu, talanoa, va, Moana, Oceania and Solwara (salt water) in new or, to use 350.org's Pacific play on words, 'niu' ways.[1] By 'key' I don't mean that these words are the same or even existent in every Pacific language, but rather that a sense of spiritual efficacy, agency and authority or power; sacred or taboo things, people and places; relational space; the ocean as material, pragmatic, connective and sacred; and the Pacific as a region shaped by shared kinship, are important across most contemporary Pacific cultures and contexts. Some call this the 'Pacific Way' (Crocombe 1976), an idea still relevant in spite of the critiques of Pacific political scientists over the years (Lawson 2010).

In spite of many scholarly assumptions about the differences between Melanesians, Micronesians and Polynesians, the concepts I have mentioned are relevant across communities who care about what they see as destructive global forces affecting the lives of people in the diaspora, in small islands, and in the highlands of the Pacific's largest islands. This is seen vividly in Pan-Pacific 350.org climate change protests across the region and in the Madang Wansolwara Dance gathering in August 2014 of artists, activists, scholars, civil society and

1 'Niu' is a common word for coconut across many Pacific languages. In Mallon and Pereira's work (see Mallon and Pereira 2002), and in popular parlance in Aotearoa New Zealand, 'niu' converts any negative connotations of the word 'coconut', signalling race or ethnicity negatively, or implying an islander is non-modern or 'fresh off the boat', into a positive term marking Pacific flavours or styles that have infused New Zealand national identities.

church leaders in Papua New Guinea, for example.[2] These concepts are thus transformed, reimagined and applied according to historical, political, environmental and economic contexts, and increasingly drive regional activism. At the heart of it is, as scholars such as Margaret Jolly have argued, an enduring sense of collective and relational personhood shaped by both indigenous heritage and Christian values and concepts (Jolly interviewed by Giggacher 2014).

While many of the contributors to this volume have explored mana in either specific cultural and linguistic contexts such as Hawaiian, Fijian, Māori, Tongan and Samoan, and in what I would call new age gaming (Golub and Peterson, this volume) and intense spiritual remix mode (Morgain, this volume), I would like to consider mana through an interdisciplinary Pacific Studies lens, and in diverse Pan-Pacific (intercultural or regional), Pasifika, diasporic and postcolonial contexts. While it is beyond the scope of my discussion here on diaspora and sport, I also have questions about how far we can take a discussion of mana and commerce or industry, mana and the commodity sign, and mana in the context of indigenous traditions, such as fa'a Samoa, or anga fakatonga, and sexuality, given the often conservative, Christian, heteronormative and ethno-nationalist values within Pacific communities. Mana is about both limits and possibilities, applications and denials within a system of specific contemporary Pacific values and ideas.

The Australian context

The topic of mana and sport is not something I sought out for research but rather something that developed as I created the undergraduate teaching program in Pacific Studies at The Australian National University (ANU) over the past seven years. We currently run the only Pacific Studies teaching program at any level in Australian higher education and there is very little visibility for the field as a potential area of study in the primary or secondary school system (Rose, Quanchi and Moore 2009). As I was trying to imagine how to grow the program

2 350.org is a global climate movement for promoting grassroots climate change activism and information. '350 Pacific' is represented by the 'Pacific Climate Warriors' in various actions and events. See more at *350 pacific*.

and attract students, I was forced to think more broadly about how the Pacific featured in the national Australian consciousness (Teaiwa 2007). Several things became clear very quickly.

Aside from the obvious and dominant pragmatic and policy context—tied primarily to Australia's regional aid, development and governance agenda—there is very little content on the Pacific in the school system in any Australian state. And while there is a wealth of writing about the Pacific Islands, very little of it is available as teaching material and most of it does not engage the Pacific diaspora (Rose, Quanchi and Moore 2009). There are just a handful of scholars who do research on Pacific communities in Australia, including research on South Sea Islanders, the descendants of Melanesians and other Pacific Islanders forced to work on Australian sugar plantations (see for example Banivanua-Mar 2007; Boucher 2012; Lee and Tupai 2009; Rose, Quanchi and Moore 2009; Vasta 2004). Thus, in Pacific Studies in Australia, which is geographically in Oceania and where there is significant Pacific research and policy work, there is a preference for engaging the Pacific out there in the Islands, but not the Pacific within Australian cities and neighbourhoods. And neither the domestic nor the island context are seen as relevant for Australian education (Rose, Quanchi and Moore 2009; Teaiwa 2007).

Furthermore, compared with New Zealand, and increasingly the United States, Pacific Islanders are not a recognised equity category or community. Statistics on the exact numbers of Islanders in Australia are not readily available, although a reasonable estimate based on census reports for ancestry, including Māori and Indo-Fijians, would put the total around 2 per cent or 400,000, which would be half a percentage less than the estimated Indigenous Australian population (see Pryke 2014; Pryor 2013; and Queensland Health 2013). Pacific communities are primarily resident in New South Wales (NSW) and Queensland and are growing in Victoria, the Australian Capital Territory (ACT), South Australia, Western Australia and the Northern Territory.

Despite Australia's long history of engagement with the southwest Pacific, particularly Papua New Guinea, and with Nauru and Kiribati, most twenty-first-century Pacific migrants are not Melanesian or Micronesian but Polynesian (Pryke 2014). The majority of migrants do not come straight from the Islands, but take advantage of the trans-Tasman agreement and move from New Zealand to Australia, drawn by the possibilities of employment within the strong Australian economy. This is certainly the case for the large Māori Australian population, sometimes referred to as 'Mozzies' in the media (Pryor 2013). Many trans-Tasman migrants regularly identify as 'New Zealander', and many Māori, duplicating structural relations with Pacific migrants back in New Zealand, prefer to be counted or imagined separately from Pacific Islanders (see Teaiwa and Mallon 2005). These factors make it difficult to get a sense of the real Pacific population size in Australia.

Because I expected that future students in Pacific Studies would include Pacific Islanders of the diaspora, I sought as much information as possible about Pacific communities in Australia and soon realised there were two dominant and highly visible arenas for positive Pacific participation on the Australian social and cultural landscape: sport and popular culture. Within these arenas, it is the Pacific Islander male, and more specifically Polynesian male, who is the most visible (Lakisa, Adair and Taylor 2014). The Melanesian diaspora by contrast is almost invisible despite the fact that there are increasing numbers of mixed heritage Papua New Guinean Australians who often come from families with PNG mothers and Australian fathers because it is still very difficult to migrate from Melanesia to Australia, compared with, for example, central and eastern Polynesia to New Zealand (see Lewis-Harris 2012; Pryke 2014).

There is a corresponding arena of negative visibility for Pacific communities, again dominated by Polynesian males, within the criminal justice system at all levels. For example, in 2008 the community liaison officer at the Woodford correctional facility in Queensland, a maximum security prison, told me that 10 per cent of their population consists of young Pacific males. And stories on Pacific Islander gangs and crime abound in Australian and New Zealand newspapers, television and online platforms (see, for example, Ansley 2012; Betz 2013; Hill 2013). The Woodford officer, however, also stressed that the Pacific population was the most organised and positive, fostering links with other inmates, especially Indigenous Australians, and creating cultural programs to connect with their families (personal communication, November 2008).

In a context where Pacific communities migrate to Australia for strong economic reasons, and where their visibility is often shaped by negative representations in the media, the corresponding 'positive' arenas of sport and popular culture become even more important as spaces in which Pacific people can counter negative stereotypes with narratives of cultural pride, agency and citizenship (Lakisa, Adair and Taylor 2014; Uperesa 2014). Such positive participation and citizenship is captured by the notion of communal mana. Brendan Hokowhitu usefully frames this convergence of mana and sport in the New Zealand context in terms of a history of colonialism, sport and European settlement:

> For a culture on the brink of extinction and subjected to explicit racism in nearly all walks of society, sport offered *tāne* a sort of salvation. Furthermore, given the national hysteria for rugby throughout the twentieth century and the consequent status of the game, it is not surprising that, for Māori men, the rugby and rugby league field was a site where they could gain their community's respect and thus mana. One need only look at the obituaries in *Mana Magazine* to recognize that *tāne* are eulogized for their sporting feat. (Hokowhitu 2004: 269–70)

Vince Diaz, in his discussion of American gridiron or football, similarly describes this phenomenon as 'beating the colonizer at his own game' (Diaz 2011: 97). While he acknowledges the positive potential of sport, Hokowhitu is critical of dominant, hypermasculine representations of what he calls the 'naturally physical' Māori man epitomised by sports such as rugby and American football circulated by mass media, and he challenges Māori men to live beyond these dominant constructs (Hokowhitu 2004: 266, 278).

While Hokowhitu was not describing a Māori diasporic context, I became interested in the idea of gaining mana through sport both in the islands and overseas and the differences between those contexts. The word mana has become quite common with a taken-for-granted meaning in English as a kind of spiritual power or potency that can manifest in persons, objects, places or acts. Mei Winitana, who does write about the Māori diaspora, describes the mana in 'Mana Wahine Māori' in Australia, with reference to the works of Maori Marsden in the 1970s and Paul Tapsell in the 1990s:

> Mana can be likened to the Greek equivalent of 'dunamai', indicating a 'capability' towards power ... This capability may be described as charisma, an indefinable 'X factor' that some people possess that influences and inspires others. Charismatic people are telegenic, that is, they project a certain look, particular warmth in their smile,

> and a personal aura or presence. They communicate in ways that touch the minds and hearts of people for both positive and negative purposes. (Winitana 2008: 2)

Media influence can enhance this telegenic quality, promoting both a provocative and reactive image for public consumption (ibid.: 2). The prominence of sport and popular culture across all forms of media, and the rise in Pacific Islander and Māori participation within these fields, coupled with the expectations of family and community (Besnier 2012; Uperesa 2014), dramatically increase the pressures on athletes and popular artists to be responsible for not just their own, but everyone's image, everyone's hopes, and everyone's mana. The expectations can be unbearable and coupled with other factors including injury or loss of contract, the suicide or attempted suicide rates of rugby league players are growing at a worrying rate, similar to their football counterparts (Cadzow 2013; Massoud 2013).

The backlash from Tongan and other Pacific communities in Australia and the United States towards Australian comedian Chris Lilley's ABC and HBO syndicated show *Jonah from Tonga* (Lilley 2014), underscores this widespread aversion to negative public representation. In reaction to Lilley, in controversial brownface, playing a young, misunderstood, delinquent Tongan teenage male with a propensity for swearing, scholars and church leaders protested, and young people mounted the counter-campaign '#MyNameisNOTJonah' across Twitter and Facebook. Leitu Havea's selfie, circulated widely on social and regular media, proclaimed:

> I am a proud Tongan
> I've NEVER spent time in prison
> I was NEVER suspended from school
> I am currently studying for my university degree
> #MyNameisNOTJonah
> #ChangeStartsHERE #ProudPoly
> (SBS 2014).

Theorising mana

In his article 'Rethinking Mana', Roger M. Keesing (1984) critiques the predominant notion—a notion based on Robert Henry Codrington's work, which he says came to dominate anthropological writing—

of mana as a spiritual essence or power that could be gained or lost (cf. Kolshus, this volume). He re-examined mana by taking a comparative linguistic perspective, arguing that it is not classically a noun but rather a stative verb. Things and human enterprises *are* mana rather than *have* mana. He argued that we can speak of the mana-ness of a thing or act, and things that are mana are efficacious, potent, successful, true, fulfilled and realised. In short, they 'work' (ibid.: 138). So, for example: a stone used magically that actually works, a fisherman's abundant catch, and a potion that heals, all are 'mana'. In all contexts, ancestors, spirits and the gods help make people and things mana. But the notion of mana as a noun denoting substantive power is, as many have observed, prominent in and beyond Polynesia and it is this definition of mana that has come to dominate our application of the term.

In 'Retheorizing Mana', Matt Tomlinson (2006) points out that Keesing did not include Christian visions of Oceanic mana and that Christianity might be the key to rethinking mana in the contemporary Pacific. He argues that mana became a standard noun not just in English-language anthropological literature but in Fijian and as used by Fijians too. The concept underwent transformation in the process of the missionary transcription of Pacific languages, and particularly in the translation of the Bible. It is now typically used as a noun, associated not only with ancestors and chiefs but also with church leaders (see also Tomlinson and Bigitibau, this volume).

Tomlinson argues that Christian transformations of mana 'were not simply grammatical, nor simply a matter of substantivizing mana … The transformations of mana were metonymic of wider political processes' (2006: 180). For example, the creation of a permanent elite chiefly class in Fiji via British colonial policy reified custom and as such this class was rationalised accordingly—they, the chiefs, must *have* mana. He further argues that by the same token, mana can slip away or be lost: he quotes Christina Toren's observation that 'a chief's mana is not what it was … because they are all Christians, and so the power of the ancestor gods has diminished' (Tomlinson 2006: 180). One particular area where this is observed is in effective speech: only God can speak with automatic effectiveness, not chiefs.

On a relevant point for my argument about masculinity and sport, Tomlinson also argues that for Fijians, when configuring mana negatively, there is seen to be a loss in male physical strength and prowess compared with the past. And while he does not mention it explicitly, I imagine this has something to do with the transformation of the warrior class into the modern institutions of sport, military and police. So Fijian mana today is often configured negatively, in terms of its disappearance, but it is clear that male sporting heroes and soldiers are viewed to an extent, in Ty P. Kāwika Tengan and Jesse Markham's (2009) terms, as contemporary warriors signalling a pre-colonial masculinity.

Diaz takes this point further, echoing the sentiments of the documentary *In Football We Trust* by stating:

> The key Polynesian concept that best captures … what is at stake in Samoan and other Polynesian performances on the American gridiron is mana. Mana is what accounts for this remarkable and unrivalled success as an ethnic or even demographic group—no other racial or ethnic group and no other similarly-sized community in the world has ever produced the number of major college and professional football players per capita. In the simplest terms possible to understand in English, mana is a powerful presence or force to be found in people, animals, and even inanimate objects, and as might be imagined in post-missionary Christianity, mana also gets ultimately linked with God, and service and obligation to God … Precisely when it is hitched to warrior traditions in powerful ways, American football can be viewed as a virtual stage for the performance of Samoan manhood and masculinity and the broader values in fa'a Samoa through mana. (Diaz 2011: 101)

The stakes of the mana of elite players in the context of the broader community are well illustrated by Diaz's analysis of gay NFL star Esera Tuaolo's public coming out on national TV (after his retirement), which resulted in a tsunami of criticism and abuse from his Samoan community. People were happy when his football enhanced their perceived collective mana but when he publicly announced his sexuality, the response from one blogger was:

> Talofa Esera, You are a disgust and menace to Samoan culture! I guess you're out of your mind! God hates gays as stated in the bible. What is wrong with you? Do not associate God with these filthy faggots and maggots. Tell your parents that you are gay and see what their reactions might be. (Diaz 2011: 97)

Setting aside my own personal judgment about such nasty comments, my question is: what happens when we add sport, the diaspora and mass media to this discussion of mana? The hysteria comes partly from the social significance and great visibility of sport and, like popular culture, its potential to uplift as well as demonise entire communities while simultaneously exposing certain values, or revealing a diversity of values, including homophobia. If mana is potency, whether individual or collective, physical or spiritual, then the immense presence of sport and media in countries where Pacific diasporic groups are most prominent means that social values—uplifting ones like strength and courage, and degrading ones like homophobia and intolerance—will necessarily be pulled into any discussion of mana.

Success in sports helps reinstate a male efficacy perceived to be lost through colonialism, migration, minority status in the diaspora, and class status (Uperesa 2014). Tengan and Markham discuss similar issues, stating that football 'becomes a site for the practice and fulfilment of family and spiritual values of faith and loyalty, especially for islanders in the diaspora. At the same time, the Polynesian male warrior becomes a commodity image to be sold for big business' (2009: 2414). Sport is marketed as hypermasculine spectacle for society as a whole. Furthermore, they discuss how the black super-athlete reinforces racial hierarchies and both glorifies and demonises primitive hypermasculinity. They argue, 'Within the present configuration of the sports-media complex, islander men, like African American and Native American men, have become commodified and consumed as racialized and hypermasculine spectacle' (Tengan and Markham 2009: 2414; see also Lakisa, Adair and Taylor 2014). There is a complex relationship between the commodified spectacle and notions of leadership, status or authority and the interpretation and significance of sport, popular culture and political icons for Pacific audiences. Within all this are both internally generated and externally integrated biases, racism, sexism, homophobia and notions of class.

In the Australian diaspora, participation in sport and popular culture is a particular area of visibility and success for Pacific peoples that holds great meaning for minority communities (Lakisa, Adair and Taylor 2014; Uperesa 2014). And this is key for Australia because the spheres of politics and higher education are not currently arenas in which Islanders are visible compared with New Zealand and the United States where there are politicians and PhDs of Pacific descent who are nationally celebrated. Sport is not just an athletic opportunity but an economic one that allows successful players class mobility, and to fulfil cultural obligations, what Fa'anofo Lisaclaire Uperesa describes as 'the opportunity to give back … [and the] privilege of performing tautua (service, in this case expanded and transnationalized)' (2014: 294–95). The achievements of elite players bring mana, as it were, not just to their corresponding Pacific communities but to their clubs and associated, and often multicultural, Australian fan base.

Revisiting Hokowhitu's analysis of why sport is seen as so significant:

> My father, like many Māori of his generation, lived for sports. He grew up in an era when sport was one of the few spheres where tāne could achieve success and compete with Pākeha men on an 'even playing field' and, accordingly, could gain mana in the Pākeha world. My father's enthusiasm for sport carried over to me, along with a definition of masculinity based on the noble, physically tough, staunch, and emotion-less Māori men we witnessed on the local, provincial, and national rugby fields. (Hokowhitu 2004: 260)

The commodification and fetishisation of Pacific bodies by diverse audiences through the sports/media complex adds another dimension to the issue. Media and the diaspora are deterritorialised spaces where agency, expression and meaning are constructed in articulation with the 'offline' sociopolitical context. And this offline sociopolitical context has its own particular sets of challenges and opportunities. Being a Pacific Islander in New Zealand or the United States, where there are named Pacific Islander agencies, programs and statutory bodies, is very different from being a Pacific Islander in Australia, where issues such as Pasifika education, health and welfare are dealt with, fairly inconsistently, at the state level. And within Australia, being a Pacific Islander in Canberra, with smaller, dispersed Pacific populations, is different from being a Pacific Islander in Campbelltown, Western Sydney, or Logan, Queensland, where they are concentrated and visible. While Pacific peoples across the globe celebrate their football, rugby union and rugby league stars, what that means to communities on the ground in their particular social and political circumstances varies considerably.

Location shapes how different agents participate and make meaning, and Australia is a particular kind of national, cultural, economic, political and geographic context compared with the United States, New Zealand or even Fiji as a migration destination. Expressions of difference, for example through distinct ethnic identities in Australia, do not always convert into social or cultural capital in the same way they might in other countries, including the United States where categories such as Native American, Asian American and Pacific Islander American exist and mean something structurally.

While there are still similar experiences of structural marginalisation and economic disadvantage, there is less to be gained, socially, for example, by being a Samoan or Tongan in a school in Melbourne, compared with being a Samoan or Tongan in a school in Auckland or Utah with their high, concentrated Polynesian populations. So while the strategies to integrate or assimilate into dominant cultures are strong in all of these contexts, the pressures and tactics in Australia are particular to this country's racial and indigenous politics. These are historically shaped by the protracted denial of Indigenous Australian rights, the 'White Australia' policy focused on populating the country with white migrants from 1901 to 1973, and a current prioritisation of 'skilled' migration. Compared with New Zealand and the United States, and in spite of relying on blackbirded labour from Melanesia on Queensland plantations from 1863 to 1904, Australia actively discouraged migration from the Pacific, including from its former colonial territories of Papua New Guinea and Nauru. Well aware of the inflow of Pacific migrants now via New Zealand, Australian policymakers continue to be concerned with the trans-Tasman agreement (see Lee 2009: 7).

Given this environment and the absence of a federal portfolio for domestic Pacific issues, Pacific Islanders in Australia have to be extra proactive in carving out safe spaces where they can celebrate their cultures and pass on their languages and values to their children. Mana is easily diffused in Australia and potentially rendered irrelevant where the pressures to assimilate, for example on sporting fields from primary school to elite levels, are strong. Pacific rugby union and rugby league players, with their large Australian fan bases, could easily play as just brown bodies in a white game, grateful they or their parents made it to Australian shores, playing in Australian professional sporting codes with all of the challenges of the migration experience. But they do not always just play the game. I propose, in a preliminary way, that there is more to the agency of elite Pacific athletes than the commodity sign. When Pacific players do not just play as brown bodies, when they draw media attention to their Pacific heritage and the centrality of 'family, faith and culture' (Lakisa, Adair and Taylor 2014: 347), the effect can be powerful.

Body Pacifica and the NRL

In January 2012, I conducted a workshop with a team of ANU Pacific Studies staff working in collaboration with the National Rugby League (NRL) Education and Welfare Office, particularly with former star and now welfare officer Nigel Vagana. Something one of the players said to me has helped me think about players' agency and transformative potential in what is regularly viewed as a violent game that epitomises dominant notions of Australian hypermasculinity and was replete with scandals over drugs, alcohol and gender-based violence (Hutchins and Mikozsca 1998).

The player told me that the Pacific players on his team would regularly get together to pray before the game and in order to do this they would have to step out of the larger group, go into their own corner and pray together before returning to finish the rest of the pre-game ritual. After a while the team coach and management flagged this as very non team-like behaviour and stressed that players needed to be strong and cohesive and not highlight their differences before the game. However, rather than asking the Pacific men to stop praying, they instead decided that if the Islanders were going to pray, everyone was going to pray. This is quite a decision in a country which is far less publicly religious than, say, the United States, but a similar thing has also happened in rugby union (see Moloney 2008).

A few years ago, sports journalist John-Paul Moloney contacted me at ANU to ask why Pacific people had to pray all the time. It was becoming quite evident within the Brumbies that their new Pacific players had very different values from the Anglo-Australian players; values that were expressed quite visibly by conducting prayers at training sessions and before games. Moloney wrote:

> Faith in a football team is no new thing. But its presence within the Canberra Super 14 team is greater than ever. Its rise has corresponded with an influx into the club of Pacific Island footballers, who almost to a man believe in Christianity, which has been indiginised within Tongan, New Zealand Māori, Fijian and Samoan communities. Flyhalf Christian Lealiifano wears his faith visibly on the field, drawing a crucifix in marker pen on strapping tape around his wrist. (Moloney 2008)

One of the main reasons the rugby league team decided to go with the Pacific Islanders' prayer ritual, and why teams like the Brumbies will have to get used to prayer, is because of the current demographic realities of both sporting codes. These were announced in the *Sydney Morning Herald* in 2006:

> Forget new rules, expansion teams and codes of conduct—the biggest influence on Australia's rugby codes has been the influx of Pacific Islanders. Some even say that it's inevitable the NRL and senior rugby union will soon be dominated by players with Tongan, Samoan or Māori blood. (Lane 2006)

The sheer numbers of Pacific players, 50 per cent of the whole junior game and over 20 per cent of the top tier, means that by demographics alone these players have the potential to transform the game from the inside and make some of their cultural values and practices mainstream, particularly if they resist the impetus to assimilate into dominant Australian culture (Lakisa, Adair and Taylor 2014; Horton and Zakus 2009; Lakisa 2011). While I agree with many of Diaz's, Tengan's and Markham's critiques in the context of the NFL in the United States, I have observed some positive and proactive efforts by Pacific rugby and especially rugby league players in Australia to infuse the game more broadly with their own values. This is also more possible in a country the size of Australia compared with that of the United States.

While some forms of fundamentalist Christianity and homophobia, for example, are hardly mutually exclusive, between sport, popular culture and this particular Australian context, new possibilities for transforming perceptions of Pacific men and Pacific communities are possible. If (niu/new) mana is about a state of being strong, efficacious, prosperous, successful, having 'status and prestige' (Palmer and Masters 2010), and doing mighty or even miraculous acts, especially when they score tries, tackle, run fast, and help win games, then I wonder if, in both senses of the word, whether noun or verb, and as 'force', players truly have the potential to increase their own and the more general 'mana' of Pacific communities, many of whom are struggling in the Australian system. Revisiting Diaz's observations about the stakes of mana, what are the direct links between mana, masculinity and sport? Is 'new mana' dependent on a still hypermasculine, 'new warrior' to reinstate authority lost in the process of colonialism and migration? Or is there another possibility within the sphere of men's sport to enhance this shared mana?

Let us take a look at three very different players who represent the most visible masculine Pacific types within the game. Someone like Samoan-New Zealander Sonny Bill Williams may not have as much potential for gaining or conferring mana as he is sometimes viewed as someone who follows the paycheck, switches back and forth between rugby league and union codes, and changes clubs at a regular rate. This is not to disconnect mana from a concept of rational economics; financial success is important to Pacific communities, as are values of stability and loyalty. But Williams' potential to be viewed as a leader, rather than just a brown body with high athletic prowess in a white game, has been undermined by a range of factors including the regular sexualisation of his image.

Tongan player William Hopoate, whose father also played league and was viewed as a 'bad boy' of the game, is practically the opposite of his dad. In spite of being one of the youngest players ever drafted into the professional tier, Hopoate gave up a $AU1.7 million contract with the Parramatta Eels to go on a two-year mission for the Church of Jesus Christ of Latter Day Saints. His decision confounded many fans and the NRL community as it was fairly unimaginable to the general public that anyone would choose the life of a missionary over being a highly paid star athlete. To Islanders, however, one could argue his choice signalled the kind of mana seen in 'a great deed', in this case, an act of Christian faith and sacrifice.

Retired Fijian player Petero Civoniceva, whose father also played rugby, is viewed as someone with incredible mana who is senior, humble, well respected and leads by example. I observed this first-hand in meetings with Civoniceva, current players and other stakeholders at the NRL Education and Welfare office in Sydney. While his Fijian surname has never been pronounced correctly—he is called 'Sivonisiva' instead of the correct 'Thivonitheva' by his teammates, fans and sports journalists—when Petero speaks, other players listen.

While Civoniceva is respected in the game, he has not always been respected by fans. In 2008, during a game against Parramatta, an Eels fan sitting very close to the field shouted that he was a 'fucking monkey'. The fan, who was later banned for five years from attending rugby league matches, said yes he'd called him a 'fucking monkey' but it wasn't meant to be racist (Read 2008). But racism is rampant within Australian sport and Pacific and Indigenous Australian players have long been targets of verbal abuse. After his incident, the usually quiet Civoniceva decided to speak up and gave several media interviews where he denounced racism within the sport and called for a change in attitudes through an NRL anti-racism campaign. Initially the NRL agreed, but apparently no campaign ever emerged, much to his disappointment. The Australian Football League (AFL), however, championed an anti-racism campaign inspired by their outspoken Indigenous players such as 2014 Australian of the Year Adam Goodes, and drew in sporting heroes from other codes (Australian Human Rights Commission 2013). Goodes experienced racism throughout his whole career and particularly towards the end. In 2015, after crowds booed an Indigenous post-goal 'war dance', he took leave and subsequently retired. This sparked a national dialogue on racism in sport which was prominent in mainstream media.

After this incident, Civoniceva and other senior Pacific players decided to get together regularly to talk about some of these problems and the group has been a catalyst for a number of new initiatives. Led by NRL Education and Welfare officer and former League star Nigel Vagana, they have come up with projects that are specifically designed to help players become better leaders and role models within and beyond the game.

The 2010 *Body Pacifica* initiative, for example, was one such project. Players used their status and popularity to promote Pacific art, culture and tangible and intangible heritage with many flow-on effects for Pacific communities in and beyond New South Wales. Produced by rugby league player turned curator Leo Tanoi and Carli Leimbach, *Body Pacifica* ran from June to August 2010 at the Casula Powerhouse Arts Centre in Liverpool, Western Sydney, and involved a diverse program of exhibitions, live performances, workshops, digital displays and sales of a very successful calendar.

The *Body Pacifica Calendar*, which sold out in advance, was art-directed by celebrated New Zealand-born photographer of Samoan heritage Greg Semu in collaboration with graphic designer Frank Puletua, a former player and the only Pacific player with a degree in fine arts. It featured NRL players of Pacific heritage: Jarryd Hayne, Fuifui Moimoi, Paul Alton, Roy Asotasi, Dene Halatau, Frank Puletua,

Nathan Cayless, Petero Civoniceva, Michael Jennings, Ruben Wiki, Manu Vatuvei, Jared Waerea-Hargreaves and Nigel Vagana, dressed in costumes sourced from the Pacific collection of the Australian Museum.

At the photo shoot a variety of objects was put out for them to choose from and then the photography session followed. Some players selected items that were not from their island of heritage and some players, like Jarred Hayne (who is Fijian, born and raised in Australia), displayed the items, such as the *tabua*, in what most Fijians would view as an incorrect manner. A *tabua* or whale's tooth is not a necklace, but is something that is held and presented ceremonially.

The players' photographs were displayed in larger-than-life—dare I say god-like—images, which lined the first-floor gallery of Casula Powerhouse. And like benevolent gods they seemed to watch over the three months of activities and over the many crowds that gathered during the opening and closing events. Some of them, however, did not actually show up in person; they instead lent their mana or spirit to the event and this was recognised and celebrated by the audience.

Body Pacifica was very well received by Pacific communities and the general public with Casula Powerhouse winning a NSW IMAGine award in public engagement for the exhibition. Thousands of people from the Pacific community, most of whom were not regular museum or gallery patrons, visited Casula during *Body Pacifica*. This helped inspire Vagana, Civoniceva and other players to take another initiative. In 2011, after almost two years of on-and-off discussions between my school's director at the time, Kent Anderson, the co-owner of the South Sydney Rabbitohs' Peter Holmes à Court, and Vagana, I was asked to join the new NRL Pacific Council as a Pacific Studies expert to help the education and welfare office come up with ideas for new ways to enhance education, leadership and positive role modelling for Pacific players.

Kent Anderson saw this collaboration as an important opportunity for Pacific Studies to strategically expand its research, education and outreach goals. We designed a Pacific Studies leadership camp where elite players from 13 professional clubs would engage with Pacific history, religion, literature and the performing arts. They went through a series of lectures and workshops and put together final performances that reflected their learning. A team of Pacific Islander scholars and

Papua New Guinean choreographer Julia Gray facilitated the three-day event with additional mentoring and inspiration from visitors to the camp such as Tofiga Fepulea'i of the internationally acclaimed comedy duo Laughing Samoans, former NFL player Richard Brown and Australian Idol contestant and Māori pop singer Stan Walker.

At the end of the camp, the players reported that the history and leadership modules had had a significant impact on their sense of Pacific history, identity and culture and they were motivated to spread this throughout their club communities. At this point, I handed the project over to other members of the team for further collaboration but I was struck by how this very short exposure to many of the core aspects of Pacific Studies learning had a reported impact on elite athletes, most of whom—unlike their NFL counterparts who play college football and therefore study throughout a significant period of their careers—had received little higher education, technical or academic. It is well known within the NRL that Pacific Islander players do not take advantage of higher education opportunities compared with their Anglo-Australian counterparts.

While the *Body Pacifica* exhibition had catalysed a much-needed public display of Pacific pride, the NRL Education and Welfare Office was keen to take this further and deepen the historical and cultural knowledge of their players. In Hokowhitu's terms, they had enhanced the mana of their communities and potentially increased their own mana by gaining respect through the lending of their regularly commoditised bodies and images to celebrate Pacific culture instead. Now Vagana wanted to ensure that they did indeed have a deeper knowledge of that culture via education.

Reflection

Migrant Pacific Islanders are transforming and applying new interpretations of both mana and tapu (taboo) in their diasporic contexts. For example, diasporic groups will apply these notions to sacred Pacific objects in museums in their new countries of residence. While they may not always understand the meaning of the objects in their original contexts, such objects have come to signify an important link to the ancestors and the Islands, bridging that distance in both time and space (Singh and Blake 2012). It is that distance from the home island context and the ways in which publicly visible bodies, acts or objects become infused with the potential 'mana'—efficacy and image—of whole communities which requires a rethinking of the stakes of mana compared with earlier studies focused on understanding its formal linguistic properties and application in the islands.

What I have done here is lay out some questions, reflected on what others such as Tengan, Markham, Hokowhitu, Diaz and Uperesa have signalled already in their research, and presented the Australian diasporic context as offering further opportunities for critical examination of the concept or effect of mana. I do not believe the word itself needs to be present or regularly utilised in Pacific diasporic discourse for its essential qualities or effects to be relevant. As argued by Diaz, mana is still the best concept to capture what is at stake in the relationship between Pacific sporting icons and the communities they represent. The deeds, words and images of an elite Pacific athlete can uplift or shame their entire cultures. This is the nature of Pacific, and especially Polynesian, relational personhood. As writer Sia Figiel has poignantly offered in her succinct characterisation of Samoan collective identity: '"I" is "we"... always' (1996: 136).

Australia is a 'new' and certainly less understood or researched diasporic space compared with the United States and New Zealand, and one that has deeply unresolved racial politics, but it is also a kind of open field for Islanders to transform and claim in their own ways. The kind of mana created by something like *Body Pacifica* or the NRL Leadership camp is both individual and collective, noun and verb, human and object, and also fleeting. A chief's or God's mana might need to be proven but is supposed to be durable, but an athlete's power is often short-term and almost always ends in one kind of defeat or another by virtue of the fact that retirement or injury means they cannot exercise athletic prowess any more in the same way.

Currently, while there are concentrations of Pacific communities and inspiring personalities and deeds evident within suburbs across several states, it remains to be seen what kind of 'niu' space Australia will become for Pacific Islanders. That is, a space infused with and informed by Pacific flavours, styles and values regardless of gender, artistic talent or athletic prowess. At the moment, in spite of the seasonal explosion of male Islander bodies across the sporting fields and flat screen televisions of countless Australian homes, Pacific peoples and the Pacific Islands still occupy the edges of Australian consciousness, especially with the intense and strategic economic, educational and political turn within the last 20 years towards Asia.

References

350 pacific. n.d. Online: 350pacific.org (accessed 2 November 2015).

350. n.d. Online: 350.org/ (accessed 2 November 2015).

Ansley, Greg. 2012. Australia's Pacific gangland. *nzherald.co.nz*. 21 January. Online: www.nzherald.co.nz/world/news/article.cfm?c_id=2&objectid=10780126 (accessed 11 October 2015).

Australian Human Rights Commission. 2013. Racism: It stops with me. Online: www.youtube.com/watch?v=ASsZ-u9YV3c (accessed 4 April 2014).

Banivanua-Mar, Tracey. 2007. *Violence and Colonial Dialogue: The Australian-Pacific Indentured Labor Trade*. Honolulu: University of Hawai'i Press.

Besnier, Niko. 2012. The athlete's body and the global condition: Tongan rugby players in Japan. *American Anthropologist* 39(3): 491–510.

Betz, Elizabeth. 2013. Unemployment not the cause of Pacific Islander violence in Logan. *The Conversation*, 18 January. Online: theconversation.com/unemployment-not-the-cause-of-pacific-islander-violence-in-logan-11650 (accessed 3 September 2014).

Boucher, Dinah. 2012. On finding our own voices: Australia's Samoan diaspora, representation and identity. B.A. Hons thesis, Griffith University.

Cadzow, Jane. 2013. The quiet one. *Sydney Morning Herald*, 30 May. Online: www.smh.com.au/rugby-league/league-news/the-quiet-one-20130422-2i948.html (accessed 9 September 2014).

Crocombe, Ron. 1976. *The Pacific Way: An Emerging Identity*. Suva: Lotu Pacifica.

Diaz, Vince. 2011. Tackling Pacific hegemonic formations on the American gridiron. *Amerasia Journal* 37(3): 90–113.

Figiel, Sia. 1996. *Where We Once Belonged,* Auckland: Pasifika Press.

Giggacher, James. 2014. Kindred spirits [interview with Margaret Jolly]. 24 March. Online: pasifika.anu.edu.au/news-events/all-stories/kindred-spirits (accessed 8 September 2014). Original, abridged article in the *ANU Reporter,* Autumn 2014: 28–29.

Hill, Bruce. 2013. Maori/ Pacific gang violence in Australia. *Radio Australia.* 15 May. Online: www.radioaustralia.net.au/international/radio/program/pacific-beat/maoripacific-gang-violence-in-melbourne/1131308 (accessed 12 October 2015).

Hokowhitu, Brendan. 2004. Tackling Māori masculinity. *The Contemporary Pacific* 16(2): 259–84.

Horton, Peter and Dwayne Zakus. 2009. Pacifica in Australian rugby: Emanant [sic] social, cultural and economic issues. *Sporting Traditions* 26(2): 67–86.

Hutchins, Brett and Janine Mikosza. 1998. Australian Rugby League and violence 1970–1995: A case study in the maintenance of masculine hegemony. *Journal of Sociology* 34: 246–63.

IFWT Productions and ITVS. 2014. *In Football We Trust* (documentary film). Trailer online: www.youtube.com/watch?v=0I6vb4XwV0o (accessed 9 October 2015).

Keesing, Roger M. 1984. Rethinking 'mana'. *Journal of Anthropological Research* 40(1): 137–56.

Lakisa, David. 2011. *The Pacific Revolution: Pacific & Māori Players in Australian Rugby League.* MA thesis, Southern Cross University, New South Wales.

Lakisa, David, Daryl Adair and Tracy Taylor. 2014. Pasifika diaspora and the changing face of Australian Rugby League. *The Contemporary Pacific* 26(2): 347–67.

Lane, Daniel. 2006. Islanders in junior leagues, it's a really big issue. *Sydney Morning Herald*. 16 July. Online: www.smh.com.au/news/league/islanders-in-junior-leagues-its-a-really-big-issue/2006/07/15/1152637922188.html (accessed 12 October 2015).

Lawson, Stephanie. 2010. 'The Pacific way' as postcolonial discourse: Towards a reassessment. *Journal of Pacific History* 45(3): 297–314.

Lee, Helen. 2009. Pacific migration and transnationalism: historical perspectives. In *Migration and Transnationalism: Pacific Perspectives*, ed. Helen Lee and Steve Tupai Francis, pp. 7–42. Canberra: ANU E Press. Online: press.anu.edu.au?p=32931 (accessed 9 October 2015).

Lee, Helen and Steve Tupai Francis (eds). 2009. *Migration and Transnationalism: Pacific Perspectives*. Canberra: ANU E Press. Online: press.anu.edu.au?p=32931 (accessed 9 October 2015).

Lewis-Harris, Jacquelyn. 2011. Dancing on the weekend: Papua New Guinea culture schools in urban Australia. *Intersections: Gender and Sexuality in Asia and the Pacific* 27 (November). Online: intersections.anu.edu.au/issue27/lewis-harris.htm (accessed 2 September 2014).

Lilley, Chris. 2014. *Jonah from Tonga* [television series]. Melbourne: Princess Pictures.

Liu, James H., Tim McCreanor and Tracey McIntosh (eds). 2005. *New Zealand Identities: Departures and Destinations*. Wellington: Victoria University Press.

Madang Wansolwara Dance. 2014. *Papua New Guinea Mine Watch* blog. Online: ramumine.wordpress.com/2014/09/01/madang-wansolwara-dance/ (accessed 3 September 2014).

Mallon, Sean and Pandora Fulimalo Pereira (eds). 2002. *Pacific Art Niu Sila: The Pacific Dimension of Contemporary Arts in New Zealand*. Wellington: Te Papa Press.

Massoud, Josh. 2013. Reni Maitua has revealed how he hit rock bottom and attempted to take his own life. *The Sunday Telegraph*. 14 December. Online: www.foxsports.com.au//nrl/nrl-premiership/reni-maitua-has-revealed-how-he-hit-rock-bottom-and-attempted-to-take-his-own-life/story-e6frf3pu-1226783159643?nk=c707862ddd0d4ad38c5ee30ad197f35b (accessed 9 September 2014).

Moloney, John-Paul. 2008. New Brumbies profess the faith. *Canberra Times*, 17 November. Online: www.smh.com.au/rugby-union/union-news/new-brumbies-profess-the-faith-20091124-j902.html#ixzz3CDkMEuI3 (accessed 2 September 2014).

Palmer, Farah and Tina Masters. 2010. Māori feminism and sport leadership. *Sport Management Review* 13(4): 331–44.

Pryke, Jonathan. 2014. Pacific Islanders in Australia: Where are the Melanesians? *DEVPOLICYBLOG*, 28 August. Online: devpolicy.org/pacific-islanders-in-australia-where-are-the-melanesians-20140828/ (accessed 2 September 2014).

Pryor, Nicole. 2013. Maori in Oz: Living the good life. *Stuff.co.nz*. 19 July. Online: www.stuff.co.nz/national/8937746/Maori-in-Oz-Living-the-good-life (accessed 12 October 2015).

Queensland Health, Queensland Government. 2013. *Pacific Islander and Maori Population Size and Distribution*. Online: www.health.qld.gov.au/multicultural/health_workers/pac-island-pop.asp (accessed 11 October 2015).

Read, Brent. 2008. Petero Civoniceva racial abuser banned from league games. *Australian*, 09 July. Online: www.theaustralian.com.au/archive/news/civoniceva-racial-abuser-banned-by-nrl/story-e6frg7mo-1111116859701?nk=c707862ddd0d4ad38c5ee30ad197f35b (accessed 3 September 2014).

Rose, Samantha, Max Quanchi and Clive Moore. 2009. *A National Strategy for the Study of the Pacific*. Brisbane: Australian Association for the Advancement of Pacific Studies.

SBS. 2014. Chris Lilley facing social media backlash over 'racist' Jonah from Tonga. 15 May. Online: www.sbs.com.au/news/article/2014/05/15/chris-lilley-facing-social-media-backlash-over-racist-jonah-tonga (accessed 3 September 2014).

Singh, Supriya, and Meredith Blake. 2012. The digitization of Pacific cultural collections: Consulting with diasporic Pacific communities and experts. *Curator: The Museum Journal* 55(1): 95–105.

Steeg, Jill Lieber. 2012. Junior Seau: Song of sorrow. *San Diego Union-Tribune*. Online: www.utsandiego.com/news/2012/Oct/14/junior-seau-real-story/ (accessed 2 April 2014).

Teaiwa, Katerina. 2007. Aussie Islanders fight ignorance. *Fiji Times Online,* 30 October (original article in *Canberra Times,* 29 October). Online: www.fijitimes.com/story.aspx?id=73247 (accessed 3 September 2014).

Teaiwa, Teresia and Sean Mallon. 2005. Ambivalent kinships: Pacific people in New Zealand. In *New Zealand Identities: Departures and Destinations,* ed. James H. Liu, Tim McCreanor and Tracey McIntosh, pp. 207–29. Wellington: Victoria University Press.

Tengan, Ty P. Kāwika and Jesse Markham, 2009. Performing Polynesian masculinities in American football: From 'rainbows to warriors'. *International Journal of the History of Sport* 26(16): 2412–431.

Tomlinson, Matt. 2006. Retheorizing mana: Bible translation and discourse of loss in Fiji. *Oceania* 76(2): 173–85.

Uperesa, Fa'anofo Lisaclaire. 2014. Fabled futures: Migration and mobility for Samoans in American football. *The Contemporary Pacific* 26(2): 281–301.

Vasta, Ellis. 2004. Community, the state and the deserving citizen: Pacific Islanders in Australia. *Journal of Ethnic and Migration Studies* 30(1): 195–213.

Winitana, Mei. 2008. Contemporary conceptions of mana wahine Māori in Australia: A diasporic discussion. *Mai Review* 3, Research Note 4: 1–8.

5

Mana, Power and 'Pawa' in the Pacific and Beyond

Alan Rumsey

In this chapter I address three interrelated topics pertaining to *mana* and how it might be understood in relation to 'power' as a social-analytical construct, and to *pawa* as a vernacular term used by some Pacific peoples.

First, I briefly review the history of anthropological and comparative-linguistic understandings of *mana*, from Robert Codrington's boldly speculative account (1891), to Raymond Firth's (1940) much more cautious one, to Roger Keesing's (1984) argument concerning what he takes to be western misconstruals of traditional concepts of *mana* held by Pacific peoples speaking Oceanic Austronesian languages. I offer some caveats about that argument and update it by reviewing some more recent work by other scholars who have tried to link those words and concepts to others that are attested in Austronesian languages across a wider region than Oceania, and even to Papuan languages extending into the interior of Papua New Guinea (PNG).

Next, turning to my field experience in PNG among speakers of a Papuan language who do not have a word like *mana* that is used in anything very close to the senses that that word has in Oceanic languages, I discuss the word that they use that comes closest to those senses, namely *pawa*, a word that has come into the Ku Waru language through borrowing from Tok Pisin, but is nowadays very frequently used by people when speaking Ku Waru as the main noun for 'power', in close relation to an inherited Ku Waru word (*todul*) meaning 'strong'.

Finally, drawing on my discussion of *mana* and *pawa* in the first two sections of the chapter, I consider some methodological and theoretical issues involved in the kind of comparative study that is pursued in this volume. I compare its overall approach with that which is taken in two other comparative exercises, the *Keywords* volumes edited by Raymond Williams (1976) and Tony Bennett, Lawrence Grossberg and Meaghan Morris (2005), and *The Gender of the Gift* by Marilyn Strathern (1988). I show that the approach taken here is closer to the former than the latter, and argue that that is the more useful approach for understanding the play of *mana* within the relatively unbounded social field in which it circulates.

Anthropological and comparative-linguistic understandings of *mana*

Concepts and practices relating to *mana* first became widely known to westerners through the writings of the Anglican missionary-anthropologist Robert Codrington in the 1880s and 1890s. Based on his missionary work in the New Hebrides and Solomons, and his knowledge of other peoples and languages including Polynesian ones, Codrington concluded that the word *mana* was 'common … to the whole Pacific' (Codrington 1891: 138) and that it referred to a kind of universal, invisible spiritual 'power or influence' which 'attaches itself to persons, and to things' (118–19). Codrington's ethnographic writings on the subject were seized upon by armchair ethnological theorists (Marett, Durkheim, Hubert, Mauss; see Introduction to this volume) who not only accepted his claims about the meaning of this word across the Pacific, but—true to the evolutionist paradigm of the day—took his account of *mana* as evidence for the nature of so-called 'primitive mentality' in general, and as the category that most nearly expressed the essence of rudimentary religion (e.g. Marett 1914: xxxii–xxvii, xxxi).

By the 1930s the evolutionist paradigm had been overturned, within anthropology at least, and in 1940 Firth published an article in which he showed that among the Tikopia people he had worked with in the southeastern Solomons, *mana* (/*manu*) was 'not spoken of as a universal force inhering in all natural objects' (Firth 1940: 505) nor as a 'metaphysical abstraction' of any kind (496). Rather, it is:

> connected with the personality of human beings, and is exercised through human agencies … The native view of *manu* may be regarded as an element in a theory of human achievement. Its thesis is that success above a certain point, the 'normal', is spirit-given. It connects an end-product empirically observed with a set of human desires by a theory of spirit-mediation and a technique of verbal utterance. (Firth 1940: 505)

More verb-like than noun-like in many of its uses, the Tikopia term *manu* is in at least some contexts best translated as to 'be effective' or to 'be efficacious' (499, 506).

Keesing (1984) took Firth's critique further by showing that similar conclusions to the ones that Firth had reached about Tikopia (a Polynesian language) could be drawn for a wide range of other languages within the Oceanic group of the Austronesian family languages (of which the Polynesian are a sub-group, see Figure 10). Through a detailed survey of Oceanic languages, Keesing showed that although cognate terms for *mana* were widespread among them, these had a much wider range of meanings than had been allowed for by Codrington et al., and that, just as Firth had found for Tikopia, these tended to cluster more around a notion of efficaciousness of human agency in specific contexts rather than of generalised supernatural power or influence.

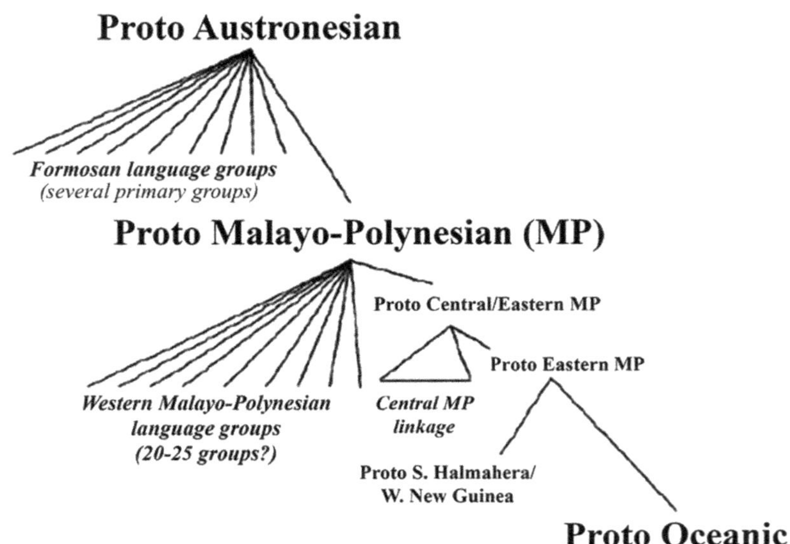

Figure 10. The high-order subgroups of Austronesian.

Source: Malcolm Ross, used with permission.

Used in the latter sense, the word *mana* had become, as Firth put it, 'a technical term describing a specialized abstraction of the theoretical anthropologist' which had 'little in common with the same term used within native phraseology' (487).[1] In the 75 years since Firth's article was published, *mana* has disappeared as a technical term in anthropology but gained a wider currency in a lay version of the older anthropological sense, that is, as the *Concise Oxford* puts it: 'power, authority, prestige; supernatural or magical power' (see the chapters by Morgain and by Golub and Peterson in this volume).

Following up on Keesing's study of **mana* words within Oceanic Austronesian languages,[2] a considerable amount of relevant new evidence has been turned up by specialists in the comparative study of those languages. Drawing on an even wider sample than Keesing had, Robert Blust (2007) showed that in many Oceanic languages there

1 Firth (1940: 487) points out that this possibility was explicitly acknowledged by at least two of those anthropologists, Marett and Hocart.

2 In line with standard practice within comparative-historical linguistics, the star before *mana* here indicates that the starred word is one that, on the basis of comparative evidence, is posited as the word in the original ancestral language (Proto-Oceanic Austronesian) from which all the cognates in the presently attested Oceanic languages have descended.

were cognate words meaning 'thunder' and 'wind'. On that basis he argued that **mana* did not originally refer to spiritual or supernatural power that could be possessed by humans, but rather to powerful forces of nature that were conceived as the expressions of invisible supernatural agency. Based on the present-day distribution of **mana* cognates and their meanings, he argued that 'as Oceanic-speaking peoples spread eastward, the notion of an unseen supernatural agency became detached from the physical forces of nature that had inspired it and assumed a life of its own' (404).

Building on Keesing's and Blust's arguments, Juliette Blevins (2008) expands their comparative base to include not only Oceanic languages, but two other higher-level sub-groupings of the Austronesian family: Central Malayo-Polynesian and South Halmahera/West New Guinea (see Figure 10). In other words, she claims to have found *mana* cognates not only in the Pacific and New Guinea but also within parts of Eastern Indonesia and Timor (Figure 11). She traces these back to a posited Proto Central-Eastern Malayo-Polynesian (PCEMP) word **mana*, to which she attributes the meaning 'supernatural power, associated with spirits of the ancestors and the forces of nature' (Blevins 2008: 253). This meaning is consistent with the one that Blust posits for Proto Oceanic, but goes beyond it in its reference to ancestral spirits. Words that Blevins cites from Oceanic languages that exemplify the meanings relating to ancestral power (all from the southeastern Solomons) are shown in Table 2.

Table 2. *Mana* words from southeastern Solomons languages relating to ancestors and inheritance.

TOQABAQITA
mamana 'be true, real, fulfilled; be successful (of a man); impart spiritual or magical power'
Mamana-a 'blessing, prosperity; **ancestrally conferred power**'
KWAIO
nanama 'be effective, fulfilled, confirmed, realised; **of ancestor**, support, protect, empower'
nanama-fa- '**of ancestor**, support, protect, empower (a person)'
Nanama-nge' e-ni '**of ancestor**, support, protect, empower (a person)'
GELA
mana '[be] efficacious; from spiritual power, obtained from charms, prayers, intercourse with [**ancestors** or spirits]'

Source: From Juliette Blevins. 2008. Some comparative notes on Proto-Oceanic *mana: Inside and outside the Austronesian family. *Oceanic Linguistics* 47: 253–74, p. 264.

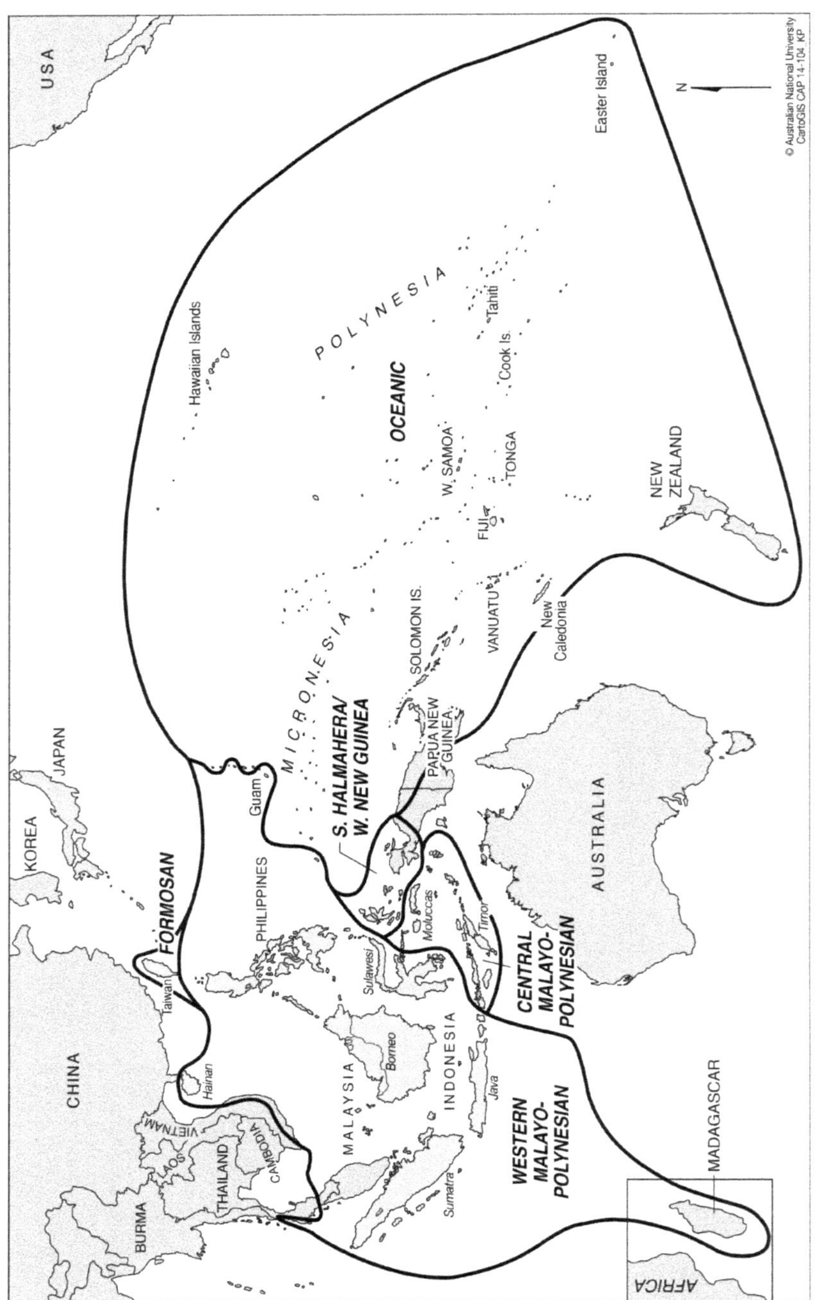

Figure 11. Approximate boundaries of the major subgroups of Austronesian.

Source: © The Australian National University, CAP CartoGIS.

Another way in which Blevins goes beyond Blust's account is by relating the posited **mana* word to another word **mana(q)*,[3] which is attested within Austronesian languages of the Western Malayo-Polynesian (WMP) group (see Tables 2 and 3), to which she attributes the meaning 'inherit(ance) from ancestors'. Based on the overlap between this meaning and that of PCEMP **mana* as shown by the boldfaced parts of the definitions in Table 2, Blevins traces both WMP **mana(q)* and PCEMP **mana* to a single posited word **mana(q)* at the level of Proto Malayo-Polynesian. In line with this scenario, Blevins (2008: 270) tentatively proposes the set of forms and meanings within the various subgroups of the Malayo-Polynesian that are shown in Table 3.

Table 3. Blevins' proposed set of etymologies for **mana(q)* words in Malayo-Polynesian languages.

(12)	PMP **mana(q)* 'supernatural power, associated with spirits of the ancestors and the forces of nature; inherit(ance) from ancestors, including qualities of spirit or body, customs and laws'
	PWMP **mana(q)* 'inherit(ance) from ancestors, including quality of spirit or body that one has from one's forebears'
	PCEMP **mana* 'supernatural power, associated with spirits of the ancestors and the forces of nature'
	PCMP **mana* 'spirit, spiritual power, ancestor spirit'
	PEMP **mana* 'supernatural power, associated with spirits of the ancestors and the forces of nature'
	PSHWNG **man-* 'bird; male, man; special power', POc **mana* 'supernatural power, associated with spirits of the ancestors and the forces of nature'

Source: From Blevins, Some comparative notes on Proto-Oceanic **mana*, p. 270. Abbreviations are: PMP, Proto Malayo-Polynesian; PWMP, Proto Western Malayo-Polynesian; PCEMP, Proto Central/Eastern Malayo-Polynesian; PCMP, Proto Central Malayo-Polynesian; PEMP, Proto Eastern Malayo-Polynesian; PSHWNG, Proto South Halmahara/West New Guinea; POc, Proto Oceanic.

Casting her comparative net even more widely, drawing in part on Aletta Biersack (1995, 1996), Blevins points to the presence of words of similar or identical form and closely related meanings among non-Austronesian languages of New Guinea. Her list of them is shown in Table 4.

3 The (q) in this form stands for a uvular or glottal stop that occurs in some of the putatively related words within the cognate set and not in others.

Table 4. Blevins' list of '*mana* lookalikes' in non-Austronesian languages of the New Guinea area.

LANGUAGE	AREA	DATA SOURCE	LOOKALIKE	GLOSS
Warembori	Yapen-Waropen, Jayapura	Donohue (1999)	ma/mana	'good'
Ipili-Paiela	Enga Province	Biersack (1996:90–91)	mana	'knowledge'
Enga	Enga Province	Lang (1973)	mána	'instruction, rule, way of doing'
Kyaka Enga	W. Highlands Province	Draper and Draper (2002)	mana mana makande	'mind, learning, capacity' 'habit, custom, trend'
Melpa, Nii	Mt. Hagen, W. Highlands	Strauss (1990)	man man-ek	'powerful, might: working through magic' 'powerful, effective speech'
Middle Wahgi	Mt. Hagen, W. Highlands Provice	Ramsey (1975)	man man (e-/to-)	'n. ritual' 'v. to perform a ritual'
			kunje man (e-/to-)	'v to work good magic; especially the ritual by which one works magic' (*kanje* 'magic, done for the purpose of helping a person')
			nu/man	'n. thought, mind, will'
			ke/man yu	'n. words of instruction, spoken request as to the disposition of one's goods after death' (*ke-* 'send', *yu* 'words, language')
			mam/bnem minman	'n. instructions, customs, source' 'n. spirit or soul of living person'
Duna	S. Highlands Provice	Modejeska (1977: 164)	mana	'custom, tradition, instructions of the elders'

LANGUAGE	AREA	DATA SOURCE	LOOKALIKE	GLOSS
Huli	S. Highlands Province	Glasse (1965), Goldman (1993)	mana	'custom, way, norms, laws; myth'
Kewa	S. Highlands Province	Franklin and Franklin (1978)	mana ta	'to advise well, give admonitions, instructions'
Pinai-Hagahai	Madang Province border	Biersack (1996:90–91)	mana	'to learn'
Hua (aka Yagaria)	E. Highlands Province	Haiman (1991)	manu manu gzo-	'n. last wishes, will' 'v. singing'
Fore	E. Highlands Province	Scott (1980)	amaná/ne amani/ne	'spirit of dead person, departed soul' 'demon, elf, spirit, spiritual, supernatural'
			amani kámanane	'folk-lore, fable, myth, legend' (cf. *kámanane* 'talk, speech, language, story, conversation, words')
Kâte	Morobe Province	Flierl and Strauss (1977)	ma/mana	'v/n. the act of hearing, feeling, understanding, knowing; knowledge'
Selepet	Morobe Province	McElhanon and McElhanon (1970)	man-manman	'to live, practice (a custom)' 'life-sustaining power'
Buin	Bougainville	Laycock (2003)	mana (N.), mara (S/)	'n. spirit, devil, nonhuman creature'
Siwai (Motuna)	Bougainville	Onishi (2002)	mo:no manu/nu	'magical corner of taro garden' 'wealth, possession'

Source: From Blevins, some comparative notes on Proto-Oceanic *mana, p. 267.

Blevins (2008: 266) points out that in two of the languages on her list, Middle Wahgi and Selepet, the range of senses of the words in question relate to both of the ones that she has posited for Proto Malayo-Polynesian, namely 'inherited supernatural power' and 'inherit(ance) from ancestors'. Given the range of these and other attested senses on her list, and the geographical distribution of the languages on it, she tentatively proposes that the apparent similarities between these '*mana* lookalikes' in Papuan languages and *mana*(*q*) words in Austronesian ones are the result of borrowing from the latter into the former. Although this proposal is an interesting one, there are two aspects of it that seem difficult to reconcile with current understandings of the prehistory of Papuan languages.

The first is that, as Blevins realises, there is another plausible source besides borrowing from Austronesian for most or all of the '*mana* lookalikes' shown in Table 4. Most of them arguably belong to a group of related languages, the Trans-New Guinea (TNG) phylum, the geographic spread of which is shown in Figure 12. In a recent unpublished paper—an earlier version of which is cited by Blevins[4]—one of the leading Papuanists, Andrew Pawley, presents two distinct cognate sets, one of which he assigns to Proto TNG **mVna*[5]- 'be, exist, live' and the other to Proto TNG **mana* 'instructions, customary practices, e.g. ritual, taboo, rule' (Pawley 2013: 9–10, 54), in addition to which he now says he 'probably should have added "speech, talk" to the range of glosses' (personal communication, September 2013). As Pawley also points out, the inference that these are distinct cognate sets is supported by the fact that 'reflexes occur as contrasting forms with contrasting meanings in the same low order subgroups (e.g. Chimbu-Waghi, Kainantu-Goroka, Rai Coast), and, in one case, in the same language: Kobon *mu̦nd*- "be, live" (*n > nd) and manø "speech, talk, language"'.

The meanings of most of the forms in Table 4 relate closely to ones that Pawley has posited for **mVna* and **mana* in Proto Trans-New Guinea. If that is indeed where they come from then there is no need to attribute them to borrowing from Austronesian languages. As has been pointed out to me by Blevins (personal communication, 16 January 2014), some of the languages represented in Table 4—Warembori, Pinai-Hagahai, Buin and Siwai—are not classified as Trans-New Guinea ones. All of those languages are located in close proximity to Austronesian ones. For the words shown on the table from them, if their meanings are

4 In the 2008 version of this paper cited by Blevins (2008: 263), Pawley had posited a single original TNG word **mana* whereas he now posits two distinct ones with different meanings as described below.

5 The V in this form designates a variable vowel in the first syllable, as distinct from the invariant *a* in both syllables of **mana*.

taken to be close enough to the others' to justify positing a common source (a debatable matter), it would seem equally plausible to attribute them to diffusion into those languages from Austronesian or from Trans-New Guinea Papuan. Regarding the words from other languages represented on the list, given their wide distribution across the TNG region—including highland areas which remained largely isolated from the outside world (including the Austronesian one) until the 1930s—it seems more plausible to attribute them to shared retention from Proto TNG.

Second, even at the level of Proto-Oceanic Austronesian, if borrowing was involved in the transmission of **mana*, I can see no reason to assume that its direction must have been from Austronesian into Papuan. As Blevins realises, the TNG phylum is likely to be much older than the Malayo-Polynesian group of Austronesian languages—indeed, much older than the Austronesian family itself (Pawley 2005: 96–97).[6] If the similarity of form and partial overlap in meaning between Austronesian and Papuan *mana* words is due to borrowing it seems possible that the borrowing could have gone in the opposite direction to the one proposed by Blevins, that is, from Papuan languages spoken in the Bismarck Archipelago to early forms of Oceanic Austronesian, including Proto-Oceanic, that are thought to have been spoken there before the movement of Oceanic language speakers into the southwest Pacific (Ross, Pawley and Osmond 2003: 15; Pawley 2008).[7]

Mana and *pawa*

In order to pursue the question of *mana* in the expansive way that is envisioned by the editors and contributors to this volume, it is important to examine not only concepts and phenomena associated with words that are etymologically related in the ways discussed above, but also to consider related concepts for which the words may differ in form. In this section of the chapter I do both of those things with respect to

6 Based on a wide range of linguistic and archeological evidence, Pawley (2008) dates Proto Oceanic at 3400–3100 BP. Pawley (2012) places Proto Trans New Guinea at 10,000–7000 BP.

7 If this is what actually happened, the borrowed word would have given rise only to Proto-Oceanic **mana*, not to the **mana(q)* that is found in Western Malayo-Polynesian languages. Such a scenario is incompatible with Blevins' attempt to trace both Oceanic **mana* and PWMP **mana(q)* to a common proto-form, but compatible with the more common position among Austronesianists that the two words are historically distinct and cannot be traced to a common source.

the Ku Wuru region of the Western Highlands Province of Papua New Guinea, where Francesca Merlan and I have been doing anthropological and linguistic fieldwork on various projects since 1981. Ku Waru lies roughly in the middle of the TNG region shown in Figure 12.

There are four words we know of in the Ku Waru language that resemble one or more of Blevins' TNG '*mana* lookalikes' in meaning and sound (although none of them exactly). One is *mani,* which combines with *ung* (word, discourse) to mean 'advice', 'warning', 'teaching' or 'lesson', and in a kind of prototypical usage refers specifically to general advice passed on by fathers to their sons.[8] This word is clearly similar in meaning to other words on Blevins' list which could be traced to Pawley's posited TNG proto-form **mana*.[9]

The second notable mana lookalike is *man,* which combines with the verb *to-* 'hit, do' to mean something like 'perform a religious ritual', and is used both in reference to the Catholic mass[10] and pre-existing non-Christian rituals such as the female spirit cult (Strathern 1970) and sacrifice to ancestors (Rumsey 2008: 458–60). This word is clearly cognate to *man* and *man to-* in the fairly closely related language Middle Wahgi, and probably to *man* in the even more closely related language Melpa, but does not correspond closely in meaning to any of the other words on Blevins' list.

The other two Ku Waru words that resemble ones on Blevins' list are *numan* 'mind', 'will', 'intention' and *mini* 'soul', 'spirit'. We do not regard the former as sufficiently close in meaning or the latter as sufficiently close in form to be identified either with Proto TNG **mana* or **mVna*, or with any of Blevins' posited proto-forms as shown in Table 3 (notwithstanding the inclusion on her list of the Middle Wahgi word *numan,* which is clearly cognate to Ku Waru *numan,* and *min̲man̲,* which is a possible cognate of Ku Waru *mini*).

8 As explained to me by our long-term Ku Waru friend and assistant Andrew Noma (in May 2014 as I was revising this paper during the course of fieldwork in PNG): 'When our father is about to die he will tell us things like "Don't get angry with your brother; be careful not to eat poison; don't touch anything that belongs to our enemies; always help out with contributions of pigs and money when your people are trying to settle a dispute; don't beat your wife or they might poison you."'

9 It is closest in meaning to words of the form *mana* in Kewa, Huli, Enga and Ipili. In order to establish it as a cognate of those words, with a presumed common proto-form **mana*, one would have to account for why its final vowel is *i* rather than *a*.

10 It is not used in reference to Lutheran services, which are called *mis*, or to other Protestant services, which are called by the Tok-Pisin derived term *lotu*.

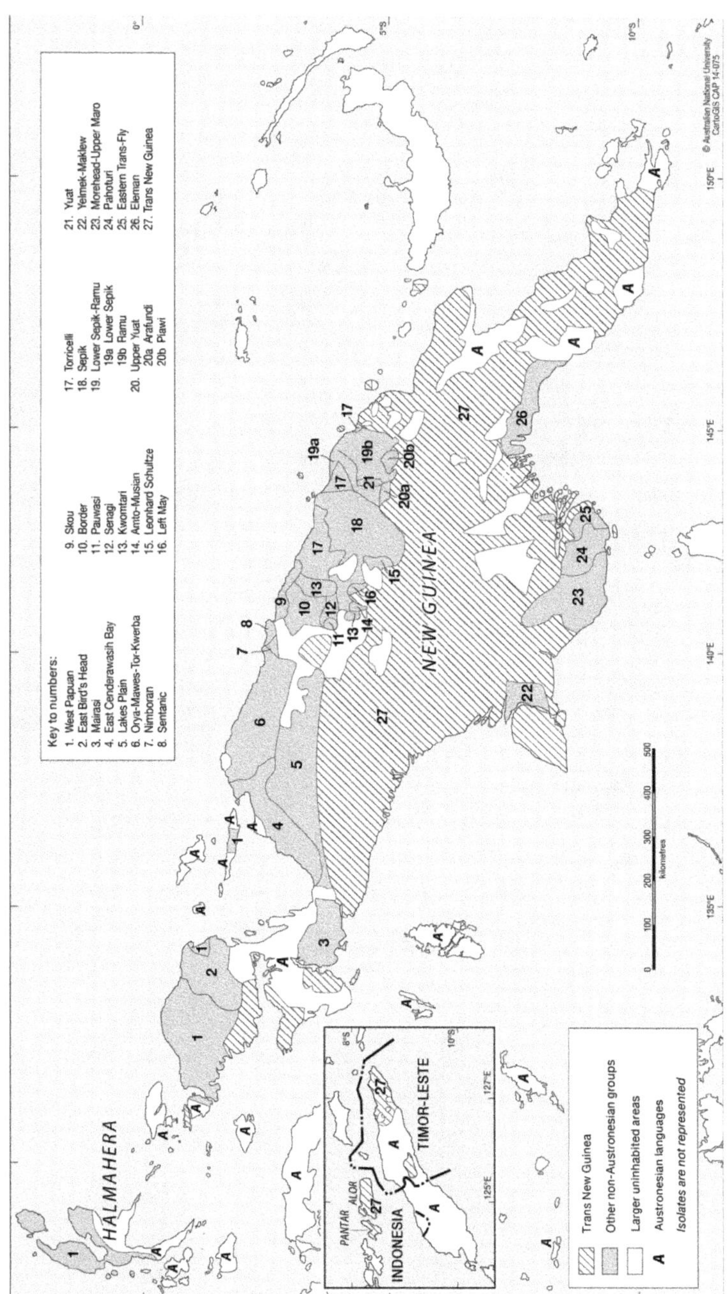

Figure 12. The Trans New Guinea Phylum and other language groups in New Guinea and environs.

Source: © The Australian National University, CAP CartoGIS.

Clearly none of the Ku Waru words discussed above is at all close in meaning to the canonical one of 'efficaciousness' that Keesing attributes to Oceanic Austronesian. The Ku Waru word that comes closest to that sense is *pawa*—a word that has been borrowed into the language from the PNG *lingua franca* Tok Pisin. Although the word derives ultimately from English 'power' it is in some ways closer in meaning to Oceanic *mana* as discussed by Firth and Keesing. To see how, let us consider two examples of its use in context.

The first example comes from a speech given in 1983 at a ceremonial exchange event that is discussed in detail in Merlan and Rumsey (1991). The speech concerned a remarkable event that had taken place in 1982. A war had broken out between two groups of tribes in the region. Before anyone was killed, the war was stopped by the intervention of a women's work group who marched out on to the battlefield between the opposing sides carrying the national flag and exhorted the combatants to call off the fight and take their weapons back home. Equally remarkably, the men did as they were told and did not do battle again for the next 23 years.

The women's actions included a payment to the men on both sides in the form of cash, trade goods and produce from the work group's market gardening activities. Having made that payment, according to local protocols, the women's group had to be given a return payment from both of the combatant sides at the exchange events which were held for the payment of compensation among the allied groups. At one such event, in August 1983, the following speech was made by a forceful leader of the women's group, Mijiyl Pokea:

(1) na ing mare awuntipa nyi naa nyibu
I will not speak at length

pilis matres na kansil na …
the village magistrates and councillors and …

pilis matres yabu lupu lupu ing ilyi-nga na-ni age nyikir
for the village magistrates' and others' invitation I say thanks

Kansil-ayl-nge ul ilyi tepa kodupa lyim
the Councillor [Kujilyi] invited us

ilyi-nga na age anum-uyl nyikir
and for that, I say, thank you very much

ya noi el tiring ilyi-nga ya ab anum mel koltal
they fought down there and so, just a few older women

kongun kubilek tiring
were working at first

tek molku-kin ilyi-nga puk noi kubu tiring
they were (working), and going down they worked at Kubu [in Tilka territory]

noi kalyke ya med palimung kolya-ma-nga tiring ilyi-nga
down at Kailge and here at Palimung they were working

ya kolya-ma-nga el-ma naa tiang
'let them not have any fights around here'

ab-ayl kongun-ayl todul pupiyl nyik pamul
saying, 'let the women's work grow strong, let's go'

wany-ayl mek ok eni-n *brukim* tiring
bringing the flag they stopped it
(from transcript in Merlan and Rumsey 1991: 171–72)

Mijiyl's speech was followed by one from a leading 'big-man', Kopia Mel, which included the following words:

wanya *plak*-ayl puk mek ok moduring ilyi-o
they went and placed the flag there

gavman-nga el *masket* kare mek pu naa puring, mol
they were not carrying government 'muskets', no!

gavman-nga *yunifom*-te pi naa pirim mol ilyi-o
they were not wearing government uniforms, no!

ilyi ab mel pangi-te nyi-pilyik ab-nga *pawa* pirim.
you may think women are a weak reed but they had determination

(from transcript in Merlan and Rumsey 1991: 178)

Note that, whereas Mijiyl (in line 11) has used the indigenous Ku Waru word *todul* 'strong' in reference to the work of the women's group, Mel (in the last line) uses the Tok Pisin derived word *pawa* in reference to their strength. This is typical of current Ku Waru usage in that although the word *todul* can be used as a noun for 'strength'[11] in fact it seldom is. Instead people use *pawa*.

A typical Ku Waru use of the word *pawa* occurs in the last line of the excerpt from Kopia Mel's speech. In our 1991 transcript as shown above we translated the word as 'determination', but when considered in relation to Firth's and Keesing's expositions as discussed above and other cases discussed in this volume, an equally appropriate translation would have been *mana*. What makes it so is that, as emphasised by Mel and other speakers who commented on the women's successful action (see Merlan and Rumsey 1991: 172–74), it was not the result of any pre-given capacities or powers, but a matter of surprising efficacy as revealed through the outcome of the action.

Now let us consider another example from 30 years later in the same community of Ku Waru people. The long peace (by local standards!) that was initiated by the women's battlefield intervention ended in 2005 when fighting broke out over a poisoning accusation. The details are too complex to go into here (see Rumsey 2009); suffice it to say that the men who were held responsible for the poisoning were from Tilka, a small tribe whose territory was adjacent to that of the Kopia tribe, to which the victims of the alleged poisoning belonged. In 2005 the Kopia and some of their allies invaded Tilka territory, drove them away from it and burned all the houses at the main Tilka settlement. Together with their much larger and more powerful allied tribe the Kulka, the Tilka then retaliated by invading Kopia territory and doing the same. The Tilka did not then attempt to reoccupy their territory but instead went back to live with Kulka and elsewhere. Nor did the Kopia attempt to occupy Tilka territory *en masse*. Rather, a few Kopia and allied families that included in-married Tilka women began coming to the area and cultivating gardens there. After the fighting stopped in 2007, one of those families built a house at the erstwhile Tilka settlement. In 2012, a Tilka family came back and did the same. The two families got along well, the Kopia one even feeding the Tilka one from their by then well-established sweet potato gardens while the Tilka family waited for theirs to come in. In 2013 a young

11 A spontaneous (as opposed to elicited) example we recorded in 1983 is *olyo-nga todul-te mol*, 'we have no strength/power' (from a dispute transcript in Merlan and Rumsey 1986: 158, line 1374).

man from the Tilka family died, for reasons unrelated to the earlier fighting. A funeral was held and the family buried the man near the house that they had built. This was a provocative move, since among Ku Waru people as elsewhere in the PNG Highlands, burying one's dead constitutes a strong claim to the land on which it is buried—stronger even than building a house on it or planting gardens there.

In response, shortly after the burial some men from the Kopia alliance came in the night, dug up the casket and left it beside the grave. The next night some other men from the Kopia alliance came and buried it again. These three actions—the burial, exhumation and reburial—for the first time forced the Kopia alliance to confront an issue that had been left unresolved until then: Would the Tilka be allowed to reoccupy their erstwhile territory, and if so, when? The question had been much discussed, at least as far back as 2009, at a peace-building workshop in which I had participated, which was the first time since the new fighting that leaders from both sides had met with each other face-to-face (see Rumsey 2009: 9–12). Some people from the Kopia alliance had been completely opposed to allowing the Tilka to move back. Others had said that in the interest of long-term peace the Tilka should be allowed to do so, but given the still-powerful memories of the poisonings and deaths in the fighting, more time would have to be allowed to pass before the move could be allowed. Now, six years after the cessation of fighting, a decisive move had been taken by the Tilka, and contradictory counter-moves taken by members of the Kopia alliance. Which position would prevail?

Over the next few weeks, after the reburial by those on the peace-making side of the issue, it became clear that they had won the day. There were no further attempts to exhume the body or force the Tilka to move it, and by the time Francesca and I returned to Kailge in August 2013 the burial was being treated as a *fait accompli*, along with a general acceptance that the Tilka would eventually be allowed to reoccupy their land. When we returned in January 2014 and visited Tilka territory we found that several more Tilka had returned, all of whom were related to Kopia, either by marriage or through their mothers. By May 2014 most of Tilka territory had been reoccupied by Tilka people, not all of whom were related to Kopia or any of the other groups who had fought against them.

During the course of our January–February 2014 fieldtrip, in a discussion that I had with a Kopia woman named Kuin about that train of events and its outcome, when referring to the reburial and the men who had carried it out she said *'eni-nga pawa pirim'* ('they had *pawa*'). In response to my questions about what she meant by that, Kuin and others made it clear that the reburialists did not have any way of compelling people to side with them. Rather, they had made a bold move which had impressed people with its decisiveness and had apparently rested on a correct judgment that the conditions were right for its acceptance. In all those respects, the reburialists' action and its efficacy resembled that of the women who had intervened on the battlefield 30 years before. And here again, as in that case, the local commentators' use of the word *pawa* in reference to the action entails a sense of retrospectively revealed efficaciousness that resonates with the understanding of *mana* that was proposed by Firth and Keesing and is exemplified elsewhere in this volume.

This is not to say that all uses of the word *pawa* in Ku Waru are like that, or that the word is never used by Ku Waru people in the more substantivising sense that Keesing claims is absent from Oceanic Austronesian uses of **mana* words. We came across a striking counterexample early in the course of fieldwork when a Ku Waru woman who was an avid card player found out that we had originally come to Australia from the United States, and had family and other contacts there. She told Francesca that she had heard about a kind of object or substance called *Amerikan pawa* which gave its possessor the ability to win every time at card games, and asked us if we could arrange to have some of it sent to us for her. To her disappointment we had to tell her that we knew of no such thing. (It is not clear whether she believed us, as she made the same request again to Francesca as we were about to leave.)

Mana, pawa and approaches to comparison

So far in this chapter I have discussed various understandings of *mana* as a word or set of presumably related words in Austronesian and Papuan languages, and the Tok-Pisin-derived word *pawa* within

Ku Waru that is used in comparable ways.[12] What I will do in this final section is to engage in a meta-level comparison to consider what is involved in comparisons of both of those kinds of cognate words and of similar meanings and compare them with another kind of comparison that has been brilliantly applied to areas of the Western Pacific, namely, the one used by Marilyn Strathern in her book *The Gender of the Gift* (1988).

As for the former, non-Strathernian kind of comparison, what I and other contributors to this volume have done is in some ways similar to what Raymond Williams did in his 1976 volume *Keywords: A Vocabulary of Culture and Society*. Starting with a number of 'keywords' which are much used within a particular discursive domain—in his case discourse about culture and society—Williams treated them not as terms to be defined but rather as sites of contestation across that domain. This volume does the same thing, not with respect to a whole analytical vocabulary, but with respect to the single term *mana*, which has been used both as term of art within anthropology and religious studies, and from the viewpoint of its vernacular uses within a range of languages and sociocultural contexts across the Pacific and beyond. Just as in Williams' approach, one thing this allows for is a full consideration of contestation and diversity in the uses of the term within given languages at particular locales, across more extensive regions within which it has circulated, and in the ways that those vernacular uses have been understood by various analysts.

Before turning to the comparison between those approaches to comparison and Strathern's, let us first briefly consider the diversity that is revealed by a keywords approach to a single word that is especially relevant for this chapter and the volume as a whole, namely 'power'. This is a word which even in strictly Anglophone discourse has been what Steven Lukes (1974) has referred to as an 'essentially contested' one, as illustrated both by the entry on it in the *New Keywords* volume by Gregor McLennan, and more extensively by

12 Although I have discussed this word only with respect to Ku Waru, there is evidence for its use as a borrowed word within at least one other language in Papua New Guinea, Guhu-Samane, which is spoken in Morobe Province about 300 km to the east of Ku Waru. Based on her extensive linguistic-anthropological research there, Courtney Handman (personal communication, 10 September 2013) reports that the word *pawa* 'was everywhere in [Guhu-Samane]'. It is of course also an everyday word in Tok Pisin, in which context there are also interesting questions about its semantics vis-à-vis *mana* and 'power'. I do not discuss those here.

Lukes in his 1986 anthology on the subject with readings from Max Weber, Jürgen Habermas, Georg Simmel, Michel Foucault, Bertrand Russell and others. Of particular relevance here is Hannah Arendt's view of power, which she sees as being inherently relational: '*Power* corresponds to the human ability not just to act but to act in concert. Power is never the property of an individual' (Arendt 1986: 64).

Now let us consider the approach to comparison that is taken in this volume in relation to the one taken by Marilyn Strathern in *The Gender of the Gift*. Interestingly, in that book, unlike this one, none of the key terms in the analysis is drawn from any indigenous language of the region. Instead, Strathern uses what she calls 'the language of Western analysis' in a way that she hopes will 'expand its metaphorical possibilities' by using it in what she calls 'incidental juxtaposition' to what she takes to be 'Melanesian' understandings. One such term is 'power', to which Strathern devotes a full chapter (1988: 98–132). Although she does not refer to Firth or Keesing, her discussion is reminiscent of their accounts of *mana* in that it stresses efficacy and the fact that it can only ever be retrospectively revealed. More particularly, Strathern stresses the importance for 'Melanesians' of the way in which efficacy is revealed *in the reactions of other people* (119, 288, 294), an idea which is consistent with her claims that 'the acting subject or agent is construed in these [Melanesian] systems as a pivot of relationships' and 'an agent is one who acts with another in mind' (272).

The convergence between Firth, Keesing and Strathern here seems telling. It suggests that, notwithstanding Strathern's disavowals on this point, the juxtaposition of a 'western' term such as 'power' with a 'Pacific' one such as *mana* need not be merely 'incidental' or 'metaphorical'. To see why, let us consider the fuller form of Strathern's claims from which the quotes near the beginning of the previous paragraph are taken:

> All I have done is to make explicit such implicit cultural comparisons as are entailed in the incidental juxtapositions of deploying one language as the medium in which to reveal the form that another, were it comparable, might take.
>
> Yet this also makes comparability disappear. Languages themselves are not generalized but specific phenomena. In expanding the metaphorical possibilities of the specific language of Western analysis, it can only be its own metaphors that I utilize. (Strathern 1988: 343)

For present purposes, the problem with this formulation is that it is too homogenising in what it assumes about the specificity of given 'languages' and too categorical in what it assumes about the differences between them. The first point is exemplified by my discussion of the 'essentially contested' nature of the term 'power' even within 'western' discourse, by the astonishingly wide range of takes on *mana* from around the world as shown by this and other chapters, and by the range of uses of the word *pawa* in Ku Waru, which includes both substantivising and non-substantivising ones. The second point can be illustrated by noting the overlap between Hannah Arendt's inherently relational (albeit 'western') view of power and the similarly relational senses of *mana* that were emphasised by Firth and Keesing and are also evident in the Ku Waru uses of *pawa* discussed in this chapter. At a more general level, the problem can be illustrated by noting that Strathern's treatment of the premise that 'an agent is one who acts with another in mind' as a specifically 'Melanesian' one is ill-founded. Something like that premise is actually shared by some 'western' theoretical accounts of agency (e.g. Gilbert 2000, Tuomela 2003) and in lay understandings of it as well, as reflected for example in the Merriam Webster online dictionary's first-listed definition of 'agent' as 'a person who does business for another person: a person who acts on behalf of another'.

The upshot of these considerations is that rather than treating the comparative exercise as one that takes place across different worlds, with 'incidental', 'juxtapositional', or 'metaphorical' kinds of understanding as the only ones that are possible between them (as opposed to some presumably more direct kind that is possible within them), it is more appropriate to treat the exercise as one that takes place within a single intercultural field within which terms and multiple forms of understanding circulate and interact with each other. The (mana-like?) efficacy of such an approach to comparison is well exemplified by the explorations of *mana* terms in this volume, by the actual results of Strathern's comparison framed in terms of 'power' (as distinct from her methodological characterisation of it), and by the interesting way in which aspects of mana and 'power' come together in Ku Waru and wider Melanesian takes on 'pawa'.

Acknowledgements

For their valuable comments on drafts of this chapter I would like to thank Juliette Blevins and Francesca Merlan. For their helpful responses to email queries about parts of it, I thank Courtney Handman, Andrew Pawley and Malcolm Ross. Thanks also to Matt Tomlinson for his meticulous editing, and to participants at the Mana Conference who responded to the version I presented there.

References

Arendt, Hannah. 1986. Communicative power. In *Power*, ed. Steven Lukes, pp. 59–74. Oxford: Basil Blackwell.

Bennett, Tony, Lawrence Grossberg and Meaghan Morris (eds). 2005. *New Keywords: A Revised Vocabulary of Culture and Society*. Malden, MA: Blackwell Publishing.

Biersack, Aletta (ed.). 1995. *Papuan Borderlands: Huli, Duna, and Ipili Perspectives on the Papua New Guinea Highlands*. Ann Arbor: University of Michigan Press.

——. 1996. Word made flesh: Religion, the economy, and the body in the Papua New Guinea Highlands. *History of Religions* 36: 85–111.

Blevins, Juliette. 2008. Some comparative notes on Proto-Oceanic *mana: Inside and outside the Austronesian family. *Oceanic Linguistics* 47(2): 253–74.

Blust, Robert. 2007. Proto-Oceanic *mana revisited. *Oceanic Linguistics* 46(2): 404–23.

Codrington, R.H. 1881. Religious beliefs and practices in Melanesia. *Journal of the Royal Anthropological Institute* 10: 261–315.

——. 1891. *The Melanesians: Studies in their Anthropology and Folklore*. Oxford: Clarendon Press.

Firth, Raymond. 1940. The analysis of *mana*: An empirical approach. *Journal of the Polynesian Society* 49(4): 483–510.

Foley, William. 1986. *Papuan Languages of New Guinea*. Cambridge: Cambridge University Press.

Gilbert, Margaret. 2000. *Sociality and Responsibility: New Essays in Plural Subject Theory*. Lanham, MD: Rowman & Littlefield.

Keesing, Roger M. 1984. Rethinking *mana*. *Journal of Anthropological Research* 40: 137–56.

Lukes, Steven. 1974. *Power: A Radical View*. London: Macmillan.

—— (ed.). 1986. *Power*. Oxford: Basil Blackwell.

Marett, R.R. 1914 (2nd ed.). *The Threshold of Religion*. New York: Macmillan.

Merlan, Francesca, and Rumsey, Alan. 1986. A Marriage Dispute in the Nebilyer Valley, Western Highlands Province, Papua New Guinea. *Studies in New Guinea Linguistics*, Series A, No. 74, pp. 69-180. Canberra: Pacific Linguistics.

——. 1991. *Ku Waru: Language and Segmentary Politics in the Western Nebilyer Valley*. Cambridge: Cambridge University Press.

Pawley, Andrew. 2005. The chequered career of the trans New Guinea hypothesis: Recent research and its implications. In *Papuan Pasts: Cultural, Linguistic and Biological Histories of the Papuan-speaking Peoples*, ed. Andrew Pawley, Robert Attenborough, Jack Golson and Robin Hide, pp. 67–107. Canberra: Pacific Linguistics.

——. 2008. Where and when was Proto Oceanic spoken? Linguistic and archaeological evidence. In *Studies in Honour of Ülo Sirk*, ed. Yury A. Lander and Alexander K. Ogloblin, pp. 47–71. München: LINCOM Europa.

——. 2012. How reconstructable is Proto Trans New Guinea? Problems, progress, prospects. In *Language and Linguistics in Melanesia*, part I, ed. Harald Hammarström and Wilco van den Heuvel, pp. 84–164.

——. 2013. Some trans New Guinea etymologies. Canberra: Department of Linguistics, School of Culture, History and Language, College of Asia and the Pacific, The Australian National University. Unpublished draft dated 8 September 2013.

Pawley, Andrew, Robert Attenborough, Jack Golson and Robin Hide (eds). 2005. *Papuan Pasts: Cultural, Linguistic and Biological Histories of the Papuan-speaking Peoples*. Canberra: Pacific Linguistics.

Ross, Malcolm, Andrew Pawley and Meredith Osmond. 2003. *The Lexicon of Proto Oceanic. The Culture and Environment of Ancestral Oceanic Society, vol. 2: The Physical Environment*. Canberra: Pacific Linguistics.

Rumsey, Alan. 2008. Confession, anger, and cross-cultural articulation in Papua New Guinea. Anthropological Quarterly 81:455–72.

——. 2009. War and peace in Highland PNG. Canberra: SSGM Discussion Paper Series 2009/7. Online: ips.cap.anu.edu.au/sites/default/files/09_07_rumsey.pdf.

Strathern, Andrew. 1970. The female and male spirit cults in Mount Hagen. *Man* (n.s.) 5: 571–85.

Strathern, Marilyn. 1988. *The Gender of the Gift*. Berkeley: University of California Press.

Tuomela, Raimo. 2003. The we-mode and the I-mode. In *Socializing Metaphysics – The Nature of Social Reality*, ed. Frederick Schmitt, pp. 93–127. Lanham, MD: Rowman & Littlefield.

Williams, Raymond. 1976. *Keywords: A Vocabulary of Culture and Society*. London: Croom Helm.

6

Mana on the Move: Why Empirical Anchorage Trumps Philosophical Drift

Thorgeir Kolshus

The mixed blessings of broader attention

At a time when the channels for academic publication seem to multiply at a staggering rate and the writer-to-readership ratio approaches 1, our fellows' gaze becomes an ever scarcer commodity. Attention-seeking behaviour has hardly been decorous in academia, and this time-honoured detached intellectualism has limited the genres for underlining novelties. But new realities require new measures. And the hullabaloo surrounding the presentation of a manifesto for an 'anthropology of ontology' at the 2013 American Anthropological Association meetings had the makings of a successful public relations campaign, gobsmacking into silence those who had regarded the various theoretical takes that are subsumed under this label as mere analytical frameworks rather than The Next Big Thing.

But for some lucky few, staying put seems to be the better option. Those of us who engage the ethnographic specificities of mana have over the decades at irregular intervals had the rare privilege of finding the attention of the academic community seeking us.

The contributions to this volume are written under a moon when mana yet again is in vogue. The introduction to the inaugural issue of the widely praised *HAU: Journal of Ethnographic Theory* (da Col and Graeber 2011), presents mana as a prime example of the theoretical promises of ethnography-derived concepts. And the influential and youthfully provocative volume *Thinking Through Things* (ed. Henare, Holbraad and Wastell 2007) gives mana a prominent place in its search for new anthropological ways of approaching the material (for a critique of the epistemological shortcomings of this volume, see Zeitlyn and Just 2014). In his chapter in *Thinking Through Things,* Martin Holbraad even seems willing to let mana decide the course for new theoretical innovations, 'by giving the transgressive potential of mana full rein so as to reach new analytical departures – thinking neither about it, nor just with it, but through it' (2007: 200).[1] He follows up the call from the volume's introductory chapter, which argues against the engrained association between theory and generalisation with universal applicability as the ultimate limit-cum-goal, and suggests that the epistemological status of anthropology is better compared to that of philosophy than that of science (2007: 190).

At first reading, I appreciated both the attention and Holbraad's magisterial overview of the mana debate. He also argues well for why mana holds particular promise, as having the capacity to move us beyond the ontological distinction between concrete things and abstract concepts (2007: 193), thus adding a somewhat new dimension to the debate while displaying a motivation that goes further than a (highly understandable) desire to stand on the shoulders of giants. Nonetheless, his conviction of mana's 'generative potency' to anthropological theory seemed hyperbolic and, I readily admit, rather bewildering. This was, in other words, fertile ground for anthropological debate, which he, tongue-in-cheek only halfway, holds is 'supposed to be motivated by misunderstanding' (2007: 191). I also found that he too casually dismisses the case against the universal application of ethnographically derived concepts, a position that he attributes to anthropology's disciplinary commitment to give ethnography right of

1 Holbraad's choice of words in this quote fits almost too neatly with Anne Salmond's assessment of spatial metaphors that characterises the Anglo-American vocabulary addressing knowledge acquisition—which she convincingly shows is highly culture-specific (Salmond 1982). A feminist reading of Holbraad's association between intellectual clarity and penetrative imagery might also have pointed out an undercurrent of axiomatic androcentrism.

way, 'so that anthropological theory has tended to disappear down the hatch of ethnographic particularism' (2007: 189). It seems that Miles's law, 'where you stand depends on where you sit', holds true also for the anthropological community, since I fail to recognise Holbraad's depiction of the current valuation between ethnography and theory. From my corner of the anthropological world, theoretical innovation (frequently in the form of rehashing old insights with new terms) consistently outranks ethnographic persistence (see Kolshus 2014 for a historic parallel to William H. Rivers' work).

In order to overcome anthropology's enduring impasse after two decades of progressively incapacitating hyper-reflexivity, attempts at theoretically rebooting the discipline are more than welcome. Even so, Holbraad's remoulding of mana, for all its virtuous intentions, appeared at first glance somewhat colonising. And with every rereading, I have found his approach increasingly nebulous. This is partly due to his philosophical agenda, which, judged from my critical realist social science standpoint, elicits a detached theological exegesis rather than an experience-near ethnography of the notion of *aché* in Afro-Cuban Ifá (cf. Keesing 1987). But even when tentatively assessed with reference to his own agenda, I find it hard to see how Holbraad's endeavour escapes rendering mana with virtually the same general applicability that is the hallmark of the science-inspired epistemological tradition he purports to challenge. And since the various theoretical and analytical stances subsumed under the 'anthropology of ontology' heading have introduced a plethora of conceptual neologisms, some of which he also engages in his analysis (2007: 209–16), I anticipate that the multiple revisits of the century-old animism/animatism debate (recent additions to the ones Holbraad mentions are, for instance, Pedersen 2011; Willerslev 2011, 2013) will bring about the conceptual tools that invite both theoretical friction and cross-cultural comparison, without the burden of culture-specific associations that expose them to the nuisance of ethnographic vetoes.

Holbraad is of course not accountable for my intellectual shortcomings. However, I cheekily suggest that my bewilderment also is due to a portion of scholarly fastidiousness that is required in order to identify not only the potential for generalisations but also its limits. Standing on the shoulders of giants like Claude Lévi-Strauss, Marcel Mauss and Émile Durkheim, to mention but a few, provides a marvellous view of the summits. But it is easy to lose touch with the continuous landscape underneath, and, possibly pushing the analogy a bit too far, this renders the giants with feet of clay. It is hard to understand how Holbraad's ambitions for mana as an analytic term can avoid leaving it empirically disembodied and consequently render the thinking that is done 'through' it no more ethnographically driven than any other form—while simultaneously providing the user with the false impression that this is less 'as if' than more intangible analytical concepts. In short, it gains legitimacy from the virtue of an ethnographic accuracy that is little but imagined, and it loses that twin purpose of analytical concepts, that is the ability to put things together and tell things apart.[2] Providing parochial correctives to these unacknowledged shortcomings is the obligation of mana scholars, however vexing they might appear.

Mota mana writ large

My approach to Holbraad's arguments is without doubt informed by academic turf-watching. Mana is very much my business. When in search of a fieldwork site in 1996,[3] I had the highly serendipitous fortune of choosing the island of Mota, from which the first ethnographic descriptions of Melanesian mana originate. Robert Henry Codrington wrote the famous passages that triggered the ongoing debate (1891: 116–21).[4] He was uniquely positioned to do so after 25 years of close association with recruits from Mota to the Anglican Melanesian Mission's central school on Norfolk Island and more than

2 In the 1960s, Isaac Schapera was invited to give a lecture series at the University of Oslo. Students who had read his works from southern Africa were unexcited by the news, since they found his writings tedious, focusing on ethnographic details and with few wider-reaching analyses. Much to their surprise, his lectures were remarkably innovative and theoretically sophisticated. When someone mustered the courage to ask why he rarely included theoretical discussions in his works, Schapera replied, 'I write for eternity' (Odd Are Berkaak, personal communication, 20 August 2014).

3 I have had two long-term fieldwork trips on Mota, 1996–97 and 2002–03, in addition to a five-week fieldtrip in 2012. These are coupled with research in the extensive archives related to the Melanesian Mission. Since the language of Mota for various reasons was used as a *lingua franca* throughout Anglican Melanesia from the 1860s to 1920, a remarkable collection of previously unaccessed material has become available to me—including the first private letters written by Melanesians, in which also is found the first mention of mana in the nominalised form by a local teacher on Nggela in the Solomon Islands (Ralph Kinogi, letter to R.H. Codrington, 2 January 1884, Rhodes House Library, Oxford, MSS Pac s5).

4 The bulk of Codrington's analysis was presented in the *Journal of the Anthropological Institute of Great Britain and Ireland* (1881), 10 years before he published *The Melanesians*.

10 stays of up to three months' duration on the island proper. This gifted scholar coupled unsurpassed language proficiency with a remarkably reflexive methodological approach, arguably turning him into the most prominent missionary ethnographer in the history of anthropology, on top of his being a pioneer linguist (Stocking 1995).[5] The fierceness in Roger Keesing's repeated charges on Codrington 100 years later (see for instance Keesing 1984, 1985, 1987, 1992) is a mark of the distinction of Codrington's work. Keesing's revisit is not paying heed to a methodologically and intellectually flawed ancestor; he assesses Codrington's work almost in a manner worthy of a contemporary contribution. Keesing's stinginess with compliments is a compliment in itself. In an article that should be read as paired with the current chapter (Kolshus 2013), I partly exonerate Codrington of Keesing's criticism by showing how the Mota version of the mana concept, which Codrington used as his point of departure for his generalisations, was influenced by a more nominalised Polynesian form of mana—through extensive pre-European relations with Tikopia, exacerbated by the first missionaries' knowledge of Maōri and their consequent search for Polynesian cognates in the Mota language.[6] Keesing's insistence that Melanesian mana never was nominalised before Codrington's misconceptions derailed the academic community's elaborations of the term, which again influenced how Melanesians conceived it, is consequently not only a colonising approach, it is also most probably historically incorrect (cf. François 2013) and is based on a seemingly wilful misrepresentation of Codrington's complex depiction of the nature of Mota mana. The Codrington/Keesing confusion is a case for caution to anyone who harbours ambitions of saying something both specific and unifying regarding the many different cloaks in which Pacific mana appears (see Firth's insightful 'methodology' for mana research in 1967: 174, 178). Keesing's search after the original

5 Many will argue that Maurice Leenhardt outranks Codrington, since he inspired the influential literature on Melanesian personhood. However, juxtaposing his *Do Kamo* (1979) with Codrington's *The Melanesians* shows a remarkable difference in ethnographic accuracy and methodological sophistication. I suspect that Leenhardt's high standing is a consequence of secondary enthusiasm rather than first-hand reading, exacerbated by the theoretical agenda of a generous biographer (Clifford 1992). For an assessment of Codrington's methodology and ability as an ethnographer, see Kolshus (2011, 2013).

6 Linguist Alexandre François, who has done research on most of the languages in the Banks and Torres groups and in the Temotu Province in the southern Solomon Islands, has recently shown that *mana is nominalised throughout the Banks and Torres (François 2013). In the Mota language, mana does operate as a noun, meaning 'a power', with a corresponding verbal form, manag, that denotes the act of imparting something with mana.

and 'untainted' Melanesian mana (1984) appears as a quixotic and rather unusual project for a social scientist to engage in. There is, of course, nothing wrong with engaging questions of origins. But in the process, Keesing loses touch with a crucial aspect of mana, namely how its conceptualisation changes with time and across space. His version of mana therefore seems atemporal and mono-spatial; it is the traditionalist Kwaio understanding writ large.

Part of Keesing's case against Codrington is facilitated by *The Melanesians*' shortage of empirical anchoring of mana. Raymond Firth, who was very appreciative of Codrington's depiction of mana, regretted that this first-class ethnographer failed to provide examples of mana in action. One reading of Codrington's take on mana suggests that his ethnographic base was so solid that he did not even consider the possibility of there being other mana notions out there. He simply read the island Melanesian world through a Mota prism, as Keesing would do for the Kwaio 100 years later.

In this chapter, I intend to rectify Codrington's omission and address the ways mana has been conceptualised and perceived on Mota during my 18 years of research engagement with Mota. I will first show the (limited) use of mana in the non-churchly domain, before moving on to its omnipresence in Mota Anglican theology and liturgy and how it renders ordained clergy with powers that are used far beyond a restricted ministerial domain. The Anglican majority's views on mana are finally contrasted with those held by the members of the Pentecostal Assemblies of God (AOG), which was established on Mota around the year 2000 and which has gradually become 'localised'—which has had consequences for their conceptualisation of mana and the work of the Holy Spirit, again showing the agility of an age-old notion. Mana is indeed on the move, spatially and conceptually.

At the outset, I would like to emphasise one aspect of particular comparative interest, namely the relation between mana and the moral. In Codrington's depiction of Melanesian mana, he insists that it is an amoral force, in the respect that there is no expectation that this extra-human capacity should be applied to the benefit of others. As we will see, this is echoed in contemporary perceptions of mana, not only on Mota but more or less throughout the Anglican area of northern Vanuatu and south and central Solomon Islands. As a consequence, within this area there is no notion that mana can be abused or misused. In short, with the capacity follows entitlement. The outcome can be cause for moral judgment, but mana in itself is not part of the assessment. This is in contrast to what Mary Kawena Pukui, E.K. Haertig and Catherine A. Lee report from Hawaii (1972) and is a twin reminder of the requirement for caution in generalising from specific instances and of the requirement for soberness in regard to the uses of experience-near notions and ethnographic concepts as analytical tools.[7]

Mana on Mota today

So then, when and in which contexts is mana made manifest on Mota 150 years after Codrington first visited the island? The short answers are 'rarely' and 'few', which to the critical eye account for Codrington's ethnographic omissions. Mana in action might simply not have been observed nor broadly addressed (however, see Codrington 1891: 57), but could easily have remained a reference for ritual specialists, for people of a philosophical disposition, and for those who had reached the top ranks of the *Suqe*-graded male society, to whom Codrington in his private journal referred as 'the old gentlemen' and with whom he reported enjoying sitting and talking—even expressing admiration for their polite but determined rejection of the Christian faith. But the historians' adage that absence of evidence is not evidence of absence has some salience here, and current praxis should not be projected retrospectively upon the past. Too, even though mana is rarely heard in everyday parlance, this could be a consequence of the term

7 In our approach to Pacific, or even Austronesian, mana, Rodney Needham's concept of 'polythetic classification' (1975) might be useful, since it refers to how a wide range of phenomena may be cognitively united without requiring any one shared trait. Apart from their sharing the four-letter structure, ABCD does not seem directly associable with EFGH. However, the two digitally disparate phenomena are analogically connected through the existence of for instance CDEF. For instance, the Mota understanding of mana as an amoral capacity is mirrored in popular Christianity on Austronesian Madagascar: 'The power of [the mana-cognate] hasina thought to permeate all living and inanimate things in the universe is fundamentally amoral and can cause good and harm, according to whether it is handled right or not' (Skeie 2011: 168; see also Bloch 1989: 64–67). This suggests that we might be dealing with a polythetic continuum, with the Mota version sharing some traits with the Malagasy form while sharing others with the Hawaiian mana-manifestation and providing a link between the two. The discussion over where the cutting point for mana-notions should be is of course highly relevant here. Should for instance the concept of *evur* from Fang of Cameroon be included, as Boyer (1986) suggests? And if so, is it sound to exclude the *aché* in the Cuban Ifá cosmology, which also has its origins in West Africa? And what about the various mana-cognates found in Native American cosmologies, etc.?

having been appropriated by the Anglican Church, and subsequently having become part of a specialised vocabulary restricted to domains where the outcome exceeds what could reasonably be expected and consequently must be of an extra-human origin. This would also be consistent with my hypothesis regarding the Polynesian influence on Mota mana, both through extensive contact with Tikopia over the centuries and through the Māori bias of the first missionaries and Bible translators (Kolshus 2013).

The first time I met mana in a non-liturgical setting was right after I had become sufficiently skilled in the Mota language to no longer have to rely on Bislama. It should be noted that this was before I had read *The Melanesians*, which even to Keesing's exacting taste should leave me untainted by what he somewhat disparagingly calls 'Codringtonian orthodoxies' (1992: 233). Judah,[8] one of the practitioners of traditional medicine, had come to examine Veronica, a 13-year-old girl who for several weeks had been suffering from fatigue and stomach pains.[9] She had already seen a diviner, but her condition had worsened after a temporary recovery, and her parents summoned Judah. He had learnt the method from his adoptive father and had decided that he eventually would pass it on to one of his sons again as part of his inheritance.[10] He charged 500 vatu, approximately $US5, for every successful treatment, which by Mota standards is a substantial extra income. Judah's procedure was widely regarded as being among the most effective on the island. Rumours even had it that he had saved patients whose hearts had stopped beating. After having administered his treatment, Judah explained to me how it worked. Before daybreak he would pick a red coconut and sing 17 different songs in archaic versions of northern Vanuatu languages. This would *manag* the coconut (bestow it with mana). In order to make sure that I got the message, he repeated the sentence in Bislama, '*givim kokonas ia fulap paoa*' ('make this coconut full of power').

8 Most of the names in this chapter are pseudonyms.

9 Her parents had sent her to an Anglican secondary boarding school on neighbouring Vanua Lava, but she had returned to Mota because of her symptoms. Parents of my disposition would interpret these as signs of homesickness mixed with school anxiety.

10 On Mota, land is transferred matrilineally while rights to trees a man plants during his lifetime go to his children. Moveable property and knowledge of traditional medicine and other zealously guarded secrets may be passed on as the holder sees fit.

Judah's initial instruction, coupled with increased language proficiency, made me more attentive to mana. But the term rarely appeared, even to a keenly listening ear. Whenever it occurred, it would be in sentences such as '*ō mana tapena apena*' ('there is mana to it'), or even '*ō mana tapena we pōa*' ('its mana is great'). Within the medical domain, mana separates remedies and treatments that have an effect from those that do not, regardless of whether these were traditional or introduced. Consequently, penicillin had mana when it first arrived along with the Mota dispensary sometime around 1970, because it so effectively combatted yaws that had been endemic on the island. But now, people say that it has lost its mana, since it has little effect on the condition due to the prevalence of penicillin-resistant strains of bacteria and other germs. And since there are no other varieties of antibiotics available, the majority seek traditional treatments or ask the clergy or the members of the Melanesian Brotherhood, an indigenous Anglican order, to pray for them (Kolshus forthcoming; see also Oroi, this volume). Panadol (paracetamol) is still widely regarded as having mana, however. According to most Motese it does not only have a palliative but also a curative effect, a conviction they continue to hold in spite of my imprudent suggestions to the contrary. When the pain from a chronic condition returns, this has a different cause and must be treated accordingly.

Every now and then I would ask different people, 'What is mana?', without further specification or contextualisation, in order to confirm the futility of questions only an anthropologist might ask (Gow 2006). Invariably they would inquire whether it was the mana associated with the Church I had in mind. Painfully aware of how unsophisticated my questioning was, on top of its being virtually unanswerable, I would proceed by asking them what their first association would be. Charitably indulging my quirks, virtually everybody pointed to the Bible. Some would not distinguish mana from the manna that the Lord showered upon the people of Israel during their exodus from Egypt (Exodus 16:4; for further discussion see Tomlinson 2006), while many brought up the Gifts of the Spirit and proceeded from these to talk about special capacities in general. Good fortune in fishing, for instance, was a sign that somebody had mana. Judging by the initial inquiries, I got the impression that there was no exegetic tradition surrounding mana outside the churchly realm. Mana seemed to be a label put on any phenomenon, capacity or talent that had an effect that exceeded the expected, consistent both with Codrington's description of mana being the cause of any 'conspicuous success' (1891: 120), Keesing's characterisation of mana as 'retrospective pragmatism' (1984: 149), and Bradd Shore's concept of 'generative potency' (1989). Likewise, to my initial disappointment, my adoptive father Paul appeared to hardly have heard the term when I first asked him about it during a communal evening meal, even though he is an expert on the *Tamate* secret male associations and the laws and procedures of the *Salagōrō*, the dwellings of these associations. Only after much deliberation was he able to relate it to 'miracles'. But his ignorance turned out to be a remarkably well-played act of deception, in order to hide one of the most zealously guarded secrets of the *Tamate* from me, as at that point I had not yet been initiated. One of the men playing a key role in the workings of the *Tamate* is indeed said to 'have mana'. This, however, is *ō gene vatnñōreag, we vatnñōreag* (a thing so very secret), that it would only be revealed to members on a need-to-know basis.

Resembling Codrington's mention of 'conspicuous success', 'luck' was an association shared by a number of Motese in relation to mana (da Col 2012; Feinberg 1996: 63). There is a range of stories on Mota and the other Banks Islands involving people who seem to have an everlasting supply of money—a trait that is highlighted by the chronically penniless state of most Mota households. Jacob, whose grandfather Clement had arrived from Tikopia, told me that he had been one of these lucky few. No matter how much he spent, he would always have 200 vatu (approximately $US2) in his pocket. His wife suspected foul play and accused him of having an affair. He adamantly denied this, but she insisted that he told her the truth—which he eventually did, grudgingly, knowing that this would put an end to his luck, since fortunes like his usually relied on the origins of the wealth being kept a secret. He rounded off his confession with shouting at his wife, 'Now look what you've done, you've ruined us!' Jacob's case was uncommon, as he was unaware of either the source of the money or how he first came to realise his blessing. Others who had been on the receiving end of enduring endowments or one-off windfalls mentioned receiving messages from deceased relatives in dreams or reported seeing an elusive figure pointing towards a particular spot where money would be found.

The Church had an ambivalent attitude towards cases like Jacob's. There was of course nothing wrong with being fortunate, particularly when this encouraged generosity rather than parsimony in the recipient. But practices that required individuals to keep secrets and withhold information from their spouses and relatives were necessarily of an antisocial nature and consequently not reconcilable with being a good Christian. Even worse, from a Church point of view, were the rare cases that involved magical procedures that paralleled those of the Church. Mark, an old man in my village, passed away a few months into my first fieldwork. People held that the cause of death was his use of a particular kind of garden magic that required stealth in order to have the desired effect. If anyone knew what he was up to before he had reached his garden to carry out the procedure, or if a particular species of bird started to sing, the magic would harm him. On this particular occasion, the priest did speak out, since Mark had shown a lack of confidence in the blessings of our Lord, the source of all life. He had also shown disregard or mistrust in the power of the 50-year-old covenant, ō *vatavata*, between the Mota people and the Lord, by which the people had sworn on the priest's consecration cross never again to use harmful magic. In return, the island gained the Lord's protection (Kolshus forthcoming). This caused any attempt to inflict injury by magical means, *ō gagapalag we tatas* (literally bad objectives), to rebound on the perpetrator while leaving the intended victim safe from harm. And even though garden magic did not necessarily qualify as harmful in itself, the requirement for silence and secrecy made it suspect nonetheless. The man should therefore have realised that someday he would pay for his hubris, which consisted in relying on the ability of unknown forces to secure a rich harvest rather than putting his fate in the hands of the Lord.

Mana and Anglo-Catholic theology

Every Mota man and woman insisted that the covenant against sorcery had saved their people from extinction. Consequently, cases like Mark's have a reassuring effect on the Motese, since they prove that the covenant is still effective and that God's mana administered by the Church is more effective than the mana that can be invoked through old practices. This realisation also brought about the conversion of the island in the first place: the Church's rituals and other procedures were found to have a greater transformative potential than those associated with the old beliefs (see Firth 1967, 1970: 342–43; Scott 2007: xxx; Tomlinson 2006: 174–75; White 1991: 166–67). It is the ordination of the Bishop, who in his turn ordains the priests and the deacons, that assures the correct transmission of ministerial powers and authority.[11] Historically, the Anglican Church's theological emphasis on the apostolic origins of the episcopacy, that is the uninterrupted chain of episcopal investiture starting with the first apostles, has wavered. And it was not until the Oxford Movement's increasing influence from the 1830s onwards that apostolic succession became more widely acknowledged as part of the dogmatic foundations of the Anglican Church. Later, it was its even more ritualistically oriented Anglo-Catholic vein that came to dominate the Melanesian Mission.[12] This theological orientation, which still dictates the liturgical practices and teachings of the Anglican Church of Melanesia, stresses the dogma of apostolic succession even more. I do not find it very far-fetched to suggest a parallel between pre-Christian notions of transfer of mana and the doctrine of apostolic succession. And the virtues of a Church established by Christ's choice of Peter as the rock on which to build it (Matthew 16:18), carrying forth the notion of successive transfers of this original endowment of powers, is a potent reminder of the powers of the clergy (see Hilliard 1978: 234). When it resonates so well with how other extraordinary abilities are believed to be transmitted, the mana of the Church is integrated into Mota cosmology, both being encompassed by and expanding Mota understandings of efficacy and agency.

11 During Firth's 1966 fieldwork, a Tikopia teacher explained the internal ranking of the clerical offices: 'Bishop, priest, deacon, teacher, brother [*tasiu*, member of the Melanesian Brotherhood]—in that order; then he added significantly: "Now, their mana is great, that of the Brothers and of the Bishop"' (Firth 1970: 342–43).

12 The Anglo-Catholic leanings were a matter of deliberate choice, for the exact same reasons that Anglican congregations in working-class parishes applied incense more liberally and otherwise appealed to other senses than mere intellect (Hilliard 1978: 233). In the periodical of the Melanesian Mission (MM), influential missionary and highly competent ethnographer Walter Durrad revealed the purpose behind the MM's gradual turn towards Anglo-Catholicism:

> The staid and sober services of half a century ago … seem to make no appeal to these emotional people, who are like Southern Europeans in love of colour and dramatic element. We need to get rid of the drab from the picture and give some appeal to the imagination and the eye. These people are children. With them laughter and tears are close together, and they are as easily moved to the one as to the other. The cold, solemn, calculating, serious, reasoning, Anglo-Saxon is surprised at such emotionalism and apparent inconsistency, but it is certain that we must strive to take account of the native viewpoint if we are ever to influence the people as a whole. (1912: 343)

It is in the Mota liturgy that mana most clearly manifests itself. The doxology of the Lord's prayer, 'For thine is the kingdom, the power, and the glory', is translated as '*Namoma ō marana, wa ō mana, wa ō leñas*'. '*God turmana*' (lit. God essence of mana) equals 'Almighty God'; and the power of God and the Holy Spirit is consistently referred to as mana. Mana also brings about the transubstantiation of the bread and wine during the Eucharist. In the eyes of the public, the celebration of the Eucharist, which takes place every Sunday in addition to the more than 100 holidays listed in the calendar of the Church of Melanesia, is a persuasive display of the priest's access to God's mana and, consequently, their full dependence on their clergy. His summoning forth the revitalising gifts of Holy Communion by uttering the right words and assuming the time-honoured bodily stances is a persuasive exhibition of mana, confirming his indispensability, while the Lord, through the successful transubstantiation, affirms the legitimacy of the priest's office and of the qualities that set him apart from ordinary men and women (see Firth 1967: 364). In the *Book of Common Prayer*, the procedures of baptism, the other major Anglican sacrament, supports the communicative aesthetics of clerical generative powers. It also clearly shows how attuned Anglican dogmatics and ritual are to Motese notions of mana. The liturgical section *Thanksgiving over the water*, during which regular water becomes Holy Water, involves the celebrant touching the baptismal font. To more evangelically minded Anglicans this act might be seen as a symbol of the transformation, but to the Motese it is done in order to *effect* this transformation. Holy Water becomes infused with, well, generative potency. It does not only have the ability to turn small children into children of God and render them with a second soul (*ō atai tape vasōgōrōño*) which carries a Christian name,[13] in addition to the soul of the world (*ō atai ta lō marama*) which is called by a Mota name (see Kolshus forthcoming). It also serves as an all-purpose medicine, and it is a means to temporarily fend off threats from malevolent beings while seeking the more permanent protection of the clergy. Consequently, every family will keep a small bottle of

13 In this context, 'Christian' refers to names associated with the world beyond Vanuatu. Historically, these have usually been missionary heroes and former Anglican bishops of Melanesia, but in recent decades, names of world leaders and soccer stars have become popular. Nixon, Clinton and Saddam Hussein all have their Mota namesakes.

Holy Water in its house. During my last fieldwork, Mama Japhet,[14] the newly appointed district priest from Ureparapa some 50 kilometres away, carefully displayed the dramaturgical consequences of this particular theology. After having read the words of the Thanksgiving prayer in a decelerating manner, he conspicuously made his finger enter the water and kept it there in silence for some very long seconds before slowly retracting it.

Also on the level of liturgical grammar, the differences between the priest and his parish are made manifest. As is the case with many Oceanic languages, Mota operates with a distinction between plural personal pronouns that include or exclude the addressee.[15] When speaking to the congregation, laypeople, catechists and (usually) deacons use the first-person plural inclusive *nina*, while the priest will use the second-person plural *kamiu*. When addressing God on behalf of the congregation, the priest refers to them as *neira*, third-person plural, while the others use the first-person plural exclusive *kamam*. This is both indicative of and informs laypeople's understanding of the clergy's capacities. Priests are people of a different kind because of their inauguration, with the ability to bring about outcomes that exceed the expected—which sums up Codrington's descriptions of the Motese understandings of mana that he encountered 150 years ago and is how mana still is conceived.

Clerical mana and moral misgivings

The folk model of clerical power holds that the clergy can distribute God's blessings and punishments at their own discretion. This perception is shared by the majority of Anglican priests with whom I discussed the matter on Mota and elsewhere. A few did

14 This equivalent of 'Father' is an abbreviation of the Mota term for 'father's elder brother', and is still used by most Anglican Melanesians when addressing a priest (see Oroi, this volume). Mama Japhet had recently come to Mota as a chaplain for the Melanesian Brotherhood household there, but since the one remaining Mota priest had been defrocked and no other replacement could be found, he was ordered by the bishop to oversee the whole island. The fact that Mota, the cradle of Anglicanism in Melanesia and source of missionaries and clergy for well over a century, was no longer self-supplied with clergy, caused much embarrassment and collective ministerial soul-searching.

15 In Mota, the renderings of 'we' (inclusive), 'we' (exclusive) and 'you' also depend on whether two, three or more-than-three people are included, which leaves Mota with 15 personal pronouns.

acknowledge the theological and ministerial awkwardness of this view, which bestows them with powers that they held rested with the Lord and for which they merely served as mediators. But they nonetheless chose not to confront these beliefs, with pragmatic reference to a greater political good. With a barely functioning local leadership structure and negligible state presence, the Church is for all practical purposes the only generally recognised authority and consequently the only institution that holds some authority over people's lives also beyond the churchly domain. Undermining public reliance on the clergy's abilities to act with efficacy upon the world might lead to a polity crisis that would aggravate the living conditions of their flock. Faced with these prospects, pastoral concerns weighed against theological exactness.

Furthermore, the minor and more substantial miracles that are attributed to the clergy and the *Tasiu*, members of the indigenous monastic order The Melanesian Brotherhood, maintain people's faith in an almighty God and His worldly representatives. Importantly, so do the occasional malicious acts committed by the same men of the cloth.[16] My initial encounter with this phenomenon took place a few weeks into my first fieldwork. It involved Cleyton, who ran a little business importing powdered kava, which was in high demand since the local kava crops had been wiped out in a drought the year before. Cleyton sold kava cheaper than anyone else, but made up for the difference by never granting credit. One of the priests, Mama Selwyn, equally known for his desire for kava as for his insolvency, wanted to buy some bags on tick. Neither flattery nor sweet promises could circumvent Cleyton's sensible business policy. When the mama realised that he was getting nowhere, he declared in the presence of several others that something bad would happen to Cleyton's body. One week later, during a football game attended by most Motese including Selwyn, Cleyton severed his big toe, with blood gushing and the digit dangling from a piece of skin. The injury left him indisposed for well over a month. Immediately after the incident, we witnessed Mama Selwyn's friends openly congratulating him on his achievement. People were indeed upset by the affair. But counter to my expectations, their grievances against the priest did not involve

16 See John P. Taylor (2008: 59–60) for an old case from north Pentecost, and Sabine Hess (2009) for a new example from Vanua Lava. Both these islands belong to the traditional Anglican area of northern Vanuatu.

any notion of abuse of power, merely regular charges of inflicting injury on a fellow citizen. It became clear that the mama's power to influence God's will was seen to be on a par with the operation of a machete or another weapon. The fact that he had made God punish a man who had done nothing wrong did not elicit resentment against either him or the Church.

I was too apprehensive to discuss this case with Mama Selwyn himself. However, during a visit to Port Vila some months later, I spent an evening with Mama Harry, who for several years had served on Mota. I knew him by reputation, since my adoptive mother's mother Hansen, who is the most renowned traditional medical expert on Mota, insisted that he had instructed God to strike her with a serious illness that almost had killed her two years earlier. A number of other families had also been adversely affected by his powers, and he was widely regarded as being responsible for the death of at least one member of his flock, in addition to allegedly withholding prayers that would have saved several others. Eventually, the parishioners' contribution to his salary trickled to virtually nothing—which is the common way to air discontent and press for a priest's resignation—and he was reassigned by the bishop. Mama Harry turned out to be a very talkative and sociable man, who soon would instruct me on his control over the weather conditions. Because of his consecration as a priest, he said, he was able to coerce the sun and the rain to follow his commands—before suddenly correcting himself and emphasising that it of course was the work of God, *through* him. Likewise, the ability to cure diseases, and even raise the dead, was granted him through the Bishop's inauguration, the evidence of which was manifest in the cross he wore hanging from a silver necklace. Harry did not mention the flip side of his influence over life and death, and I was reluctant to ask. I still regret this omission, and I am quite certain that he would have answered my questions. Because even though our exchange of anecdotes showed that I had close relations with some of those who held him responsible for their tribulations, he showed no signs of embarrassment. Quite the opposite, he almost seemed to invite questions regarding his role in their hardships. I was only prevented by my entrenched understanding that a priest's mana could only be used for good, which would make suggestions to the contrary highly inappropriate. In other words, my initial reaction to what I regarded as blatant abuse of mana by Harry and other members of the clergy made me read such acts as being of an antisocial nature. In hindsight, I realise how flawed this deduction is. The allotment of blessings and misfortunes is a priest's pastoral right. Sickness and even death brought about by the clergy are a consequential part of the introduction of the more potent mana of the Church, enhanced by the monopoly on generative potential that followed from the covenant. And even though people respond with distress when men of the Church use their mana to harm others, the situation is after all much more predictable when the ability to impart injury by non-corporeal means lies exclusively with a handful of people who are known to all. More importantly, this 'darker' side of the clergy's abilities assures the congregation that they have rightful access to God's mana—which means that the required blessings will also flow through the clergy whenever need be.

Pentecostalism and the mana of the Holy Spirit

The distribution of mana through the Anglican clerical hierarchy puts laypeople in a position of dependency and consequently exposes them to the idiosyncrasies and whims of individual members of the clergy. Frustration over this privileged access to generative potency was a prime mover behind the single greatest change on Mota since the covenant that eradicated sorcery, namely the conversion of Garamal village to the Assemblies of God, an American Pentecostal Church with a global outreach. This was the first non-Anglican Church to have a presence on the island that is widely regarded as the cradle of Anglicanism in Melanesia. During my second long-term fieldwork in 2002–2003, I spent much time discussing the background for the schism two years before, as well as how the AOG members experienced their new life. As far as theological deliberations were concerned, the leading characters behind the split were remarkably candid, stating matter-of-factly that the choice of AOG had been purely accidental. Andrew, the elected Garamal village headman, had gone to the provincial capital on Vanua Lava in anger, following the sudden climax of a longstanding land conflict involving an Anglican deacon, in search of a new Church. The only requirement was that it had to be non-Anglican. The clerk of the provincial court happened to be the leader of the local AOG congregation, and she gave him an outline of their history and practices. Andrew readily admitted that he had not paid much attention to dogmatic specificities. The main attraction had been the fact that the Church was American. After he returned, with promises of a new church building to go with the new faith, along with a few bags of second-hand clothes, the approximately 40 Garamal villagers converted en masse. Soon, other disgruntled Anglicans had joined them and the village almost tripled in size, going from being the smallest to the second largest in little over a year.[17]

During the many conversations I had with people in Garamal about their relationship with the Anglican majority, they emphasised repeatedly that their only desire was to be on friendly terms. The most important thing was that they all believed in the same one God, they said, even though some Anglicans acted as if this was not the case. I knew that the actions of some Anglican clergy had affected several of the converts particularly harshly, with Mama Harry allegedly being responsible for the death of at least one of their relatives. But I never heard them openly criticise Anglican clergy. However, much of the praise for their own spiritual leader, Pastor Walter from neighbouring Mota Lava, seemed to be founded on a negation of the qualities of Walter's Anglican counterparts, emphasising his good nature (*matevui*), as a generous man who was in control of his temper. When I asked what the main differences were between their current denominational association and their lives as Anglicans, many mentioned the feeling of proximity to the acts of worship. The service was more of a companionship where people got together to praise the Lord rather than a gathering where they depended on middle-men to take responsibility for the proceedings. Sarah, an elderly woman whom I knew well from my first fieldwork, said that even though she had been an Anglican her entire life, she never had understood much of what was going on during Mass. She sang the hymns but did not know the meaning of many of the liturgical procedures. Worse, she said, was that the clergy did not seem to mind people's ignorance. The AOG, on the other hand, depended on her taking part. She concluded, coyly but proud, '*Wa lōkenake ō lölömaran me kalō galean*' ('So now I feel a bit brighter').

17 A clear majority of these were associated with one particular political party, the Union of Moderate Parties (UMP), which historically is closely connected to the Francophone parts of Vanuatu. This party also claimed stewardship of Mota's 'community boat', a 16-foot aluminum dinghy, since it was donated by the French on the eve of independence. Consequently, the dinghy was relocated from the only natural landing place on the island to a site that is much more exposed to wind and weather, making landings a hazardous business for boat and people alike.

I asked them rather bluntly whether they felt somewhat closer to God now that they no longer depended upon the clergy as officiators. Again, they politely dodged the question. Joel, Sarah's husband, started talking about a subterranean water source they recently had discovered, which along with the rain they had been receiving provided them with more than enough water—in stark contrast to the rest of Mota, which in 2003 suffered yet another serious drought. Given the context and his choice of wording, he seemed to attribute their abundant supply to blessings brought them by their more direct relation with the Lord. Others seconded Joel and mentioned that during the past couple of years, they had on a number of occasions witnessed how rain had fallen exclusively on the western part of Mota, where Garamal was the only village to benefit from it. They stressed that they did not keep this blessing (*sōgōv*) to themselves, but did their best to share with those who were in need of or requested their help. As part of their diaconal service, the AOG regularly sent water to the school and the teachers, most of whom came from islands with ample water supply and therefore threatened to leave whenever their water tanks at irregular intervals would run dry.

An important part of the office of the Anglican clergy is to use his rapport with the Lord to manipulate the weather (Kolshus forthcoming). Droughts were frequent and nobody would blame these on the Church. But a mama is expected to bring about sufficient rain when water shortage jeopardises a major feast or when the non-Motese teachers threaten to leave the school and the island. He should also do his best to divert the course of devastating cyclones. During Christmas 2002, when Category 5 cyclone 'Zoe' was moving towards us after wreaking havoc on Tikopia, the resident priest Mama Malakai led a late-night service asking the Lord that this cup should pass us by. Anglicans felt reassured that Mota would not be harmed—until news reached us that immediately after the service, Malakai had left for a cave on his wife's matrilineal land that served as a cyclone shelter. People were in disbelief. Open criticism of a mama is rarely heard and particularly not in a time of crisis when faith in the measures at hand, which includes a mama's mana, is of the essence. But several men made subdued remarks disputing whether Malakai trusted his powers to sway the Lord's will. And if he did not have faith in their privileged relationship, then how could we?

It was precisely this being at the mercy of clerical caprice that the AOG members had escaped through their conversion. And they obviously felt empowered by their move. They also pointed to their services as testimonies of the presence of the Holy Spirit, again by implication indicating that this was not the case with the modes of worship of their old Church. While the Anglican liturgical order ensured the repeated display of the transformative powers of the clergy, the spontaneity (albeit already ritualised) of the AOG services was proof of a living Church, with people falling over with convulsions, entering trance-like states, and speaking in tongues. In addition, the preferred posture of the Anglican parishioners, heads bowed in a subordinate manner, was inverted by the AOG members, standing upright, heads high, raising their hands towards Heaven. I tried to pursue the nature of the gifts of grace and whether these in any way could be related to mana, but my questioning was much too contrived even for these very forthcoming respondents. They were also reluctant to use the word mana in any sense. And since they also preferred to say 'Holy Spirit' instead of the time-honoured '*Ō vui we rōñō*', I saw this as expressing a desire to theologically detach themselves from their Anglican backgrounds by applying a new vocabulary befitting their new creed.

Mana anew, again

When I returned in 2012, I met a Pentecostal Church that seemed to have come of age. Some 80 members remained, and they professed to have almost worn themselves out carrying sand and material for an impressive 200 square metre concrete building that served the dual purpose of church and school. My first impression confirmed the view of many Anglicans I had talked to prior to my visit; namely that the days of vibrant spiritualism were long gone. A pastor had recently arrived from Mota Lava to look after the congregation, assisted by his wife from Epi, an island much further south, who also was responsible for the kindergarten. But the vigorous passion with which the two led the Sunday service I attended was far from being mirrored by the assembly. People in Garamal had also become lax on punctuality, a marked difference from what had been the case nine years before, when their strict timekeeping and ability to synchronise their efforts and movements had been key points of AOG pride. The worship also had an unmistakable air of following a script, albeit unwritten.

And there was no speaking in tongues or possessions by the Spirit, which once was commonplace. Numerous appeals from the pastor and his guitar-playing and lead-singing wife that 'whoever feels like it' should worship with their hands in the air was only answered by one elderly woman, indulging them by raising her right arm half-way. I could not help feeling sorry for the couple, who responded to the seeming lack of resonance with even more frenzied attempts to ignite the assembly, thus highlighting the difference between their fiery selves and the apparent tepidity of the congregation.

However, after having spent the day in the village after the service, my initial understanding that AOG had moved from stirring revolution to stale convention had to be adjusted. During conversations with AOG members of both sexes and of various ages, I was impressed both by their theological savvy as well as their ability to convert dogmatic principles into practical ethics. But even more striking was their reflective attitude towards my nebulous question on the nature of their relationship with the Holy Spirit—whom they now, significantly, referred to as '*Ō vui we rōñō*' rather than 'Holy Spirit'. Tonna, a man in his 30s, explained that whenever the Spirit made its presence and its will known, it felt like a whisper in one's ear. When many others confirmed his version with enthusiastic nodding, Tonna was quick to emphasise that apart from these whispers, he himself had not had any major experience of *ō mana tape Ō vui we rōñō* (the power of the Holy Spirit). This far in our conversation, I had deliberately avoided any mention of mana, in part because they had been so reluctant to use the term during my last visit. So I was quite surprised when Tonna referred to it so casually, thinking it to be either an idiosyncrasy or an attempt to accommodate my interests in traditions and purist Mota language. But the others followed suit, and 'mana' was used whenever our talk touched upon the work of the Holy Spirit. Their sense of being empowered was also more articulated than during my last visit. People talked about making direct appeals to the Spirit, and unlike nine years earlier they explicitly contrasted this with their Anglican kin's dependence on their clergy. In their community, women and men, young and old, might channel mana. After all, the effects of mana should reflect the will and wisdom of the Lord rather than the moods of a mama.

Mota mana on the move

I left Garamal village with questions that I still struggle to come to terms with. In order to understand this increasing 'localisation' of the AOG theology, I find it helpful to return to the first Mota conversion, which took place between 1860 and 1880. The Christianisation of Mota did not substitute the existing mana beliefs. Quite to the contrary, Anglican dogmatics entail motifs that are highly adaptable to these very beliefs. What the new teaching brought was simply access to an even more powerful source of mana. And since the Melanesian Mission during the latter half of the nineteenth century subscribed wholeheartedly to Henry Venn's influential missiology (see Williams 2000), which insisted that God was not an Englishman and consequently that His words and wills could be revealed in all tongues and in many different cultural cloaks, this was realised also by the missionaries themselves—and capitalised upon by Codrington in his translations of the liturgy and the Bible into Mota. With reference to a principle of 'appropriation', by which only polygamy and infanticide were directly confronted by the European missionaries, they sought the practical realisation of Venn's aim for a 'euthanasia of the mission' (Darch 2009: 8–10). Appropriation meant that mana retained its basically amoral qualities. If you have it, you can use it. Undesired consequences attributed to the application of mana are definitely seen as ill-willed and 'bad', so it is not free from moral evaluation. But there is no expectation that acts should be benign simply because they involve mana. Mana is simply that, an ability to bring about outcomes that exceed what could be expected.[18]

With the AOG's emphasis on the individual relationship with God, the Mota version of mana has in a certain sense come full circle. Codrington's descriptions of how mana was distributed show that knowledge of how to bring about mana effects was a carefully guarded secret, usually passed on towards the end of a person's life. With the introduction of the mana of the Church, access to the most coveted transformative potential was through the Anglican hierarchy—

18 Since Mota was used as a *lingua franca* throughout Anglican Melanesia, these interpretations of the mana of the Church were introduced to areas with slightly different understandings of the nature of mana (Kolshus 2013) and have consequently become widely shared throughout Anglican Melanesia. This cosmological theme provides a comparative axis through an otherwise culturally and linguistically diverse area (Scott 2007; White 1991).

which, incidentally, is not very different from the classic Polynesian understanding of mana as an attribute of, and constituting, social rank (see for instance Howard and Borofsky 1989b; Shore 1989). The most recent understanding of mana among the AOG members seems to include aspects of both the old and the new and renders it much more accessible to everyone: it is independent of the Church hierarchy sphere and is no longer a carefully guarded secret. As such, it brings to mind the emphasis on individualism that frequently is referred to as characterising charismatic and Pentecostal churches. The AOG understanding of mana implies full empowerment of the individual member, by which fortune and blessing become a property of the state of a person's faith. In other words, Mota mana remains on the move.

Epilogue: The boundaries of mana motion

The salient feature of mana as an analytic concept is its ethnographic groundedness. And since a general ethnography is an oxymoron, we inevitably must return to the question of where to draw the line of inclusion and exclusion, with reference to the age-old academic balancing act between simplicity and simplicisticism. At what point does 'thinking through mana' produce the 'world in general' that Clifford Geertz's apposite truism reminds us no one lives in? (1996: 262). This 'world in general' would turn mana into a concept 'at the servitude of all thought' (MacClancy 1986: 148), and consequently deprive it of exactly the experience-near qualities that made people look to mana in the first place. The promise of ethnographic theory lies not in its general applicability but in the ways it helps us pose different sets of questions. In other words, it is closely affiliated with the comparative method, with which it also shares challenges and shortcomings. Obstacles to generalisation have always kept anthropological theory on its toes. And I hold that the necessary nuisance of the ethnographic veto is as important as ever before in our disciplinary history. Steamrolling mana into ethnographic pulp in the manner of Holbraad does little to set anthropology on a more productive course. Quite the contrary, it dilutes the gains from an ethnographically informed discussion and threatens to bring us back to square one by arguing for a mana concept that might include all and everything and consequently becomes nothing in particular.

So, flattering though the wider anthropological community's attention may be, it should not make us scale down our fastidiousness in order to accommodate overstretched claims. We should reclaim mana for the benefit of the social sciences rather than compartmentalising it by putting it in the service of 'turns' of mainly philosophical value. The service of mana researchers is to provide informed bumps in the intellectual road by our staying put and carrying on with our parochial business—so that whenever mana yet again comes into vogue and we again enjoy a wider readership, we can show how it has moved since mana's last call and remain uniquely positioned to identify the limits of its analytic potential.

References

Archival repository

Kinogi, Ralph, letter to R.H. Codrington, 2 January 1884. MSS Pac s5, Rhodes House Library, Oxford.

Books, journal articles and chapters

Bloch, Maurice. 1989. *Ritual, History and Power*. London: Athlone Press.

Boyer, Pascal. 1986. The 'empty' concepts of traditional thinking: A semantic and pragmatic description. *Man* (n.s.) 21: 50–64.

Cannell, Fenella (ed.). 2006. *The Anthropology of Christianity*. Durham, NC: Duke University Press.

Clifford, James. 1992. *Person and Myth: Maurice Leenhardt in the Melanesian World*. Durham, NC: Duke University Press.

Codrington, R.H. 1881. Religious beliefs and practices in Melanesia. *Journal of the Anthropological Institute of Great Britain and Ireland* 10: 261–316.

——. 1891. *The Melanesians: Studies in their Anthropology and Folk-lore*. Oxford: Clarendon Press.

da Col, Giovanni. 2012. Natural philosophies of fortune—luck, vitality, and uncontrolled relatedness. *Social Analysis* 56: 1–23.

da Col, Giovanni and David Graeber. 2011. Foreword: The return of ethnographic theory. *HAU* 1: vi–xxxv.

Darch, John H. 2009. Missionary Imperialists? *Missionaries, Government and the Growth of the British Empire in the Tropics, 1860–1885*. Eugene, OR: Wipf & Stock.

Durrad, Walter J. 1912. Banks Islands report. *Southern Cross Log* (Australia/New Zealand version) 17: 337–43.

Feinberg, Richard. 1996. Sanctity and power on Anuta: Polynesian chieftainship revisited. In *Leadership and Change in the Western Pacific. Essays Presented to Sir Raymond Firth on the Occasion of His 90th Birthday*, ed. Karen Ann Watson-Gegeo and Richard Feinberg, pp. 56–92. London: Athlone Press.

Firth, Raymond. 1967. *Tikopia Ritual and Belief*. Boston: Beacon Press.

——. 1970. *Rank and Religion in Tikopia*. Boston: Beacon Press.

François, Alexandre. 2013. Shadows of bygone lives: The Histories of Spiritual Worlds in Northern Vanuatu. In *Lexical and Structural Etymology*, ed. Robert Mailhammer, pp. 185–245. Boston: De Gruyter.

Geertz, Clifford. 1996. Afterword. In *Senses of Place*, ed. Steven Feld and Keith H. Basso, pp. 259–62. Santa Fe, NM: School of America Research Press.

Gow, Peter. 2006. Forgetting conversion: The Summer Institute of Linguistics in the Piro lived world. In *The Anthropology of Christianity*, ed. Fenella Cannell, pp. 211–39. Durham, NC: Duke University Press.

Henare, Amiria, Martin Holbraad and Sari Wastell (eds). 2007. *Thinking Through Things*. Oxon: Routledge.

Hess, Sabine. 2009. *Person and Place*. New York: Berghahn.

Hilliard, David. 1978. *God's Gentlemen*. St Lucia: University of Queensland Press.

Höem, Ingjerd and Reidar Solsvik (eds). 2011 *Identity Matters: Movement and Place*. Oslo: The Kon-Tiki Museum Occasional Papers, vol. 12.

Holbraad, Martin. 2007. The power of powder: Multiplicity and motion in the Divinatory Cosmology of Cuban Ifá (Or *Mana*, Again). In *Thinking Through Things*, ed. Amiria Henare, Martin Holbraad and Sari Wastell, pp. 189–225. Oxon: Routledge.

Howard, Alan, and Robert Borofsky. 1989a. Social organization. In *Developments in Polynesian Ethnology*, ed. Alan Howard and Robert Borofsky, pp. 47–94. Honolulu: University of Hawaii Press.

Howard, Alan, and Robert Borofsky (eds). 1989b. *Developments in Polynesian Ethnology*. Honolulu: University of Hawaii Press.

Hviding, Edvard and Cato Berg (eds). 2014. The Ethnographic Experiment: Rivers and Hocart in Melanesia, 1908. New York: Berghahn.

Keesing, Roger M. 1984. Rethinking 'mana'. *Journal of Anthropological Research* 40: 137–56.

——. 1985. Conventional metaphors and anthropological metaphysics: The problematics of cultural translations. *Journal of Anthropological Research* 41: 201–17.

——. 1987. Anthropology as interpretive quest. *Current Anthropology* 28: 161–76.

——. 1992. Some problems in the study of oceanic religion. *Anthropologica* 34: 231–46.

Kolshus, Thorgeir. Forthcoming. Faith and demography: Sorcery, migration and Anglican *mana*. *Journal of Pacific History*.

——. 2011. Letters from Homes: Maintaining Global Relationships in the Victorian Age. In *Identity Matters: Movement and Place*, ed. Ingjerd Höem and Reidar Solsvik, pp. 51–62. Oslo: The Kon-Tiki Museum Occasional Papers, vol. 12.

——. 2013. Codrington, Keesing and Central Melanesian *Mana*: Two historic trajectories of Polynesian cultural dissemination. *Oceania* 83: 316–27.

——. 2014. A house upon Pacific sand: W.H.R. Rivers and his 1908 ethnographic 'survey work'. In *The Ethnographic Experiment: Rivers and Hocart in Melanesia, 1908*, ed. Edvard Hviding and Cato Berg, pp. 155–76. New York: Berghahn.

Leenhardt, Maurice. 1979. *Do Kamo: Person and Myth in the Melanesian World*. Chicago: University of Chicago Press.

MacClancy, Jeremy. 1986. Mana: An anthropological metaphor for Island Melanesia. *Oceania* 57(2): 142–53.

Needham, Rodney. 1975. Polythetic classification: Convergence and consequences. *Man* (n.s.) 10: 349–69.

Nielssen, Hilde, Inger Marie Okkenhaug and Karina Hestad Skeie Skeie (eds). 2011. *Protestant Missions and Local Encounters in the Nineteenth and Twentieth Centuries*. Leiden: Brill.

Pedersen, Morten A. 2011. *Not Quite Shamans: Spirit Worlds and Political Lives in Northern Mongolia*. Ithaca, NY: Cornell University Press.

Pukui, Mary Kawena, E.K. Haertig and Catherine A. Lee. 1972. *Nānā i ke Kumu* (Look to the Source). Honolulu: Hui Hānai.

Salmond, Anne. 1982. Theoretical landscapes: On a cross-cultural conception of knowledge. In *Semantic Anthropology*, ed. D. Parkin, pp. 65–87. London: Academic Press.

Schneider, David M. 1980 (2nd ed.). *American Kinship*. Chicago: University of Chicago Press.

Scott, Michael W. 2007. *The Severed Snake: Matrilineages, Making Place, and a Melanesian Christianity in Southeast Solomon Islands*. Durham, NC: Carolina Academic Press.

Shore, Bradd. 1989. *Mana* and *tapu*. *Developments in Polynesian Ethnology*, ed. Alan Howard and Robert Borofsky, pp. 137–73. Honolulu: University of Hawaii Press.

Skeie, Karina Hestad. 2011. Mission appropriation or appropriating the mission? Negotiating local and global Christianity in nineteenth and twentieth century Madagascar. In *Protestant Missions and Local Encounters in the Nineteenth and Twentieth Centuries*, ed. Hilde Nielssen, Inger Marie Okkenhaug and Karina Hestad Skeie, pp. 157–86. Leiden: Brill.

Stocking, Jr., George W. 1995. *After Tylor. British Social Anthropology 1888–1951*. Madison: University of Wisconsin Press.

Taylor, John P. 2008. *The Other Side*. Honolulu: University of Hawai'i Press.

Tomlinson, Matt. 2006. Retheorizing mana: Bible translation and discourse of loss in Fiji. *Oceania* 76(2): 173–85.

Ward, Kevin and Brian Stanley (eds). 2000. *The Church Mission Society and World Christianity, 1799–1999*. Grand Rapids, MI and Cambridge: William B. Eerdmans Publishing Company/Richmond, Surrey: Curzon Press.

Watson-Gegeo, Karen Ann and Richard Feinberg (eds). 1996. Leadership and Change in the Western Pacific. *Essays Presented to Sir Raymond Firth on the Occasion of His 90th Birthday*. London: Athlone Press.

White, Geoffrey. 1991. *Identity through History: Living Stories in a Solomon Islands Society*. Honolulu: University of Hawai'i Press.

Willerslev, Rane. 2011. Frazer strikes back from the armchair: A new search for the animist soul. *Journal of the Royal Anthropological Institute* 17: 504–26.

——. 2013. Taking Animism seriously, but perhaps not too seriously? *Religion and Society* 4: 41–57.

Williams, Peter. 2000. 'Not transplanting': Henry Venn's strategic vision. In *The Church Mission Society and World Christianity, 1799–1999*, ed. Kevin Ward and Brian Stanley, pp. 147–72. Grand Rapids, MI and Cambridge: William B. Eerdmans Publishing Company/Richmond, Surrey: Curzon Press.

Zeitlyn, David and Roger Just. 2014. *Excursions in Realist Anthropology. A Merological Approach*. Newcastle: Cambridge Scholars Publishing.

7

'Press the Button, *Mama*!' Mana and Christianity on Makira, Solomon Islands

Aram Oroi

Almost tearful, a 65-year-old widower in a rural Anglican parish on Makira Island, Solomon Islands, requested in Solomons Pijin: *'Presem baten nao, Mama!'* (Press the button now, *Mama*!).[1] A valuable tribal heirloom in his possession had gone missing. The item had been passed on from his ancestors and legitimised tribal ownership of a certain disputed land. So the request to 'press the button' referred to a perceived 'spiritual switch' that when triggered would make 'something happen', and the item would be recovered.

In this chapter, I discuss the implicit theology of *mana* in the context of that 'spiritual switch' in Makiran Christianity. *Mena* is the native Arosi word for *mana*. To explore the implicit theology of *mena/mana*, I begin with examples of events I have experienced as an Anglican priest serving the community. Next, I review selected literature on *mana*, considering the usefulness of scholarly accounts for the Makiran context. Finally, I pose questions about *mana* and efficacy in relation to the idea of pressing buttons and the work of the Holy Spirit. I argue that a proper understanding of *mana* is vital to the continuing efforts

1 *Mama* is the Makiran word for father or dad, and also the title used for a priest.

of contextualising the Gospel in Makiran Christianity and clarifying Makiran contextual theology for scholars interested in the social dynamics of Solomon Islands religion.

Background

My approach is that of a *maamaani* (story/storytelling) based on the *hinihini* (strong belief) of Arosi people on northwest Makira Island. *Hinihini* refers to what Arosi hold to be true, our views of reality. *Maamaani* refers to an important story and the act of sharing this story. I further contextualise this *maamaani* as coming from the *raronai ruma* (inside of the house) in an Arosi *hanua* (home, land, place), the opposite of a view from an *abau'omaa* (outside of the house) perspective that is associated with visitors to Arosi. The two perspectives, *raronai ruma* and *abau'omaa*, are mutually supportive and involve a continuous dialogue. My *maamaani* shares in that dialogue about *mana*.

Fieldwork data for this *maamaani* comes from interviews and pastoral experiences during the Christmas periods of 2010, 2011 and 2012. Thirty-two informants were interviewed in 2011, with follow-up interviews conducted in 2012 and 2013. Although the view I express in this chapter is specifically from the context of Arosi, for the purposes of comparative analysis I also interviewed informants from Ugi, Bauro, Santa Ana, Kirakira (the provincial capital of Makira/Ulawa Province) and Honiara, the national capital located on Guadalcanal Island.

The people of Arosi number around 10,000 in the recent population census (Solomon Islands Government 2011: 12). The Pijin word *kastom* (custom), found in Solomon Islands, Vanuatu and Papua New Guinea, is also used in Arosi with similar meanings to the Arosi word and concept *ringeringe*. The anthropologist Michael Scott, who did fieldwork for his doctoral dissertation in Arosi, gives a useful discussion of *ringeringe* (our way of doing things) as it is used interchangeably with *kastom* (Scott 2007: 6–10; see also Lindstrom 2008).

The main Christian churches to which Arosi belong are the Anglican Church of Melanesia (ACOM), the South Seas Evangelical Church (SSEC), and the Seventh-day Adventists (SDA). ACOM is rooted in the Melanesian Mission (MM), begun by George Augustus Selwyn, Bishop of New Zealand, who took the first Melanesians to New Zealand in 1848 and later consecrated John Coleridge Patteson as the first Bishop of Melanesia (killed on Nukapu in 1871). After many years of missionary work, MM gained independence from the New Zealand 'parent' church in 1975 and became the Church of Melanesia. In the Provincial Synod held at St Nicholas High School, Honiara, in 2008, the present name the 'Anglican Church of Melanesia in Solomon Islands, Vanuatu and New Caledonia' was adopted.

Meeting *mena*

My engaging with *mana* arises out of the need to understand how *mana* is applied in the mission and ministry of the church in Arosi and the wider ACOM context. We, Arosi, hold the *hinihini* that *mana* at work in the church comes from God. This belief is held in tension within a *hanua* where views about God are a mixture of pre-Christian and Christian ideas. This mixture affects how we contextualise Christianity. For example, our beliefs about *mana* and spiritual power, being *abu* (sacred), *mamaunga'a* (deep religious spirituality), being *maea* (holy), and *hairaru* (spell, charm) are pre-Christian concepts that affect our pragmatic approach to life. Arosi pragmatism influences expectations of efficacy and agency that are loosely configured in the popular Oceanic concept of *mana*. To be able to press a button is an example. Mama Jeffrey Mata described that button in the following way:

> A battery is in this torch [holds out a torch (flashlight)]. The battery has *mana*, because there is power in it. But that *mana* cannot act unless you turn on the switch. That is *mana*. *Mana* is power where you apply something [switch], and then it [*mana*] will act [and have an effect]. (Interview with Mama Jeffrey Mata, 'Umara village, Ugi Island, 7 November 2011)

Although the torch used analogically in this example is an item bought in a trade store, the concept of 'activating *mana*' existed before torches and batteries were introduced to Makira, as can be seen in the words/concepts of *tagorahia* (to work) and *biringia* (activate; lit. to press). *Mana* that is working in that perceived spiritual switch is assessed by spiritual evidence that is manifest physically. Such evidence can come through either Christian or non-Christian means. Within Christianity, *mana* from God manifests through the clergy, members of religious orders such as the Melanesian Brotherhood (known as *Tasiu*), their companions, *ha'ausuri* (catechist-teachers), and in the lives of ordinary Christians who believe in God's *huuna i mena* (true and everlasting *mana*).[2] Evidence from local *kastom* comes from *adaro* (ancestral spirits) and *kastom* magic or *hai'uaasi* (sorcery).

Simply put, if I don't press a button, then *mana* is not present in my interactions. I am ineffective as a church worker. The ability to press a 'button' connected to the spiritual wiring system of God is more readily seen in someone who is *mamaunga'a*. Such a person is *to'o mena* (has *mana*) and is able to control and direct events. As Charles E. Fox noted, the purpose of Arosi religion after all is 'to receive and use helpful *mena*, and to avoid or overcome harmful *mena*' (Fox 1962: 62).

How, then, does one approach or use helpful *mana* in contemporary Christianity? Such a question challenges contextual approaches to theology within Makiran Christianity. Consider the following selected stories of my encounters with *mana*.

Saudaria was a married woman in her late 50s. Although I did not interview her, I recorded her story because of her request. Seven years ago, Saudaria's husband left her. She reasoned that he had worked his *madu* (love magic) to 'capture' the heart of a much younger woman. I could not independently verify the use of love magic, but other villagers that I spoke with said the couple separated because she was plagued with harmful jealousy. It got to a point where the husband was never free to speak to his sisters without being accused of impropriety, which was unacceptable in Arosi *ringeringe*. Despite the best efforts by a succession of parish (and retired Arosi) priests, the Mothers Union, the Melanesian Brothers, the Sisters of Melanesia, the Sisters of the Church, and chiefs from both sides—from prayers to counselling to

2 The *Tasiu* (short form of *Retatasiu*), a 'Company of Brothers' (Fox 1962: 67), is an all-male religious order in Melanesia began by Ini Kopuria in 1925. *Tasiu* Kopuria is from the island of Guadalcanal. The companions to the *Tasiu* are a Church-wide group with thousands of members who support the work of the *Tasiu*. To become a companion, one is admitted by a *mama*, and makes a vow to the effect that a companion must always offer support in prayer and almsgiving to the *Tasiu*. A companion member makes promises as lifelong vows. Many former members of the *Tasiu*, commonly referred to as ex-*Tasiu*, have become companions, as well as members of the Roman Catholic Church, United Church in Solomon Islands, and South Seas Evangelical Church. A *ha'ausuri* (catechist-teacher) is a person who conducts daily morning and evening worship services. Excepting the celebration of the Holy Eucharist, a *ha'ausuri* also acts on behalf of a priest in many instances. A *ha'ausuri* is therefore quite an important figure in the spiritual life of Arosi villages because he is usually the first person that people run to for help in times of need, especially in situations where a priest is not immediately available.

kastom reconciliation of *ha'anagu* (to make a peaceful relationship)—Saudaria and her husband remained separated.[3] She turned up a few days after I arrived in Arosi in 2011 with her candid but disturbing request.

> I want you to pray for my husband so that something will *to'o* [happen] to him ... a big sickness, a heart attack ... that will make him lie in bed, helpless ... to make him realise [his] mistakes and then turn back to me ... his real wife ... When he is sick ... the woman he is with will leave him. But I will not [desert him] ... I will go to him and care for him. (Discussion with Saudaria, Tawaatana village, Arosi, Makira Island, 24 November 2011)

Saudaria then followed through with the Gospel verse in Mark 10:9 that priests say during church weddings: 'What God has joined together, let no one separate' (Church of Melanesia 1982: 243–49; Church of Melanesia 1985: 263). In Saudaria's emotive reasoning, her husband had lied to God, the angels in heaven, the *mama* who conducted the wedding, and to the Arosi public. He should be smitten with 'a big sickness, a heart attack' so that 'he can repent' and renounce his perfidy. And in all of that, I was to be the person to *biringia* my spiritual 'button' in order to make 'something' happen to her man.

If pressing the button can cause sickness, it can also heal. Another story concerns healing that was done by a certain *ha'ausuri*. A family of five was kept awake half the night as a teenage daughter suffered from horrible abdominal pains. The nearest rural health clinic was about three hours' walk away. However, they were unable to get medical help because a tropical cyclone was raging outside and kept the family indoors. Under such circumstances travel was dangerous. They finally managed to approach the village catechist at about 3:00 in the morning. As the girl's father said, 'The *ha'ausuri* came, pressed [a] button only ... [and] my daughter was healed'.

A second set of stories relates to the pastoral work of Colson Anawelau, an ex-*Tasiu* (Melanesian Brother), Mama Jeffrey Mata, and Mama Clayton Maha, Diocesan Mission Secretary in the Anglican Diocese of Hanuato'o. In Arosi there is a practice called *tongo* (off-limits) that is done on properties such as betel nut trees, coconut plantations and

3 A *ha'anagu* (to make a peaceful relationship) is an exchange of shell money by both parties to restore relationships.

bush gardens. I have seen examples of how this is done in *kastom* before I became a priest. First, a person takes an object of spiritual significance such as bone scrapings, hair, or fingernail clippings from a deceased relative. Pebbles from pre-Christian shrines have also been used. Then he utters a *haiaru* (charm) to invoke the *adaro* associated with the object. He then places this in a plantation, garden, or even in a dwelling. The spirit associated with the object becomes what is called a *didiusi* (protective spirit) or a *suura'i* (defensive mantle) that guards against potential thieves (in the case of a garden) and intruders (in a dwelling). A coconut palm frond or a bunch of dried grass is tied around a tree in a plantation to show that 'something' is placed in that area.[4]

A Christianised version is called a *tongo maea* (holy off-limits; that is, a *tongo* that is placed using Christian prayers). In some cases, a *mama* or *ha'ausuri* simply makes an announcement in chapel to inform villagers, followed by Christian prayers to *ha'aabu* (make a tabu) on a property. In other instances, a strip of red cloth or a bottle of *wai maea* (holy water) is tied to a stick and conspicuously placed in a betel nut grove or cocoa plantation to let the public know of the *tongo maea* (see Figure 13).

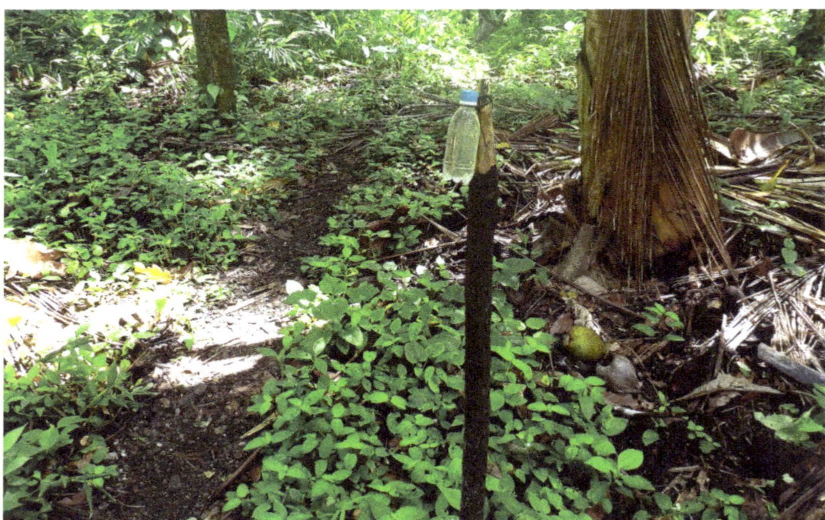

Figure 13. Tongo maea.

Source: Photograph by Aram Oroi, 'Ubuna village, Arosi, Makira Island, 23 November 2011.

4 Fox has given some pre-Christian examples in his writings (see Fox 1924: 254–64).

I checked with Mama Mata about this practice and he admitted initial skepticism and hesitance in doing it. Asked why, he replied that people often 'tested' a *tongo maea* to see if it was *mana*; that is, whether there was potency in the practice or not. In other words, people were 'putting to the test a perceived button' that was associated with the practice. 'When they do that, they end up getting hurt or even killed.' Mama Mata then shared an incident involving a man who harvested a bush garden over which a *tongo maea* had been placed. 'He came to my house in the middle of the night, mourning painfully. His private parts were so enlarged as a result … they were as big as that thing', sighed Mama Mata while pointing to a reasonably large soot-blackened kettle that he used to boil water for tea. In harvesting the garden, this man had triggered 'a button', the results of which were clearly painful to him. Mama Mata prayed over the man for restoration to normalcy (which happened) and then followed through with teachings about the practical results of disobedience. The consequences of blatantly disregarding a *tongo maea*, blessed in the name of God who is/has *mana*, are physical as well as spiritual.

Colson Anawelau and Mama Clayton Maha were involved in what is called a Clearance Mission. This is a time towards Christmas when the Melanesian Brothers go out into villages to set up what is referred to as a Binding, a practice similar to a *tongo maea*. The idea of a Binding began to be formally accepted in some ACOM dioceses in the 1990s in order to address sorcery.

First, the *Tasiu* (Melanesian Brothers) went to villages and talked to people in order to discover the practices that were associated with elements of *mana* from *kastom*. Second, the *Tasiu* would collect and destroy the items that they discerned to be associated with sorcery, sometimes filling up a whole sack with an assortment of animal and human bones, dried herbs and *ria* (ginger), cloth, hair and magical lime from burnt coral or river shells. After that, they would ritually cleanse a village with prayer and holy water before setting up a Binding.

The Binding consisted of an *ariari* (stone enclosure) of about two metres square. In a Binding that I saw, a blessed pebble called *hau maea* (holy stone) was placed inside a three-inch waterproof container, and then buried in the centre of the *ariari*. Angels were then invoked to stand guard at the *ariari* in a spiritual radar-system that kept harmful spirits at bay and maintained peace and well-being in a village.

Arosi experiences have confirmed that people have been affected by a Binding, including instances where *adaro* from other parts of the Solomons were brought into a village where a Binding is in place.

For Anawelau, *mana* that was working with the Clearance Mission team enabled them to carry out their mission, including that of 'finding out' the *ria* planted for use in sorcery. For example, *mana* in a Brother's walking stick had a gravitational pull towards sorcery *ria*, a sort of 'zeroing-in' effect on *ria* planted in bush gardens. After clearance prayers, Anawelau said that he double-checked the next day just to be sure. He confirmed that the *ria* that they visited had wilted, which was a sign that *mana* had taken effect. They had activated something through their prayers.

On another occasion, Mama Maha went with two members of the *Tasiu* following requests by a certain rural parish to address sorcery. Rural Melanesian parishes consist of a number of villages. It took about one and a half months to visit every village and complete the Clearance Mission. Halfway through the mission, Mama Maha's team found out through prayers of Christian exorcism that a certain feared sorcerer was named in most cases of spiritual possession. Babies as young as two months old, who could not speak, even uttered the sorcerer's name. When the mission team came to the feared sorcerer's home village, they took him to the village chapel for questioning. He argued that his *kastom* magic was for healing. When requested to reveal the *kastom* objects and *ria* he used in his healing practices, he refused. Moreover, he demanded, 'If you want to prove me wrong, make me die, now, right now! If I am in the wrong, I would like to see it, now. If you are wrong, I would like to see it, too!' (Interview with Mama Maha at Alangaula, the Administrative Headquarter for Ugi Parish, Diocese of Hanuato'o, Ugi Island). One of the *Ta*siu took his walking stick, threw it in the air (above a chapel pew) where it hung on its own, and then said in Pijin, '*Babae yumi lukim*' ('We will see it'). They left the matter at that. The phrase 'we will see it' refers to the *hinihini* that the truth will be revealed.

The sorcerer reportedly collapsed three months later outside his house. He died instantly. His death was viewed as a situation in which he had requested a 'button' and had in the end triggered it. The community reported to Mama Maha that the sorcerer's tongue spilled out to about a metre from his mouth. This was taken as a demonic sign of his having lied to the Clearance Mission team. The tongue is meant to tell the truth, but a refusal means it will be spilled out to 'reveal' the truth.

In these stories, *mana* is recognisably Christian—it depends on a church leader metaphorically pressing a button—but it also evidently has ties to pre-Christian *hinihini*. In the next section, I examine traditional interpretations of *mana* and consider its philosophical basis.

Mana and the anthropological literature

Mana has been debated ever since scholars first learned about it, with a massive literature and many controversies regarding interpretation, description and definition. Writing in 1940, Raymond Firth commented that 'despite sixty years of discussion and a bulky literature', arguments about the nature and meaning of *mana* 'are still far from settled' (1940: 483). The controversies go back to Robert Henry Codrington, who defined *mana* as 'a supernatural power or influence' that 'works to effect everything which is beyond the ordinary power of men, outside the common processes of nature; it is present in the atmosphere of life, attaches itself to persons and to things, and is manifested by results which can only be ascribed to its operation' (1891: 118–19). For Codrington, *mana* is spiritual power that, in its presence or absence, shows in results experienced by the human senses. Many other scholars have followed this general interpretation, including Friedrich Rudolf Lehmann, R.R. Marett, Henri Hubert and Marcel Mauss, and Émile Durkheim. *Mana* was interpreted as a substantivised force or power. In other words, an understanding of *mana* as spiritual power can lend itself to a view of *mana* as a metaphorical substance.

Recent scholars have been skeptical about Codrington's interpretation of *mana*. For example, Ben Burt states that there are 'serious doubt[s] on the way many writers, mission scholars and anthropologists, Solomon Islanders and Europeans' follow Codrington's interpretations (1994: 54), and Darrell Whiteman writes that 'Western scholars, including Codrington, have made far more of it [*mana*] philosophically and intellectually than would Melanesians' (2002: 74). Firth clarified this by saying:

> too often it is the European's own conception of the meaning of the term that has been placed on record and not an exact translation of texts spoken by the natives themselves … The observation and analysis of actual native behavior in situations where *mana* has been used as an explanatory concept is at a minimum. It is particularly to be regretted that Codrington, who knew his Mota people well, did not base his exposition on the analysis of examples which he actually recorded or observed, but instead composed some of them for his purpose. (Firth 1940: 488)

Firth's argument is taken up further in Roger Keesing's article, 'Rethinking Mana', where he argues that Codrington used 'insecure ethnographic evidence' that was 'deeply flawed' and 'fundamentally erroneous' (1984: 138). Keesing counters that *mana* is:

> canonically a stative verb, not a noun: things and human enterprises and efforts are mana. Mana is used as a transitive verb as well: ancestors and gods mana-ize people and their efforts. Where mana is used as a noun, it is (usually) not as a substantive but as an abstract verbal noun denoting the state or quality of mana-ness (of a thing or act) or being-mana (of a person). Things that are mana are efficacious, potent, successful, true, fulfilled, realized: they 'work.' Mana-ness is a state of efficacy, success, truth, potency, blessing, luck, realization – an abstract state or quality, not an invisible spiritual substance or medium. (Keesing 1984: 138)

Keesing further emphasises that to philosophise or theologise spuriously about 'mana as a diffuse *substance*, an invisible medium of power that humans sought from ghosts, spirits, and gods' is a metaphysical 'creation of European, not native, theologians' (Keesing 1985: 203). For Keesing, contemporary linguistic and ethnographic evidence suggests a 'tripartite usage of mana as stative verb, active verb, and abstract noun' (Keesing 1985: 203). Recent scholarly writing on *mana* generally agrees with Keesing (Blevins 2008; Blust 2007; Keesing et al. 1989; MacClancy 1986; Tomlinson 2006).

Taking a similar approach to Keesing's, Esau Tuza, a theologian and minister in the United Church in Solomon Islands who comes from the Western Solomons, writes that *mana*:

> is often spoken of in terms of 'impact' made on man and its sources … Suppose you came across a dead tree that suddenly falls and almost hits you in the face. You were missed by inches. Mana is not spoken of as some power or person felling the tree, but rather as the force that directs the tree to 'miss' you and so save you. (Tuza 1979: 102)

Tuza then explains three ways in which *mana* is accessed. First, *mana* is 'determined by a person's own skills or gifts in life' and is transferrable, from mother to daughter for instance; second, it is a gift from the supernatural world, and exists as part of a blessing of creation; and third, it is accessed through the *Sope* ritual (1979: 104–05). The *Sope* is a *kastom* house, built with rituals and charms in which ancestors imbue their descendants with *mana*.[5]

Tuza is a significant author because he is a native Melanesian. Most well-known interpretations of *mana* have been made by non-Melanesians and contribute to Keesing's concern about issues of cultural mistranslation. Additionally, *mana* as a force that directs a tree to save a person indicates that one can 'use and direct' *mana* through 'a reality [that] involves a living relationship' connecting spirits and humans (Tuza 1979: 103). Tuza's explanation correlates with Codrington's, that 'this power, though itself impersonal, is always connected with some person who directs it; all spirits have it, ghosts generally, some men' (Codrington 1891: 119).

For a spirit to potentiate *mana* there needs to be a living relationship with a human being. Only through that connection can one witness the idea of having *mana*, or have the quality of being *mana*-ised (Keesing), which is what we Arosi refer to as *to'o mena*. On that note, in Western Christianity a traditional and strongly held viewpoint suggests that a living relationship between spirits and humans is un-Christian, wrong and unhealthy. Codrington did not suppress this important idea about spiritual connections. Tuza therefore brings additional clarity to the argument about how *mana* is interpreted, and so can be seen to give credibility to Codrington as an observer, whose views represent in some ways a Melanesian perspective that can be respected and not dismissed as a western misinterpretation (see also Kolshus, this volume).

5 In some ways, the *Sope* house resembles the sacred space and place that a contemporary church building offers to Melanesian Christians, where God who is/has *mana* is met daily in the Liturgical life of a community.

Closely aligned with Tuza is Fox, who defines Arosi *mena* as 'spiritual power' (Fox 1970: 254).[6] As Fox writes: 'certain places are impregnated with *mena*', 'words handed down from old times possess *mena*' and 'certain men can manipulate it and cause it to pass into objects' (Fox 1924: 252). Arosi refer to Fox's third example—to make *mena* pass into objects—as the ability to *ha'atarauhia i mena* (to make *mena* move). The idea that *mana* can be manipulated strikes a chord with Tuza's view that *mana* can be inherited/bestowed and used/directed/transmitted. I argue that the idea of directing *mana* is dependent on a spiritual connection, a living relationship that is perceived as a stringed-connection that can take place through *manawa* (breath), *haiaru* (spells, charms), and *'iirara* (to find out; as in divination). In a certain sense, this accords well with physical metaphors of buttons, cords, electricity, and the idea that *mana* is made to move through connections (see also Mills, this volume). In the context of Melanesian priestly ministry in ACOM, which is rooted in teachings about Apostolic Succession, a *ha'atarauhia i mena* takes place during a priest's ordination with the laying on of hands with prayer.

I checked with my non-ordained informants about how they have access to *mana*, and the answer given was that *mana* from God is made available to Christians during baptism, making a living connection between baptism and God's mantle of protective *mana*. Sister Catherine Rosa, a member of the Sisters of Melanesia, also mentioned that she was given access to *mana* during her baptism, but added that her admission into a religious order has 'empowered' her with 'more *mana*'. As a result of this *mana* from God, she was able to enter as a woman into a shrine on her island of South Malaita and 'nothing happened to her'. That is, the spirits in the shrine did not attack her or make her sick.

Fox also mentioned *mana*'s use as a transitive verb, as in *ha'a mena* (cause to be *mena*) or 'to make a thing [to be] *mena*' (Fox 1970: 254). However (and here is where Keesing's argument about abstract metaphysical constructs becomes an issue), Fox went beyond simply understanding *mana* as a verb. In doing that, he risked defining *mana*

6 Charles Elliot Fox (1878–1977), an Anglican missionary-priest and scholar who spent nearly 70 years with the Melanesian Mission, lived on Makira for about 15 years, with the better part of that time spent in Arosi. We respect his views because he came to Arosi and did what we call *mono* (to live a lifetime), instead of doing on-and-off visits.

as a substance or force that could have similarities to the Biblical concept of the *ruach* of God. James D.G. Dunn describes the Hebrew sense of *ruach* as 'an invisible, mysterious, powerful force' that 'can be disturbed or activated in a particular direction, can be impaired or diminished and revive again', and is meaningful when understood as 'a supernatural force taking possession' of a charismatic person or a prophet (Dunn 2006: 5–6). It appears that Dunn's explanation of *ruach* is applicable to the idea of *mana*-isation—the quality or state where someone is *to'o mena*.[7]

Having said that, to fully understand the power of the term *mana*, one needs to understand the power of the sacred or spiritual that both underlies the concept and also helps constitute it. Fox viewed *mana* not just as a verb but also as 'something' that could be linked to the Christian God. In doing so, Fox was able to convey a far better understanding of *mana* to the people of Arosi because he fully understood the sacred in a way that Keesing was perhaps unable to.

I also sense that Keesing's difficulty in understanding *mana*'s spiritual dimensions comes from a hesitation to commit his *hinihini* in the face of western rationalism. He did enter the *raronai ruma* in Kwaio to observe *mana* at work (Keesing 1978: 246–56). But having done so, he was held back by the rationalistic approach that guided his anthropological enquiry. This might not have been a weakness on Keesing's part, but the problem is that it made him appear to watch from either a 'doorstep' or a 'window' of a Melanesian *ruma*. In addition, Keesing's disregard of *mana* in Christianity mirrors the general attitude of hostility towards Christians by non-Christian Kwaio. For a Christian to enter non-Christian Kwaio territory without invitation and proper *kastom* protocol is, even in contemporary Malaitan society, nothing short of asking for serious trouble.[8]

7 Drawing on Fox and Keesing, as well as my own knowledge, I can offer a contemporary Arosi tripartite understanding of *mana*: first, as a stative verb when we speak of *'a mena*, 'it' works; second, *mena* as an active verb when we speak of *'e mena*, a word/action that involved *mena* or was brought about because of *mena*; third, as a noun, *i mena*, a word/action that was possible through a quality or state of being *mana*.

8 A group of westerners were lucky to escape with their lives after breaking all ancestral *tabu* by taking toilet paper with them into a non-Christian Kwaio village (Montgomery 2004: 198–99).

Given that both Keesing and Fox had a deep respect for Melanesians, one can hazard a suggestion that they wrote from two opposing perspectives. Keesing argued as an anthropologist with a low opinion of Christianity who refused to accept that *mana* is a contemporary social 'force' worthy of understanding, and Fox wrote from a Christian spiritual view influenced by his *mono* (living a lifetime) in Melanesia. In interpreting *mana*, they faced two conceptual difficulties: (a) the difficulty of proving *mana* empirically using linguistic evidence; and (b) the difficulty of disproving *mana* when there is spiritual evidence. Citing Paul Radin's arguments (1937: 13), Robert Blust reasons that these differing interpretations point 'to differences in the data rather than to differences in the approach or temperament of the investigators' (Blust 2007: 405). Blust has a point, but the differing views proposed by Fox and Keesing suggest that their beliefs did affect their interpretation of *mana*.

It is noteworthy that when both Fox and Keesing died, their mortal remains were returned to the people with whom they lived and had come to love and respect. Fox was buried at Tabalia, headquarters of the *Tasiu*. Keesing's ashes were given to the people of Kwaio (Macintyre 1995).

Mana and contextualising Christianity

What does the above suggest about contemporary Arosi understandings of *mana* when viewed through the work of the Holy Spirit?

From a *raronai ruma* perspective, I argue that western concepts of *mana* as a force or power are just part of the story and do not fully explain or understand *mana* when based on observations excluding spiritual experiences. Failure to fully understand the spiritual dimensions of *mana* is problematic, although Keesing's insights into *mana* as a verb—as doing something, not as a thing—are important. In other words, it is one thing to observe *mana* at work. It is also another thing to actually become an instrument of *mana* to direct and manifest *mana*.

During my conversation with Anawelau, I was using a small audio recorder that could fit in the palm of my hand. At the same time, I was also charging a mobile phone as a standby recorder in case I ran out of batteries. The mobile phone was plugged into a small convertor and connected to a portable five-watt solar panel placed in the sun a few metres away from where we were sitting. Anawelau looked at the gadgets and then said, 'You see, that is *mena* at work. In the past, if you want to send an important message to Kirakira, you have to walk or paddle. Nowadays, you simply go outside of your house, press buttons, and then you talk to people through that mobile phone.'[9]

Anawelau could not have been more right in picturing *mana* through the buttons of a mobile phone. Moreover, he highlights Tuza's point about *mana* and relationships. Buttons connect to somewhere. Human relationships beget a movement of 'something' being transmitted through the airwaves and connected to a device held in one's hand. *Mana* as that 'something' must move in order for 'it' to manifest or show out. Without that movement through connections *mana* will have no effect.

That is to say, Makiran understandings of Christianity find validity in Whiteman's comment about religion being 'more experiential than it is cerebral. It is a religious experience that people feel more in their livers or their stomachs, than in their heads' (Whiteman 2002: 66). On that note, Christianity in Arosi is not the kind that is necessarily buoyed with systematic explanations of complicated theories about *mana*. An Arosi *maamaani* that could credibly be ascertained within Arosi *hinihini*, their *ringeringe*, and a walking stick that could hang in midair because of *mana* from God is what matters to Arosi Christians. In that regard, my attempt at deconstructing *mana* is enmeshed in what Solomon Mamaloni termed 'the foreign Jesus Christ culture' that brought Christianity to Arosi (Mamaloni 1992: 14) and raises tensions in contextual Arosi theological constructs. One main area has to do with the need to be clear about *mana* that forms the core of the Gospel message as it is contextualised. This is challenging in Arosi when spirits and spiritual forces continue to find some form of manifestation

9 In 2011, a telecommunications company called Solomon Telekom had set up solar-powered telecommunication towers at Alangaula on Ugi, at Pakera in Bauro, and Aboru in Arosi. These offered a limited form of communication via mobile phones, but only on some areas along the coast of north Makira. For some villages, connecting to the network meant walking for up to two or three hours to a 'hotspot' in order to catch the signal from the tower. Other people paddled out in small canoes to 'specific locations' on the open sea to catch the signal. Mobile phones are also expensive items for rural peoples and only those who can afford them have one. Also, Solomon Islands is probably one of the most expensive places in the Pacific to make domestic and international phone calls.

in a *hanua* that must be attentive to *kastom* magic, syncretism and animism as viewed from the standpoint of teachings about the work of the Holy Spirit.

What I can say about *mana* in Arosi is that how *mana* works and moves and has an effect depends on the context, the individuals inside the context, and what they ascribe to be *mana* or to have the quality of being *mana*. The *hinihini* that we, Arosi, hold about God, spirits and/or spiritual forces affect these understandings. Additionally, *mana* exists independent of actions/words, but is only realised when *mana* is made manifest, shows out, makes a display. That is to say, *mana* exists both inside and outside of words/actions, but *mana* can only be known as *mana* when *mana* is working and moving and having an effect.

Conclusion

To sum up, interpreting and ascribing *huuna i mena* (true and everlasting *mana*) to the work of God's Holy Spirit is meaningful within an Arosi *hanua* in distinctive ways. First, *huuna i mena* is that which existed before creation. No human effort can bring about its existence, because it is part of the blessing of creation. In this sense, *mana* and its connections to natural phenomena like thunder and lightning (Blust 2007: 415–16) are meaningful because the world is God's creation. Second, *mana* that is associated with the mysterious workings of God is capable of acting all at once as a noun, a verb, and an adjective. We cannot describe it because, as Serah Gede Tanara, an informant, explained to me, 'I see the effect of *mena*, but I don't know where *mena* comes from or where it is going' (compare this to the New Testament idea of wind and Spirit in John 3:8 and Acts 2:1–4). Third, *mana* and the movement of the Spirit is meaningful to Arosi in the sense that *huuna i mena* is capable of manifesting inside and outside of hierarchical human structures and is not restricted to a particular class of people. This leads to the fourth point, that *mana* is associated with relationships and connections. The metaphor of *mana* as electricity (Fox 1924: 252; Handy 1927: 28) appears useful and fitting in this sense. Without connections, batteries in torches cannot be activated. In like manner, God's Spirit thrives in relationships, a Spirit that moves and manifests within human connections. Identifying *mana* that is of/from God remains a challenge in Arosi contextualisation of Christianity.

References

Blevins, Juliette. 2008. Some comparative notes on Proto-Oceanic *mana: Inside and outside the Austronesian family. *Oceanic Linguistics* 47(2): 253–74.

Blust, Robert. 2007. Proto-Oceanic *mana revisited. *Oceanic Linguistics* 46(2): 404–23.

Burt, Ben. 1994. *Tradition and Christianity: The Colonial Transformation of a Solomon Islands Society*. Chur: Harwood Academic Publishers.

Church of Melanesia. 1982. *Na Book Ni Rihunga'i: Book of Common Prayer in the Language of Arosi, San Cristoval, Solomon Islands*. Honiara: Church of Melanesia.

——. 1985. *A Melanesian English Prayer Book with Hymns*. Honiara: Church of Melanesia.

Codrington, R.H. 1891. *The Melanesians: Studies in Their Anthropology and Folk-lore*. Oxford: Clarendon Press.

Dunn, James D.G. 2006. Towards the Spirit of Christ: The emergence of the distinctive features of Christian pneumatology. In *The Work of the Spirit: Pneumatology and Pentecostalism*, ed. Michael Welker, pp. 3–26. Grand Rapids, MI: William B. Eerdmans Publishing Company.

Firth, Raymond. 1940. The analysis of mana: An empirical approach. *Journal of the Polynesian Society* 49(4): 483–510.

Fox, Charles E. 1924. *The Threshold of the Pacific*. London: Kegan Paul, Trench, Trubner & Co.

——. 1962. *Kakamora*. London: Hodder & Stoughton.

——. 1970. *Arosi-English Dictionary*. Canberra: The Australian National University.

Handy, E.S. Craighill. 1927. *Polynesian Religion*. Honolulu, HI: Bishop Museum.

Keesing, Roger M. 1978. Politico-religious movements and anticolonialism on Malaita: Maasina rule in historical perspective. *Oceania* 48(4): 241–61.

——. 1984. Rethinking mana. *Journal of Anthropological Research* 40(1): 137–56.

——. 1985. Conventional metaphors and anthropological metaphysics: The problematic of cultural translation. *Journal of Anthropological Research* 41(2): 201–17.

——. 1989. Exotic readings of cultural texts [and comments and reply]. *Current Anthropology* 30(4): 459–79.

Lindstrom, Lamont. 2008. Melanesian kastom and its transformations. *Anthropological Forum* 18(2): 161–78.

MacClancy, Jeremy. 1986. Mana: An anthropological metaphor for Island Melanesia. *Oceania* 57(2): 142–53.

Macintyre, Martha. 1995. Obituary: Roger Martin Keesing 1935–93. *Oceania* 65(3): 193–94.

Mamaloni, Solomon. 1992. The road to independence. In *Independence, Dependence, Interdependence: The First 10 Years of Solomon Islands Independence*, ed. R.C.a.E. Tuza, pp. 7–18. Honiara: The Institute of Pacific Studies, University of the South Pacific Honiara Centre and the Solomon Islands College of Higher Education.

Montgomery, Charles. 2004. *The Last Heathen: Encounters with Ghosts and Ancestors in Melanesia*. Vancouver: Douglas & McIntyre.

Radin, Paul. 1937. *Primitive Religion: Its Nature and Origin*. New York: Viking.

Scott, Michael W. 2007. *The Severed Snake: Matrilineages, Making Place, and a Melanesian Christianity in Southeast Solomon Islands*. Durham, NC: Carolina Academic Press.

Solomon Islands Government. 2011. *Report on 2009 Population and Housing Census: Basic Tables and Description*. Honiara: Solomon Islands Government.

Tomlinson, Matt. 2006. Retheorizing mana: Bible translation and discourse of loss in Fiji. *Oceania* 76(2):173–85.

Tuza, Esau. 1979. Spirits and powers in Melanesia. In *Powers, Plumes and Piglets: Phenomena of Melanesian Religion*, ed. Norman C. Habel. pp. 97–108. Bedford Park, SA: Australian Association for the Study of Religions.

Welker, Michael (ed.). 2006. *The Work of the Spirit: Pneumatology and Pentecostalism*. Grand Rapids, MI: William B. Eerdmans Publishing Company.

Whiteman, Darrell L. 2002. *Melanesians and Missionaries: An Ethnohistorical Study of Social and Religious Change in the Southwest Pacific*. Eugene: Wipf and Stock Publishers.

8

The State of Mana, the Mana of the State

Alexander Mawyer

Introduction

At this point, few in our field could be surprised to hear that there is reason to be dissatisfied with an unqualified Codringtonian definition of the term mana and its extensive anthropological uptake as an 'invisible medium of power, a spiritual energy manifest in sacred objects, a potency radiated by humans' (Keesing 1984: 137; Shore 1989; Tomlinson 2006).[1] Nevertheless, contemporary and historical uses of this concept in French Polynesia's Society and Gambier Islands suggest that the term continues to bear careful consideration. In the Society Islands, mana is not well attested in historical documentation reflecting everyday speech in the nineteenth century nor in mid-twentieth-century ethnographers' experiences (Oliver 2002). However, today the term demonstrates extension into numerous contemporary contexts, including a significant popularisation and commercialisation. In comparison, in the Mangarevan speech community in the Gambier

1 In Codrington, mana is famously 'what works to effect everything which is beyond the ordinary power of men, outside the common processes of nature; it is present in the atmosphere of life, attaches itself to persons and to things, and is manifested by results which can only be ascribed to its operation' (Codrington 1891: 118).

Islands, mana is also remarkably absent in the limited record of nineteenth-century texts, and is today not much more visible in contemporary use and then only within a narrow range of expression. In this regional contrast—increasing usage of mana in speech on Tahiti in comparison with an enduringly limited everyday usage on Mangareva, processes I describe as a 'quotidianisation of mana' on Tahiti and a culture of 'anti-quotidianisation' on Mangareva—I examine a moment in which mana came into visibility for one Mangarevan man grappling with issues of personhood, legal status and state authority. I argue that this instance reveals something about the tension between the disciplinary uptake of Robert Henry Codrington's formulation of mana as indicative of 'supernatural' powers which are 'outside the common processes of nature' and 'beyond the ordinary power of men' (Codrington 1891: 118) as opposed to vernacular conceptions of remarkable worldly power. At the same time, this pragmatic inflection of contemporary mana sheds interesting light on its sometimes changing trajectories of regional use.

Bare mana

With astonishing regularity, mana's lightning-like and thunderous bursts onto the anthropological scene have seen it deployed along Codringtonian lines or in conversation with them. Marshall Sahlins' (1985) work on the life and death of James Cook might be seen to capture the century-long drift of the disciplinary commonsense in which mana appears to have a substantial, supernatural and mobile quality that imbues persons and things with heightened salience or potency. Sahlins suggests that the spiritual, indeed ineffable, character of the experience of persons and their external relations to objects and others is calibrated by the concept of and term for godhood or divinity, in Hawaiian *akua,* from whom all mana flows. Thus, at first glance, the special status accorded to the stranger-king/British naval officer seems to be a question of his divinity and not of his quotient of worldly power. Sahlins writes with typical piquancy, 'Nothing human was truly foreign to the Hawaiians—if not always the other way around' (Sahlins 1985: 30). However, if Cook was the *akua* Lono among men, Sahlins' account actually shows it to be his mana that they were after. Thus, 'the mana of the sacrificed Cook devolved on the Hawaiian chiefs as a sign of their legitimacy' (Sahlins 1985: 74).

That is, in *Islands of History* mana plays the key role in the analysis, in a story which after all seeks to account for an economy of spectral force, not an economy of godliness.[2]

A later passage beautifully captures the way this term is framed as significant to the category of human beings, setting out types of persons, social roles and implications for action. 'On the other hand, Cook's hubris was as much Polynesian as it was European … He would have died, then, a truly Polynesian death: the death reserved for the man who has accumulated so much mana, he is tempted to defy the rules that govern ordinary men' (Sahlins 1985: 134). Mana serves then as the anthropological measure for evaluation between kinds of beings or entities. Mana invokes a metaphysical market, or exchange, in which words, things and the persons who possess them calculate their value through the machinations of a literally invisible hand. It is the gold standard against which everything stands comparable, a 'native theory' that stands 'Marx on his head by its insistence that ("in the final analysis") the economic base depended on the spiritual superstructure' (Sahlins 1985: 8). Mana is heady anthropological stuff—on one hand strong evidence of the necessity of culture for describing and explaining the perception, conception and experience of human affairs in specific social contexts, and on the other hand a readily deployable model for universalised arguments about the intersection of religion, psychology and politics in the ordering of the social. Even as weighty interpretive purchase on mana was sought and re-sought over the last century more or less along Sahlinsesque lines, it is curious to note that it was also perceived, for at least half that time, as something of a conceptual nullity, a hollowed out semantic vessel to be filled by the interpretive bias of the anthropological

2 According to Valerio Valeri,

> It is clear that in the Maori notion of *mana* as reconstructed by Johansen the idea of efficacy is prominent, particularly as it applies to social relations. But contrary to what happens in Melanesia according to Keesing, this efficacy is grounded in a philosophy of life based on the idea of growth—that is to say, a concept much more encompassing than 'luck'. Moreover, the hierarchical and relational dimensions of mana are emphasised: although from the point of view of an individual *mana* is life turning outward, influencing less vital beings, it is also and more importantly a relation linking all of them and therefore not located in that individual only. Mana is, in a sense, the efficacy of a system of relations personified by an individual (for instance a chief): it is the notion that the system 'works'. This notion of *mana* perhaps confirms Hubert and Mauss' intuition that *mana* identifies more with the 'circle' connecting the terms said to be *mana* than with the terms as such (Valeri 1985: 97).

commentator (Lévi-Strauss 1987). Cloaked as it is in the ambiguity rising from too much or too little semantic content being reserved for it (Holbraad 2009; compare Kolshus, this volume), there is a real risk of throwing out the concept with the bathwater of critique (Shore 1989; Tomlinson 2006).

Table 5. Attestations of mana in Mangarevan.

Mana 1. Powerful, mighty; 2. Miraculous, marvelous, supernatural; 3. Existence, being; 4. Provocation; 5. Divination; 6. A quoit used in a game resembling hop-scotch; 7. To hold a higher card of the same suit.
'Akamana [+caus] 8. To make powerful; to give authority to a person.
Managa [+nom1] 9. A mighty action, something marvelous and extraordinary.
Manaraga [+nom2] 10. Power, might; 2. Omnipotence.
Manamana [+redup] 11. To send to fetch anything without the consent or authority of its owner; 12. The conqueror in a race, competition, or trial of skill; 13. The object of divination, of research.
'Akamanamana [+caus, +redup] 14. To divine; to foretell. To propose to foretell.
Mamana [+ partial redup] 15. To prevent one being employed on certain duties; to prohibit. 16. To respect oneself; to respect each other.
Manamanaua [+redup, +mod] 17. Many, said of 40 persons and more.

Source: Compiled from Tregear 1899 and [Janeau] 1908.

In French Polynesia's speech communities mana is alive and well. Traditional syntactic and semantic regularities of use resonate with long enduring regional and super-regional cultures of mana (Blevins 2008; Blust 2007; compare Rumsey, this volume) and also point to entirely contemporary cultural formations. Although questions remain about the relationship between the general and the specific, between putative definition and cultural use, and between the over- or under-determined theoretical model and specific local conceptions and experiences, anthropological purchase on the term seems possible. For instance, examination of the lexicographical traditions stemming from the work of nineteenth- and early twentieth-century Catholic missionaries on Mangareva—the primary island of one of the five archipelagos that comprise French Polynesia—offers partial evidence for the enduring character of mana in part of Oceania (see Table 5).

With respect to significant previous work on mana's lexicographical tradition and the various controversies over its status (Keesing 1984; Shore 1989), I want to draw attention to several features of these records. Comparable to lexical work elsewhere, such traces of nineteenth-century Mangarevan certainly suggest mana as ontologically lush and semantically verdant. At the same time, syntactical elaborations of mana do not point to quite the same breadth or verdant lushness. In Mangarevan, the causative, nominalised and reduplicative forms indicate a narrower primary semantic field of pragmatic authority and practical powers. Moreover and despite the clarity of the dictionary entries, surviving nineteenth-century Mangarevan texts, the manuscripts and commentaries on traditional histories called *atoga* (Pacific Manuscript Mangareva; see Buck 1938 for a partial history of their provenance), have few uses of this term applied to a narrow range of entities even though the extraordinary characters, actions, and things of pre-Christian gods, heroes and chiefs are all but their only subject (see Table 6).

Table 6. Use instances of mana in Mangarevan *atonga* (traditional histories).

Instance	Gloss	Application
18. O te vaka o Niu, tau ki 'Avaiki, aruara ta Turiakainoa ki ā toa, e mea **mana**, (MPM 3.3:61)	*Of the canoe of Niu … a thing of mana,*	Canoe
19. Ko **mana** i Tautoro ara noti, 'ā marae tana i 'akatu i 'Akamaru, (MPM 3.3:66)	*… mana at [of] Tautoro himself,*	Man
20. O te vaka o Niu, tau ki 'Avaiki, aruaru ta Turiakainoa ki ā toa, e mea **mana**, (MPM 3.3:83)	*Of the canoe of Niu … a thing of mana,*	Canoe
21. I reira, kua tagi ko Turi-a-kainoa ei toa **mana** ko Ina-Raurega te toa i te vehine ona (MPM 3.4:27)	*Then, Turi-a-kainoa wanted a woman of mana …*	Woman
22. Ena i te toa **mana** ko Aumea (MPM 3.4:28)	*There is a mana-woman Aumea*	Woman
23. Putuputu ke te karokaro me te patuga, e ko roa e akoako no **manamana hua**. (MPM 3.4:51)	*… the manamana'ua (assembled mass) [of combatants] practiced crying out.*	Collective
24. Ko Pakoiti nei hoki e toa tagata noti, kakore tona **mana**. (MPM 3.4:65)	*Of Pakoiti truly a woman, her mana negated.*	Woman
25. Ku takaohia kia Teriki **mana** e tinai. (MPM 3.4:83)	*… Teriki mana in the striking.*	Man
26. Ki atu ko Te Magi ki tona teina ko Korotauiti, 'Aia to etua ka igogo, me hakatere vaka o taua. Ite koe te **mana**.' (MPM 3.4:88)	*… 'You stretched out to the mana.'*	Man

Instance	Gloss	Application
27. Ovatu ki te teina ta Te Akariki-tea, **mana** e hakauta. (MPM 3.4:98)	*… mana [of] causing to go upland.*	Action
28. Paru ta Toa-pere ki ana, aruaru. Kakore ra koia ei hao ki te tagata ke a noti e toa tuhuga **hakamamana**. (MPM 3.4:119)	*… a wise-woman 'akamamana [prevented, ie dis-authorized] it.*	Action
29. E kore te etua e tiki ki te haga **mana** me turu ki te hu Aieretiko.' (MPM 3.4:124)	*… The tiki of the gods are not works of mana that supported the Heretical people [of pre-Christian times].*	Tiki (carved figure)

Given this tradition of use, recorded in both the *atoga* and lexicographical contexts, a bare bones sense of mana's invocation and application in nineteenth-century speech in this community looks something like Table 7.

Table 7. Summary of mana's ascriptions from Tables 5 and 6.

Ascription	Domain
Game-of-chance pieces, canoe, tiki 6, 7, 18, 20, 29	Objects
Women and Men 12, 19, 21, 22, 24, 25, 26	Persons
Groups 17, 23	Collectives
Empower, authorise, task, prohibit 8, 11, 14, 15, 27, 28	Actions

In the scant surviving textual evidence of Mangarevan traditions of use there is thus a remarkable tension between the seeming possibility of semantic extension, applicability, appropriateness and felicity in the lexicographical tradition for possible use of the term and evidence of actual application. In recorded discourse, mana appears in secular qualities of practical powers and regimes of authority, in material properties of objects, and in natural notions of force that are not 'outside the common processes of nature' or 'beyond the ordinary power of men' (*pace* Codrington), but manifest in the crispness of everyday life and the concrete social powers of human beings working in unison. There is no strong evidence that mana was regularly expressed in this speech community, nor does it appear to have been particularly ambiguous in its application to certain kinds of objects (things, persons, actions). Its attested use in the nineteenth century appears to have been limited, circumspect and rare.

How does this pattern of limited use compare elsewhere within this part of Polynesia? Douglas Oliver for instance notes:

> in fact, *mana* occurs quite infrequently in utterances attributable to 18th and early 19th century Tahitians. One example of such was characterization of a village council as being *e pupu mana*, a group having legitimate authority and positive coercive power. Another was reference to a canoe as having been well-laced and ornamented with sacred coconut-fiber cordage, and thereby possessed of mana, i.e., sturdiness, stability, and speed of passage. (Oliver 2002: 23)

By way of further comparison, Valerio Valeri observes a similar absence in early surviving Hawaiian texts, especially the *luakini* temple rituals which were 'the most important occasion for the transmission of mana from the divine to the human realm' (Valeri 1985: 97). Notably, Valeri argues that perhaps we should not be surprised that the object of the ritual itself (mana) goes, relatively, unnamed; 'to think otherwise would be to confuse the texts with the complete accounts of what happens in ritual and especially of what is presupposed throughout it and therefore does not have to be explicitly stated' (1985: 98).[3]

In Tahiti, Oliver's examples of mana attributed to political collectives and individuals or things of dependable, effective and practical powers are still normative and common. Thus, as Jean-François Baré records in contemporary Tahiti, there is Ia Mana te Nuna'a (Power to the People), a political party, and Feia Mana (People of Mana), both of which seem to indicate something about the secular potency of civil society. Indeed, Baré's account of mana strongly points to a pragmatic and nominal understanding of the term, although he claims, citing Max Weber's notion of the disenchantment of modernity, that the authentic magical-political function and understanding of the word was corrupted by contact with the West. Furthermore, he claims this depletion theory corresponds to an important modernist current of local experience in the region (Tomlinson 2006). Thus, he gives as an example the *Ma'ohi* (Tahitian) politician Pouvana o O'opa's comments in a postwar speech to the French Polynesian leaders assembled to consider a postcolonial future that *'notre mana n'etait pas tres fort (puai) a ce moment-la'* ('Our mana was not very strong at that time')

3 This argument would perhaps seem less forceful coming from anyone else.

and *'quand on a du/un mana sur (i ni'a) une terre, c'est en fait des droits sur cette terre'* ('when one has mana over a land, that is in fact rights over this land') (Baré 1987: 480).

In addition to such weighty usage enduring from the past and greatly resembling attested uses in the closely related but distinct Mangarevan context, perhaps the most remarkable thing about Tahitian mana emerges in its contrastive appearance in contemporary use. Today on Tahiti mana is increasingly deployed in popular cultural contexts. Mana-saturated shopping, mana-enhanced t-shirts, mana-infused internet or wifi access, popular musical groups, mana-effervescing beverages, mana-enhancing pearls, tattoo parlours (and presumably their tattoos), imported industrial-mana machinery, and mana-mediating dance have all emerged in recent years.

Available from dedicated boutiques on the island of Tahiti, as well as from numerous other venues, pareu and shirts designed and dyed in Tahiti have been offering wearable mana for years (Figure 14). According to their Facebook page, Te Mana

> signifies the universal force present in everything and every being. It is also the name of a celebrated brand of Tahitian shirts. The label Te Mana is everywhere celebrated for its shirts for persons of great qualities, available in a multitude of styles and colors ... Te Mana also sells clothing for women and children also designed with Pacific motifs, and fabricated with the attention to detail and quality.

The conspicuous consumption of mana is not limited to terrestrial fabrics. Several pearl producers and boutiques index mana in their firm name and attach the term to their wearable products (Figure 15). Indeed, you too can be a Mana-Boy (or Mana-Girl), by acquiring a 'pearl of mana' and 'discovering the secrets of the "Le Chemin de la Perle ©" (the path of pearl)' (Manapearl 2015).

Figure 14. Te Mana clothing brand.
Source: Photograph by Alexander Mawyer, June 2014.

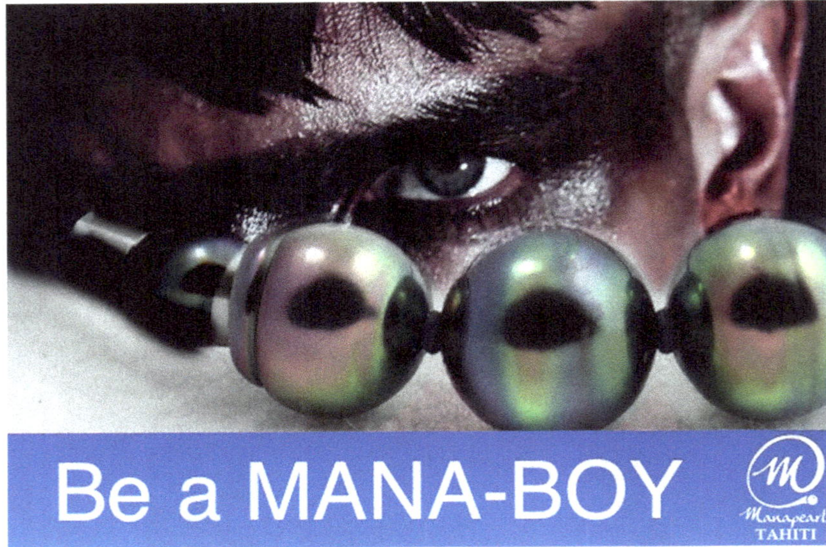

Figure 15. 'Be a Mana-Boy'.
Source: Manapearl Tahiti 2014, used with permission.

The proposed absorption or transfer of mana is not limited to acquired possessions. Experiences too, are being attached to the mana 'brand'. Mana Rock Café (Figure 16), long noted in regional guidebooks for evening entertainment in Papeete, is contextualised by other mana-rocking venues and experiences, including massages, hostelries and tattoo parlours.

Figure 16. Drinking mana.
Source: *Mana Rock Café* website 2014.

Perhaps the most quotidian encounter with mana in contemporary French Polynesia is mediated by the VINI Corporation's internet arm with its several mana-infused (and infusing?) subsidiaries including Mana L'Internet Polynésienne (Figure 17) and its separate business ManaSpot offering 'The Polynesian Wi-Fi connection, in all liberty, it's ManaSpot!' Other offerings include the rental of a Manabox™ router and the Manamail service, 'Rediscover the pleasure of communicating!'

Figure 17. Mana-infused communications.

Source: Photograph by Alexander Mawyer, June 2014.

Mana is not only found in the things and experiences one can now, with daily regularity, consume; it also supports the very sites of consumption. Still under construction in 2014, the Mana Nui Shopping Mall (Figure 18), also known as the Takau Plaza Shopping Center in Papeete, is not the only commercial shopping centre to take this name. The major French grocery chain Carrefour's (crossroads) building in Fa'a is also the Mana Nui Building.

Figure 18. Mana shopping.

Source: Photograph by Alexander Mawyer, June 2014.

Profoundly historically and socially charged collective associations such as the political party Ia Mana te Nunaa (Power to the People) formed in 1975 by Henri Hiro and other leaders in the Tahitian cultural and political renewal of that era, are not the only popular associations to assert the mana of collectivity. For instance, Mana o te Reo (Mana of the Language) works commercially to provide Tahitian translations for various public and private entities, the Mana o te Moana (Mana of the Ocean) foundation supports marine conservation and public education in the region, and a popular mana-enhanced and enhancing Tahitian dance association has been active in France and Tahiti since 2006 (Figure 19).

Figure 19. Choreographing mana (Mana Ori Tahiti 2015).

Do advertisements seeking to enhance claims about the potency of products demonstrate that, on Tahiti, mana is being corrupted by the West, hollowed out even as it expands in its reach? Do they suggest that a western corruption—the disease of someone else's culture—has tainted mana at its source or in its expressive realisation? Contra Baré, I note that modernity and its playing-out is not everywhere identical (Appadurai 1996). While it may be entirely accurate that the march of modernity in the West included this process of disenchantment, it may also be true that western disenchantment was in part made possible by various displacements and transferences which resulted in a heightening of the senses of the potent and the occult elsewhere—which is to say that I am not at all convinced that whatever mana has been in Tahitian contexts it has now been stripped and etiolated of past potency. Rather, the fact that mana, whatever it signifies, is in ever-greater extension in everyday contexts may well point to a process of *quotidianisation* but not necessarily of etiolation and depletion. The argument that the semantic extension to cover a broader range of situations, goods and aspects of personhood than in the past must mean that the term is increasingly emptied out—as opposed to the possibility that this range of situations, goods and everyday contexts have taken on meaningful cultural inflections—is a judgment with which I am not comfortable. That is, from the point of view of lived experience, and in contrast to Baré's interpretive stance, some aspects of contemporary life in the French Polynesian regional center of Tahiti now seem more enchanted, not less.

But what might quotidianisation suggest about the underlying culture of mana, and is this pattern of quotidianisation playing out in the same way across the region? To answer such questions with sensitivity to the emplacedness of culture, fieldworkers and critical commentators alike are better served by attending to the term's everyday economies of usage in specific social and historical contexts. On Mangareva, as shown in the next section, an account of mana in enduring and contemporary culture suggests a markedly different trajectory of usage than in Tahiti—one in which the term's semantic extension is scarcely broader than in the past but is, as yet, resisting quotidianisation.

Indeed, on Mangareva, over the course of multiple visits between 1999 and 2009, and particularly during my doctoral fieldwork in 2002 and early 2003, I only witnessed the term 'mana' used on a small number of occasions. These included several references to the *'aga mana*

(mana-works) of ancient culture heroes and chiefly persons, and on a number of occasions to *e mea mana* (mana-things or doings) when referring to objects and public works whose purpose and meanings are either lost to record or memory, obscure, or understood with difficulty relative to the amount of labour involved in their construction. Such mana-works include the cathedral and certain other works of the early mission period. Massive works that predate the construction of the cathedral were also often couched in terms of *'aga mana*: the rolling of a massive coral boulder to the top of the ridge where a paved road now crosses over the ridge line, the raising of several massive platforms (termed *paepae*) in the mountains, the now lost *marae*, and the hand-hewn and polished stone benches and massive stone anchors used for the ritual sea-burial of certain prestige-filled remains (not those of high chiefs, however, who had a specific burial site on land). Several senior speakers with whom I worked on a dictionary project initiated by the Association Culturelle Reo Mangareva (Mangarevan Language Cultural Association) also spoke with me about *naue* (divination) and the *tapa'o* (signs) of natural events, doing so with reference to the persons capable of such acts as *tagata mana*, people of mana.[4] These instances could be tallied on my two hands. When speaking with a Mangarevan colleague about this pattern of scarce use, he observed, 'This is not surprising, *mana* is a *tapu* word',[5] one set aside, one that should only be invoked when appropriate.

Although all of these instances of use might indicate something like the sense of mana's second definition above (miraculous, marvelous, supernatural) and are notably identical to the scant uses recorded in the Mangarevan *atonga*, I suggest something else lingers in the semantics besides the supernatural and extraordinary—something more in line with the sense of practical powers and authorities. In my fieldwork, there was a singular context of use that puzzled me and that suggested the practical and worldly place of mana on the landscape of contemporary (and perhaps past) Mangarevan discourse.

4 The attachment of *mana* to the parapsychological evidenced in these usages is locally worrisome, however, in its potential motivation by the slender and regionally much read and referred to book *Mana* by an itinerant French aristocrat and new-ager who interpreted the concept along western occult lines (Putigny 1993). Robert Putigny is, coincidentally, the father of one of my Mangarevan informants who taught me something rather profound about local conceptions of 'silence'—quite a small world as it turns out.

5 Ena Manuireva, personal communication, Skype, Spring 2014.

Herangi means Pitcairn

Having written on the *Bounty* and its various instantiations in film several times since entering graduate school, I was conscious of how close Pitcairn (called 'Erangi' in Mangarevan) was to the Gambier Islands of French Polynesia. Prior to the construction in the 1960s of an airstrip on one of Mangareva's *motu* sand islets dotting the 100-kilometre reef, both islands shared their commercial and transportation regimes to a great degree. Ships hailing at one island hailed at the other and a vigorous trade of goods, resources, and news was maintained. I was delighted early in my fieldwork to 'discover' that the historical relationship between these two islands survived into the twentieth century. However, the cold-war advent of French nuclear testing had changed much, and an invisible wall seems to have been thrown up between the islands, greatly complicating what had been enduring inter-island kin groups, exchange networks and, more interestingly, inter-island property rights. I heard reports of disincentives for Mangarevans to travel to Pitcairn or other nearby islands (Henderson, Ducie, Oeno) where many persons claimed traditional rights of access and use earlier in the century—including explicit prohibitions on travel imposed by the gendarmes.

Despite such obstacles as changes in the material infrastructure of island lives and the ethereal superstructure of state politics (n.b. Pitcairn, a British Colony to this day, is administered by New Zealand, generally governed by a High Commissioner operating out of New Zealand—a state that staunchly opposed French nuclear testing, proposed the South Pacific as a Nuclear Free Zone, and was the outraged host of the Greenpeace flagship *Rainbow Warrior* scuttled by French special forces in Auckland Harbour in 1985), I discovered not long after my arrival that some individuals on Mangareva are commonly understood to be 'Pitcairners' despite, in some cases, having been raised on Mangareva and also being of Mangarevan descent, in addition to the Tahitian and Tubuaian *toto* (blood) that all Pitcairners have through the maternal line. Later, when by pure coincidence a senior member of the Christian family,[6] Charles, arrived on Mangareva en route with his

6 From what I gathered first-hand on Pitcairn during a brief visit in 2002 and from Charles Christian on Mangareva, the social organisation of Pitcairners on Pitcairn, Norkfolk Island, New Zealand and elsewhere is felt to be closely aligned to certain Polynesian precedents including a sense of ranked superiority by birth order and 'family' (clan) arrival order, e.g. the Christians take precedence over Adams and others, who all in turn take precedence over the several families of American-descended jump-ships.

wife to visit Pitcairn and was kind enough to invite me to dinner and to taste her 'famous' Pitcairn pie (a freshly grated coconut crème/dried banana masterwork), I learned that other folks on Mangareva, not merely those who were socially marked as 'Pitcairners', maintained family and economic ties of various sorts with Pitcairn mediated by the occasional yacht passing in the countervailing direction. In some cases such ties, I learned, extended back three or four generations and were rooted in the commercial relations of merchants, copra traders and ships' pilots. Many Mangarevan adults are deeply sensitive to what Pitcairners are likely to be wanting at any season of the year, especially with respect to the potentially many-months cargo cycle of that island. In comparison, Mangareva is served by weekly flights and two cargo ships that circle through French Polynesia on alternating three-week cycles. Thus cargo arrives optimally every two weeks, but sometimes twice in two days, and sometimes not for six weeks or more if there is a delay, resulting in palate-numbing culinary boredom, hoarding and quite a rush on the day when the bakery is understood to be putting its last loaves in the oven until the cargo's next arrival.

After long months in the field wishing for a suitable yacht to offer serendipitous passage, I had begun to wonder if that year's sailing season would see anyone bucking tradition and sailing the 400-odd nautical miles from Mangareva to Pitcairn and back—about 50 yachts made the trip that year heading in the other direction, generally en route from Rapanui (Easter Island) or the Galápagos to Tahiti, the Marquesas, the Cook Islands, or some combination thereof. Finally, eight months into life on Mangareva, my chance all but drifted into the village bay on high tide, under gentle coral-anxious power, in the form of the Brazil-machined solid steel hull of a 60-foot yacht that was to collect a BBC television personality and fetch him to Pitcairn to conduct interviews for a book on far-flung British possessions, imperial jewels that shine the brighter for having been retained into the postcolonial era, but also 'the meanest inhabitable rocks in the seven seas', as he put it. I was tremendously gratified when the captain—the only person aboard and an internationally known sailor famous for solo cape-navigations, as it turned out—offered my wife and me the journey if I would crew and she cook a bit. So, with the lessons and admonitions of Charles Christian resounding in my head, before embarking I went around asking what folks might like to have taken to or collected from Pitcairn.

At least a half-dozen different requests were made for watermelons which grow plentifully on Pitcairn, along with whatever other produce the horticulturally industrious Pitcairners happened to have a surplus of, which was thought to be whatever is in season since there were only so many Pitcairners then in residence (48 at the time) and the island's plateau is basically a single extended garden/orchard. Also, we were asked to post several letters—normally a letter posted to Pitcairn must travel to Tahiti, thence to New Zealand, and there suffer the vicissitudes of freight and fate, perhaps to depart on the multi-week journey to Pitcairn all but immediately, perhaps to rest in informational stasis for six months while the cargo cycle arrives at the next departure. In the most fruitful case, one of the island's three main store operators, Edmund, asked us to port two sacks of baguettes, about 100 in all, specially ordered and freshly baked. On Mangareva, the bakers generally know how many loaves will be wanted, purchased and consumed on the island on any given day to within a few loaves and are loath to overbake since flour is white gold. Edmund also asked us to carry two breadfruit saplings of a particular variety not under cultivation on Pitcairn that had been requested years earlier and were conveniently in season for transplantation.[7] Now, obviously this struck us as deliciously ironic given the history of Pitcairn's settlement.[8]

7 Breadfruit is not readily transplanted out of a certain developmental season (Oliver 1988).

8 Pitcairn is famously the final stopping point of the mutinous dream-ship of libidinous liberty, HMAV *Bounty*. The *Bounty* mutineers had been fed up with Bligh's overbearing character and displacement of all human affection and existential concern onto the breadfruit saplings they had laboriously collected at Tahiti for transport to the West Indies (Dening 1992). Among other indignities early in the return voyage, the *Bounty* crew had to deal with an under-rationing of water as it was learned that breadfruit was intolerant of salt and must be regularly wetted down with fresh water to prevent early and rapid desiccation, defoliation and death. Of course, the first thing the mutineers did was throw the damned saplings overboard all the while jeering Bligh for his chlorophylliac inhumanity—in his defence, the man incontestably was green-thumbed and green-minded as he showed in his successful second breadfruit voyage (Dening 1992; Oliver 1988). In any event, the saplings had been requested by one of Pitcairn's residents, a sculptor, and would have been much appreciated had they not been intercepted at the landing by the High Commissioner himself, not usually in residence, who happened to be on the island, entomologist in tow, among other reasons for the very purpose of enforcing and promulgating stricter rules for the debarking of goods and the insects that stowaway in them—particularly the Cicadella 'pissing fly' now endemic in French Polynesia. On arriving, into the sea went our saplings too.

Aside from such pleasantries, a more serious request arose, one which cast a personal light onto the notion of *mana*, which, as I noted above, had been bothering me for months and months due to the irregularity or near invisibility of its use.

Warren is a hard-working and not particularly affluent man who lives on the fringe of village life, about 1 kilometre in the *i mua* direction.[9] Warren and I saw one another and exchanged words daily as I passed his homestead and small pearl operation on my run, generally a shouted greeting and his comment on my form. Sometimes we would stop and chat at the far store. Once or twice we exchanged a few words of Pitcairnese (the particular speech community of that island developed out of English, Jack-Speak and 'Polynesian' in the late eighteenth, nineteenth and early twentieth centuries, e.g. *you must have kill'd me for jump* (you scared me)).

Warren is the son of Sterling Warren and Aunoa, a Mangarevan woman. Sterling and a group of other Pitcairners aboard the *Pro Patria* had been marooned on Temoe atoll in September 1933, and were rescued by Mangarevans after their presence on this atoll was discovered by a fishing expedition—coincidentally, James Norman Hall was also aboard the *Pro Patria* and recorded this event in his *The Tale of a Shipwreck* first published in the *Atlantic Monthly* in 1934. On a clear day, Mangareva can be seen from Temoe but rarely the reverse and then only from Taraetukura and Aororotini, the island's highest peaks. It was quite some time before a boat could be arranged to carry the Pitcairners back home—as I heard the story, no captain could be found at the time to undertake the voyage without a payment that was simply not available, and a number of unions were formed in the interim.

When a Captain Johnston of the commercial vessel *Yankee* finally agreed to transport the Pitcairners home, one of the couples that had formed in the meantime, Sterling and Aunoa, refused to be separated and Aunoa departed with the men for their home island. She was not the first Mangarevan woman so to do. They were married aboard the *Yankee* by Capt. Johnston, who noted in a letter of attestation to the

9 One of the non-cardinal directional orientations ordering normal transit on Mangareva, corresponding to travel away from the centre of town along the coast in a counter-clockwise direction.

marriage, dated 1954 and stamped 'Certified True Copy' by the Island Secretary of Pitcairn in 1994,[10] that both parents had certified their willingness for Aunoa to be taken off the island despite her tender age (perhaps she was as young as 13).

Once on Pitcairn, the couple produced three children, two of whom returned with their mother to Mangareva, where they settled on family land and have remained to the present. Here the story intersects with the problematics of land tenure. Despite the passage of over one and a half centuries (longer on Tahiti) since colonial and commercial interests began to transform the rule of land in these islands from the traditional collective property rights rooted in tribe/clan-based membership, and complex land tenure (Newbury 1980; Finney 1965), only the last few years have seen any serious headway made in achieving transparency in, and the motivated dissolution of, collective proprietorship and usufruct rights (Bambridge and Neuffer 2002; Bambridge 2009). It is hard not to speculate that countervailing strategic interests resisted the reformation of land tenure with the tacit understanding that what happened in Hawai'i or New Zealand could happen in French Polynesia should a western fee simple/title system be implemented in these islands; and that it is the contemporary achievement of local quasi-sovereignty, termed autonomy, under a French constitution that has motivated various influential interests to expedite the process of legal reform after 150 years of delay (Bambridge 2009, 2012). In the years since the 1996 Statute of Autonomy, and intensively since the 2004 expansion of the autonomy framework, such reforms as have been implemented have led to a scramble for documents that could prove, or at least suggest to a judge, that you were one of a group of inheritors of rights over any particular piece of land as the demonstrably senior man or woman in a descent line (that is, the inheritor of a patronym which folks bear on Mangareva in quasi-titular manner, such as

10 The date is telling as it points to the time depths in which the family has been entangled in working to establish a legal identity and the evident decade (or longer) that Warren himself had been struggling to do so. I could add that I know Warren had approached others with similar requests both before and after the events described here. In 2006, notably, he was still in the process of advocating for his legal rights and of collecting evidentiary supports to legitimate his status and claims as evidenced in a remarkable blog posted to the SEA following news of the vessel SSV *Robert C. Seamans* (Sea Education Association 2006).

'E Paeamara' and 'E Mamatui'), or, even better, the sole authentic proprietor of a particular land—among which documents a birth certificate was necessary.[11]

Which brings us to Warren's problem. He had no birth certificate on Mangareva demonstrating, legally, what everyone knew but some cousins were not willing or able to legitimately certify—that is, that as Aunoa's son he has legitimate rights (by birth, common agreement, customary law) to use of certain lands. Consequently, the previous few years had been increasingly anxious, as his perennial failure to prove descent to a series of French courts and judges—the 1954 attestation of his parents' marriage notwithstanding—had put his descendants' and his own titles, positions and economic futures on the line as cousins would step forward with their own rights to certain lands which will, in the future, become theirs exclusively should Warren not produce the proper evidence prior to the statutory limit set for this process.[12]

So, when on my daily run several nights before embarking, I stopped at Warren's to ask if I could take a letter or anything to Pitcairn for him, I was surprised to get an earful, a version of the situation I've just described along with a most personal request. In brief, he asked me if I would get a birth certificate made there for him, one that was specifically authorised by the state, a legitimate one that could serve as evidence for the various legal processes in which he was currently involved.

11 The problem of descent deserves its own extensive treatment. Folks sometimes today joke that there are only three families (Paeamara, Mamatui, Teapiki), though a number of other patronyms are still very much present (Teakarotu, Kopunui, Mamatamoe, among others). Members of the primary three gradually acquired large portions of the rule of the land since the collapse of the *'ati* system.

12 The legislature has changed this ultimate date for the entire region several times, extending it on each occasion. I was initially told that 2005 was the limiting year, but understand that that changed while I was in the field, and the judge who visited Mangareva twice during my fieldwork to preside over various legal processes almost entirely devoted to land issues told me that he did not personally believe that some of the local land disputes would be resolved much sooner that 2020 or 2030. We discussed Warren's case as an example. The judge's rationale for this claim was both occult, in that he would not share it publicly, and perverse in that he expected but would not publicise that many of the concerned, with evident rights and a certain degree of knowledge about the traditional constitution of those rights, would have to pass away in order to clear the ground for the re-assignment of specific rights to a smaller number of more easily identifiable individuals. His entropic presupposition, quite possibly erroneous, is that over time fewer individuals will be able to demonstrate that they have land rights 'before' the law based on customary knowledge. In fact, by 2009, many disputes had been settled far more concretely than anticipated.

The conversation, impassioned on Warren's part and, on mine, nervous with the sense of responsibility and improbability that a Pitcairn authority would hand over a birth certificate, revolved around one term. Surprisingly, he used a singular conceptual frame to cover all of the different qualities of the object, cause, effect, event and the various tasks involved. Warren used *mana* and its causative form *'akamana* to refer to what the Pitcairn authorities needed to do for this document—that is, to empower it, to legitimately authorise Warren's claims, in some sense his (legal) existence. At the same time, he referred to the document as *mana* and to *mana* as a character or quality of the incipient document. *'Na koe i 'akamana 'ia toku kaie, toku [birth] certificat'* ('You will have made-mana (stamped, authorised) my paper, my birth certificate') he repeated while gesturing the action of stamping, with his hand serving as a virtual stamp.

A following conversation when I returned the next day to pick up a brief letter from Warren to be delivered to the Pitcairn authorities, stating his request in his own words, reconfirmed the pattern of his use of this concept—that is, the secular (or perhaps, considering the character of states, profane) or bio-political use of the term stuck out. Other senior speakers consulted in my language working group noted that Warren's usage was quite correct: *'akamana*, to give authority to a document, was in fact exactly how this term should be used in everyday talk when appropriate.

What might be called the 'great works' uses of the term 'mana' described at the end of the last section accorded perfectly with what I expected to encounter as the actual use of this term in everyday speech, indeed virtually identical to the historically attested extensions of mana discussed at the outset in the section on bearing mana and its limits. I did not, however, expect such uses to be so rare or to be so parsimonious given the lushness of mana's semantic potential from either existing dictionaries or years of reading in the ethnography and history of Polynesian studies. Warren's conversation further challenged my sense of mana's semantic range or, rather, what that range reveals. Warren's speech and affirmations of it by others made me anxious about the seeming simplicity of previous usages. Contextualised by Warren's meaning, they seemed less indicative of a diffuse and ethereal supernatural force imbued in some things and persons than of the pragmatic powers of states and their agents manifest in the materiality of the everyday.

The mana of the state: *Homo sacer* in Polynesia?

As amply demonstrated by Warren's usage above, mana is not always used in a manner to suggest the ineffable, metaphysical, flowing (or non-flowing) of some chthonic energy or supernatural quality (like 'luck') adherent to some persons and not others, or to certain things. Given these other uses of the term, the puzzle emerges of how this active 'mana' relates to mana in other contexts where it appears to be playing a descriptive role and what, if anything, this instance says about the scarcity of other uses or perhaps about the quotidianisation or anti-quotidianisation of mana across regional speech communities.

Bradd Shore (1989), in his major analysis of the term, certainly draws attention to the practical quality of mana as part of his analysis, but he also argues that mana's source can be shown to rest in the ineffable and the divine. Power is inherent in this world because it is transported here, authorised and legitimated from elsewhere or elsewhen. In addition, *mana* as a general principle of action in the world is relatable to fecundity. Shore notes that there is a ubiquitous linkage between the act, human or divine, and social reproduction as a matter of both physical and metaphysical import. Elsewhere in Polynesia, persons of mana literally inseminate the land in order to secure its future fertility, just as every application of potent force in human activity (re)produces some sort of social relation as did Tiki, on Mangareva, when he made the world meaningfully human through copulative acts (Buck 1938). 'In a number of Traditional societies, the high *ariki* endowed the land with his Mana, making it fruitful. This too, as we have seen, was a relationship of honor to the land' (Goldman 1970: 512).[13] And, as a sort of *tertium quid*, Shore notes of the nature of mana that 'although western analysts have chosen to view mana as some kind of general and abstract force, Polynesians seem to emphasise a variety of particular powers, or at the very least specific manifestations of a general concept' (Shore 1989: 138). Is mana

13 'The specific quality of Fijian chiefly power (*kaukawa* [sic] or *mana*) is masculine potency, a virility that has more than one representation in common custom. It appears directly, for example, in the paramount's privileged access to nubile women of his domain; symbolically, in the correspondence between the rites of chiefly investiture and the initiation of young men to sexual and warrior status by circumcision' (Sahlins 1976: 26).

a field of force or a flowing current of power, or a simple substance which, like dark matter and dark energy, is nowhere visible but latent in the cosmic order of things? Or is mana something else, a word in use that indexes or summons into contextual relevance a local, culturally nuanced bundle of understandings about the ordering of things and the forces (more or less authorised) behind or in front of that ordering?

The tension between the ineffable spiritual and the practical and administrative is highly visible in Warren's request for a state document, a certificate legitimating his birth and being, one that must literally be fabricated and authorised, by stamp and seal, as valid in the context of highly sensitive micro-political social processes, as when at law. Equally suggestive is the presupposed lack of absence or insufficiency of mana in Warren's existing documentation. This state of affairs, at once personal and impersonal, local and extralocal, legal and extralegal, strikingly resembles the condition of *homo sacer* identified by Giorgio Agamben (1998) as an extraordinary tool for making visible regimes of sovereign state power. While I do not propose a close exegesis of Agamben's *Homo Sacer* cycle, I do want to pursue several points in relation to it that clarify several of the tensions in understanding contemporary mana, its relations to the past, and its transformations in French Polynesia.

In Roman law, *homo sacer* is a person whose *bios* (political life) has been legally stripped away and who is thus reduced to *zoe* (bare life, animal life). Such beings are subject to the capricious whims of those around them who may kill them (or impede lesser rights also derived from *bios*) as they will. However, with dark irony, *homo sacer* may not be sacrificed. Presumably a human sacrifice requires recognition of *bios*, the value of a fundamentally social and political being equivalent to the significance of the sacrifice, and the *homo sacer* has been reduced to bare life or *zoe*. Agamben himself locates mana within the analytical framework of the fraught condition of *homo sacer*. The central passage is worth quoting in its entirety.

> An enigmatic archaic Roman legal figure that seems to embody contradictory traits and therefore had to be explained thus begins to resonate with the religious category of the sacred when this category irrevocably loses its significance and comes to assume contradictory meanings. Once placed in relation with the ethnographic concept of taboo, this ambivalence is then used – with perfect circularity – to explain the figure of homo sacer. There is a moment in the life of

> concepts when they lose their immediate intelligibility and can then, like all empty terms, be overburdened with contradictory meanings. For the religious phenomenon, this moment coincides with the point at which anthropology – for which the ambivalent terms *mana*, taboo, and sacer are absolutely central – was born at the end of the last century. Levi-Strauss has shown how the term *mana* functions as an excessive signifier with no meaning other than that of marking an excess of the signifying function over all signifieds. Somewhat analogous remarks could be made with reference to the use and function of the concepts of the sacred and the taboo in the discourse of the social sciences between 1890 and 1940. An assumed ambivalence of the generic religious category of the sacred cannot explain the juridico-political phenomenon to which the most ancient meaning of the term sacer refers. On the contrary, only an attentive and unprejudiced delimitation of the respective fields of the political and the religious will make it possible to understand the history of their intersection and complex relations. (Agamben 1998: 51, emphasis added)

What then does an attentive and unprejudiced inquisition of mana at the intersections of the political and religious framed anew through the lens of *homo sacer* achieve (with delicious parallel to Mauss' use of Roman law in 'the discourse of the social sciences between 1890 and 1940')? Perhaps it raises the question of the source of the power to reduce a person (or persons) to bare life, to remove their *bios* or political being and subject them to existential contingency without the protections of social order. Agamben observes that this power, which can be reduced to the right to kill, is the essence of sovereignty. Which is to say, it is a power whose source cannot be found in nature, identified as *imperium* in Roman law, and which was (and continues to be) wielded by state agents, persons personifying political regimes such as magistrates who through *auctoritas* enacted the rule of law ultimately grounded in *imperium*. *Homo sacer*, this curious or enigmatic condition, is specifically interesting because its enactment makes visible the fundamental tension between the absolute limits of power, *imperium* (sovereignty, authority over the death of *bios*-constituted beings), the legitimated powers of state agents wielding *auctoritas*, and the everyday powers of lesser agents or citizens enacting their own political or social powers as *potestas*.

My point in drawing attention to Agamben is to emphasise that the history of mana's uptake in anthropology can come into focus as a point of disciplinary and cross-disciplinary fetishisation of the numinous and ineffable in the perception, conception and experience of the exercise of power over human entities (those bearing *bios*) and culture-specific explanations thereof. Coming out of my experience of seeking to honour Warren's request in friendship, what strikes me most about mana's anthropological uptake is how the concept-in-use appears to be far more readily translatable under most or possibly all of its actual contexts into more familiar cultural terms than suggested by all of the ink spilled over its presupposed 'numinous' content. The practical contexts of mana's rare but forceful appearance in everyday speech on Mangareva has left me skeptical of anthropology's lingering willfulness to ascribe to Polynesian (or Oceanic) mana a greater degree of mysticism, amazement, or miraculousness than ascribed to western conceptions of legal authority and the powers of states through their agents and objects, for instance in legal documents processed through more or less bureaucratised institutions. Recalling the derived forms of mana pointing to collective powers, of the authority of the social or of the 'state' broadly defined as those regimes of power (authority) bearing effects on any given community, mana thus might be seen to be a culturally specific working out of issues of authority, power and social force that have been worked out in other parts of the world in terms of *imperium* and *auctoritas* (the authority of sovereigns, states, political regimes, collectives, or their agents).

To the best of my knowledge, there is only one other instance of the use of mana in the entire corpus of traditional Mangarevan texts—one highly suggestive of this reading. Mana appears one time in the 58 pages of the Code Mangarévien, the books of laws enacted and published in the dusk of the Mangarevan Kingdom in 1881, a process entangled in the historical incorporation of the kingdom into a French territory. Including the Constitution, civil code and code of justice of the land, in both a French (first) and Mangarevan (second) version, this document invokes mana only once, in the fifth line of the Mangarevan version, in the first article of the constitutional accord.

> TE UGA NEI: Art. 1. Ka akamana tapu kehekehe hia, ki roto i a mau Kaiga Mangareva nei, a mau Ture Mangareva i akatu hia mei te makararaga i rotopu i te mau Tagata ao o te kaiga nei, me to Komagata Kaireo o te Repupirika Harani. (Richard 2001: 127)[14]

> BE IT KNOWN: Art. 1. By utter sacredness [*tapu kehekehe*] 'akamana-ed, inside all Mangarevan lands, the Mangarevan Laws [are] hereby made-to-stand in the deep (absolute depths, rotopu) of the minds (thoughts) of the People of these lands, and the Commandant [*Komagata*] Commissioner (*kairea*: 'a deputy; an envoy; a delegate. One who is embued with the authority of another', in Tregear [1899]) of the French Republic [my translation].

In this context, as in Warren's uses of the term described above, the potency and authority of the state is the significant (non-ambiguous) and semantic heart of the term, one reinforced—just in case any of the *Tagata ao o tera kaiga ra* (local citizens) somehow missed the *imperium* involved—with an explicit assertion of the *tapu kehekehe* (utter sacrality; hence force) of these *akamana*-ed words (see also Silva, this volume).

This re-reading stands in contrast to Sahlins (1985) and a century of other scholars who I suggest could be productively re-read in conversation with Agamben's attempt to produce an 'attentive and unprejudiced delimitation of the respective fields of the political and the religious [that] will make it possible to understand the history of their intersection and complex relations' (Agamben 1998: 51), one that does not over-emphasise the supernatural and extraordinary majesty of individuals instead of their magisterial authority derived from *imperium* or *auctoritas* (whether legendary heroes, or chiefs, or British naval officers who overstepped their mana to disastrous results, or Colonial Commissioners, or everyday bureaucrats). In this reading, other reflexes of mana are semantically rooted in the same field of significance, one in which mana is evident in every marvellous or amazing or unlikely human act not because of the supernatural, beyond-the-common, or otherworldly dimension of spectral power, but because it takes a state, an authorised regime, to move a boulder uphill, to erect an edifice, to achieve a victory, or to compel others to

14 The passage in the French version: 'ORDONNE: Art. 1. Est promulgué dans l'archipel des Gambier (Mangareva) le Code mangarévien établi d'un commun accord entre les représentants du pays et le Commandant Commissaire de la reunion de la République Française' (Richard 2001: 96).

follow an everyday command from a singular individual. *E mea mana* (all these things), including the simple act of a mayor in a British colony in the post office building, making a photocopy of a birth certificate, signing a short letter attesting its validity, enclosing it in an envelope, signing the flap, and sending it across the sea. This is mana.

Conclusion: Quotidianisation and anti-quotidianisation

In conclusion, my premise is that on Mangareva most speakers are like Warren in their regularities of usage regarding this term. Friends and colleagues on Mangareva rarely speak *about* mana-things and mana-works (in French or Tahitian or Mangarevan) in contexts that suggest a heightened quality attached to certain things and superlative persons. However, as a matter of everyday speech acts and semantics, on no occasion did any speak as if they perceived spectral and flowing supernatural qualities inherent in persons or acts. All of which leaves me exceedingly sceptical about whether Mangarevan persons today conceive of mana as a sort of universal field of supernatural energy, the force par excellence, that is by the ontologically otherworldly status of some persons and certain things beyond normal efficaciousness. Warren's usage and others' confirmation of it suggested, however, that certain acts of mana did in fact produce effects and changes in the world, and did in fact have a special quality. As a Mangarevan colleague put it in a phrase perhaps worth repeating, 'mana is a tapu word' and there is a significant and enduring culture of anti-quotidianisation of invocation of the term in everyday speech. It seems to me that mana on Mangareva prototypically summons into real-time discourse certain local and culturally nuanced understandings of the practical and pragmatic powers of *imperium* and *auctoritas*, thus making visible the clash between *potestas* and these higher order regimes of power. Such contexts are, of course, utterly weighty, and perhaps point to the 'setting aside' (tapu) of the use of this term in everyday life. English too, and many other languages, have set aside terms reserved for the lightning-wielding (*auctoritas*-bearing) agents of the state's *imperium*, for example, 'Your Honour' or 'Your Majesty'. Mana thus resonates with its ethnological use as a conceptual *origo* which calibrates and allows one to make sense of 'specific notions about kinship, relationships between human beings and ancestral gods, and a host of related beliefs' (Kirch and Green 2001: 59) in the material outcomes of collective acts, including those of individuals who, in some sense, represent the state or, in elder days, their prevailing regimes of power and authority.

As discussed at the outset, my own first-order experience of the term *mana* surprised me by the scarcity of its use. Recall, Warren's possessions, rights, and those of his descendants had been put at risk because of a problematic lack of paper documentation of his existence as a byproduct of his birth on Pitcairn. In brief, he asked me if I would get a birth certificate made there for him, one that was specifically authorised by the state, a legitimate one that could serve as evidence for the various legal processes in which he was currently involved. Surprisingly, Warren used *mana* and its causative form *'akamana* again and again to refer to what Pitcairn authorities needed to do for this document—to empower it, to authorise his claims and, from the point of view of the French state, his legal existence. At the same time, he referred to the document's legitimacy as a question of *mana* (previous letters of attestation secured through correspondence with the Pitcairn administration and presented to the land judge on Mangareva were said to be without legitimacy) and to *mana* as the 'stamp' of authority by the Pitcairn administration and by the authority of the French judge who presided over the long-running land crisis in this part of Polynesia (complete with gestural mime of the 'stamping process' and indexical fingering of the stamp itself).

I suggest that Warren's mana and that of his Mangarevan community is clarifying. This discussion of mana casts light on the local value of certain heightened terms in everyday talk over time. In the Society Islands, where the power of the state to regulate collectives and to arbitrate *bios* has been under decades of active contestation and legal (re)negotiation, is it any surprise that mana is quotidianising? In the Gambier Islands, as elsewhere in French Polynesia's outer islands, where the experience of and response to the fact of enduring French colonialism has included a greater degree of ambivalence about a regional future independent from or autonomous within France, and despite massive language shift and loss, the use of mana in everyday speech appears to be resisting change—at least in the sense of increased invocation. Perhaps this too is unsurprising inasmuch as the everyday economies of linguistic power can track and index broader political tensions and struggles.

The sense of mana as miraculous, flowing power is an excellent example of what might be called a metaphorical figuration of a more straightforward conception of a majestically complex thing (the *imperium* of past and present states and their agents). Did past speakers conceive of mana as miraculous and supernatural or as worldly and very much the possession of certain men and women within particular regimes of authority? Men, women and collectives who possessed mana possessed *auctoritas* or represented *imperium*. Extraordinary things require extraordinary labours and the organisations and administrations of authorities to achieve them. Conspicuously, this does not make them less amazing or marvellous, or even less miraculous. With an eye towards the chronotope of past powers and marvels and a seeming diminution implicit in mana's regular expression about things-of-yesterday (Tomlinson 2006) on Mangareva, from something like Warren's point of view, Mangarevans would not be wrong to claim that their ancestors had more *mana* than they do today. As practical, pragmatic power, as literally the 'rule of the land', *mana* was indeed a possession of the ancient *tupuna* as a government administered by both chiefly and priestly ancestors with *imperium* and *auctoritas*. In a difficult position on a small island on the fringe of a global colonial empire, it is clear that states do not always or easily lend citizens their lightning. Today, it can be tragically difficult to *'akamana* local political initiatives and practices. But, with reference to the quotidianisation of mana on Tahiti, and the fact that some contemporary mana may be caught up in global and regional capital logics notwithstanding, perhaps there is reason to be hopeful for a relocalisation of *imperium* and *auctoritas*.

Throughout, I have noted that mana is used differently in Tahiti and Mangareva. Indeed, it is hardly used in Mangarevan conversations or contexts relative to those of Tahiti, where it was once invoked far less frequently than one would think given all the anthropological ink and its present visibility on the communicative landscape, or given its attested semantic lushness and imputed verdancy. I suggest the change in the semantic extension of the term over time on Tahiti represents a process of quotidianisation whose activity tracks a desire for the democratisation of sovereignty in an enduringly colonial situation. This is not the case on Mangareva where many continue to avoid the use of this term in everyday life except in highly rarefied circumstances such as when discussing the *imperium* of state powers or the *auctoritas* of government officials, a process I describe as anti-quotidianisation. Certainly it is easy to wonder how mana's trajectories of use are changing elsewhere in the region—what roles mana might be playing in conceiving and experiencing and responding to contemporary states and other regimes of power such as transnational commerce and potent local currents of social and political renewal. An interesting result of mana's movements in French Polynesia is that, *contra* Weber, some aspects of social and cultural life have remained or become progressively more enchanted in an age of westernisation, bureaucratisation and modernisation. Moreover, this process may indicate a resurgence of 'new' mana even as it harks back, sometimes wistfully, to the potency of the old.

Acknowledgements

I offer a heartfelt thanks to Matt Tomlinson and Ty Tengan for organising the New Mana initiative and for their generous support and encouragement. A hearty *maroi* is also due to Erwin Warren and many others in the *punui* of Rikitea for sharing their *mana* and for gifts of words about the present and the past, and particularly to Nikola Mamatamoe, Daniel Teakarotu and Bruno Schmidt. Many thanks too to Ena Manuireva for sharing his *mana o te reo* Mangareva.

References

Archival Repository

British Museum Archives:

MS PAC Mangareva 3.3. [MPM 3.3.], n.d.

MS PAC Mangareva 3.4. [MPM 3.4.], n.d.

Books, journal articles and chapters

Agamben, Giorgio. 1998. *Homo Sacer: Sovereign Power and Bare Life*, trans. Daniel Heller-Roazen. Stanford, CA: Stanford University Press.

Appadurai, Arjun. 1996. *Modernity at Large: Cultural Dimensions of Globalization*. Minneapolis: University of Minnesota Press.

Bambridge, Tamatoa. 2009. *La terre dans l'archipel des Australes*. *Étude du pluralisme juridique et culturel en matière foncière*. Papeete: Institut de Recherche pour le Développement (IRD) et Aux Vents des Îles.

——. 2012. Le foncier terrestre et marin en Polynésie française: L'étude de cas de Teahupoo. *Land Tenure Journal* 2: 119–43.

Bambridge, Tamatoa and Philippe Neuffer. 2002. Pluralisme culturel et juridique: le foncier en Polynésie française. In *La France et les Outre-Mers*, ed. Tamatoa Bambridge, JeanPierre Doumenge, O. Bruno, J. Simonin, D. Wolton, pp. 307–15. L'enjeu multiculturel, CNRS Éditions, Hermès, no. 32–33.

Baré, Jean-François. 1987. *Tahiti, Les Temps et Les Pouvoirs: Pour une anthropologie historique du Tahiti post-européen*. Paris: Éditions de l'Orstom.

Blevins, Juliette. 2008. Some comparative notes on proto-Oceanic *mana: Inside and outside the Austronesian family. *Oceanic Linguistics* 47(2): 253–74.

Blust, Robert. 2007. Proto-Oceanic *mana revisited. *Oceanic Linguistics* 46(2): 404–23.

Buck, Peter H. [Te Rangi Hiroa]. 1938. *Ethnology of Mangareva*. Honolulu: Bernice P. Bishop Museum Press.

Buse, Jasper with Raututi Taringa. 1985. *Cook Islands Maori Dictionary*, ed. Bruce Biggs and Rangi Moeka'a. Canberra: ANU Printing Service.

Codrington, R.H. 1891. *The Melanesians: Studies in their Anthropology and Folk-lore*. Oxford: Clarendon Press.

Davies, John. 1991 [1851]. *Tahitian and English Dictionary with Introductory Remarks on the Polynesian Language and a Short Grammar of the Tahitian Dialect: With an Appendix*. Tahiti: Editions Haere Po.

Dening, Greg. 1980. *Islands and Beaches: Discourse on a Silent Land: Marquesas 1774–1880*. Honolulu: University of Hawai'i Press.

——. 1992. *Mr. Bligh's Bad Language: Passion, Power and Theatre on the Bounty*. New York: Cambridge University Press.

Dordillon, Mgr. I.R. 1999 [1904]. *Grammaire et Dictionnaire de la Langue des* Îles *Marquises*. Tahiti: Société des Etudes Océaniennes.

Finney, Ben, 1965. *Polynesian Peasants and Proletarians: Socio-economic Change among the Tahitians of French Polynesia*. Wellington: Polynesian Society.

Firth, Raymond. 1940. The analysis of mana: An empirical approach. *Journal of the Polynesian Society* 49: 483–510.

Goldman, Irving. 1970. *Ancient Polynesian Society*. Chicago: University of Chicago Press.

Hall, James Norman. 1934. *The Tale of a Shipwreck*. Boston: Houghton Mifflin Co.

Holbraad, Martin. 2009. The power of powder: Life-force and motility in Cuban adivination. *Bedeutung* 1(3): 42–56.

Hubert, Henri and Marcel Mauss. 1902–1903. Esquisse d'une théorie générale de la magie. *L'Année Sociologique* 7: 1–146.

[Janeau, Vincent Ferrier]. 1908. *Grammaire et dictionaire Mangaréviens, par les Missionaires Catholiques de cet Archipel*. Members de la Congrégation des Sacres-Cours de Picpus, Braine-le-Comte.

Keesing, Roger M. 1984. Rethinking 'mana'. *Journal of Anthropological Research* 40(1): 137–56.

Kirch, Patrick Vinton and Roger C. Green. 2001. *Hawaiki, Ancestral Polynesia: An Essay in Historical Anthropology*. Cambridge: Cambridge University Press.

Lévi-Strauss, Claude. 1987. *Introduction to the work of Marcel Mauss*. London: Routledge.

Manapearl. 2015. Be a MANA-BOY. Online: www.maison-perle-tahiti.com/manapearl-tahiti/ (accessed 16 October 2015).

Mana Ori Tahiti. 2015. Online: tahitienfrance.free.fr/associations/assosculturelles/mana_ori_tahiti.htm (accessed 16 October 2015).

Mana Rock Café. 2015. *Mana Rock Café*. Online: facebook.com/rock.mana1 (accessed 16 October 2015).

Newbury, Colin. 1980. Tahiti Nui: Change and Survival in French Polynesia, 1767–1945. Honolulu: University of Hawai'i Press.

Oliver, Douglas. 1974. *Ancient Tahitian Society*. Honolulu: University of Hawai'i Press.

——. 1988 [with William Bligh]. *Return to Tahiti: Bligh's Second Breadfruit Voyage*. Honolulu: University of Hawai'i Press.

——. 2002. *On Becoming Old in Early Tahiti and in Early Hawai'i*. Tahiti: Societe des Etudes Oceaniennes/Haere Po.

Putigny, Robert. 1993 [1975]. *Le mana: ou, Le pouvoir surnaturel en Polynésie*. Paris: Editions R. Laffont.

Richard, Vahi Sylvia (ed.). 2001. *Code des lois [Cahiers du Patrimoine: Histoire]*. Tahiti: Ministère de la Culture ed de l'Enseignement supérieur.

Sahlins, Marshall. 1976. *Culture and Practical Reason*. Chicago: University of Chicago Press.

——. 1985. *Islands of History*. Chicago: University of Chicago Press.

Sea Education Association. 2006. *Following Sea*. Online: www.sea.edu/followingsea/3-06/f2_2_3-06.aspx (accessed 2 October 2015).

Shore, Bradd. 1989. Mana and tapu. In *Developments in Polynesian Ethnology*, ed. Alan Howard and Robert Borofsky, pp. 137–73. Honolulu: University of Hawai'i Press.

Tomlinson, Matt. 2006. Retheorizing mana: Bible translation and discourse of loss in Fiji. *Oceania* 76(2): 173–85.

Tregear, Edward. 1899. *A Dictionary of Mangareva (or Gambier Islands)*. Wellington: John Mackay.

Valeri, Valerio. 1985. *Kingship and Sacrifice: Ritual and Society in Ancient Hawaii*. Chicago: University of Chicago Press.

9

Theologies of *Mana* and *Sau* in Fiji

Matt Tomlinson and Sekove Bigitibau

Nineteenth-century Methodist missionaries saw something miraculous in Fijian *mana*. David Hazlewood's pioneering dictionary defined *mana* as a noun meaning 'a sign, or omen; a wonder, or miracle' and an adjective meaning 'effectual; efficient, as a remedy; wonder-working' (Hazlewood 1850: 85). Thomas Williams, who wrote the first major ethnography of Fijian society, explained the name of the god Kanusimana (*kanusi* means 'spit') by writing that he '"spits miracles," i.e., does them easily' (Williams 1982 [1858]: 218). And when the Bible was translated into Fijian, the noun phrases *cakamana* and *cakacaka mana* (working *mana*) and (*vei*)*ka mana* (*mana* thing/s) were often used for the English word 'miracle/s'.[1]

Both missionaries and (potential) converts operated in a world where spiritual power was expected to be made visible and tangible. Yet the missionaries' use of the term 'miracle/s' suggests that *mana* was seen by them as a kind of going-beyond, a transgression of the normal order of things, when in fact it might well have been woven into that normal order in pre-Christian Fiji. What if there was nothing

1 For early published references to *mana* in Fiji that do not come from the pens of missionaries, see Charles Wilkes (1845: 209) and Horatio Hale (1846: 399). The former describes the pairing of *mana* and *dina* (true) in ceremonial language, which we discuss below; the latter, similar to the missionaries, defines *mana* as 'a miracle'.

miraculous about Fijian *mana*? Indeed, each of the examples given in the opening paragraph raises questions about how missionaries' presuppositions might have shaped their treatment of *mana*. First, after Hazlewood offered the two definitions quoted above, he added another for *mana* as an adverb 'used when addressing a heathen deity—so be it, let it be so: also used after uliaing a report expressive of confirmation, as above' (Hazlewood 1850: 85).[2] This third definition, despite mentioning 'a heathen deity', is less theologically freighted than the first two; it is simply an affirmative and performative speech act, and is no more miraculous than saying 'amen'. Second, Williams' explanation of Kanusimana's name is flawed. In 'Kanusimana', *mana* is not a grammatical object of spit (*kanusi*). The name is a verb phrase, and can be translated more accurately as '[his] spit is prophetic' (that is, his spit makes things come to pass), or more compactly as 'magic spit'.[3] Kanusimana is not spitting miracles, but his spit makes things happen—which, although extraordinary, is quite a different portrayal of magical mechanics than Williams'. Finally, *mana* in older Fijian accounts is strongly associated with acts of speaking, as we describe below, but the Methodist missionaries who favoured *mana*-based terms for translating 'miracles' in the Bible used the term *vosamana* (speak *mana*) more often to denigrate the lying speech of false prophets than to exalt the effectiveness of divine speech (Tomlinson 2006: 178).[4]

Our purpose in this chapter is not to argue over translations, however. As more than a century of scholarship has shown, isolating the word *mana* to search for a context-free meaning is not a productive enterprise, and there is an obvious danger in what Michael Lempert (2010: 394) has called 'word prospecting'—pulling terms out of context and treating them as emblems, or fetishising them. There is significant variability in how *mana* is used in different contexts within a society, between societies, and over time—and the larger point is that terms in language never precisely map onto concepts, practices,

2 By 'uliaing' he means 'to receive a message respectfully; to assent to, or return an answer to a report, or message' (Hazlewood 1850: 157).

3 The translation '[his] spit is prophetic' was suggested in personal communication by Paul Geraghty.

4 Coincidentally, but with suggestive resonance, they also used the term *mana* for the homonym 'manna' (food from heaven) (see also Kolshus, this volume). Karen Brison writes that Fijian Pentecostals do not often use the term *mana*, and quotes an interlocutor who says, 'Hmm, man[n]a. That's not really a Fijian word, is it? I think it comes from the Bible and means something like bread' (Brison 2012; cf. Ryle 2001: 233).

or effects. We focus, rather, on the ways that *mana* has become an object of analysis by indigenous Fijian Methodist theologians. In the first half of this chapter, we examine *mana*'s association with speech and with the term *sau*, a word with which *mana* is often paired and sometimes contrasted. In the second half, we turn to Fijian Methodist theologians' analyses of *mana* as well as *sau*, especially as they compare the authority and effectiveness of church leaders with that of hereditary chiefs. Ultimately, we aim to rethink Fijian *mana* as something which is not necessarily miraculous, but is instead a poetic expression used to articulate and evaluate models of divine and human speech.

Speaking *mana*

The first monolingual Fijian dictionary, published a decade ago, defines *mana* as 'achieving its intended purpose' (*yaco dina na kena inaki*; Tabana ni Vosa kei na iTovo Vakaviti 2005: 356). This sense of *mana*, hinted at in Hazlewood's third definition from 1850 ('so be it, let it be so'), is regularly made clear in indigenous Fijian communities during ceremonial speeches. For example, during *isevusevu* (offerings of kava between guests and hosts), the speeches made by those receiving the presentation feature aspirational phrases such as 'Let fish be abundant' and 'Let chiefly authority be maintained', and those who have given the presentation often respond '*Mana*' to these lines; the Methodist theologian Savenaca Vuetanavanua (2009: 35) writes that *mana* in this context translates as 'May it be so'.[5] Some events may feature context-specific wishes, such as a wedding's invocation, 'may the couple live happily together for the rest of their lives'. At the end of the speech of acceptance, all those present often chant together '*Mana, e[i] dina, a muduo*'.[6] '*Mana, e dina*', means '*Mana*, it is true'; '*a muduo*' does not

5 The Fijian phrases which Vuetanavanua translates as 'Let fish be abundant', and 'Let chiefly authority be maintained' are *Cabe tu na ika mai takali* and *Dei tikoga na itutu vakaturaga*. A more literal translation of the first would be '[Let] fish rise from the sea'.

6 Eräsaari (2013: 154) writes that in Naloto village, Verata, *mana, e dina* is presented as a dialogue, with the individual speech-giver announcing '*mana*' and other participants then responding '*e dina*'. In comparison, Bigitibau has observed that a speaker's cadences and voice quality, as well as the specific phrases the speaker uses, can signal to the audience that the speech is about to conclude; if audience members recognise the cues, they are likely to join the speaker in chanting '*mana, e dina*', but if they miss the cues, they will chime in with '*e dina*' only after '*mana*' has been said. On the differences implied by *e dina* and *ei dina* in one part of Fiji, see Tomlinson (2009a: 69n5).

have a literal translation, but is a poetic closure followed by rhythmic clapping and sometimes repetition of *'muduo'*. In chanting *'mana, e dina'*, the thing that is true (*dina*) is not *mana* itself. Rather, the thing that is (becoming) true are the words spoken before the chant; for example, the fish will be abundant, chiefly authority will be maintained, and the married couple will live happily ever after.

In such speeches and chants, *mana* has illocutionary force, per J.L. Austin (1975: 13): 'in saying these words we are *doing* something'. It also manifests the 'poetic function' of language, per Roman Jakobson, displaying a 'focus on the message for its own sake' (1960: 356). As a formula, *'mana, e dina'* follows the previously mentioned metonyms of the good life in traditional Fiji—plentiful food, strong leadership, a happy couple, and so forth—and ties them together with the affirmative and performative chant that aligns *mana* (may it be so) with *dina* (what we have said will come to pass). *Mana* and *dina* are an irreducible dyad whose utterance ties together and accomplishes what has been said, emphasised by the rhythmic, unified clapping and repetition of *muduo* which generally follows, with styles varying in different regions of Fiji.

Mana is also linked with speech in the verb phrase *vosamana* (speak *mana*). In the 1920s, Methodist minister Epeli Rokowaqa published an account of ancient Fiji in a mission magazine, and of the 20 times his history mentions the term *mana*, 13 times it is linked with the verb *vosa*, either in the phrase *vosamana*, as in 'He was a good man and spoke *mana* [i.e. he determined the future by speaking]' (*'Sa turaga vinaka ka dau vosa mana'*), or in more complicated expressions such as 'Those words came to pass' (*'A mana na vosa ko ya'*; Rokowaqa 1926: 16, 54). In two other cases, Rokowaqa mentions the *'mana, e dina'* formula, meaning that in three-quarters of his examples, *mana* is connected to speech.[7]

7 Rokowaqa's 75,000-word account of Fijian history was published as *Ai Tukutuku kei Viti* (meaning *Stories of Fiji*) in 1926. His text contains tales of Fiji's origins, the migrations and wars of the great chiefdoms, and explanations of how the present social order came into being—the chiefly system, orders of hierarchy, and clans' traditional obligations. Rokowaqa had attended the Methodist mission school at Navuloa in the early 1890s (France 1966: 111), and his account of Fijian history has 'a style reminiscent of the Book of Revelation' (Geraghty 1977: 28).

In looking for early appearances of *mana* in the Fijian literature, we have found references to it in the Methodist missionary Jesse Carey's survey of his 'native teachers' in Kadavu Island in the mid-1860s. Of the six times that Carey's texts mention *mana,* it is always used as part of the phrase '*mana, e dina*'. In three of these instances, the phrase is attributed to people attending a healing session who are responding to the words of a traditional priest. In two cases, the speaker's identity is not clear. In one case, from the lyrics of a chant (*meke*), it is a spirit or god who says the words.

Carey's examples from healing ceremonies, which were reported to him by the teacher Joeli Nau, are worth examining for the way they differ on a crucial matter of detail. In the first example, Nau describes a priest praying for a sick person:

> E dua mada na yaqona e laki cabo vua a sa ta[ra]i au tara ga ka bula ga na baca, ni sa oti ko ya ka mama, ka lose ni sa tauya, sa qai masu lakina ka vaka, Ai sevu kei Ravouvou ... kei ira kece ga na Kalou mai na tui cake mai ra tale ga mo dou yalovinaka, ka me bula na mate, era qai vaka, mana e dina, ka sa dina.

> Kava is presented to him, and when received [he says], 'I receive it, and the sick will get well'; after that [the kava] is chewed and mixed. Upon receiving it, he then prays for it like this: 'The offering for Ravouvou ... and all of the gods from the east and from the west as well. Be merciful and let this sick person be cured'. Then they say, 'mana, it is true', and it is true. (Carey 1865: 198)[8]

Thus, this event concludes with the performative utterance of '*mana, e dina*' making the healing effective. In comparison, when '*mana, e dina*' is mentioned in a discussion of sacrifice (*isoro*) made for a priest who is sick, there is a coda added:

8 This passage is also quoted in Tomlinson (2006: 175). While conducting research for that article, Tomlinson worked from a transcript of the original document prepared by an anonymous researcher. Since then, he has consulted a microfilmed copy of the original at the Mitchell Library in Sydney and noticed numerous transcription errors which do not, however, change the meaning of the passage. The Fijian versions of the Carey texts presented here are reproduced verbatim except for bracketed inserts and the deleted names of various traditional gods (indicated by ellipses); the idiosyncratic phrasing and (lack of) punctuation in the originals is retained, as well as the inconsistent verb tenses. The English translation of the first example is a refinement of that presented in Tomlinson (2006).

Nai soro e na vuku ni dua sa tauvi mate, sa vaka oqo. Ke dua na Tabua se liga sa mudu, ka kauta e dua na turaga e na mataqali s[a] yacana nai qaravi, ka laki cabora, ka vaka, Oqo Ratu nai soro e na vukuna na nomu batiniyaqona sa tauvi mate no, ia keitou sa vakawirimadigi, a sa qara vua sa tauvi mate, ia na kenai soro oqo mo lomavinaka me bula, ia, ke vaka ko sa tiko e keri mo vosa mai. Sa qai kaila na bete ka vaka Ai valu! Koi au, a cava talega ko dou tawa kilai au kina? Au sa cakacakava vaka10 ga vei kemudou, ka dou tawa kila ga, e na sega sara ni bula na mate. A sa masu tiko ga na turaga ko ya mo yalovinaka ga me bula, ke vaka e na bula, au na qai tara e dua na nomu Bure vou. Sa qai vakadonuya, io, sa na qai bula; sa qai laki tara na tabua ka vaka au tara ga oqo ka bula ga [na] mate sa qai vaka ko ira kece sa tiko, mana e dina ka sa dina, sa qai masu laka na kamunaga, ka vaka, Au sa qai taura na kamunaga sa kauta mai oqo na qau i qaravi; ka kila ko yau kei Vuetiono…kei ira kece na Kalou vaka [ya]dua ga mai Natuicake, mai ra tale ga meda loma vata me bula na mate. Era qai kaya tale mana e dina, ni sa oti sa qai lako na Bete ka tara na mate me bogi va.

The sacrifice for a sick person is like this. If a whale's tooth or a cut-off hand is taken by a man of a clan, it is called a *qaravi*, and is formally presented as, 'Ratu, this is the sacrifice for your kava priest who is sick, we have cast lots and it pointed towards the sick, hence this is a sacrifice [on his behalf] that you may grant him mercy and let him live. If you are there, may you speak.' The priest then shouts and says, 'A war! It is I, how come you don't recognise me? I have worked ten times already for you and you still don't recognise me, the sick shall not recover.' But the man continued pleading, 'Be merciful and let him live; if he shall live, I shall build you a new temple.' He then conceded and said, 'Yes, he shall live'; then he went and took hold of the whale's tooth and said, 'I touch this, and the sick shall recover'. All those present said, '*mana*, it is true', and it is true, then he prayed over the whale's tooth, 'Now I take this whale's tooth, brought by my servant [or brought as a sacrifice]; and I know, as well as Vuetiono … and all individual gods from the east and the west as well, let us be of one spirit for the sick to get well.' They all said again, '*mana*, it is true', then the priest left to attend to the sick for four nights. (Carey 1865: 201)

Whereas in the first example the words are automatically effective, in the second example the priest leaves to attend to the sick person (another priest) for the ritually significant period of four nights, and this physical attention helps to effect the healing. Thus, in the first example, '*mana, e dina*' is performative in and of itself: people show their agreement and support by chanting the formula after the words of the priest, and the healing comes to pass. In the second example, by comparison, effectiveness seems to depend partly on the healer making sustained contact with the sick.[9]

Because the utterance of *mana* concludes ceremonial speeches so prominently, it is easy to imagine how it might be treated as an indigenous emblem, something that defines Fijian spirituality. Indeed, as we discuss below, the Methodist theologian Ilaitia Sevati Tuwere approaches *mana* in this spirit. Moreover, Sekove Bigitibau has observed how, in his homeland of Nakelo, it is traditional for a person receiving a presentation of kava on others' behalf to say '*kaloumana i dina*', linking traditional deities (*kalou*) to the previously spoken words. (Those on whose behalf the kava is received respond '*mana i dina, sa dina*', confirming and supporting what has been said.) Linking pre-Christian spirits, kava and *mana*, these speech practices are apparently traditional, pre-Christian forms.

Mana? *What* mana?

However, several ethnographic reports tell of other Fijians who consider *mana* to be a foreign term. Buell Quain, who conducted research in Vanualevu in the 1930s, wrote, 'The term *mana*, impersonal supernatural power, is understood at Nakoroka [in Vanualevu] and occurs in ceremonial chants. But the equivalent in the local dialect is *sau*' (1948: 200n30). In other words, people in Nakoroka knew what *mana* meant for other indigenous Fijians, and chanted it; but their term for what

9 Over a century after these reports were written, the anthropologist Barbara Herr wrote a doctoral dissertation on psychology and healing in Fulaga which resonates with Nau's second example. Herr wrote, 'The skilled, mature female vuniwai [healers] know medicines in great detail, and they reported receiving intentional instruction. They also, however, believe that the power to heal in their "fingers" is supernaturally dictated. One vuniwai who was also a good friend emphatically stated on several different occasions "sa bau mana a ligaqu!" (lit. my hands really work), to explain the quickness of a cure at her administration' (Herr 1983: 181). She adds 'or "my hands really have mana"' as a possible second translation, but this is misleading, as there is nothing in the Fijian phrase to indicate that *mana* is a possession.

Quain knew his audience would consider to be *mana* was not *mana*, but *sau*. (Unfortunately, Quain did not elaborate on what he meant by 'equivalence', nor on the local pragmatics of *sau*.) A second example comes from a forthcoming book chapter by the French anthropologist Françoise Cayrol based on her research in Vitilevu. She offers the following observation: 'Nasau people insist that the term mana does not belong to the language of the region. Formerly, this term did not exist there; only the idea of sau was present (Cayrol, n.d.).'

Sau can be defined specifically as 'chiefly power' (Eräsaari 2013: 49) or generally as 'powerful and effectively influential to cause ill or good' (Ravuvu 1983: 120). Bigitibau has observed how *sau* typically refers to individual chiefs and the way their instructions and plans to their people must be followed or else misfortune (accidents, sickness and so forth) will afflict those who have disrespected the chiefs' words.

Theologian Savenaca Vuetanavanua writes, 'On many occasions, *sau* is used interchangeably with mana (especially in Lau) [eastern Fiji]' (Vuetanavanua 2009: 67; see also Ravuvu 1983: 86). Similarly, anthropologist Steven Hooper, also writing of Lau, states that 'the word *sau* is often used as an equivalent to *mana*, although in discussions there was some uncertainty as to whether their meanings were precisely the same' (Hooper 1996: 262). Matt Tomlinson, working in Kadavu, has observed how *mana* and *sau* are spoken of together in Methodist discourse, used as a pair in statements meant to glorify God by emphasising God's ultimate power (see Tomlinson 2009b: 76). Bigitibau, who has extensive research experience throughout Fiji, has come to conclude that although indigenous Fijians distinguish between *mana* and *sau* in speech, understandings of their differences generally remain unarticulated.

Mana is now prominent in the writings of Fijian authors, and is generally treated in the ways that people from Nakoroka and Nasau seemingly distrust. That is, it is treated as a thing—as spiritual power. As Tomlinson has argued elsewhere (2006), and as suggested above, *mana*'s notional transformation into a thing—the kind of transformation that Roger M. Keesing (1984) accused anthropologists themselves of generating—seems to have been influenced by Methodist missionaries' Bible translations.

In becoming thinglike, *mana* has also become strongly associated with the power of chiefs. For example, education scholar Unaisi Nabobo-Baba, in her monograph on indigenous Fijian social science research methodology, writes, 'Daily life among the Vugalei [people] includes talk of the mana of chiefs, which is said to be divine' if they have been installed by the people of the land (Nabobo-Baba 2006: 51). Similarly, Asesela Ravuvu wrote that direct or indirect physical contact with a chief was forbidden to lower-ranked people because in making such contact, 'one is not only undermining the veneration and sacredness accorded to the chief, thus weakening his authority and prestige, but one is also being contaminated and affected adversely by his *mana*' (Ravuvu 1983: 92). Semi Seruvakula, writing in Fijian, cautions that 'it is very dangerous for us to touch the heads and necks of our chiefs, because those are the site of *mana* and the seat of the *sau* of the land and people' ('*Ia na uludra li se domodra na noda gone turaga sa qai ka rerevaki sara meda bau tara yani, ka ni oya na itikotiko ni mana ka idabedabe ni sau ni vanua*') (Seruvakula 2000: 36).[10]

10 The three most incisive recent anthropological treatments of chiefliness and *mana* in Fiji have been those of Steven Hooper, John D. Kelly and Matti Eräsaari. Hooper deftly observes the complications of analysing Fijian *mana* and provides useful summary characterisations, noting *mana*'s connection with chiefs' effective speech, with healing, and with places like the sea (Hooper 1996: 257–59). He also provides useful lengthy transcripts in Fijian of indigenous Fijians' own statements about *mana* (see also Hooper 1982).

Kelly argues that the *mana* of Fijian chiefs must be understood as a term dialogically co-constituted with Indo-Fijian *shanti* ('a conception of religious peace and well-being, the calm after the storm and the experience of grace') (Kelly 2011: 236). The most inspired part of Kelly's argument is his claim that the relative lack of lethal violence in Fiji's coups is due 'almost entirely to the valorization of *shanti*' by Indo-Fijians, more than three-quarters of whom were Hindus in the mid-1990s and who were the main targets of physical aggression by militant Fijian Christians during the coups of 1987 and 2000 (Kelly 2011: 245). The least convincing part of his argument is his poetic claim that where power (as *mana*) is truth for indigenous Fijians, truth (as *shanti*) is power for Indo-Fijians (see also Kelly 2005). The equation of *mana* with truth, as stated above, is based on the misleading equation of the terms *mana* and *dina* due to their use together in ritual speech (see Kelly 2011: 240; see also Hocart 1914; Sahlins 1985; for a critique see Tomlinson 2009a). Kelly's most provocative statement, not yet developed into a full argument, is that 'devotional Hindu values have fundamentally challenged and are altering the practices and significances of ethnic Fijian *mana*' (Kelly 2011: 246n4); he adds teasingly, 'here lies the truest scandal, if it is true'. This claim, as phrased, is unquestionably true to the extent that indigenous Fijian and Indo-Fijian histories have developed in dialogue with each other since the late nineteenth century: with long-term engagement, there is necessarily challenge and alteration. But an in-depth argument with supporting ethnohistorical and linguistic detail on interactions between those speaking of power in terms of *mana* and those speaking of truth in terms of *shanti*, with an eye to reciprocal indigenous uptake of *shanti* and Indo-Fijian uptake of *mana*, has not yet been made.

Finally, Eräsaari analyses *mana* and *sau* with reference to objects in ceremonial exchange, namely kava and whales' teeth, and notes that when *mana* is seen as a practice, 'it appears much less "supernatural" or religious than commonly understood. Observed within a sequence where an intention is first declared, then accepted and finally announced, *mana* becomes the outcome of strictly controlled conditions that ensure the performative quality of these rituals'—with nothing, in short, miraculous about it (Eräsaari 2013: 156).

It is important to emphasise that *mana* is not tied exclusively to chiefliness. As seen in the examples above, traditional priests could speak in dialogue with their audiences to act (with) *mana*. In another example, from a tale told by Rokowaqa, carpenters speak *mana* when a man named Cameletamana steals an axe from them. The carpenters tell the thief's fellow villagers: 'Whoever stole our axe, he and his descendants will not be able to build boats.' Hence, according to Rokowaqa, 'Those words came to pass [*A mana na vosa ko ya*], enduring until today, the descendants of Camelematana, who live at Navunivesi, do not know how to build boats' (Rokowaqa 1926: 54).[11] It is also important to note that much discourse in modern Fiji characterises history in terms of loss, implying that the ability to act with *mana* is waning for humans, as described at length in Tomlinson (2009b). In the old days, many Fijians indicate, the ancestors were socially unified and acted with strength and propriety under truly authoritative chiefs. Today, in contrast, many people say that chiefs are unable to act in the powerful ways they once did and the social order is breaking down. Figures who can act more effectively are the ancestral spirits who sometimes curse the living. In short, *mana* in contemporary Fiji is often a diagnostic of what people feel they are losing or have lost.

Methodist theologians do not fully endorse this diagnosis of the decline of *mana*. Instead, they present *mana* as something to which they have a special claim as God's representatives. The balance of power between church leaders and hereditary chiefs, all considered to be under God's ultimate authority, is the site of theological argument to which we now turn.

Methodist theologies

The Methodist Church in Fiji has had a close relationship with many of Fiji's high chiefs for more than a century and a half, but it has had a problematic relationship with the national government in recent years. Fiji became independent from Great Britain in 1970 and has suffered four coups d'état since. In the coups of 1987 and 2000,

11 In the original: '*O koya sa butakoca neimami matau, e na sega sara ni kila na ta waqa, me yacovi ira sara nona kawa … A mana na vosa ko ya, sa yaco tikoga edaidai, ko ira ga na kawa i Camelematana [*sic*], era tiko oqo mai Navunivesi era sega sara ni kila na ta waqa.*'

conservatives in the Methodist Church tended to support the actions of coup leaders by justifying them in the name of indigenous rights and against the rights of non-indigenous citizens, primarily Indo-Fijians, the descendants of indentured immigrants who arrived in Fiji between 1879 and 1916. Progressives and moderates in the Methodist Church were marginalised. In the most recent coup in 2006, however, the Methodist leadership opposed the takeover of government—it was a coup in which the indigenous-dominated military removed an indigenous-led government—and since then the Church has suffered serious repercussions, including the arrest of leading ministers and repeated cancellation of its annual conference.

In this political context, defining the proper relationship between divine and human power is a matter of urgent concern for many citizens. A theological analysis of the *mana* or *sau* of chiefs versus that of church leaders is thus a pressing task, not simply an academic exercise. It is a task that needs to attend to Christianity's profound engagement with the *vanua*, which means 'land', 'people under a chief', and 'chiefdom', and connotes the system of chiefly leadership, land ownership and ritual exchange which is 'tradition' writ large and publicly displayed. The term *vanua* is often heard in Fijian religious and political discourse, and it carries strong emotional resonance: the *vanua* is a homeland, a gift from God, and a group identity, but it is also under threat from modern forces which threaten to dissolve indigenous Fijian unity and compromise land ownership. 'The *vanua* and the Methodist church are regarded as inseparable by most Methodist church members', as Bigitibau has observed (see Degei 2007: vi), but chiefs, who lead the *vanua*, also incarnate ancestor gods and therefore might plausibly derive at least some of their efficacy from a non-Christian source (Hooper 1996: 260; see also Nayacakalou 1961: 7; Quain 1948: 200–201).

The foremost thinker on the subject of Fijian *mana* is theologian Ilaitia Sevati Tuwere, who has served as principal of the Pacific Theological College in Suva (1982–88), president of the Methodist Church in Fiji (1996–98), and an honorary lecturer at the School of Theology at the

University of Auckland.[12] In 1992, Tuwere earned his doctorate from the Melbourne College of Divinity with a dissertation on the theology of the Fijian *vanua*. In 2002, he published a revised version of his dissertation as *Vanua: Towards a Fijian Theology of Place*; here, we discuss this book rather than the dissertation.

In *Vanua*, Tuwere devotes an entire section to *mana* (the book's other three sections are 'Birth', a general introduction; 'Face', on God's emplaced presence; and 'Ear', on the need to listen and to respect silence). In his discussion of *mana*, Tuwere uses the term to articulate various contradictions in Fijian understandings of spirituality. He writes that it 'involves a semantic domain that includes a number of other terms such as *tabu*, presence, blessing, success, creative force, fertility and more', but also writes that it is integral to sorcery (Tuwere 2002: 142, 161). *Mana* is implicated in social control, but also in ultimate freedom: Jesus 'is the source of all life-giving *mana*', and in sacrificing himself on the cross he gave 'lasting *mana* for all those who believe' and 'for the whole world to have healing and integrative *mana*'; *mana* is power, but also powerlessness as seen in Jesus' humility and despair (136, 141, 155, 156, 164, 166–68). Keeping these irreconcilable meanings in tension, Tuwere writes that '*Mana*, illustrating the reconciling work of God in Christ … does not exhaust the nature of God but … is the only meaningful way of describing God and what his power may mean in the Fijian context' (165).

In his radically inclusive approach to *mana*, Tuwere, curiously, does not say much about *sau*. He mentions that the concepts are 'related' and observes *sau*'s resonance with Māori *hau* (72–73, 147), but does not firmly distinguish the terms. He does, however, cast a politely critical eye on the authority of chiefs, writing:

> Chiefs are vital as ritual brokers between spirits and people … But *mana* is not simply vested in someone's person or self. It demonstrates itself outwardly through chiefly qualities or *i tovo vakaturaga* [chiefly customs/behaviour]. I often hear young men in the village saying,

12 We refer to people as theologians if they have earned a Master's or Doctorate in theology. Savenaca Vuetanavanua received his Master's in 2009 from the University of Auckland for a thesis on chiefly installation ceremonies, and three others mentioned in this chapter received their Master's degrees from the Pacific Theological College in Suva: Lesila Raitiqa in 2000 with a thesis titled 'Jesus: Healer of Vanua Sickness and Mana of the Vanua', Apete Toko in 2007 with a thesis on post-coup reconciliation, and Lisa Meo in 1993 with a thesis on garment industry workers.

> *Ke ra vinaka walega na noda i liuliu* (if only our leaders were good), referring to traditional leaders in general and implying that *mana* is slipping away from its source. In pre-Christian time[s], lack of *mana* indicated a defect in the chief's relation with the gods so the rule of the club [i.e., murder] was applied. Today, no action is taken, people merely grumble and speculate. (Tuwere 2002: 138)

In Tuwere's theology, those old gods do have *mana* (162), but it is a misused *mana* that is life-destroying rather than life-affirming. To really belong to the land, he argues, Fijians must seek 'new *mana* in Christ' (158–69): new *mana* which can overcome the nationalist, pro-chiefly forces that have led Fiji into multiple coups; new *mana* to straighten out misguided Church leaders who have enabled and even exacerbated the political turmoil in Fiji.

A Methodist theologian whose understanding of *mana* echoes Tuwere's in some ways, but who emphasises a distinction between *mana* and *sau*, is deaconess Lesila Raitiqa. In her Master's thesis, she refers to Jesus as 'the True *Mana* of the *Vanua* [land and people]', and writes that '*Mana* is something wholesome and good … [and] belongs to the spirit or the divine realm', even as it is manifest in human qualities (Raitiqa 2000: 53, 63). These human qualities include markedly aesthetic ones as well as ones associated with raw power. For example, Raitiqa identifies *mana* with 'the quiet dignity of a chief or royal person' and 'the beauty of kinship' as well as special strength and survival (52–53). *Sau*, for Raitiqa, is dangerous and frightening, and discovered only when one is afflicted (58). She quotes from an interview she conducted with scholar Pio Manoa in which he stated that '*mana* is the fruit of the *sau*', but Raitiqa characterises the relationship somewhat differently: '*sau* is the executor of *mana* … A chief would utter an angry word or pronounce a blessing, but it is the *sau* which [affects] the one for whom the blessing or curse was intended' (58–59). Ethically, for Raitiqa, *mana* is entirely positive—'wholesome and good'—but *sau*, as executive power, is ethically ambiguous.

Another theologian whose understanding of *mana* resonates with that of Tuwere is Apete Toko, whom Tomlinson interviewed on 10 June 2009 when Toko was the Secretary for the Men's Fellowship of the Methodist Church. Asked about *mana* and *sau*, Toko mentioned the performative use of *mana* in ceremonies—he summarised it as 'Let it be. *Me yaco mai* [Let it be]. *Emeni* [Amen]. So be it'—and then moved on to a second meaning:

> E vaka e jiko e dua na, e dua na vakabauta ni tu e so na mana. Na mana ni vanua, na mana ni lotu.... Jiko na mana ni vanua. Na mana rau veiwekani jiko kei na karua ni vosa e vatokai na sau. Na mana ni sau, e dua sa buli me turaga se me tui me liuliu ni, ni dua na vanua. Ah, na mana ni na italatala. Baleta na cava? Baleta ni o koya sa, sa buli, sa lumuji me tamata ni Kalou, talai ni Kalou. Talatala is a person of God. Not only that, but he is anointed. Kevaka sa tu kina e dua na mana levu se sa tu vua e dua na sau, e rawa ni vosa e na yaco na ka e tukuna. Se kevaka e masu me da qarauna na nona masu. Na ka sa na tukuna mai sa na yaco. Ia kena ibalebale na mana vata kei na sau e vaka e sema tu kei na dua na, kei na dua na kaukaua levu e jiko.

> It's like there is a, a belief that some *mana* exists. The *mana* of the land and people, the *mana* of the church ... There is the *mana* of the land and people. *Mana* is related to a second word, *sau*. The *mana* of *sau*, when one is installed as a chief or paramount chief in order to be the leader of a land. Ah, the *mana* of the church minister. Why? Because he is, he's installed, he's anointed to be a person of God, messenger of God. The church minister is a person of God. Not only that, but he is anointed. If there is a great *mana* or he has *sau*, he can speak and what he said will happen. Or if he prays, we should pay attention to his prayer. What he says, it will happen. This means that it's like *mana* and *sau* are joined in a, in a great power that exists.

Like Tuwere and Raitiqa, Toko ties *mana* to both God and humanity: it is 'of the land and people' as well as 'of the church'. He mentions chiefs in order to explain *sau*, but then, observing that church ministers are installed or anointed in their positions like chiefs are (or at least as they are supposed to be—many chiefs today are not actually installed; see Eräsaari 2013: 222–23), Toko focuses on the position of the minister, who as a 'person of God' is linked to *mana* and *sau* alike 'in a great power that exists'. In short, Toko begins with a Tuwere-style model of *mana* rooted in the land and, like Tuwere, goes on to suggest that church ministers are now the ones with the most effective connection to divine *mana*, which is to say ultimate *mana*. In this way, Toko's discussion of *mana* and *sau* resonates with an earlier discussion that Tomlinson had with a Methodist catechist who stated bluntly, '*Mana* and *sau* is with the people of God [i.e., church officials]. Less is with the chiefs of the land of Fiji' (see Tomlinson 2009b: 76).[13]

Lisa Meo, another Fijian Methodist theologian, wrote an entry for the *Dictionary of Feminist Theologies* in which she describes the Pacific Islands as patriarchal places but does not mention chieftainship specifically. She does, however, explicitly prise open a gap between *mana* and *sau* in the same way as Raitiqa. Meo also emphasises the distinction's ethical aspects, drawing a sharper line than Raitiqa does:

> For Pacific Island people, theologies are an integration of traditional and Christian beliefs of the nature of God and gods, and a craving for God's power. God's power brings blessings, *mana*, and to be without God's power means a curse, or *sau*. One can interpret feminist theologies as an acknowledgment of God's power that will bring forth empowerment for the powerless, especially, in this case, women. (Meo 1996: 109)

For Meo, the key distinction between *mana* and *sau* is the ethical evaluation of *mana* as blessing and therefore inherently good, and *sau* as cursing and therefore inherently bad. *Mana* is godly and *sau* is godless. Her identification of both *mana* and *sau* as Pan-Pacific concepts is highly problematic (see also Vamarasi 1987), but her theology is noteworthy for making a clear, explicit break that the

13 This catechist's life had been profoundly influenced by Toko, which is one of the reasons Tomlinson sought out Toko for an interview (see Tomlinson 2009b: 200–202). On *mana* in relation to chiefs and church leaders, see also Nabobo-Baba's discussion of 'public *mana* providers' who 'are people who must be present before a function is considered *dodonu* (correct); they provide *mana* and blessings to an occasion'; such public *mana* providers include chiefs and elders, she observes, but also 'increasingly today, a church minister' (Nabobo-Baba 2006: 67–68).

scholars quoted above do not make: *mana* is ultimately a thing of the Church and *sau* is not, meaning the Church has an ethically grounded right to claim power on behalf of the powerless.[14]

Conclusion

What does this wealth of information actually tell us?

At the very least, it reveals that some indigenous Fijians think *mana* is foreign and irrelevant, and others think it is the key to the order of the universe and eternal spiritual salvation. *Mana* cannot be understood without *sau*, but whether they draw together in similarity as 'a great power' or diverge in opposition as blessings versus curses is not something on which all indigenous Fijians agree. *Mana* has key aesthetic dimensions, both in its poetic chanting at ceremonies and in theological characterisations of it in terms of dignity and beauty (Raitiqa 2000: 52). It has key ethical dimensions, too, especially when opposed to *sau*, as in Meo's feminist theology, which explicitly associates *sau* with the power to curse. These aesthetic and ethical dimensions should both expand and nuance scholarly equations of *mana* with power and, reading against the grain of early Methodist missionary translations, should trouble any equation of *mana* and

14 In 2009, Tomlinson also interviewed two Christian ministers who were not theologians but who offered especially thoughtful contributions on the topics of *mana* and *sau*. A Seventh-day Adventist minister in Suva, Timoci Beitaki, said that:

> *mana* is God's, it comes from Him, eh? … *Mana* belongs to God in heaven because he made things out of nothing. But people in positions of leadership because they are leading, are respected in a chiefly way, and are considered to be sacred chiefs because they are appointed by God, are installed by God, but *mana* is not with them [the chiefs] … it is with God, *sau* is with them [the chiefs] (*ki vua na Kalou koya e nona na mana, e? … Na mana e nona na Kalou ni lomalagi e, baleta o koya e cakava na ka mai, mai na sega ni dua na ka. Ia na tamata na itutu ni veiliutaki baleta ni sa mai veiliutaki sa rokovi vakaturaga ka namaki ni tamata e turaga tabu saka yani era sa mai vua na Kalou, e buli tiko [ira] na Kalou, ia, e sega ni tiko vei ira na mana … e tiko vua na Kalou, e tiko vei ira na sau*). (Interview, 8 June 2009)

A Fijian Methodist superintendent minister (*talatala qase*), Maika Sorowaqa of the Matuku district in Lau, eastern Fiji, equated *sau* with cursing like Meo does, explaining, 'here's an example. You say something, it happens. It's like this, if I should curse you. You will go out today, even if you haven't heard what I said, you will meet with misfortune. You'll go and get hurt, eh? … That's one translation of *sau*' ('*kena vakatautauvata oqo. Mo cavuta e dua na ka, yaco. E va beka qo, me'u cursetaki iko. O na lako nikua, ke o sega ni rogoca noqu vosa, o na sotava e dua na ka rarawa. O lako ga, mavoa, e? … Ya dua na ivakadewa ni sau*'). When asked whether *mana* and *sau* were similar or different, Sorowaqa replied that in his opinion they are 'in the same family' (*matavuvale vata*) (Interview, 2 June 2009).

truth or *mana* and miracles. As we have suggested in this chapter, Methodist theologians who attempt to claim the moral authority of the church against the executive authority of chiefs, speaking (with) *mana* as they do, face the dilemma of valorising tradition and the chiefly system as keystones of indigenous Fijian identity while both depending on and trying to supersede them.

References

Archival Repository

Carey, Jesse. 1865. Manuscript in the Methodist Overseas Mission Collection, reel CY509. Mitchell Library, Sydney.

Books, journal articles and chapters

Austin, J.L. 1975 (2nd ed.). *How to Do Things with Words*, ed. J.O. Urmson and Marina Sbisà. Cambridge, MA: Harvard University Press.

Brison, Karen. 2012. From mana to anointing: Reformulating Indigenous Fijian agency through global Pentecostalism. Paper presented at the American Anthropological Association meeting, San Francisco, 16 November.

Cayrol, Françoise. n.d. How would we have got here? Unpublished book chapter.

Degei, Sekove Bigitibau. 2007. The challenge to Fijian Methodism—the *Vanua*, identity, ethnicity and change. M.S.Sc. thesis, University of Waikato, Hamilton.

Eräsaari, Matti. 2013. 'We are the originals': A study of value in Fiji. PhD dissertation, University of Helsinki.

Firth, Raymond, Richard Feinberg, Karen Ann Watson-Gegeo (eds). 1996. *Leadership and Change in the Western Pacific: Essays Presented to Sir Raymond Firth on the Occasion of His Ninetieth Birthday*. London: The Athlone Press.

France, Peter. 1966. The Kaunitoni migration: Notes on the genesis of a Fijian tradition. *Journal of Pacific History* 1: 107–13.

Geraghty, Paul. 1977. How a myth is born—the story of the Kaunitoni story. *Mana* 2(1): 25–29.

Hale, Horatio. 1846. United States Exploring Expedition during the Years 1838, 1839, 1840, 1841, 1842: *Ethnography and Philology*, vol. 6. Philadelphia, PA: C. Sherman.

Hazlewood, David. 1850. *A Feejeean and English Dictionary*. Viwa, Fiji: Wesleyan Mission Press.

Hermann, Elfriede (ed.). 2011. *Changing Contexts, Shifting Meanings: Transformations of Cultural Traditions in Oceania*. Honolulu: University of Hawai'i Press in association with the Honolulu Academy of Arts.

Herr, Barbara. 1983. Gender and illness among Lauan Fijians: Somatic and affective disorder. PhD dissertation, University of California, Los Angeles.

Hocart, A.M. 1914. Mana. *Man* 14(46): 97–101.

Hooper, Steven. 1982. A study of valuables in the chiefdom of Lau, Fiji. PhD dissertation, University of Cambridge.

——. 1996. Who are the chiefs? Chiefship in Lau, Eastern Fiji. In *Leadership and Change in the Western Pacific: Essays Presented to Sir Raymond Firth on the Occasion of His Ninetieth Birthday*, ed. Raymond Firth, Richard Feinberg, Karen Ann Watson-Gegeo, pp. 239–71. London: The Athlone Press.

Jakobson, Roman. 1960. Closing statement: Linguistics and poetics. In *Style in Language*, ed. T.A. Sebeok, pp. 350–77. Cambridge, MA and New York: Technology Press of Massachusetts Institute of Technology and John Wiley & Sons.

Keesing, Roger M. 1984. Rethinking 'mana'. *Journal of Anthropological Research* 40(1): 137–56.

Kelly, John D. 2005. Boycotts and coups, *Shanti* and *mana* in Fiji. *Ethnohistory* 52(1): 13–27.

——. 2011. *Shanti* and *mana:* The loss and recovery of culture under postcolonial conditions in Fiji. In *Changing Contexts, Shifting Meanings: Transformations of Cultural Traditions in Oceania*, ed. Elfriede Hermann, pp. 235–49. Honolulu: University of Hawai'i Press in association with the Honolulu Academy of Arts.

Lempert, Michael. 2010. Review of Gluck and Tsing, *Words in Motion*. *The Australian Journal of Anthropology* 21(3): 393–94.

Meo, Lisa. 1996. Feminist theologies, Pacific Island. In *Dictionary of Feminist Theologies*, ed. Letty M. Russell and J. Shannon Clarkson, pp. 108–10. London: Mowbray.

Nabobo-Baba, Unaisi. 2006. *Knowing and Learning: An Indigenous Fijian Approach*. Suva: Institute of Pacific Studies, University of the South Pacific.

Nayacakalou, R.R. 1961. Traditional Authority and Religious Sanctions in Fiji. Unpublished seminar paper delivered at the London School of Economics, November 3. Typescript at Pacific Collection, Hamilton Library, University of Hawai'i–Manoa.

Quain, Buell. 1948. *Fijian Village*. Chicago: University of Chicago Press.

Raitiqa, Lesila Taranatoba. 2000. Jesus: Healer of vanua sickness and mana of the vanua. M.Th. thesis, Pacific Theological College, Suva.

Ravuvu, Asesela D. 1983. *Vaka i Taukei: The Fijian Way of Life*. Suva: Institute of Pacific Studies, University of the South Pacific.

Rokowaqa, Epeli. 1926. Ai Tukutuku kei Viti. *Methodist Missionary Magazine* (April): 1–84.

Russell, Letty M. and J. Shannon Clarkson (eds) 1996. *Dictionary of Feminist Theologies*. London: Mowbray.

Ryle, Jacqueline. 2001. My God, my land: Interwoven paths of Christianity and tradition in Fiji. PhD dissertation, School of Oriental and African Studies, University of London.

Sahlins, Marshall. 1985. *Islands of History*. Chicago: University of Chicago Press.

Sebeok, T.A. (ed.). 1960. *Style in Language*. Cambridge, MA and New York: Technology Press of Massachusetts Institute of Technology and John Wiley & Sons.

Seruvakula, Semi B. 2000. *Bula Vakavanua*. Suva: Institute of Pacific Studies, University of the South Pacific.

Tabana ni Vosa kei Na iTovo Vakaviti (Institute of Fijian Language and Culture). 2005. *Na iVolavosa Vakaviti* (Fijian Dictionary). Suva: Institute of Fijian Language and Culture.

Tomlinson, Matt. 2006. Retheorizing mana: Bible translation and discourse of loss in Fiji. *Oceania* 76(2): 173–85.

——. 2009a. Efficacy, truth, and silence: Language ideologies in Fijian Christian conversions. *Comparative Studies in Society and History* 51(1): 64–90.

——. 2009b. *In God's Image: The Metaculture of Fijian Christianity*. Berkeley: University of California Press.

Tuwere, Ilaitia S. 2002. *Vanua: Towards a Fijian Theology of Place*. Suva and Auckland: Institute of Pacific Studies at the University of the South Pacific and College of St John the Evangelist.

Vamarasi, Jotama. 1987. The *mana* of the word. In *South Pacific Theology: Papers from the Consultation on Pacific Theology, Papua New Guinea, January 1986*, pp. 48–51. Parramatta and Oxford: World Vision International South Pacific and Regnum Books.

Vuetanavanua, Savenaca. 2009. Veibuli (Chiefly Installation): A theological exploration. M.Th. thesis, University of Auckland.

Wilkes, Charles. 1845. *Narrative of the United States' Exploring Expedition, during the Years 1838, 1839, 1840, 1841, 1842*, condensed and abridged. London: Whittaker and Co.

Williams, Thomas. 1982 [1858]. *Fiji and the Fijians*, vol. 1, ed. G.S. Rowe. Suva: Fiji Museum.

10

Claiming *Pule*, Manifesting *Mana*: Ordinary Ethics and Pentecostal Self-making in Samoa

Jessica Hardin

Mid-week at a week-long revival at an Assemblies of God Church in a village near Apia, Pastor Keni began his sermon by saying, 'When you fellowship with God, he pours His spirit and *pulea* [governs] the people who believe in God. This will begin the spiritual life and the righteous life'. The relationship, he explained, 'is warm and close, and He moves'. Especially when 'you pray and fast, He keeps you warm and will do things for His people'. He continued, 'we have this revival to ask the *mana* [power] to come down and to renew our life. We sing in the *mana*. We dance in the *mana*.' He finished by saying 'remember our church is a Pentecostal church. A Pentecostal church is full of the *mana* of the Holy Spirit, where we see the signs of the *mana*, where we see the miracles of the church, where we see changes in lives, where we see love and togetherness from God'. This revival sermon aimed to teach congregants how to bring the *pule* (authority) of God into the world and the blessings of God into individual lives through the bestowal of *mana*. The congregants were told that through faith and a personal relationship with God, divine *pule* is brought into being. They must pray and fast to bring about this relationship as a way to bring *mana* into their lives. Through celebrating, witnessing and manifesting *mana*, individual lives as well as communities would change.

Mana is defined in Samoan as divine power or God's grace (Anae 1998; Schoeffel personal communication, 2 November 2015). The Samoan definition resonates with Hawaiian definitions of *mana* as 'power originating from a spiritual source' (Silva 1997: 91) and the Māori notion of *mana* defined as 'power, prestige, authority, control, "psychic force," spiritual power, charisma' (Salesa 2011: ix). Wende Elizabeth Marshall, also writing of Hawai'i, suggests that *mana* is 'more than a theory, *mana* is a relationship and a practice that in precolonial times was the source of health, vitality and abundance, in which a thriving world was the co-creation of divinity, humanity, and nature: fractal and indivisible' (Marshall 2012: 88). Most broadly, *mana* 'is an indigenous ontology' (Marshall 2012: 88; see also Kame'eleihiwa 1992; Shore 1989; Valeri 1985) and 'a pan-Polynesian concept of divinely sanctioned power and efficacy' (Henderson 2010: 310); it is spiritual power and prestige (Tengan, Ka'ili and Fonoti 2010) and spiritual authority and sovereignty (Meleisea 1997: 469). In this chapter, I examine the related meanings and uses of *pule* and *mana*, which, when invoked together, help to configure each other.[1] The relational invocation of *pule* and *mana* is a strategic, yet ordinary, everyday ethical practice for Pentecostal Christians.

While *mana* and *pule* are concepts shared among Christians in Samoa, I focus on two everyday uses of the terms: first, how Pentecostal Christians are taught to manifest *mana*, which is a capacity that is supposed to be available to all born-again believers; second, how *mana* and *pule* are invoked in interdenominational contexts. Claiming *pule* and channelling *mana* mediates tensions surrounding Pentecostal Christians striving for individual agency and indigenous notions of flexible and context-specific notions of agency, which are also expressed in mainline Christianity. Pentecostal Christians are explicitly taught how to manage individual agency in ethical ways through cultivating a personal relationship with God, which enables supplicants to become agents of *mana*. Claiming *pule* and channelling

1 Others have also argued that *mana* is relational with other terms such as *tapu* (Samoan) and *sau* (Fijian). Bradd Shore argues that *tapu* 'point[s] to alternative conditions of *mana*' (Shore 1989: 148). *Tapu*, according to Shore, is 'symbolically formalized and thereby focused *mana*' (1989: 150); it implies potency, respect, and danger. *Tapu* 'represents generative power (*mana*) in its contained form' (Shore 1989: 149). *Tapu* thus refers to the productive containment of *mana* in the bodies of *matai* (titled chiefs). Matt Tomlinson (2006; see also Tomlinson and Bigitibau, this volume) argues that *sau* (spiritual power) is a term used in parallel to *mana* (efficacy) in Fijian discourse.

mana are thus discursive tools for managing tensions surrounding agency by allowing born-again Christians to de-centre individual agency and foreground God's agency. In everyday life in Samoa there is a hierarchical imperative of defaulting to titled or high status people. The three most widely circulating criticisms in Samoa—*fiapalagi* (to try or want to be white), *fiapotu* (to try or want to be smart), and accusations that suggest pride, including *fiamaualuga* (wanting to be high) or *mimita* (to be boastful)—suggest that claiming authority and power is difficult because of a general bias against individual agency and non-titled authority (see also Gershon 2006: 145). The personal and individual relationship with God encouraged in Pentecostal Christianity heightens these already present anxieties about individual agency and authority (see also Eriksen 2014).

I examine *mana* and *pule* through the lens of what Michael Lambek calls 'ordinary ethics' to explore how claiming divine *pule* and *mana* is a strategic and ordinary way to deflect individual agency. Focusing on '"ordinary" implies an ethics that is relatively tacit, grounded in agreement rather than rule, in practice rather than knowledge or belief and happening without calling undue attention to itself' (Lambek 2010: 2). Similarly, selfhood requires embodied and discursive labour that is often a tacit, taken-for-granted, orientational process (Csordas 1994: ix) and an embodied and historically situated practical knowledge (Battaglia 1995: 3). Manifesting *mana*, and its pair *pule*, are discursive tools of everyday ethical practice that enable believers to speak and act with culturally recognised authority. Claiming divine authority and channelling divine power through the self are everyday ways that Pentecostal Christians in Samoa carve out distinct (i.e. different from mainline Christianity) and ethical ways of generating power in ways that are legible and valued across Christianities.

Mana and *pule* are evidence of the extraordinary qualities of God, and channelled into everyday life events that are also extraordinary—healing, sickness—yet Pentecostal Christians are taught to tend to *mana* and *pule* in ways that are *supposed* to be ordinary and available to every born-again believer. As the preacher noted at the beginning of this chapter, 'Remember our church is a Pentecostal church'; Pentecostal Christians are encouraged to see their connection to the Holy Spirit as something special to them but also something they should learn to take for granted. Thus in this case, the ordinary aspects of ethics point to an ideal way to relate to God and God's immanence, which in practice is often a 'precarious achievement' (Lempert 2013: 371). I draw on Michael Lempert's (2013) recognition that there is a great deal of discursive and embodied labour involved in ethical practice. As such, I trace how in claiming *pule* and harnessing *mana* these practices are a way to negotiate tensions surrounding individual agency. While claiming *pule* and channelling *mana* ought to be ordinary and taken for granted, my interlocutors 'strain[ed] to make the ethical not just effective but intersubjectively evident' (Lempert 2013: 371). In other words, claiming *pule* and manifesting *mana* are discursive ways of deflecting individual agency in order to bring ethical personhood into being.

To develop this argument, I focus on how claiming *pule* and harnessing *mana* are basic skills taught in sermons and practiced in healing prayers. In the first section of this chapter I present excerpts from sermons at a Pentecostal church to analyse how Pentecostal Christians are taught to manifest *mana* in their own lives through the everyday practices of prayer and fasting. These sermons show how Pentecostal Christians are explicitly taught what *ought* to be taken-for-granted and ordinary. In the second section, I analyse how healing leaders carefully proclaim the *pule* of God as a way to explicitly harness the *mana* of God. This section shows the discursive labour involved in authorising individuals as agents of God. Together, these two sections show how through practice Pentecostal Christians bring *mana* into being through cultivating and representing a direct and personal relationship with the divine. In the third section, I briefly present the wider context of anthropological investigations on self-making in Samoa to argue that by articulating a relationship between *mana* and *pule*, Pentecostal Christians de-centre individual agency while revealing the divine as the source of efficacious action. I trace the ways that born-again Christians are encouraged to harness divine power through ethical self-making, which in turn helps to shape a social world that is suspicious of individual (and non-ranked) authority.

Background

Samoa is marked as a Christian nation—the oft-sighted motto of Samoa is '*Fa'avae i le Atua Samoa*' ('Samoa is founded on God'). Christianity is embedded in Samoan hierarchies, as *matai* (titled chiefs) are often the elders or deacons of mainline congregations. Church institutions reflect missionisation strategies, which privileged local autonomy and Samoan strategies of accepting Christianity in ways that served local hierarchies and rivalries. Cluny Macpherson and La'avasa Macpherson write, 'The church is not seen as having inserted itself in and dominating Samoan custom. It is seen rather as something that Samoans inserted into the Samoan hierarchy in ways that ensured they maintained control of both institution and hierarchy' (Macpherson and Macpherson 2009: 108). The original missionary churches, now mainline churches, including Congregational, Methodist and Catholic, maintain the majority of adherents. The Congregational Christian Church Samoa (n.d.) reports having 192 churches and, according to the 2011 Census (Samoan Bureau of Statistics 2012), 51,131 members or 31.8 per cent of the population over age five.[2] The World Council of Churches reports that the Methodist church in Samoa has a membership of 35,983 and 279 pastors (World Council of Churches n.d.); the 2011 census recorded membership to be 22,079 (Samoan Bureau of Statistics 2012). The 2011 census recorded Catholic membership to be 31,221 or 19.4 per cent of the population (Samoan Bureau of Statistics 2012).

Evangelical churches are marked as *lotu fou* (new churches) or *lotu patipati* (clapping churches), referring to the worship style. The first evangelical churches arrived in both Samoa and American Samoa in the 1950s (Ernst 2012). The most prominent of the evangelical churches is the Assemblies of God (AOG). By the 1970s, AOG churches began to grow rapidly and by 2002 there were 64 churches (Ernst 2012; Pagaialii 2006, 2012). The AOG reports having three Bible schools, 108 pastors, and 18,000 adherents (World Assemblies of God Fellowship, 2010). The 2011 census recorded AOG membership to be 12,868 or 8 per cent of the population (Samoan Bureau of Statistics 2012). There are several evangelical churches local to Samoa, including Worship Center and Peace Chapel, as well as others that originate elsewhere, including the Church of the Nazarene and Open Brethren (Figure 20). Membership for these churches is difficult to assess because the 2011 census includes all these evangelical churches as 'other'.

2 The total Samoan population is just under 190,000 and the population over age five is approximately 160,000.

Figure 20. A pastor from Glory House preaches at a tent revival in Apia, 2012.

Source: Photograph by Jessica Hardin.

What is apparent from the census data, however, is that membership for mainline churches (Congregational, Methodist, Catholic) is slowly declining while membership in evangelical churches and other *lotu fou* (The Church of Jesus Christ of Latter-Day Saints (LDS), Jehovah's Witnesses, Seventh-day Adventists) is slowly increasing (see Samoan Bureau of Statistics 2012 for comparative data from 1981 through 2011). The slow exodus from mainline churches to evangelical churches is usually explained by two factors: changed worship styles and giving practices (Thornton et al. 2010; Besnier 2011; Macpherson and Macpherson 2011).[3] Despite the growth of Pentecostal churches, leaving mainline churches for Pentecostal churches is difficult because, as many of my interlocutors have said, 'if you leave the [family] church, you leave the family'. Additionally, the centrality of (mainline) Christianity to everyday life in Samoa cannot be overstated: morning prayers in government ministries are common, and each evening across Samoa families gather for the *sa* (literally, 'sacred'),

3 Mainline churches practice public gift-giving while Pentecostal churches practice private tithing. The demands of mainline church giving are rigorous as congregants express their commitments to their family and village through the public display of gifts to pastors and the church. Tithing, on the other hand, is private and calculated based on income (10 per cent of income).

which is a time when families gather to say evening prayers. Tracing how *pule* and *mana* are invoked illuminates some of the ways that interdenominational difference is managed in everyday life.

Data and methods

The data for this paper was collected during 14 months of ethnographic fieldwork in independent Samoa in 2011–12. Data is from church services, evangelising healing work at the national hospital, and prayers in a health clinic (Figure 21). I worked in two primary church fieldsites, the first an Assemblies of God church community in a peri-urban village and the second a Samoan-founded Pentecostal church in the urban area of Apia. During this time I audio and video recorded sermons, healing services, household prayers, and Bible study meetings. Over the course of fieldwork I worked with 10 research assistants transcribing and translating all the data presented here. The data selected for this chapter was then back-translated by one research assistant.

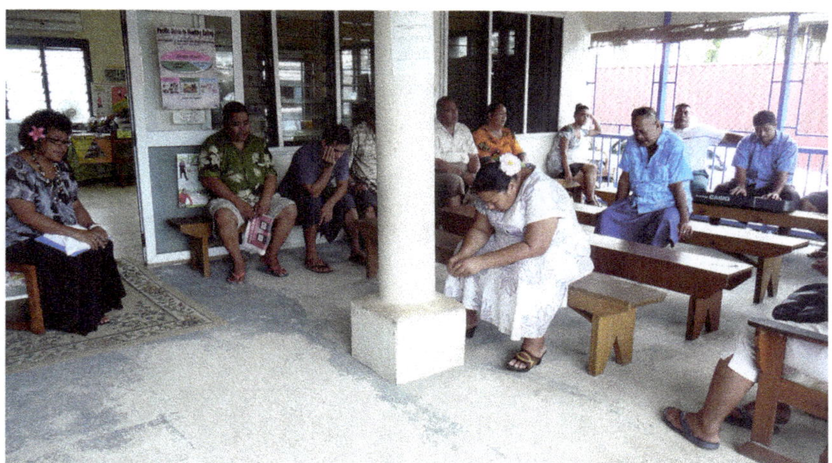

Figure 21. Morning prayers at a clinic, 2012.
Source: Photograph by Jessica Hardin.

I also participated in and observed at a diabetes clinic where I audio and video recorded morning prayers. Every morning at the clinic, the head nurse, who was also a Pentecostal pastor's wife, would ask the eldest man present to lead a prayer before clinical services began for the day. These prayers varied from brief prayers lasting a few minutes to prayers lasting up to 20 minutes. Prayers were always followed by a song. The head nurse, indexing her born-again Christianity, would end the morning prayers by saying in English, 'To God be the glory forever and ever, amen', while pumping her fist in the air. After the prayers I would ask the supplicant his denomination and also others in the clinic to learn perceptions about prayer styles and formulas. I only include prayers identified as *lotu fou*. The other main source of data I draw from is healing prayers among a group of female healers from an institution I call Glory House. The healing team have been evangelising during visiting hours in the hospital in Apia for over two years. They work in pairs. Some are pairs of more senior women with novices and others are teams that have been working together for long stretches of time; each has their own style developed over time through mentorship. These pairs approach women and men, young and old, and in most cases they do not know the denomination of the sick person and her family. Sometimes sick persons looked away to indicate they were not interested in interacting while others eagerly invited the pair over to their beds.

In order to understand *pule* and *mana* as concepts operating in everyday life rather than theoretical or philosophical abstractions, I searched all of my transcriptions for '*mana*' and '*pule*'. The data set included in this chapter is comprised of the 43 transcripts (out of 63) in which I found '*mana*', '*pule*', or both.

The twins: Prayer and fasting

While scholars are increasingly investigating prayer (Corwin 2012; Luhrmann 2012), fasting has received little attention (Hardin 2013). Prayer is 'a discursive act that bridges human limitation and the spiritual realm' (Baquedano-Lopez 2000: 197). Fasting is an embodied act that seeks to make the same connection. In Samoa, however, among evangelical Christians, prayer or fasting alone are not considered efficacious ways of bringing God's power into everyday life but must be co-practiced. Alo, an AOG preacher in his 50s, started his sermon by saying, 'Bible scholars say that prayer and fasting are brothers, or twins. They work together. They are of one heart' (3 November 2011). 'Twins' refers to the complementary linguistic and embodied labour involved in harnessing *mana*. Through sermons, Pentecostal Christians are trained to understand their prayer and fasting practices as essential to channelling divine *mana* and the blessings that accompany it. They learn to embed these practices in everyday life so they become taken for granted.

Alo said that 'God's *pule* over the world' begins with 'the individual spiritual life' (3 November 2011). He emphasised that individual embodied and discursive practices bring God's *pule* into being. Through these practices believers allow the divine to 'pour His *mana* and *pulea* [govern] the people who believe in God'. Believers' practices of prayer and fasting are intended to create a world governed by the divine. In turn, *mana* will manifest blessings in everyday life. He continued:

> Fa'atumu, e fa'afou, o uiga nei o le upu fa'aolaolaina. O le toe fa'amalosia o 'oe ma a'u, toe fa'afou 'oe ma a'u, toe fa'atumu 'oe ma a'u. Fa'atumu i le a? Ia toe fa'atumu i le mana o le Agaga Pa'ia. A fai tatou galuega, ole'a ia fa'amalosi ia tatou. Na te toe fa'atumu tatou. Ole'a toe sau e fa'afou ma fa'a'atoa i tatou. Ole'a toe sau e fa'atumu le tatou malosi. O le aso lenei olo'o tatou anapogi ma tatalo. Olo'o tatou vala'au i le mana ia afio mai i lalo e toe fa'afou tatou olaga. O lou tatalo ma lou anapogi ole'a tali mai e le Atua. Tatou te tilotilo i lona tali fa'aāliali mai. E fa'aaliali mai ana galuega ona o le mana lea. E va'aia i le autalavou, i tatou tina, i tatou tama. O le mana lea e fa'afouina ma fa'atumuina le fa'apotopotoga.

> Refill, to renew, these are the meanings of revival. To re-strengthen you and me, to renew you and me, to refill you and me. Refill with what? To be refilled with the mana of the Holy Spirit. When we do work, He will strengthen us. He will refill us. He will come to renew and complete us. He will come to refill our strength. This day we are fasting and praying. We are asking the mana to come down and to renew our life. Your prayer and your fasting will be answered by God. We look at His obvious response. It is obvious in His work because of this mana. It is seen in our youth, in our mothers, in our fathers. This mana it renews and refills the congregation.

This message was met with enthusiastic responses of 'hallelujah' and 'amene' (amen). Prayer and fasting are practices that are ways of seeking divine strength. Alo suggests symmetry between prayer and fasting and asking for divine *mana* when he says: 'This day we are fasting and praying. We are asking the *mana* to come down and to renew our life.' Everyday religious practice establishes the believer as a conduit of divine blessings, and permits communication of needs to which the divine will answer. *Mana* is the generative means through which needs and prayers are answered. In this case, Christians are taught how to bring the abundance of God's potential into their lives by connecting to the *mana* of God through prayer and fasting. These may be individually oriented activities and achievements but supplicants are meant to understand the good things in their lives as the result of God's *mana*, not individual effort ('We look at His obvious response. It is obvious in His work because of this *mana*. It is seen in our youth, in our mothers, in our fathers. This *mana* it renews and refills the congregation').

Mana thus also manifests community well-being. Alo finished his sermon by saying:

O lou fa'atuatua olo'o koneti i le mana o le Atua, vavega e tutupu, o maumaga ua tele ua tutumu kapoti mea'ai, ua tumu lou ato tupe, ua fa'amaloloina lou tino. Fa'atafe atu au fa'amanuiaga ia i latou.	Your faith is connected to the mana of God, miracles happen, plantations are abundant, pantries are full, your wallet is full, your body is healed. Let your blessings flow to them.

Prayer and fasting establish a connection to the divine. Another preacher referred to this as a spiritual telephone. The connection, which requires faithfulness and dedication to mindful practice, enables the *mana* of God to flow, which remains inactivated without these practices (see also Oroi, this volume). Sermons are explicitly aimed at teaching Pentecostal Christians what ought to be taken for granted and specifically how to become an ethical self. Congregants are reassured that when flow is established, material, psychological and embodied needs are met. Combined prayer and fasting are thus a way of seeking divine power and its potential effect in the world. By focusing on individual practice, these sermons were a practical guide to bringing the *mana* of God into one's own life without the assistance of pastors. This is also a tacit way that born-again Christians critique mainline Christianity and the presumed authority of pastors over congregants (Handman 2015).

'Your power continues to work in us': Claiming *pule*, manifesting *mana*

Born-again Christians in Samoa bring *pule* and *mana* into being through their personal prayer and fasting practices. These embodied practices are aimed at creating a direct connection between believer and divine that funnels *mana* into everyday life. Discursively, born-again Christians also work to authorise themselves as vehicles of *mana* to act on behalf of others. This effort to harness *mana* reveals the discursive labour involved in addressing extraordinary circumstances through ordinary practices. Performatively claiming divine *pule* enables healing *mana* to manifest.

Anthropologists have long explored the performative force of language in evangelical Christian practice (Coleman 2000; Harding 1987). Pentecostal religious language, particularly when it comes to healing, privileges speech acts that transform bodies and worlds through their utterance (Austin 1962). Simon Coleman writes, 'Words come to create the very reality which they purport to describe' (2000: 131). Claiming healing, or speaking healing, brings it into being for Pentecostal Christians around the globe. There were two ways I observed claiming *pule* in order to bring healing *mana* into being: first, in clinic-based prayers where supplicants interceded on behalf of both sick persons and medical professionals asking for healing power to be channelled through medical interventions; second, in healing prayers performed in the hospital where female healers, who were also evangelising, would claim divine *pule* over the world and seek to act as agents of healing *mana*.

Claiming *pule* has the capacity to release *mana* to believers and medical practitioners. These prayers render the medical work about to take place at the clinic efficacious. Manu, a diabetes patient in his 60s, led the morning prayer at the clinic one morning, saying:

Ole'a ou ta'ita'ia tatou i se tatalo. Sa matagi, ma malulu ma timu le aso lenei, 'ae o le matou mana'o aua o 'oe o le na faia, o le pule o ō matou olaga ma mea 'uma. O 'oe o le matou leoleo mamoe e gaioi. E te le moe. Matou te fa'afetai mo lenei aso ua e aumaia. Matou te le faitio auā o 'oe olo'o iai le pule o o matou olaga aua e leai se matou malosi. O matou olaga olo'o i ou 'a'ao. O 'oe o le Atua soifua. Le Atua, matou te vaala'au ia oe ia fa'asusulu mai lou alofa i luga ia te'i matou nei ua potopoto i lenei fale. O matou tama, o matou tina, matou te si'itia atu ia te oe e auala i lima o foma'i ma teine tausi ma'i olo'o fesoasoani ia te'i latou ia toe malolosi. Fa'amanuia ia te'i latou uma. Matou te manatua lenei fa'apotopotoga ina ia iai lou mana fa'amalolo i luga o i latou e ala i vai ua saunia. (19 January 2012)

I will lead us with a prayer. It's been windy and cold and rainy this day, but it's our wish because you are the creator, the pule (ruler) of our lives and everything. You are our active shepherd. You never sleep. We thank you for this day you have brought, we don't have to complain because you have the pule for our lives because we don't have the strength. Our lives are in your hands. You are the living God. God we call on you to shine your love upon us who are gathered here in this house. Our fathers and our mothers, we carry them to you through the hands of doctors and nurses who are helping them get better. Bless all of them. We remember the ministry that your healing mana will be upon them through the medicine they have prepared.

Tasi, another diabetes patient who was in his 60s, began his prayer by saying:

E fia momoli atu le agaga fa'afetai ia te oe ona o le ola ma le malosi i tama ma tina matutua ua matou fa'atasi ai i lenei itula. Le Atua, alofa mai ma fesoasoani i foma'i i le fa'atinoina o latou tiute ina ia iai le mana o ou fa'amanuiaga ia i latou. Ia iai le malamalama i le fa'atinoina o latou tiute a'o matou ōmai mātou te mo'omia se fesoasoani. (12 January 2012)

We would like to give our thankful hearts to you for the life and the strength to the old fathers and mothers. We are together this hour. God, love us and help the doctors with their duties so the mana of your blessings comes to them. Let them have understanding for their duties as we come wanting to get some help.

Recognising authority in order for *mana* to be released is a dynamic performative interaction. In each example, the supplicant begins by claiming divine authority over the world ('You are the creator, the *pule* (ruler) of our lives and everything', or 'We would like to give our thankful hearts to you for the life'). God is represented as all-powerful and omnipresent ('We thank you for this day you have brought, we don't have to complain because you have the *pule* for our lives because we don't have the strength'). Supplicants also represent themselves as powerless and dependent upon that animating authority for strength ('Our fathers and our mothers, we carry them to you through the hands of doctors and nurses who are helping them get better' and 'Let them have understanding for their duties as we come wanting to get some help'). By claiming divine *pule* and recognising the limitations of humanity, supplicants positioned themselves as seekers. In seeking and appropriately asking for divine *mana,* individual believers could channel that *mana*. *Mana* is channelled into medicines and doctors so that both objects and persons may be efficacious in their healing capacities.

Prayers are structured in such a way so as to create a world of divine authority over the lives of supplicants, and the nation of Samoa, in order to ask for healing power. *Mana* is power that is derived from appropriate divine authority and then channelled through, in this case, physicians and nurses to administer their medications. Physicians, nurses and medications are efficacious because the world is orchestrated in the appropriate fashion: divine authority is the source of all blessings; healing power is channelled to those with knowledge who act as conduits for efficacious healing. Through the performance of prayer an ideal cosmic order is established, which in turn enables divine intervention.

Patients authorise medical practitioners and imbue their work with efficacy in clinic prayers. Conversely, hospital-based healers must actively authorise themselves as efficacious healers; this is a difficult process in Samoa when healers do not have the usual trappings of authority, including titles, wealth or education. On their weekly visits to the hospital, the healing team often began with a conversation about the sicknesses facing the patient and then switched to evangelising. If the patient agreed to say a salvation prayer, which was often quick and formulaic, the ministry team members would either perform deliverance and healing or only a healing prayer. Before even entering the hospital the ministry team would pray. The prayers were led by the ministry team leader, Hana, and they were often also short and formulaic.

Matou te vala'au i lau pule ina ia e fesoasoani mai ia matou. O au galuega le Atua, matou te mo'omia lau fa'au'uga mana. Ia e alofa i le matou vaega i le mana o lou Agaga Paia i lenei taeao. (8 May 2012)	We call upon your pule so that you can help us. Your works God, we need your holy anointing, have mercy on our team through the mana of your Holy Spirit this morning.
Matou te vala'au atu mo le mana o lou agaga. O lau fanau lea ole'a galulue i le falema'i i le aso. Matou te vala'au i le mana o lou Agaga e foa'i le matou fesoasoani sili. Lo matou faia'oga fa'amolemole afio mai e fa'amatala o matou gutu ina ia tautatala o matou laugutu, tatala o matou loto ina ia mafai ona matou momoli lau upu i totonu o si matou atunu'u pele o Samoa. Ia iai lau mana i totonu o i matou uma i lenei falema'i ina ia tatala taliga o lou atunu'u aua lau Upu olo'o laugaina e au 'au'auna i le aso. Ia iai 'oe ma i matou ma ia e fesoasoani mai Agaga Paia i lau fanau, ma ia fa'afoi atu le vi'iga ia te 'oe. (5 June 2012)	We ask you for the mana of your spirit. Your children will be working in the hospital today. We ask for the mana of your spirit to give our best help. Our teacher please come to open our mouths and let our lips speak, open our hearts so we can deliver your Word inside our dear country Samoa. Let your mana be with all of us in the hospital to open the ears of your country in order for your Word, that is delivered by your servants this day, to fit. Be with us Father and may your Holy Spirit be with your children and we should return the praising back to you.

In both examples *mana* animates: it opens ears, minds and mouths to be efficacious in the delivery of a divine message or reception of such a message. Through their prayers the healers establish divine *pule* in order to render themselves efficacious conduits for divine healing *mana*. In claiming divine *pule*, individual agency is backgrounded while individuals and objects (supplicants, medical practitioners, medicines) become the conduits of divine *mana*. Efficacy is centred in the ability both to channel divine healing power and to speak effectively so as to affect potential believers, to make them effective message-bearers.

Before the hospital visits, the women in the healing team would often discuss how entering the hospital was difficult. Speaking to strangers and experiencing the potential antagonism of interdenominational differences was difficult and sometimes painful. The prayers quoted above were one way the group performatively constituted themselves as effective and authoritative actors. In this example, *mana* works materially through the imagery of the blood of Jesus. Louisa, one of the senior members of the healing team, prayed over a patient in the hospital who was suffering from stomach pain:

> Le Atua, Tama, tatala o matou loto ina ia fa'alogo i lau Upu, le Upu o le ola. Matou te vala'au atu ia oe i lenei itula, ia fufuluina i matou e le mana o le toto o Iesu mai o matou ulu se'ia o'o i o matou tamatama'i vae. Fufulu o matou loto e fa'alogo. Tama, ia e fa'amanuia i o matou uso, matou te vala'au atu i lenei taeao e leai se mea e te le mafaia. E alu lau upu ma le mana ia te i lātou. Matou te avatu le fa'afetai ma vala'au atu ia e suia o latou loto. Matou te fa'afetai ona ua e tusia o latou loto i le tusi o le ola. Tama, O oe ua iai le pule. E te silafia mea uma mai le ulu se'ia o'o i vae. Oute vala'au atu ia 'oe Tama e te afio i totonu o le manava i le mea olo'o iai le fa'afitauli. Tama matou te vala'au atu ia 'oe, i le mana o lou toto ia 'a'apa atu i o matou uso. Lo matou Tama, matou te vala'au atu ia 'oe, e leai se mea e faigata ia 'oe. Ua ia'i matou le pule ma le mana e fa'aleagaina ai ma'i. Matou te tutu i le pule ma le mana ua e aumaia e fa'aleaogaina ai le suka. (21 February 2012)

> God, Father, open our hearts to listen to your word, the Word of life. We call you this hour, let the mana of your blood Jesus clean us from our heads to our toes. Clean our hearts to listen. Father bless our brother, we call this morning Father because there is nothing you can't do. Your Word goes with the mana to them. We give you thanks and ask you to change their souls. We give thanks that their souls are written in the book of life. Father, you have the pule. You know everything from the head to the toe. I ask you Father to go inside the stomach where there's a problem. Father we call you, the mana of your blood to reach our brother. My father, we call you. Nothing is impossible for you. We have the pule and the mana with us to destroy this sickness. We stand and believe in the pule and mana you gave us to destroy the sugar.

In this example, Louisa claims divine authority and asks that God heal inside the body. The blood of Jesus Christ is thought to be the material of *mana*, that which covers bodies and protects them or that which heals bodies. *Pule* here is associated with divine omniscience and healing is a process of recognising that omniscience and human inadequacy. As conduits for divine *mana*, though, healers direct the potentiality of this healing power. By extension healers have access to divine authority and towards the end of the excerpt above, Louisa indicates a switch from directing the divine, 'You have the *pule*', to a collective 'we' who as healers manifest divine *mana*: 'We have the *pule* and *mana* with us.' Claiming *pule* and invoking the blood of Jesus Christ, these healers instantiate what is referred to as the believer's authority. This healing prayer also brought a newly born-again person into a community of believers with the deictic marker 'we' by extending this authorisation and animating power into each believer. By sharing this authority with the whole group, healers worked against the imperative of mainline Christian hierarchical authority where divinely originated authority and power are thought to rest in pastors and *matai* only.

Through the performative forces of language, and as a result of healers' harnessing of *mana*, efficacious healing is possible. These are not extraordinary prayers, although the circumstances are extraordinary, but are everyday embodied and discursive practices available to all believers to channel and direct divine *mana*. These methods reveal the ways that *mana* is harnessed with care, revealing the effort involved in acting appropriately, and therefore ethically, in interdenominationally diverse contexts.

De-centring agency and self-making

Scholars of Christianity in the Pacific have recognised a basic tension between Christianity and indigenous orientations towards ideas about the individual (see Robbins 2004; Keane 2007). Christian practices are associated with cultivating individual subjectivity, responsibility, and, for evangelical Christians, a personal relationship with God. This contrasts with the ways that most societies in the Pacific tend to 'de-emphasize individualism' (Tomlinson 2011: 155). In Samoa, Bradd Shore (1982) suggests a concept of self with multiple sides, as opposed to an imagined western self that is cohesive and acontextual. 'Lacking any epistemological bias that would lead them to focus on "things in themselves" or the essential qualities of experiences', Shore writes, 'Samoans instead focus on things in their relationships, and the contextual grounding of experience' (1982: 136). Selfhood can be considered a way of enacting the well-known Samoan expression *teu le va* (taking care of the relationship) (Lilomaiava-Doktor 2009, Ka'ili 2005). Albert Wendt writes, 'Important to the Samoan view of reality is the concept of *Va*. *Va* is the space between, the betweenness, not empty space, not space that separates, but space that relates' (Wendt 1999: 402). Taking care of the *va* then is an expression that highlights how Samoans 'value group unity more than individualism' (Wendt 1999: 402). Alessandro Duranti also writes that Samoans privilege social context in determining self-identity and action and suggests that Samoans are not concerned with knowing intentions but with 'the implications of the speaker's actions/words for the web of relationships in which his [sic] life is woven' (1992: 42). It can be argued then that agency is not located within the individual to act based on emotion, motivation, or intention but 'Samoan behavior is (externally) "caused"' (Shore 1982: 136). In other words, context drives the particular aspects of self that are highlighted or inform action in any given moment. Again, Shore writes, 'This Samoan emphasis on correct perception of social relations and their requirements goes far beyond a concern for etiquette or tact. It is a moral and epistemological axiom' (1982: 137). Perception of social relations is a moral and epistemological axiom because it informs how one will self-identify and self-present, which informs how one will act. Here I briefly explore anthropological approaches to selfhood in Samoa because when *pule* and *mana* are invoked they mediate the tensions of Samoan orientations towards a flexible selfhood informed by social relations-in-context and the Christian imperative for faith and Christian action that is individual and consistent across contexts.

As part of Christian self-making practice, claiming *pule* and invoking *mana* reflect a cultural and social context that is skeptical of individual intentional action. Among evangelical Christians, taking credit for healing or demonstrating pride in one's spiritual work is looked down upon and actively avoided. Generally in Samoa, as Ilana Gershon recognises, pride is 'one of a small number of motivations' Samoans attribute to one another (Gershon 2012: 56). Accusations of *fiapoto* or *fiamaualuga* are in constant circulation. These accusations suggest arrogance and incompetence about appropriate matching of behaviour with social expectations (see Gershon 2012: 146). Fears of these accusations are apparent in Pentecostal Christian spiritual practice where individuals are accused of identifying healing efficacy with the healer and not God. Consistently invoking *pule* and *mana* is one way that individual agency is deflected but not rendered invisible. Deflecting individual agency is thus one way to bring ethical selfhood into being, but it requires discursive labour.

Hirokazu Miyazaki argues that Christian faith in Fiji emerges as the 'capacity to place one's agency in abeyance' (2000: 32). Claiming *pule* and channelling *mana* work in a similar way, as Pentecostal Samoans de-centre individual agency while foregrounding divine agency. In these cases the efficacy of individuals and groups is not hidden but only represented as a shadow of the real source: God's *mana*. Individual agency is de-centred when supplicants bring attention to the inefficacy of their own action without divine *mana*. Sam, a diabetes patient in his 60s, led the morning prayer by saying:

> Le Atua lo matou Tama, matou te 'avatu lenei taeao, e pei ona e taga'i mai ua matou omai ma o matou ma'i ia 'oe. O 'oe 'olo'o iai le Pule, ioe Tama, o 'oe olo'o iai le Pule, i mea 'uma. O foma'i olo'o iai le poto i o latou tiute, ae a leai lou mana, ma au vavega e leai se mea e mafai ona matou faia. O le matou tatalo lena ia 'oe lo matou Tama, alofa Tama fesoasoani mai ia matou. Ia aoga latou vai ma togafitiga, ina ia fa'aali mai ai lou mana ina ia matou maua ai lau fa'amalologa mai ia oe. (17 February 2012)

> God our Father, we give you this morning as you can see that we are coming with our sicknesses to you. You have the pule, yes Father you have the pule, over everything. The doctors have their wisdom and their duties, but without your mana, and your miracles there's nothing we can do. That is our prayer to you our Father, loving Father help us. May their medicines and their treatments be useful, in order to show us your mana in order for us to receive healing from you.

God's authority is established here, and doctors are represented as having wisdom. However, wisdom alone cannot bring about healing, animating *mana* is required. Prayers are thus the means of activating that efficacious power. This is also expressed by the healing team, who also prayed together as a group after leaving the healing ministry. Hana said:

Fa'afetai mo le fa'ataunu'uina o lau upu i loto ma mafaufauga o lau fanau a'o asiasi mai i le falema'i i le aso. E tatau ona matou fa'afetai ia oe ona o le 'au'aunaga a au 'au'auna fa'atauva'a aua e leai se mea matou te mafaia pe a aunoa ma lou mana. Fa'afetai Tama, matou te vala'au atu ia e fa'amagalo ia matou vaivaiga ma agasala i le mana o lou toto Iesu. Ia e foai mea e mo'omia e i mātou ta'ito'atasi, i lona lava loto le Atua ia e foa'i. (5 June 2012)	Thank you for keeping the words in the hearts and the thoughts of your children as they visited the hospital today. We should thank you for the humble service of your servants, because there's nothing we can do without your mana. Thank you Father, we ask you to forgive us for our weaknesses and our wrongdoings with the mana of your blood Jesus. Let you Lord meet all the needs of each person, her own heart may you Lord meet it.

Here Hana said bluntly: 'There's nothing we can do without your *mana*.' Both examples demonstrate how supplicants, physicians and healers are ineffective without divine *mana*. *Mana* is positioned as the source of efficacious action, which requires recognition and appropriate ways of relating to that source. Speaking of ineffectiveness is essential to bringing about effective action.

Mana also creates futures for individual persons that imbue the life course with efficacy to fight against evil in everyday life. At times beyond the recognition of individuals, *mana* is the material of the divine within the person to act in a divinely orchestrated plan. The following examples are taken from closing prayers of the healing team. Hana led both prayers:

> E tatau ona tatou tau fa'asaga i le ti'apolo o lenei lalolagi olo'o taumafai e fa'asalavei i le fa'atinoina o lau vala'auga. Ua e vala'auina i matou. E pei ona e fetalai ia matou tutū i luga ma e, matou te talitonu o lou mana e fa'aauauina le galuega i totonu ia'i matou ma ole'a iai le taimi i le lumana'i ole'a mātou saunia lelei ai o ni au fanau. Ona matou o'o atu lea i le isi tulaga ma va'ai i lou mataoutia, ma au faoamanuiaga ona o lau valaoauga ia'i matou. (15 May 2012)

> We need to fight against the devil of this world who tries to get in the way of your calling, you have called us. Just like you have spoken to us rise up and go forth, we believe that your mana continues to work in us and that there will be a time in the future when we will be well-prepared as your children. Then we will reach another level and see the wonders of you and the blessings of being called by you.

> Aumai ia te'i matou le malosi i totonu o matou aiga matou te alolofa ai ia'i latou ma i latou e pele ia te'i matou, tusa pe olo'o iai le fa'anoanoa ona latou te le iloa oe Tama. Silasila mai ia'i matou i le alofa, o lau fanau, fa'afaigofieina e lou malamalama ma lou mana ona 'a'apa atu i o matou aiga ina ia latou iloa mea moni ia e fa'aalia i o matou loto, aua o le mea lea na e vala'auina ai i matou ina ia mafai ona latou mulimuli i lea fa'ata'ita'iga. (15 May 2012)

> Give us the strength in our families for us to love them and all those that are dear to us even if it's with sadness to know that they do not know you Father. Look upon us with love, your children, make it easy for your light and your mana reach into our families so that they may come to know the truth that you have revealed to our hearts, which is why you have called us so that they may be able to follow this example.

Mana works in the moment it is claimed, as with the medicines of doctors, but it can also set into motion a divine plan. In each of these examples, *mana* is not only credited for past effective action but also sets forth a future of effective action. *Mana* then has the capacity to propel healers into the future not only as they heal in the hospital but as they evangelise in their own families. In this way, *mana* enhances self-efficacy in difficult contexts of interdenominational kinship. Managing *pule* and *mana* in prayer and fasting form a set of discursive and embodied practices that highlight how to maintain ethical individual relations with the divine. Through these taken-for-granted practices, individual supplicants represent themselves as powerless without the animating capacity of *mana*. In revealing human inefficacy, ethical practice is brought into being.

Conclusion

For Pentecostal Christians, *mana* must be carefully brought into being through specific practices, including prayer, fasting and specific linguistic handling of *pule* and *mana*. In this process divine agency is recognised, which in turn animates human capacities. De-centring human agency is important to maintaining the divine as source and also circumspectly managing a Samoan prejudice against individually mandated authority. De-centring human agency does not render invisible human agency but instead indicates appropriate and ethical ways of acting. Louisa shared with me that when she was first born again, she kept receiving a single word message from God. Like a highlighted word on a computer screen, she recounted, YIELD flashed as she prayed, as she dreamed, and as her mind wandered during the day. Surrendering to divine agency then is an active and ethical human capacity in relation to which divine *mana* is enabled, requiring embodied and discursive labour.

Harnessing *mana*, according to Pentecostal Christians, is available to all born-again believers. This is an instance of the ways Christianity 'as an institutional force' has 'created [a] new sense of *mana*' (Tomlinson 2006: 182). Claiming *pule* and harnessing *mana* mediate the widely recognised tension between a relational model of Samoan selfhood over that of an individually driven model of self, which Christian practice aims to cultivate (see Tomlinson 2011; cf. Schram 2013). In a resonant comparative example from Papua New Guinea, Joel Robbins (2004) argues that the dyad of sin and salvation mediate Urapmin tensions between individual and relational notions of self. In particular, 'spirit disko' rituals are instances where Urapmin work to cultivate collective salvation while in everyday life they focus on monitoring individual sin. In these rituals of redemption, 'indigenous and Christian understandings [are] working in concert rather than at cross-purpose' (2004: 287).

Individuals from across station and rank in Samoan society may harness *mana* and its animating capacities through practice and language, not through conferral of title by family. *Mana* mediates the tension between the ideal individual agentive Christian believer and Samoan orientations towards prioritising relationships and context over individual intention by rendering individuals' effectiveness dependent upon divine power. By claiming *pule* and channelling *mana*, Pentecostal Christians create the possibility for effective action by foregrounding the divine as source for current and future action. In this process, individual agency recedes but does not disappear. This de-centring of agency permits recognition of individual work only insofar as this work is appropriately linked to the animating *mana*. Claiming *pule* and harnessing *mana* are thus part and parcel of developing an ethical Samoan Christian self.

'Everything is possible through the *mana* of God', Louisa said to me as we walked out of the intensive care unit after praying over a woman dying as a result of complications arising from a stroke. 'We can do nothing without Him', she said sadly as she comforted the sister of the dying woman (5 March 2012). Whispered to comfort, and repeated in prayer, sermons, and elsewhere in everyday life, the divine is the source of *mana*. All born-again Christians have this ordinary capacity, which they heighten through prayer, fasting, and their authorising uses of *pule* and *mana*. When born-again Christians recognise their own authority and capacity to connect with the divine, they challenge mainline Christianity in Samoa which centres the priest or minister as the divine conduit between God and congregants. Claiming *pule* and channelling *mana* is thus one way that born-again Christians in Samoa bypass hierarchies in mainstream Christianity. Not only do born-again Christians in Samoa personalise faith and a relationship with the divine but they teach believers how to manifest divine power in their everyday lives.

Acknowledgements

This research was funded by a Wenner Gren Dissertation Grant. I would like to thank the staff at the clinic where I recorded for their generosity and patience with me. Many thanks to Christina Kwauk for her comments on an earlier draft and to Mafiosamoa Palepoi for her help with translations. Finally, I am grateful to Matt Tomlinson and Ty Kāwika Tengan for their generous feedback throughout the writing of this chapter.

References

Anae, Melani. 1998. Fofoa i Vaoese: Identity journeys of New Zealand-born Samoans. PhD thesis, University of Auckland.

Austin, J.L. 1962. *How to Do Things with Words: The William James Lectures Delivered at Harvard University in 1955*, ed. J.O. Urmson and Marina Sbisà. Oxford: Clarendon Press.

Baquedano-Lopez, Patricia. 2000. Prayer. *Journal of Linguistic Anthropology* 9(1–2): 197–200.

Battaglia, Debbora. 1995. Problematizing the self: A thematic introduction. In *Rhetorics of Self-Making*, ed. Debbora Battaglia, pp. 1–16. Berkeley: University of California Press.

Besnier, Niko. 2011. Reconfiguring the modern Christian. In *On the Edge of the Global: Modern Anxieties in a Pacific Island Nation*, pp. 205–30. Contemporary Issues in Asia and the Pacific Series. Stanford: Stanford University Press.

Coleman, Simon. 2000. *The Globalization of Charismatic Christianity: Spreading the Gospel of Prosperity*. Cambridge: Cambridge University Press.

Congregational Christian Church Samoa. n.d. Parishes. Online: www.cccs.org.ws/index.php (accessed 2 November 2015).

Corwin, Anna. 2012. Changing God, changing bodies: The impact of new prayer practices on elderly Catholic nuns' embodied experience. *Ethos* 40(4): 390–410.

Csordas, Thomas J. 1994. *The Sacred Self: A Cultural Phenomenology of Charismatic Healing*. Berkeley: University of California Press.

Duranti, Alessandro. 1992. Intentions, self, and responsibility: An essay in Samoan ethnopragmatics. In *Responsibility and Evidence in Oral Discourse*, ed. Jane H. Hill and Judith T. Irvine, pp. 24–47. Cambridge: Cambridge University Press.

Engelke, Matthew and Matt Tomlinson (eds). 2006. *The Limits of Meaning: Case Studies in the Anthropology of Christianity*. New York: Berghahn Books.

Eriksen, Annelin. 2014. Sarah's sinfulness: Egalitarianism, denied difference, and gender in Pentecostal Christianity. *Current Anthropology* 55(S10): S262–S270.

Ernst, Manfred. 2006. Samoa. In *Globalization and the Re-Shaping of Christianity in the Pacific Islands*, ed. Manfred Ernst, pp. 539–77. Suva: Pacific Theological College.

——. 2012. Changing Christianity in Oceania: A regional overview. *Archives de Sciences Sociales des Religions* 157: 29–45.

Gershon, Ilana. 2006. Converting meanings and the meanings of conversion in Samoan moral economies. In *The Limits of Meaning: Case Studies in the Anthropology of Christianity*, ed. Matthew Engelke and Matt Tomlinson, pp. 147–64. New York: Berghahn Books.

——. 2012. *No Family Is an Island: Cultural Expertise among Samoans in Diaspora*. Ithaca: Cornell University Press.

Handman, Courtney. 2015. *Critical Christianity: Translation and Denominational Conflict in Papua New Guinea*. Berkeley: University of California Press.

Hardin, Jessica A. 2013. Fasting for health, fasting for God: Samoan Evangelical Christian responses to obesity and chronic disease. In *Reconstructing Obesity: The Measures of Meaning, the Meaning of Measures*, ed. Megan McCullough and Jessica A. Hardin, pp. 107–30. New York: Berghahn Books.

Harding, Susan F. 1987. Convicted by the Holy Spirit: The rhetoric of fundamental Baptist conversion. *American Ethnologist* 14(1): 167–81.

Henderson, April K. 2010. Gifted flows: Making space for a brand new beat. *The Contemporary Pacific* 22(2): 293–315.

Hereniko, Vilsoni and Rob Wilson (eds). 1999. *Inside Out: Literature, Cultural Politics, and Identity in the New Pacific*. Lanham, MD: Rowman & Littlefield Publishers.

Hill, Jane H. and Judith T. Irvine (eds). 1992. *Responsibility and Evidence in Oral Discourse*. Cambridge: Cambridge University Press.

Howard, Alan and Robert Borofsky (eds). 1989. *Developments in Polynesian Ethnology*. Honolulu: University of Hawaii Press.

Ka'ili, Tevita O. 2005. Tauhu va: Nurturing Tongan sociospatial ties in Maui and beyond. *The Contemporary Pacific* 17: 83–114.

Kame'eleihiwa, Lilikalā. 1992. *Native Land and Foreign Desires: Pehea Lā E Pono Ai? How Shall We Live in Harmony?* Honolulu, HI: Bishop Museum Press.

Keane, Webb. 2007. *Christian Moderns: Freedom and Fetish in the Mission Encounter*. Berkeley: University of California Press.

Lambek, Michael, ed. 2010. *Ordinary Ethics: Anthropology, Language, and Action*. New York: Fordham University Press.

Lempert, Michael. 2013. No ordinary ethics. *Anthropological Theory* 13(4): 370–93.

Lilomaiava-Doktor, Sa'ilemanu. 2009. Beyond 'migration': Samoan population movement (malaga) and the geography of social space (va). *The Contemporary Pacific* 21(1): 1–32.

Luhrmann, T.M. 2012. *When God Talks Back: Understanding the American Evangelical Relationship with God*. New York: Knopf.

Macpherson, Cluny and La'avasa Macpherson. 2009. *The Warm Winds of Change: Globalization in Contemporary Samoa*. Auckland: Auckland University Press.

——. 2011. Churches and the economy of Samoa. *The Contemporary Pacific* 23(2): 304–37.

Marshall, Wende Elizabeth. 2011. *Potent Mana: Lessons in Healing and Power*. Albany: State University of New York Press.

McCullough, Megan and Jessica A. Hardin (eds). 2013. *Reconstructing Obesity: The Measures of Meaning, the Meaning of Measures*. New York: Berghahn Books.

Meleisea, Leasiolagi Malama. 1997. *The Cambridge History of the Pacific Islanders*. Cambridge: Cambridge University Press.

Miyazaki, Hirokazu. 2000. Faith and fulfillment: Agency, exchange, and the Fijian aesthetics of completion. *American Ethnologist* 27(1): 31–51.

Pagaialii, Tavita. 2006. *Pentecost 'To the Uttermost': A History of the Assemblies of God in Samoa*. Baguio City: Asia Pacific Theological Seminary Press.

Robbins, Joel. 2004. *Becoming Sinners: Christianity and Moral Torment in a Papua New Guinea Society*. Berkeley: University of California Press.

Salesa, Damon. 2011. *Racial Crossings: Race, Intermarriage, and the Victorian British Empire*. Oxford: Oxford University Press.

Samoan Bureau of Statistics. 2012. *Population and Housing Census 2011*. Apia, Samoa.

Schram, Ryan. 2013. One mind: Enacting the Christian congregation among the Auhelawa, Papua New Guinea. *The Australian Journal of Anthropology* 24: 30–47.

Shore, Bradd. 1982. *Sala'ilua: A Samoan Mystery*. New York: Columbia University Press.

——. 1989. Mana and tapu. In *Developments in Polynesian Ethnology*, ed. Alan Howard and Robert Borofsky, pp. 137–73. Honolulu: University of Hawaii Press.

Silva, Kalena. 1997. The adoption of Christian prayer in Native Hawaiian pule. *Pacific Studies* 20(1): 89-99.

Tengan, Ty Kāwika, Tevita O. Ka'ili and Rochlle Tuitagava'a Fonoti. 2010. Genealogies: Articulating Indigenous anthropology in/of Oceania. *Pacific Studies* 33(2–3): 139–67.

Thornton, Alec, Maria Kerslake and Tony Binns. 2010. Alienation and obligation: Religion and social change in Samoa. *Asia Pacific Viewpoint* 51(1): 1–16.

Tomlinson, Matt. 2006. Retheorizing mana: Bible translation and discourse of loss in Fiji. *Oceania* 76(2): 173–85.

——. 2011. The true me: Individualism and Biblical types in Fijian Methodism. In *Managing Modernity in the Western Pacific*, ed. Mary Patterson and Martha Macintyre, pp. 147–71. St Lucia: University of Queensland Press.

Valeri, Valerio. 1985. *Kingship and Sacrifice: Ritual and Society in Ancient Hawaii*, trans. Paula Wissing. Chicago: University of Chicago Press.

Wendt, Albert. 1999. Afterword: Tatauing the post-colonial body. In *Inside Out: Literature, Cultural Politics, and Identity in the New Pacific*, ed. Vilsoni Hereniko and Rob Wilson, pp. 399–412. Lanham, MD: Rowman & Littlefield Publishers.

World Assemblies of God. n.d. Samoa – Participating Member. Online: worldagfellowship.org/fellowship/countries/wagf-participating-member-s-z/samoa-2/ (accessed 2 November 2015).

World Council of Churches: A Worldwide Fellowship of Churches Seeking Unity, a Common Witness and Christian Service. n.d. Methodist Church of Samoa. Online: www.oikoumene.org/en/member-churches/methodist-church-of-samoa (accessed 20 October 2015).

11

Mana for a New Age

Rachel Morgain

From chakra healing to African drumming, sweat lodges to shamanic journeys, New Age movements, particularly in North America, are notorious for their pattern of appropriating concepts and practices from other spiritual traditions. While continental Native American and Asian influences are perhaps most familiar as sourcing grounds for New Age material, the traditions of Pacific Islanders, particularly Hawaiians, have not escaped New Age attention. In particular, the movement known as 'Huna' has introduced Hawaiian-sounding words and concepts to the New Age vocabulary. Chief among these is the concept of 'mana', controversially subsumed within what is often a large laundry list of non-western religious and philosophical nomenclature, under the generic category of 'energy' or 'life force'. Continually adapted through succeeding generations of Huna teachings, and further adopted into sections of the related contemporary Pagan movement through the tradition known as 'Feri', the concept of 'mana' displays some consistent themes across these traditions, quite different from its meaning in Hawaiian contexts. In being adopted into these movements, it has been transformed to fit within a field of ideas that have developed in western esoteric traditions from at least the late eighteenth century.

In this chapter, I trace some of the ideas that have come to be attached to the concept of mana through several iterations of New Age movements in North America. Beginning with the foundational works of Max Freedom Long, I look at the spiritual practice known as Huna, popularised from the late 1930s through a series of Long's texts and his Huna Research organisation. I then go on to examine how these ideas have been developed in the works of one of Huna's most influential contemporary teachers, Serge 'Kahili' King, who not only substantially expanded the conceptual vocabulary connected with the notion of mana in Huna, but whose spiritual and healing methods have been 're'-introduced into Hawai'i through sites such as the Kalani Retreat Center, located on the island of Hawai'i. Finally, I explore how mana has been adopted into the contemporary Pagan movement through the tradition known as Anderson Feri.

Feri tradition, created by Victor and Cora Anderson in California during the middle decades of the twentieth century, drew on ideas drawn from Huna including the concept of mana as it had been written about by Long. As an orally transmitted tradition, Feri concepts and practices are potentially subject to many sometimes contradictory interpretations among those from different lineages, taught by different teachers, or by the same teachers at different times, suggesting that there is likely to be no single, unified understanding of mana within Feri. My research here focuses on interviews with a group of Feri practitioners in San Francisco who also have ties to the closely related Reclaiming movement, with whom I have a long-standing research relationship. While their ideas may be idiosyncratic in some respects compared with other Feri lineages, certain threads can nevertheless be identified in how mana is understood and spoken about that are consistent with Huna ideas, pointing to a widespread adoption of particular conceptions of mana across New Age and contemporary Pagan movements. Here, I trace these ideas back to cosmological conceptions that have a long genealogy within western esoteric traditions, particularly since the work of Franz Mesmer in the late eighteenth century and that of the Theosophical Society established in the later decades of the nineteenth century.

Max Freedom Long and Huna

'Mana' entered the New Age movement primarily through the spiritual practice known as Huna, the invention of white American teacher and writer Max Freedom Long. Long claimed to have met with the Curator (later Director) of the Bishop Museum in Honolulu, William Brigham, suggesting Brigham was the main source of his insights on Hawaiian tradition. Long worked as a teacher on the island of Hawai'i from 1917 to 1920. According to the historical work of Makana Risser Chai, who has examined the evidence of Long's time in Honolulu, assessing his claims for the 'Hawaiian' roots of his system of Huna, he arrived in Honolulu some time in late 1920 or early 1921, making a bare living working in a photographic shop (Chai 2011: 104). From his earliest time there, he spent his spare time trying to talk to as many people as he could, learning what he could of Hawaiian life. Chai quotes a personal correspondence with author and former researcher at the Bishop Museum, Pali Jae Lee, who suggests, 'Every moment he could get away from work and try to find something out from someone, he did so' (quoted in Chai 2011: 115). In the process, he tried to find a kahuna who would share secrets with him, to no avail.[1]

After returning to the mainland United States from 1939 to 1941, Long wrote a number of mystery novels set in Hawai'i, drawing from his experiences and his rich imagination. But from the mid-1930s, he also wrote a series of books on Huna claiming knowledge of 'ancient Hawaiian secrets'. Pali Jae Lee, in research conducted in the 1970s, carefully traced Brigham's personal journals over the period of Long's residence in Honolulu. As she demonstrates, from the man who kept a detailed account 'even to the lists and receipts of groceries he purchased, the laundry he sent out and received back', there is no note of Brigham ever having met with or spoken to Long (Lee 2007: 92). As Chai suggests, based on Brigham's character and his consciousness of his superior class, it is highly unlikely he would ever have deigned to meet with Long, and less so that he would have taken in Long as a student (Chai 2011: 105). Nor are the stories Long shares in his works, which he claimed to have sourced from Brigham, reflected in Brigham's writings (Chai 2011: 106–108).

Interestingly, Chai suggests that it is possible Long may have nevertheless had some legitimate sources for his writings on Hawai'i. In particular, she points to the role of Lahilahi Webb, a Hawaiian woman from a chiefly family, who had participated in the coronation

1 This is hardly surprising given Long's brief time in Hawai'i and status as an outsider, and, as Lee points out, even less so considering the climate of fear, suspicion and legal prohibitions against use of the Hawaiian language and culture among Kanaka Maoli at this time (Lee 2007: 90).

of Kalakaua and served as lady-in-waiting and nurse to Queen Lili'uokalani. During the period of Long's stay in Honolulu, Webb worked as a guide in the Bishop Museum, and met Long during his visits there. Webb was so respected during her time at the museum that she became the informant of many of its resident scholars. Webb was a source of much information on Hawaiian traditions, including on healing, traditional wisdom and kahuna. However, according to museum workers interviewed by Pali Jae Lee, she was also inclined to 'tell the haole lots of foolishness' (Chai 2011: 116). Chai suggests that it is possible that Webb was the source of many of the stories Long attributed to Brigham, which she describes as 'relatively accurate descriptions of Hawaiian traditions' albeit containing some errors, possibly as a result of 'little jokes [Webb] played on him' (Chai 2011: 116).

Despite these sometimes accurate depictions dotting Long's work, Long left Hawai'i with little more in source material for his Huna system than these few stories and the 'old Hawaiian dictionary' of Lorrin Andrews, which he pored over intently to glean from it what he could (Long 1981: 38; see also Lee 2007: 92, for a critique of Long's dictionary method of learning about Hawaiian concepts). The most sympathetic Hawaiian account, from scholar and Living Treasure of Hawai'i Charles Kenn, highlights the limitations of a genuinely Hawaiian influence in Long's work. Kenn was a friend and long-time correspondent of Long, who spent some time as one of his Huna Research Associates (HRA) in Los Angeles in the late 1940s. In 1949, having returned to Hawai'i, he wrote in a letter to a member of the HRA that, 'I have no doubt about Long's sincerity, but he may have introduced some non-huna factors on account of his white-man's mind' (Chai 2011: 109). Ten years later, he wrote to his friend, author and scholar Leinani Melville Jones, that 'Max Long was "*auana*" [to stray morally or mentally]. I too cannot swallow his "*huna*" stuff, and I told him so … Max means well but, being a *haole* … is unable to comprehend the inner meaning of the kahuna philosophy' (quoted in Rodman 1979: 131).

Far from being able to learn of Hawaiian spiritual traditions, which it seems he originally hoped to do, in the end the Huna method that Long developed was a western esoteric system dressed up with a few Hawaiian terms and some scattered stories and imagery. He drew his core ideas almost wholesale from the traditions of early twentieth-century spiritualism, and in particular those of the Theosophical Society, with whom he had trained prior to his time in Hawai'i (Long 1981: 1). Other western philosophies that pervaded the intellectual landscape of the early twentieth century can also be traced in Long's writings. In particular, Long introduced a concept of 'three selves', which he claimed as part of kahuna lore, but which instead drew clear influences from Freudian psychology:

> The 'unihipili' (akin to Freud's id), which he describes as the 'low or animal spirit in us' which 'has inferior powers of reason'
>
> The 'uhane' or 'conscious mind spirit' (akin to Freud's ego), which 'cannot remember for itself but can use the full power of inductive reasoning'
>
> The 'aumakua' (akin to Freud's superego), which he describes as the 'superconscious' or 'parental spirit', the 'oldest and most highly evolved of men's three spirit selves' (Long 1954: 47).[2]

In *The Key to Theosophy*, Helena Blavatsky had written in 1889 that the consciousness is comprised of four components: the Lower or Personal Ego, including 'animal instincts, passions, desires, etc.'; the Inner Ego or 'permanent *Individuality*'; the Spiritual Soul; and the Higher Self or 'inseparable ray of the Universal' (Blavatsky 2006: 99). In Long's model, Blavatsky's latter two selves were merged into the 'aumakua' or 'superconscious', which takes on a more Freudian flavour in his somewhat supercilious notion of a 'parental spirit'. Thus Long adapted these Theosophical notions into a tripartite model of the self (remoulding them in a way that more closely resembles Sigmund Freud's framework); he lent each aspect a Hawaiian name, but retained an essentially Theosophical underpinning.[3]

2 Mary Pukui Kawena and Samuel H. Elbert's Hawaiian dictionary give the following translation of these terms:

> 'unihi.pili: Spirit of a dead person, sometimes believed present in bones or hair of the deceased and kept lovingly (Pukui and Elbert 1986: 372)
>
> 'uhane: Soul, spirit, ghost (363)
>
> 'au.makua: Family or personal gods, deified ancestors who might assume the shape of sharks … owls … hawks … [other forms listed] (32).

3 Indeed, Freud's ideas themselves were heavily influenced by the ferment of spiritualism in the late nineteenth century, and by the practices of Mesmerism, which served as a precursor to both Theosophy and psychoanalytic theory (Crews 1996).

The concept of mana in Huna

The concept of mana as elaborated by Long likewise has its roots in Theosophy. Blavatsky had earlier identified the word Prana with the notion of 'life or vital principle': '"*Prana*," or "Life," is, strictly speaking, the radiating force or Energy of Atma [the Universal Life]—ITS lower or rather (in its effects) more physical, because manifesting, aspect. Prana or Life permeates the whole being of the objective Universe' (Blavatsky 2006: 99). Opening a discussion on mana, Long writes:

> In the psycho-religions, both ancient and modern (with the exception of Huna) there is little to be found that gives us a clear idea of the POWER that turns the wheels of life or that moves the machinery of prayer …
>
> In the beliefs of India, much is said of *prana* (which may have been an idea drawn from a source similar to that from which Huna was drawn). Prana was held up as a tool of value in the early Theosophical writings … The shining example of a force of this kind was found in the legendary 'serpent force' supposedly rising at the base of the spine in response to certain exercises … and rising in spirals along the spine until the top of the head was reached. There the force caused the 'open consciousness' and one 'saw God' … I spent several months trying to get proof of these mechanisms when young and a member of the [Theosophical Society]. I also tried for some years to find any person who gave evidence of having learned to arouse and use this force, but without success. (Long 1981: 1)

It is this 'vital force' or essence of life that Long identifies as mana in his writings.

Images of flowing water are often used to express his understanding of mana. In one of Long's most influential works, *The Secret Science Behind Miracles*, he states:

> They [kahunas] knew the force as a thing which had to do with all thought processes and bodily activity. It was the essence of life itself. The kahuna symbol for this force was water. Water flows, so does the vital force. Water fills things. So does the vital force. Water may leak away—so may vital force. (Long 1954: 31)

In this context, then, mana is something that exists within the natural world, independent of the human activity that might direct it or express it. It has a pseudo-substantive quality, with the capacity to flow, fill up or leak away.

As with the spiritualist traditions of the nineteenth century, this 'flow' is also often described in metaphors of electricity and magnetism:

> We suppose that gravity is akin to magnetism, and that magnetism is to be found where there is a current of an electrical nature … The kahunas recognised the magnetic and the opposite, repulsive, nature of vital force or motricity but, unfortunately, they left no detailed exposition of the subject. (Long 1954: 31)

Developing this electromagnetic imagery further, Long suggests that mana has three levels or 'voltages', which connect with and operate through the three selves:

> The vital force or mana of the kahunas has three strengths. If it is electrical in nature, as modern experiments have demonstrated, we may safely say that the three strengths of mana known to the kahunas equal three voltages.
>
> The kahuna words for the three voltages were mana, for the low voltage used by the subconscious spirit, and mana-mana for the higher voltage used by the conscious spirit as 'will' or hypnotic force. There was a still higher voltage known as mana-loa[4] or 'strongest force,' and this was thought to be used only by a superconscious spirit associated with the two lesser spirits to complete the triune man. (Long 1954: 52)

The popularity of electromagnetic imagery in spiritual traditions reflects a nineteenth century cross-fertilisation of language between the emerging sciences of electromagnetism and spiritualist ideas, which trace back at least to Franz Mesmer's notions of 'animal magnetism': what he thought of as a universal, permeating magnetic fluid. By the twentieth century, many like Long with interests in the esoteric viewed themselves as engaged in experiments aimed at establishing the scientific basis for their ideas about such a universal, potent substance, now often referred to as 'vital force', and described these ideas in language borrowed heavily from these sciences.

4 Pukui and Elbert include mana.mana as a reduplicated form of mana; no form of mana loa is recognised among their translations; loa translates as: distance, length, height; distant, long, tall, far, permanent (Pukui and Elbert 1986: 236, 209).

Despite its quality as a universal substance, the implications of recognising this substance in New Age movements centre largely around the person, and in particular the individual, who is able to engage with this force to transform her- or himself. A great deal of Long's writings are dedicated to what he describes as processes of 'accumulating a good surcharge of mana and sending it to the High Self' for healing, personal goals or other purposes (Long 1981: 38). The psychoanalytically oriented three-part self points to Huna's focus as a spirituality of self-transformation, a fact that highlights one of the most important points of departure in how mana has come to be understood within New Age movements: that it is primarily about individual transformation, a source of power from within.

Building on the base of Long's writings, many authors from the continental United States have expanded upon the tradition of Huna and core concepts such as mana. Chief among these contemporary proponents of Huna is Serge 'Kahili' King, a prolific writer and teacher of Huna in New Age workshops, including in Hawai'i. King is Anglo-American and a former student of Long's, who claims to have been adopted into the Hawaiian Kahili family by his Hawaiian teacher (King 1992), although this has been disputed (K.L. Walker 2005). He describes Huna as 'the Polynesian philosophy and practice of effective living' (King n.d.), demonstrating the way in which the ideas of Huna fit with the broader New Age movement in focusing first and foremost on self-improvement of the individual. This individualisation is clear in the 'seven principles' of Huna identified by King, and widely listed among authors of Huna books and websites. These are:

1. **IKE** – the world is what you think it is
2. **KALA** – there are no limits, everything is possible
3. **MAKIA** – energy flows where attention goes
4. **MANAWA** – now is the moment of power
5. **ALOHA** – to love is to be happy with

6. **MANA** – all power comes from within
7. **PONO** – effectiveness is the measure of truth (King 2009: 53–57).[5]

By the twenty-first century, these principles were being reproduced in images posted on the Facebook page of the Kalani Retreat Center, which claims to be 'the largest retreat center in Hawai'i' (Kalani 2010). In the poster for the sixth principle, 'Mana: All power comes from within', the words are superimposed upon an image of a woman holding a yoga pose on a cliff overlooking the ocean. Kalani is a well-loved destination for yoga, wellness, and Hawaiian culture, personal retreats, and volunteer vacations. In 2011, the centre ran a Huna workshop, which was promoted as follows:

> According to the ancient Hawaiian Huna philosophy, all illness is a result of stress. Modern medical research continues to prove this relationship—linking stress to everything from high blood pressure to weight gain. If you know how to relieve tension, the body's healing energy can flow and you can achieve 'instant healing.' This workshop reveals ancient secrets to managing stress as well as the latest information on achieving optimal health. (Kalani 2011)[6]

5 Pukui and Elbert give the following translations for these terms:

'ike: To see, know, feel, greet, recognize, perceive, experience, be aware, understand; to know sexually; to receive revelations from the gods; knowledge, awareness, understanding, recognition, comprehension and hence learning; sense, as of hearing or sight; sensory, perceptive, vision. (Pukui and Elbert 1986: 96)

kala: To loosen, untie, free, release, remove, unburden, absolve, let go, acquit, take off, undo; to proclaim, announce; to forgive, pardon, excuse; … prayer to free one from any evil influence (120)

mā.kia: Aim, motto, purpose; to aim or strive for, to concentrate on (229)

manawa: Time, turn, season, date, chronology, period of time (237)

aloha: Aloha, love, affection, compassion, mercy, sympathy, pity, kindness, sentiment, grace, charity … (21)

mana: Supernatural or divine power, mana, miraculous power; a powerful nation, authority; to give mana to, to make powerful; to have mana, power, authority; authorization, privilege; miraculous, divinely powerful, spiritual; possessed of mana (235)

pono: Goodness, uprightness, morality, moral qualities, correct or proper procedure, excellence, well-being, prosperity, welfare, benefit, behalf, equity, sake, true condition or nature, duty; … in perfect order, accurate, correct, eased, relieved; should, ought, must, necessary (340).

6 The fee for the workshop was over $US2,000, although this included accommodations, meals and use of the resort's luxury accommodations.

The focus on physical and psychological healing through allowing the body's healing energy to flow, and the idea that the concept of mana tells us that 'all power comes from within', points critically to how the focus on individual transformation in New Age settings likewise individualises the concept of mana.

At the same time, mana, for King, as for other Huna authors, exists objectively within the natural order of the cosmos. Building on the experiments in orgone energy conducted by followers of Wilhelm Reich,[7] King elaborated methods for measuring and collecting mana, using objects known as manaplates and manaboxes. His work in this field began in the early 1970s, and although he claims his ideas stemmed from visiting West Africa and 'studying the life force that some Africans call mungo', it is telling that around this time he also began studying the works of Reich (King 1999), whose unusual psychological theories gained traction with esoteric and alternative spiritual movements in the 1970s (Clifton 2006: 62–64). King describes how he learnt to build plates that give off 'energy' from metal sheets such as copper and insulating material such as acrylic. Although he experimented with different shapes and arrangements, he describes his breakthrough in this area in interspersing the metal and insulating material. He likens these to a capacitor, with more folds or layers increasing the charge (King 1992: 70–71). By using these to construct plates, boxes or other shapes, he suggests, it is possible to build devices that sharpen razor blades, clarify and purify water, charge batteries and provide physical and spiritual healing (King 1992: 72–83). As with Long's writings, these early experiments of King's reveal a concept of mana as a cosmic energy, understood through electrical metaphors of charge, voltage and capacitance.

King's later writings reflect a growing awareness of the critiques of such a concept of 'mana' being subsumed alongside other non-western concepts under the generic rubric of life force. Perhaps influenced by emergent anthropological critiques of earlier conceptions of mana in ethnographic writings, particularly that of Roger Keesing (1984), in 1992 King wrote:

7 Orgone was a term coined by Reich, a psychoanalyst engaged in experiments in alternative healing during the middle of the twentieth century, to describe what he saw as a substance of innate life force within the cosmos, and particularly living beings, which moved through all things and could be passed through objects and from person to person for the purposes of healing.

> Many books that deal with esoteric energy tend to list *ch'i, ki, prana* and *mana* together as if they are the same thing. While the pairs do rhyme nicely, it must be stated that *mana* does not belong in the list. *Mana* is a Polynesian word that basically means divine or spiritual power and authority or influence. It is the ability to direct energy, rather than the energy itself. (King 1992: 12)

King accounts for his earlier writings that equate mana with 'life force', for example in his discussions of manaplates and manaboxes, by stating that they were written at a time 'when I was still equating the word "mana" to life energy in order to simplify the introduction of Hawaiian concepts to the general public' (King 1999). Nevertheless, behind this conception of mana as human capacity, King retains a notion that there is an 'energy' that can be directed in this way, reflecting the widespread influence of these ideas in western esoteric traditions. This remains the hegemonic understanding of mana within New Age spirituality.

Mana in neopaganism

The concept of mana has entered into contemporary Paganism in North America primarily through the influence of Victor and Cora Anderson's Feri tradition. Feri was founded in the late 1940s in a similar period to the emergence of Wicca in Britain. The Andersons claimed their traditions represent an independent North American witchcraft practice pre-dating British Wicca, a claim which historian Chas Clifton suggests, inconclusively, is possible, although it is clear that the Andersons corresponded with Gerald Gardner, the founder of British Wicca, and read his books, incorporating many Wiccan elements into their practice (Clifton 2006: 130–32). Nevertheless, Feri has drawn some of its inspiration from sources apart from Wicca, including the incorporation of 'Hawaiian' elements.

Many claims are made about Victor Anderson's knowledge of Hawaiian beliefs. One Wiccan practitioner suggests that 'during his youth Victor also had many native Hawaiian teachers and through his training with them, he grew up to become an expert in ancient Hawaiian beliefs, a Kahuna' (Knowles 2009). Somewhat more plausibly, a Feri initiate and student of Cora Anderson writes on a website dedicated to Feri: 'Cora Anderson mentioned that Victor had a Hawaiian girlfriend when he was in his early teens (to whom one of the poems in *Thorns* was dedicated), and was presumably exposed to Huna at that time' (V. Walker n.d.). While it is possible that such an early association could have sparked Anderson's interest, it is clear that Victor Anderson drew his 'Hawaiian' ideas from Long's work. This is particularly clear in Feri's three souls model of consciousness, which mirrors Long's system, and was sometimes taught using the names attributed by Long.

Since Feri is an orally transmitted initiatory tradition, the Andersons never systematised their ideas in writings, but rather transmitted different teachings at different times. Interviews I conducted with Feri practitioners in San Francisco in 2013 therefore display somewhat disparate understandings of Feri concepts, including Feri ideas on mana. Nevertheless, like the three souls model of consciousness, many of the characteristics seen in Long's writings on mana form consistent threads through the descriptions of these Feri initiates.

As in Huna, mana in Feri can be moved on the breath or 'ha'.[8] One of the most fundamental exercises in Feri is the 'Ha Prayer', designed to draw in mana to align the three souls. Similarly, the 'Kala Rite' draws mana into a bowl of water held between the hands to purify the water, which can then be drunk to cleanse the soul. Cress, a new initiate, explained these commonplace exercises that she has been taught, through which mana is deployed:

> So, you're breathing in the mana [in the Ha Prayer] … It works better for me if I open my heart and go 'hhhh'. Because then it creates those blessings kind of just raining down on me and the Earth and everybody gets it. And I'm bringing it from everything, and I'm sending it back to everything, charged with who I am and what I'm doing.
>
> … But there's also making kala, which is another way to align … There's a … blowing into the egg, and then changing it, blessing it, drinking it, which … it seems to me that it's used for the same clearing and alignment, but it also seems to me to be used a little differently in my practice. Mostly because when I'm doing this, I have stuff to let go of. There's a cleansing that needs to happen before I can align. So it's much more focused on that than on bringing it in from my surroundings. (San Francisco Bay Area, 31 August 2013)

8 Hā: To breathe, exhale; to breathe upon … breath, life (Pukui and Elbert 1986: 44).

While Cress's description of the Kala Rite is more personally focused, both of these practices reflect the fundamental idea, drawn from Huna, that 'mana', or 'life force', can be breathed in or otherwise drawn from its pervasive presence in the cosmos, and used for spiritual effect.

In these interviews, 'mana', 'life force' and 'energy' were generally used interchangeably to describe the fundamental force used to work magic. Starhawk, a Feri initiate who later became a founder and leading priestess in the Reclaiming community, wrote in the early 1980s:

> This is where our language begins to break down ... Even if we were to speak of *ch'i* or *ki* or *mana*, or *the force* ... perhaps any name, any noun, would be a lie, because energy cannot be separated ... So I will now speak in these metaphors, as if energy were a thing rather than moving relationships, until we evolve the nounless language that would let us speak more truly. (1988: 29)

Mana, then, is interchangeable in Starhawk's writings for the complex of terms appropriated from a range of religious and spiritual traditions worldwide, yet which cannot quite capture the sense of 'moving relationships' she sees as the essence of spiritual activity. Nevertheless, she also wrote of these in substantive terms:

> No modern English word quite conveys the meaning of *energy* in the sense I'm using it. The Chinese *ch'i*, the Hindu *prana*, and the Hawaiian *mana* are clearer terms for the idea of an underlying vital energy that infuses, creates, and sustains the physical body; it moves in our emotions, feelings and thoughts, and is the underlying fabric of all the material world. (1988: 51)

In this description, mana signifies an almost tangible substance that permeates the cosmos. Speaking to me in an interview, Starhawk stated:

> There's the concept that kind of goes through western esotericism of energy and different etheric bodies and astral bodies. And I think that is similar to more the Huna idea of mana. But it's this idea of some kind of subtle energy that you're moving and shaping, and that moves through the universe. And that ritual is a process of kind of orchestrating a movement of that energy toward an intention that's embodied usually in an image or some sensual image to make things happen.

It's like a fluid in a way, in that it is a real thing, you know. You feel it, you can feel it around somebody, you can direct it, you can shape it. (San Francisco Bay Area, 27 August 2013)

This attribution of substantive qualities to mana is commonplace, echoing Long's understanding of mana as a substance which flows like water.

Feri practitioners describe a range of sensory experiences through which they detect the presence of mana. Aurora, who at the time of our interview had been studying Feri for approximately six years under multiple teachers, explained how she senses mana visually:

We usually seem to draw Blue Fire mana,[9] so it's like we take a lens of mana, and we pull one type of energy … we're just taking one slice of the pie.

… oh, my healing, when I do massage, we'd do a lot of like bringing in the golden light. I think that's very good for healing … it's very protective and—how does it feel? It's like—I think of Apollo, it just feels very warm and—yeah that's a good one, it's a good one for healing.

And—or orange is—some of it relates to chakras—maybe it's because of my own experience of being trained in chakra energies … but I do feel like the orange was more sexual, and the violet as being more ether and spirit. When we were doing work in ether and spirit realms, I did breathe in and connect a lot with violet and purple, and—yeah. Yellow's very golden and the East and bright.

Oh, and lime green, light green—the color of bright blades of grass is super-fey … the fey, like the little people. (San Francisco Bay Area, 29 August 2013)

A more common way of sensing mana is through feeling it with one's inner feelings. As Thibaut describes his experience:

So the way that I feel it, breath is the tool to bring in … And then I feel it in my belly, like I feel my belly filling up, and then it expands outside of my belly, like it takes more space, and so I have this external mana belly, if you wish, it's kind of this huge thing. And then I feel movement.

9 In Feri Tradition, mana used for rituals and spellcasting is widely imaged as blue, a conception that pre-dates the imaging of mana as blue or blue-green in gaming contexts (see Golub and Peterson, this volume). It is unclear that there is any direct relationship behind this same choice of colours between these two settings, but notable that an attribution of colour to mana, with its implications for the conception of mana as a fluid substance, is consistent between them.

> … So it's very physical feeling of like energy moving. It's like, you know when you breathe in, and you push your breath into a limb, there's that feeling of something moving, it's kind of—that's the way to describe it.
>
> And it can pool at extremities. Like I can feel it pool here [in his hands]. Or I can gather it in balls, and then I feel these balls at my extremities, and use it.
>
> Yeah, like here [his gut], or in my hands. Like when I do the kala, I store the energy in my hands, going into the water, like it's very—some people say it's 'heat', some people say it's 'pressure'. (San Francisco Bay Area, 29 August 2013)

Mana then can be felt with inner feelings, or seen with an inner eye, or indeed (though more rarely) detected with a crackling in the ear or a smell in the air. In this way, mana is something bordering on tangible and physically substantive, discernable through an array of supersensory modalities.

Many of the explanations given of mana in Feri are expressed through similar metaphors of electricity which Long used in his work. Gwydion told the story of the first time he had seen what he called a 'physical manifestation' of working with mana, beyond his own internal perception of feeling it 'energetically'. As a young practitioner, at a restaurant in Berkeley, his mentor was explaining to him the process of charging water in the Kala Rite:

> I think I said something like, 'Does that work?' You know, some naïve question. And she's like, 'Well yeah, watch this!' And she charged the glass of water and then just stepped back and she was like, 'watch'. And the waiter came over and picked up the glass to go and refill it and got a shock. And set it back down. (San Francisco Bay Area, 25 August 2013)

Likewise, Starhawk gave the following description of her teaching practice in Reclaiming, when I asked her about whether she saw mana as potentially dangerous:

> Certainly in Reclaiming, what we try to do is encourage people to be grounded, and stay grounded. So it's when you're grounded, it's like you have a lightning rod. So if there's too much energy floating around, then it goes into the earth, and it sort of passes through you. (San Francisco Bay Area, 27 August 2013)

As with Long's work, these metaphors of electricity speak to ideas of the power or force seen to lie behind particular magical or ritual acts. As Aurora explained, this power is related to the amount of mana accessed:

> Part of being able to charge your intentions or charge your spells, or be proactive is how much oomph you have behind it. If you're raising a cone of power,[10] your juju,[11] it's very related to it. I mean part of it is the structure of how you're casting the spell, or putting your intention, saying or writing the correct thing that's actually what you mean to say is really important … And the structure of that ritual or spell, so it's how you contain the vessel. But you still need the battery. The battery is very important.
>
> And you can use other batteries … like a candle or create a servitor[12] to do the work for you, like there's other ways to create batteries. But if you're the one charging the spell, you know, absolutely … the more energy you have, the more power you have to do the things you want to do. (San Francisco Bay Area, 29 August 2013)

In many of these interviews, respondents switched freely between 'mana' and terms they see as related, particularly 'energy' and 'life force'. Mana has thus come to be associated in these New Age and contemporary Pagan systems of thought with a concept that holds a very central place in western esoteric traditions: a substantive vital essence that infuses the whole cosmos and serves as the source of power in prayer or ritual. Since Mesmer's work from the late eighteenth century, and emerging as a spiritualist concept in parallel with the science of electromagnetism, the metaphors, imagery and ideas of electricity and magnetism have become central means for explaining and apprehending this vital essence. The language of electric forces, voltages, grounding and batteries has thus become familiar for those seeking to explain the workings of their magic. As the concept of mana has been drawn into this theoretical schema, it too has come to be understood through similar metaphors of substance, flow and electromagnetic power.

---

10 A cone of power is an energetic field seen as being raised at the heart of rituals and spells and directed towards a particular, focused purpose.

11 Juju is used informally among Pagans to describe their magical drive or vitality.

12 A servitor is an energy form created to carry out a particular task.

As in Huna, mana in Feri can be directed toward the self, used for healing, 'alignment' or other spellwork. Thibaut described how he directs the mana he feels within himself, in a version of the soul alignment exercise:

> So I put it in my Fetch [the animal self], and then I move it so I feel this conduit being created. And then when I push it to align the Goddess-self, it kind of there's this rush of energy going through, that goes up and then feeds the God-self, the Holy demon, the Goddess-self, and that falls down, and I feel it falling down. (San Francisco Bay Area, 29 August 2013)

But because it is understood as permeating every corner of the cosmos, for Feri practitioners, mana can also be used to connect with one's surroundings and infuse it with blessings. Using a similar notion of creating a conduit through which mana can move, Cress described this process of feeding mana back into the surroundings at a Feri camp she attended:

> We were doing a cone [of power], and we were feeding the spirits, and feeding the land with it, and we were also collecting it up and sending it back up again, and making another cone. And it seems that the energy and the blessings that come from that—that connection between spirit and land. (San Francisco Bay Area, 31 August 2013)

Such processes express a sense of interconnection with the cosmos, and, more immediately, with the land of the immediate environment and its attendant spirits.

Thus mana in Feri is seen as a relational phenomenon. Yet, in sharp contrast to the mana of Hawai'i and many other regions of Oceania, the relationships mana encapsulates in Feri (or in Huna) are rarely located at a social level. A telling contrast can be found in the writings of Wende Elizabeth Marshall in *Potent Mana*, where she explores the centrality of Hawaiian ideas of healing for a Kanaka Maoli population suffering from poverty, illness and the effects of colonisation and dispossession:

> The healing practices and epistemologies of late-twentieth-century Native Hawaiians invigorated and applied methods and ways of understanding illness from the ancestral past … By expanding the meaning of health to include the impact of politics, economics, and culture on the bodies of the colonized, health and political power were decisively linked. (2011: 7)

Marshall then situates the reclaiming of mana taking place through this healing work as part of the broader sovereignty movement aimed at decolonisation: 'Reclaiming mana as ontology is crucial for decolonization and is an exigency for the survival of indigenous Hawaiians' (2011: 6). Very different from that of New Age and Pagan conceptions, the mana of Kanaka Maoli healing evokes a collective power mobilised for the purposes of transforming a whole community. While many New Age and Pagan practitioners are concerned about the alienating effects of oppressive social structures, rarely would one find the mana of healing spoken about in such expressly social terms.

Concluding remarks

Lisa Kahaleole Hall, in a scathing critique of appropriation of Kanaka Maoli tradition by non-Hawaiians, writes:

> 'Hawaiians at heart' are joined by 'Hawaiians of the spirit' in the New Age spiritual industry's marketing of 'huna' practices … They are an eclectic bunch, however; Huna.com notes, 'We also offer Training in Neuro-Linguistic Programming, Hypnosis, Time Line Therapy®, The Secret of Creating Your Future®, & Ancient Hawaiian Huna.' The problem with this, of course, is that it bears absolutely no resemblance to any Hawaiian worldview or spiritual practice. Some of these Huna practitioners, including the extremely popular Serge 'Kahili' King, claim a lineage that comes from 'Starmen from the Pleiades', which would be fine if they would just leave Hawaiians out of it … The disrespect, exploitation, and cultural distortion and appropriation of Hawaiian culture and identity would be hard enough to deal with in the best of times—but these are not the best of times for Hawaiians. (Hall 2005: 411–12)

The idea of Huna as a Hawaiian tradition has a significant impact on Kanaka Maoli and their understandings of Hawaiian tradition, as the founders of the website and Facebook page 'Huna is not Hawaiian' suggest. In an interview explaining why they started this project, Kelea Levy described attending a class at college in which she was shown a video they were told represented Hawaiian traditional healing practices:

> Right away, when I saw in that video in class what the lady was doing, something didn't seem right. I got really turned off when I had to turn in a paper on the video and I said that Huna was not Hawaiian

> and from this made the analysis that maybe nothing in the video was real and could be used as a basis for determining a universal way of diagnosing and treating disease in the world—and I was graded down for this. (Levy, Ka'upenamana, Chai and Auvil 2012)

Makana Risser Chai, a contributor to the website, states as one of the main reasons for her involvement: 'I wish that people, especially Hawaiians, would realize the Huna [sic] is insidiously destroying Hawaiian culture. There are so many Hawaiians today who are using Huna words and/or concepts, thinking they are Hawaiian' (Levy, Ka'upenamana, Chai and Auvil 2012).

Hall uses the term 'Plastic Shamans' to describe practitioners of Huna, adopting Lisa Aldred's (2000) term critiquing widespread appropriation of American Indian culture by New Age movements. It is certainly true that appropriation of indigenous spiritual, religious and traditional concepts is rife, and often uncritical, in New Age and contemporary Pagan contexts. There are exceptions to the rule. During my interviews, Cress stated that most of her teachers used the term 'life-force' rather than 'mana'. In some cases at least, this avoidance may be a deliberate recognition of problems of appropriation, a recognition I have heard expressed by a small minority of practitioners in other contexts. With regard to the ideas of Huna in Feri tradition, Cress went on to reflect:

> I've no idea how that relates to what the Pacific Islanders do. I know that—you know, I know that—what's his name? – Anderson, Victor, studied the somebody in Hawaii … other people can clearly delineate, and I don't know whether he stole a bunch of stuff, whether he read a bunch of stuff and put it in his practice, I don't know. (San Francisco Bay Area, 29 August 2013)

The concept of mana in Feri is now at many steps removed from Long's appropriation of Hawaiian-language terms, with most practitioners unaware of this genealogy. Thus the concept of mana, and related ideas, has come to take on a new form within these western esoteric traditions, not completely disconnected from, but certainly generally apart from, how their meanings take shape and transform in Oceania. Many New Age and contemporary Pagan practitioners have a very deep blind spot around issues of appropriation, and continue to use terms such as mana unaware of the potential impact this misappropriation has on those from whom the ideas were originally adopted. It is also the case that some non-Native practitioners are making substantial money from the perpetuation of these ideas as 'native wisdom'. Nevertheless, I would suggest that the term 'plastic shaman'—implying inauthenticity, pretence and commercialisation—does not capture well the full spectrum of those engaging with the ideas and practices explored here. Many New Age and Pagan practitioners are also often very serious in their spiritual practices, dedicating a great deal of thought, time and experience to their traditions. It may well be hoped that a much greater level of critical awareness and caution be seen in the adoption of language, concepts and practices within these movements, but in my research, I would suggest that those who adopt concepts of mana are deeply committed and genuine in their pursuit of spiritual practices. They are not 'fakes'.

The concept of 'mana', for better or worse, has thus been transformed through its adoption into New Age and contemporary Pagan spiritual traditions. One of the key ideas in this transformation is that of mana as a force of the cosmos, likened to electrical and magnetic forces and flows. Such an idea, as Roger Keesing pointed out in his 1984 paper 'Rethinking "Mana"', has also been central to interpretations of mana as they have appeared in ethnographic literature since the foundational writings of the Reverend Robert Henry Codrington. Keesing suggests that Codrington was influenced in his conception of mana by western metaphors, in particular by the science of the nineteenth century (compare Kolshus, this volume). He states that 'mana as invisible medium of power was an invention of Europeans, drawing on their own folk metaphors of power and the theories of nineteenth-century physics' (Keesing 1984: 148), elaborating that:

> Because of the way we metaphorically substantivize 'power', the term was adopted to label quantifiable electrical energy as a medium whose flow could be channeled through cables and directed to human ends. This physicalist conception of electrical energy as power … has affected characterizations of mana. (Keesing 1984: 150)

Such physicalist metaphors have also had a powerful bearing on western esotericism, informing ideas about cosmic 'energy' and 'life force' that took shape through the spiritual traditions of the nineteenth century. This in turn seems to have affected Long's interpretation of 'mana', echoed in the metaphors of mana as 'voltage' and 'power' and the idea that mana 'flows' and 'charges' objects, can be stored and channelled. As Long wrote:

> In the bulky literature which has grown up around psychic phenomena and spiritualism during the century just past, scattered postulations are to be found covering the possible part magnetism may have in the action of motricity on objects. This is a most exciting and promising line of thought and, because of the unexplored territory which it still surrounds, it is recommended to the reader as a fine place to begin working with a view to helping to forward the general investigation of magic. (Long 1954: 31)

In New Age conceptions, this idea of mana as a force or flow goes hand in hand with its perceived role in spiritual healing and individual transformation. What is notably absent in this conception is much emphasis on mana as a collective attribute, or on the role of others in attributing mana to those seen as most effective or powerful. In the New Age and Pagan contexts, mana is a spiritual substance that exists independently of human activity, and can thereby be accessed by individuals for their own healing, influence or spiritual work. It has substantive qualities that can be sensed through touch, breath, colour, and in many other ways, and can be used to enhance personal power. But its relationship to the social world is at one remove; it is not so much part of a social system, as a key component of a cosmic system to which all people potentially have access as individuals, regardless of their social context.

References

Aldred, Lisa. 2000. Plastic shamans and astroturf sun dances: New Age commercialization of Native American spirituality. *The American Indian Quarterly* 24(3): 329–52.

Blavatsky, Helena. 2006 [1889]. *The Key to Theosophy: Being a Clear Exposition in the Form of Question and Answer of the Ethics, Science, and Philosophy*. Theosophy Trust Books. Online: www.theosophytrust.org/Online_Books/The_Key_to_Theosophy_V1.5.pdf (accessed 27 July 2014).

Chai, Makana Risser. 2011. Huna, Max Freedom Long and the idealization of William Brigham. *Hawaiian Journal of History* 45: 101–21.

Clifton, Chas. 2006. *Her Hidden Children: The Rise of Wicca and Paganism in America*. Lanham, MD: AltaMira Press.

Crews, Frederick C. 1996. The consolation of theosophy II. *The New York Review of Books* 43 (15). Online: www.nybooks.com/articles/archives/1996/oct/03/the-consolation-of-theosophy-ii/ (accessed 27 January 2014).

Hall, Lisa Kahaleole. 2005. 'Hawaiian at heart' and other fictions. *The Contemporary Pacific* 17(2): 404–13.

Kalani. 2010. Kalani Retreat Center Facebook Page. Online: www.facebook.com/Kalani.Oceanside (accessed 13 September 2013).

——. 2011. Mastering stress for optimal health. *Kalani Retreat Center*. Online: www.kalani.com/workshops/2011/mastering-stress-optimal-health (accessed 27 January 2014).

Keesing, Roger M. 1984. Rethinking 'mana'. *Journal of Anthropological Research* 40(1): 137–56.

King, Serge. n.d. Serge King's biodata. *Serge's Cybership*. Online: www.sergeking.com/skbio.html (accessed 26 January 2014).

——. 1992. *Earth Energies: a Quest for the Hidden Power of the Planet*. Wheaton, IL: Quest Books.

——. 1999. The amazing manabloc. *Serge's Cybership*. Online: www.sergeking.com/Psience/manabloc.html (accessed 26 January 2014).

——. 2009. *Urban Shaman*. New York: Simon and Schuster.

Knowles, George. 2009. Victor Henry Anderson. *Controverscial.com*. Online: www.controverscial.com/Victor%20Henry%20Anderson.htm (accessed 27 January 2014).

Lee, Pali Jae. 2007 (2nd ed., large print). *Ho'opono: The Hawaiian Way to Put Things Back Into Balance*. Mountain View, HI: I.M. Publishing, Ltd.

Levy, Kelea, Maija Athena Ka'upenamana, Makana Risser Chai and Jolene Uyehara Auvil. 2012. The women of 'Huna Is Not Hawaiian': Part 2. Interview by Adam Kinau Manalo-Camp. *The Examiner*. Online: www.examiner.com/article/the-women-of-huna-is-not-hawaiian-part-2 (accessed 22 October 2015).

Long, Max Freedom. 1954. *The Secret Science Behind Miracles*. Santa Monica, CA: DeVorss.

——. 1981 (6th ed.). *Mana or Vital Force: Selections from Huna Research Bulletins*. Cape Girardeau, MO: Huna Research Association.

Marshall, Wende Elizabeth. 2011. *Potent Mana: Lessons in Healing and Power*. Albany: State University of New York Press.

Pukui, Mary Kawena and Samuel H. Elbert. 1986 (revised and enlarged edition). *Ulukau: Hawaiian Dictionary*. Honolulu, HI: University of Hawaii Press. Online: www.ulukau.org/elib/cgi-bin/library?e=d-0ped-000Sec--11en-50-20-frameset-search-h%e4-1-010escapewin&a=d&p2=book (accessed 28 January 2014).

Rodman, Julius Scammon. 1979 (1st ed., 1st printing edition). *The Kahuna Sorcerers of Hawaii, Past and Present*. Hicksville, NY: Exposition Press.

Starhawk. 1988. *Dreaming the Dark: Magic Sex and Politics*. Boston: Beacon Press.

Walker, K. LeslyAnn. 2005. Call for Help! *New Age Frauds and Plastic Shamans Forum*. Online: www.newagefraud.org/smf/index.php?topic=316.msg1334;topicseen#msg1334 (accessed 26 January 2014).

Walker, Valerie. n.d. Feri FAQs. *Feri Tradition: Articles, Exercises, Lore*. Online: www.wiggage.com/witch/feriFAQ.8.html (accessed 27 January 2014).

12

How Mana Left the Pacific and Became a Video Game Mechanic

Alex Golub and Jon Peterson

One of the key insights of this book is that 'mana' is not, despite what anthropologists might think, a concept that is uniquely tied to their discipline. True, the term has been important at foundational moments of anthropology, but it is not currently a topic that is the subject of much attention in anthropological theory. Indeed, it appears that mana has the most import amongst non-anthropologists, such as Pacific Islanders pursuing cultural revival (Tengan, this volume) or in Pacific Christian theology (Oroi, this volume). But as we will demonstrate in this chapter, even these uses of the term 'mana' are hardly the most common. In fact, the most widespread use of the term 'mana' today comes from game players. In video games, trading card games, and tabletop role-playing games, 'mana' is a unit of energy used to cast spells. It is this usage, employed by tens of millions of people who participate in the global culture of fantasy game play, that is most common today.

How did an Austronesian concept become a game mechanic? In this chapter we present a Boasian culture history (Sapir 1916) of the diffusion of mana from the Pacific into the western academy and American popular culture. Tracing the diffusion of mana is difficult because there are multiple lines of influence, and teasing them apart would require a close analysis of the biographies of dozens of people.

Here we will tell this story in broad outlines only, choosing as our end point how mana ended up in the massively multiplayer online game *World of Warcraft* (or *WoW*). We describe how mana left Island Melanesia and entered the Victorian world of letters in the nineteenth century. As this diffuse world of intellectual production hardened into discrete disciplines, knowledge of mana was incorporated into the disciplines of anthropology and the history of religion. After World War II, this work was read by the creators of early role-playing games. Game designers then grafted the idea of mana onto a pre-existing mechanic of 'spell point'. Once the idea of mana as a unit of magic energy was established, it transferred easily to early computer games.[1]

In addition to this historical account, we aim to make a theoretical contribution to debates on diffusion (or, as it is now known, 'globalisation') and the politics of culture in the Pacific. Today the ethics of cultural appropriation are central to anthropology both in the Pacific and beyond. We conclude by arguing that anthropologists seeking to study mana must come to terms not only with Pacific Islanders, but with majority populations in their own countries, who often pursue their own 'quasi-anthropological' interests in ways that are as detailed or more detailed than anthropological work, and equally worthy of commemoration and documentation.

Mana as a unit of spell power

Let us begin by describing the most common use of the term 'mana' today, which is mana as a resource possessed by characters in video games who use it to cast spells. This is mana as part of a 'game mechanics', the set of rules and definitions that structures video games and shapes the action that occurs in them.

A good example of mana as a unit of spell power is its use in the video game *WoW*. *WoW* is set in a 'high-fantasy world' in which players pay a monthly fee to create characters of different 'races' (orcs, dwarves) and 'classes' (mage, warrior) and then play them with thousands of

1 At a late date in the production of this chapter, we learned of Nicholas Meylan's earlier work tying together the history of mana in video games and the history of religions (Meylan 2013). We thank him for sharing his work with us.

other people who are logged on concurrently. Players kill monsters and complete quests in order to gain experience and 'gear', or armour and weapons (Nardi 2010).

WoW is the most popular online virtual world in the United States of America. At its peak, the game was played by 2.5 million people in the USA and 11 million players worldwide. It has been translated into seven languages and is played in North America, Europe, Australia, New Zealand, South Korea, mainland China, Taiwan, Singapore, Hong Kong and Macau (Blizzard Entertainment 2008). This is more people than the combined population of Tonga, Fiji, Vanuatu, Samoa, New Zealand (including pakeha), and all the Pacific Islanders in the US.[2] If there is a hegemonic definition of mana today, it is that used in *WoW*.

In *WoW*, mana is a magical energy possessed by druids, mages, paladins, shamans, priests and warlocks. All characters possess a certain amount of mana, which is measured in points. Different spells cost a certain per cent of a character's total mana pool. Thus, for instance, the shaman spell 'Riptide' (which heals fellow players) costs 16 per cent of a character's mana (*WoW* experts will observe that we are glossing over the difference between base and total mana). When a character has used up all of its mana, it is said to be 'oom' or 'out of mana'. Much of the game mechanics revolves around managing and using mana wisely: casting spells often enough to achieve your goal, but not so often that you go oom.

Mana is featured heavily throughout *WoW*'s fantasy world. Characters can replenish their mana by drinking mana potions or eating mana-filled foods (created by mages) such as mana strudels and biscuits. Mana oil can be applied to weapons to increase the rate that their bearers regenerate mana. Mana looms are required to weave enchanted cloth. Magical beasts such as mana leeches and mana serpents roam the land. Clearly, mana as a magical energy is central not only to the mechanics of this game, but to the fantasy world in which it is set.

2 We estimate that 7,149,515 million people live in these areas. Census figures come from Central Intelligence Agency of the United States (2016), with the exception of Pacific Islanders in the United States, which comes from Hixson, Hepler and Kim (2012).

Mana outside of anthropology: Eliade and Jung

Mana began its journey towards *WoW* in the late nineteenth century. As Matt Tomlinson and Ty Tengan point out in their introduction, the works of Robert Henry Codrington, especially his 1891 book *The Melanesians*, were a key pathway by which mana entered the late Victorian world of letters. But it would be wrong to assume that this meant that the study of mana would be exclusively carried out by anthropology. Today, anthropologists look back at this period as the period when anthropology was institutionalised as a discipline (Kuklick 1991; Stocking 1987). But Codrington's audience did not know, as we do, that our present was their future, and they were not anthropologists in our sense of the term. Many of the lines of transmission of mana from anthropology to the game-playing community come through what we will call 'quasi-anthropology', the disciplines and semi-disciplined intellectual fields which inherited the same world of letters as anthropology and studied similar things in similar ways to anthropology, and yet which were clearly not anthropology. These include disciplines such as German *völkerpsychologie* ('folk psychology') and *völkerkunde* (which later become something like 'ethnology'), which were arranged in disciplinary configurations quite different from those that currently exist today.

A key 'quasi-anthropological' discipline in this story is the 'history of religions' (sometimes called 'comparative religion' or 'religious science'). History of religions had its origin in the eighteenth century's focus on enlightenment and rationalism. It began as a Dutch Protestant endeavour that sought to undertake a modern, critical study of the textual sources of Christianity in order to free Jesus' true teachings from the oppressive and inaccurate corpus of texts and traditions that had been grafted on to it by the Catholics (de Vries 1977: 19–20).

By the time Codrington published his works on mana, history of religions became a sort of proto-area studies discipline, providing an institutional home for those studying Europe's Others in ways that could not be accommodated by the traditional mediaeval disciplinary arrangement that still organised the western academy (Fournier 2006: 38–40). Philology (Turner 2014) and archaeology had revealed thousands of years of history in the ancient near east that predated the world described in the Torah. Missionary and ethnological work provided accounts of 'religious' beliefs (for so were they labelled) of colonial subjects. And translations of Buddhist, Hindu and Confucian texts—as these traditions came to be labelled in the West—revealed entire worlds of thought. It was at this time that the concept of 'world religions' as a phenomenon to be studied was first formulated (Masuzawa 2005; Nongbri 2012). Max Müller, who first published Codrington's findings on mana (see Tomlinson and Tengan, this volume), was a key figure in this area.

One of the main thinkers who helped transmit mana to the gaming community was the Swiss medical doctor Carl Gustav Jung. Jung combined a modern, rational training in medicine and science with a Protestant, spiritualist background that was deeply influenced by romanticism and he took seriously occult and paranormal phenomena (Douglas 1997). Although briefly in Sigmund Freud's orbit, Freud and Jung parted ways and Jung constructed his own system of 'analytical psychoanalysis'. But to call Jung's work merely a version of psychoanalysis is to miss the audacity of his vision. Jung was a synthetic thinker whose voluminous work combined *völkerpsychologie*, history of religion, philosophy, literature and various mystic and hermetic streams of thought into a single overarching picture of the human condition. Indeed, Jung bears comparison to authors such as Ernst Cassirer (Skidelsky 2008) and Eric Voegelin (Webb 1981) in that he attempted to present a comprehensive explanation of mind, culture and religion in an age when such synthetic accounts were being replaced by specialised and modern scientific disciplines.

Jung was conversant with the ethnographic reportage of his day, and drew connections to it that strike us as unfamiliar given the current disciplining of our field. Jung read E.B. Tylor and James Frazer, and participated in at least one seminar in the United States with Franz Boas (Shamdasani 2003: 274–78). He read *L'Année Sociologique* and shared with Émile Durkheim the intellectual influence of Wilhelm Wundt. He cited Marcel Mauss and Henri Hubert's discussion of mana eight times in his work (Jung 1960: 293–94), and was a correspondent and friend of Lucien Lévy-Bruhl (Shamdasani 2003: 323–28). His interest in cross-cultural psychological universals led him to travel to Africa on something like an ethnographic expedition (Burleson 2005), as well as the American Southwest (a hotbed of Boasian anthropology at the time (Stocking 1982), where he was chaperoned by the semi-Boasian Jaime de Angulo, who eventually became his patient (Bair 2003: 332–40).

What role did mana play in Jung's work? Unlike Freud, Jung believed that the contents of the unconscious derived not just from individual experience, but from a species-wide and millennia-deep collective unconscious that Jung's writing brought increasingly into reflexive, articulated consciousness. Thus, for instance, he claimed that 'the concept of energy ... is ... an immediate a priori intuitive idea' (Jung 1960: 28). He continued:

> The idea of energy and its conservation must be a primordial image that was dormant in the collective unconscious ... the most primitive religions in the most widely separated parts of the earth are founded upon this image. These are the so-called dynamistic religions whose sole and determining thought is that there exists a universal magical power [a footnote here reads: 'generally called mana'] about which everything revolves. Tylor ... and Frazer ... misunderstood this idea as animism. In reality primitives do not mean, by their power-concept, souls or spirits at all, but something which the American investigator Lovejoy has appropriately termed 'primitive energetics.' This concept is the equivalent to the idea of soul, spirit, God, health, bodily strength, fertility, magic, influence, power, prestige, medicine, as well as certain states of feeling which are characterized by the release of affects (ibid.: 68).

In his discussion of 'the primitive concept of libido' ('*Über die Energetik der Seele*' perhaps more properly translated as on the energetics of the soul), Jung moved quickly through about a dozen ethnographic accounts, mostly from North America, Africa and Australia, discussing 'how intimately the beginnings of religious symbol-formation are bound up with a concept of energy' (Jung 1960: 61). This, his most sustained engagement with ethnography, cites Codrington ('so rich in valuable observations' (ibid.)) as well as other authors who have summarised the literature on mana, such as Friedrich Lehmann (1922), J. Röhr (1919), Arthur Lovejoy (1906), and Nathan Söderblom and Rudolf Stübe (1916). After around four pages of discussion he concludes that 'we cannot escape the impression that the primitive view of mana is a forerunner of our concept of psychic energy and, most probably, of energy in general' (Jung 1960: 65). Jung's longest discussion of mana comes in a section of his long essay 'The Relation Between the Ego and the Unconscious' entitled 'The mana-personality', but here as elsewhere in his work, it is really the authors cited above (Lovejoy, Mauss and Hubert, Lehmann, and so forth) who are his main sources on mana.

Jung's work strikes the contemporary anthropologist as paradoxical—massively researched and yet reliant on secondary sources, incredibly erudite and yet fundamentally stuck in the nineteenth century in the way that it juxtaposes decontextualised ethnographic reportage. Edward Sapir described Jung's Psychological Types as 'almost defiantly bare of case-material' (Sapir 1999: 715).

Another major quasi-anthropological thinker who drew on the concept of mana was Mircea Eliade, who was present for the collision of anthropology, mana and the history of religions at the École Pratique des Hautes Études (EPHE) in Paris. In 1886—five years before Codrington's *The Melanesians*—the École expanded to include a fifth 'section' in 'sciences religieuses'—section here meaning something like 'centre' or 'department' in an Anglophone academic organisation. Founded during France's Third Republic, the fifth section was designed by the secularist, bourgeois and progressive government of the day to increase France's eminence abroad through rational improvement of the country within. The institution was highly controversial in Catholic France, where challenges to priestly authority could still meet with stiff resistance.

The fifth section of the EPHE became important in the history of anthropology because it was home to several key figures in the discipline: Marcel Mauss was there from 1901 to the early 1920s, and Claude Lévi-Strauss worked there in the early 1950s. Both dealt extensively with the concept of mana (see Tomlinson and Tengan, this volume). In 1947, a sixth section of the EPHE was created to study social sciences (*sciences sociales*) and in 1975 this section became its own organisation: the École des Hautes Études en Sciences Sociales, which is now where many French anthropologists find a home. The original section of religious sciences continues to exist at the EPHE, although this work is not often read by anglophone anthropologists. This history demonstrates the complexity of academic disciplinarity and its relationship to the concrete institutional structures of academic life.

Teaching alongside Lévi-Strauss was Georges Dumézil, a scholar who worked on the comparative mythology of Indo-European societies. Dumézil has had a direct impact on anthropology, influencing Lévi-Strauss and Marshall Sahlins. As a key patron of Michel Foucault, his influence on anthropology was often indirect as well. Central to our story here, however, is Dumézil's patronage of another scholar: Mircea Eliade, whom Dumézil invited to the fifth section of the EPHE in 1945.

Eliade is a complex figure with a colourful biography (see Wedemeyer and Doniger 2010). Briefly, he was a Romanian intellectual who originally specialised in Yogic techniques in South Asia. By 1945 he had expanded his scope to a broader synthetic account of the history of religions. At the École, he produced two books which summarised his thought—*Traité d'Histoire des Religions* (translated as *Patterns of Comparative Religion*) and *Le Mythe de l'Éternel Retour* (translated as *Myth of the Eternal Return*) were both published in 1949. Drawing originally on Gerardus van der Leeuw (1938) and later Rudolf Otto (1923), Eliade argued that all humans shared a species-wide experience of divine power. Because such power was ineffable, our experience is shaped by culture and history. Eliade thus proposed a global comparative study of the culturally distinct shaping of hierophany, or this universal experience of the sacred. This study, a 'new humanism' (Eliade 1961) was pluralistic and inclusive of cultural difference even as it organised its study under a single, all-embracing academic discipline.

Eliade's longest discussion of mana takes place in the *Traité* and in *Myths, Dreams and Mysteries* (Eliade 1967 [originally 1957]). The latter reiterates almost exactly Eliade's discussion in his *Traité*. In this work, Eliade argues that the experience of mana is 'kratophonic'—an experience of the sacred in which the element of power or efficacy is primary. Eliade was especially concerned to make two points. First, he argued against R.R. Marett that mana 'is not a universal idea, and therefore can hardly be taken to represent the first phase of all religions' and, second, that 'it is not quite correct to see mana as an impersonal force' (1958: 20). For Eliade, mana is an elementary form of kratophany not because it is historically earlier or ontogenetically simpler, but simply because it is 'a simple and undisguised modality of the sacred made manifest' (1958: 20). Such a force could not be 'impersonal' because such a concept 'would have no meaning within the mental limits of the primitive' (ibid.: 23)—anything that had mana, he argued, must exist and therefore have some sort of identity. As a result, an 'impersonal force' could not exist.

Eliade was especially wary of attempts to conceive of mana as a universal concept of power or efficacy, which was how it was portrayed in the sources that Jung read and used. 'The idea of mana is not found everywhere', he argues—indeed, he points out that 'mana is not a concept of all Melanesians' (Eliade 1958: 20–21). In his description of similar terms from North America and Africa, Eliade is quick to point out that 'all these words [*wakan, orenda, zemi, oki, megebe* and so forth] mean the same sort of thing as mana' but that 'even among the varying formulae ... there are, if not glaring differences, certainly nuances not sufficiently observed in the early studies' (ibid.: 21–22).

In this work Eliade drew largely from Codrington (1891) and Jørgen Prytz-Johansen (1954), the two authors he excerpts in his massive sourcebook *From Primitives to Zen* (Eliade 1967). But he was also a regular reader of the journal *Oceania* and cites H. Ian Hogbin (1936) and Arthur Capell (1938), whose work is recognisably modern when compared to Codrington's. On the one hand, Eliade continued to reuse this material a quarter century after it was written without consulting more up-to-date sources, which was hardly ideal. On the other hand, his work is more nuanced than that of thinkers who saw in mana a universal or primitive conception of spirituality.

Mana, California counterculture and fantasy gaming

How did mana move from these high-academic, largely European, and quasi-anthropological schools of thought into role-playing games? The key moment for this movement was post-war America—and particularly California—where a growing higher education system helped create the American counterculture and its hobbies.

After World War II, higher education began a massive expansion that continued until the mid-1970s (Menand 2010). Veterans, members of what is called the 'silent generation', used the GI Bill and America's new affluence to pursue college degrees. Soon their children, the baby boomers, followed their parents to college. Between 1965 and 1972 there was a new community college opening once a week in the US (ibid.: 65). As many humanities and social science dissertations were written in the US between 1956 and 1965 as were written from 1890 to 1956 (Abbott 2014: 32). The 1950s also saw the rise of paperback book publishing, which made specialised academic work easy to access (Abbott 2011: 75). This included series such as Harper Torchbooks, 'the first series of a trade publisher specifically designed for the religious interdenominational market' (Schick 1958: 240) and which published Eliade's work. As early as 1950, publishers began marketing these paperbacks to the college market (ibid.: 83). Like the rest of the country, California witnessed rapid expansion in public education in the postwar era, particularly after 1960, when the Donohoe Higher Education Act was made law, creating a massive expansion of the University of California system (Starr 2009: 217). Both Jung and Eliade benefited from this massive growth in higher education.

Jung spent most of his career outside higher education, benefiting instead from the Bollingen Foundation, a nonprofit organisation funded by the Mellon family (McGuire 1982) and dedicated to creating an entire scholarly infrastructure of publication and conference organisation to support Jung and his fellow scholars. Joseph Campbell was one of the best-known members of the Bollingen circle, but it should be noted that the Boasian Paul Radin received financial support from Bollingen (McGuire 1982: 168–69), particularly during the years he was hounded by the FBI (Price 2004: 199–206). Importantly, Bollingen helped support the publication of many early popular anthologies of Jung's work. The first major anthology of Jung's work, *Psyche and Symbol*, was published in 1958. *The Basic Writings of C.G. Jung* came out the following year, while *The Portable Jung* appeared in 1971, edited by Joseph Campbell.

Eliade also used the higher education boom in the US to his advantage. He moved to the US in 1956 where he took up a position at the University of Chicago. There, Eliade used his position at the Divinity School to become a hegemonic force in the history of religions. In addition to training students, Eliade founded the journal the *History of Religions* (see Eliade 1961), wrote an ambitious three-volume synthesis of the history of religious ideas, edited a major encyclopedic reference work (completed in 1986), and published an anthology of readings for classroom use (Eliade 1967) which, due to its size, was reissued in three shorter books. He frequently produced books of essays, many of which repeated his earlier writings. These then were in turn reanthologised and edited by Eliade's students and followers.

Jung's analytical psychoanalysis and Eliade's new humanism respected cultural difference while exploring its most exotic details—a role that anthropologists often assume is uniquely their own. As a result it struck a chord with baby boomers seeking an escape from the dullness of their everyday lives. 'Strange worlds, man', remarked game designer Steve Perrin in an interview with Alex Golub, 'that's where we were going' (Skype interview between Hawai'i and California, 6 June 2013). Psychedelica and humanistic psychology, popular incitements to self-exploration at the time, thus combined with an interest in exotic cultures, which were seen as reservoirs of usable difference. Disentangling all of these threads is beyond the scope of this paper. But at least in the case of California, we can say that South Asia, East Asia and the European past (particularly the medieval period) were key reference points. Outposts of South Asian and East Asian mystic traditions, as well as Medievalist antiquarianism, had been established in Marin, Big Sur and the Southern California desert in the early decades of the twentieth century (Starr 2009: 314–51). These prepared the ground for the reception of Jung and Eliade, who focused largely on these same ethnographic areas.

The Pacific, however, was not a 'strange new world' for baby boomers. Rather, it was a source of exotic liberation for their predecessors, the silent generation. World War II ended almost exactly a century after the publication of Herman Melville's *Typee: A Peep at Polynesian Life*, which was arguably the moment when America's romance with Oceania truly got underway. The late nineteenth and early twentieth centuries saw the appeal of the Pacific wax and wane under the influence of authors such as Robert Louis Stevenson and Margaret Mead, as well as the fad for 'Hawaiian' music in the 1920s (Imada 2012). But, especially after World War II, the Pacific truly became the object of American pop primitivism (Kirsten 2003). James Michener's *Tales of the South Pacific* was published in 1947 and turned into the musical *South Pacific* in 1949 (Lovensheimer 2013). Thor Heyerdahl's *Kon-Tiki* appeared in the US in 1950. 'Tiki' bars and entertaining date back to the 1930s, but Tiki culture really came into its own in the 1950s and matured in the 1960s. As Sven Kirsten notes:

> Just as Tiki fever reached its peak, the big generational divide of the 60s put an end to it. The children of the Tiki revelers decided to create their own Nirvana where Free Love and other-worldly happiness became an immediate reality. Alcohol was no longer the drug of choices as marihuana [sic] and psychedelics became recreational avocations and the sexual revolution seemingly did away with all Puritan notions of monogamy. Together with the tropical cocktails, the greasy sweet faux-Chinese cuisine termed 'Polynesian' clashed with the growing health food consciousness. The 'British Invasion' shifted the young generations' attention toward another strange Foreign cult, the Beatles. The Kinks lamented a plastic Polynesia in 'Holiday in Waikiki' whining 'even all the grass skirts were PVC'. (2003: 47, 50)

In an earlier piece (Golub 2014) we emphasised the importance of Eliade to this moment, but with further research we feel that Jung may ultimately have been more effective at transmitting the concept of mana. Early Jungians settled in California as early as the late 1930s, and by the time the C.G. Jung Institute was established in 1964, there had been over a decade of interest in Jung in the Bay Area (Kirsch 2000: 74–91).

Moreover, it is difficult to over-estimate the role of Joseph Campbell in popularising Jung's thought. Although a scholar in his own right, Campbell drew heavily on Jung in the books and television shows that made him a household name. With the exception of the hero figure of Maui, Campbell wrote little about the Pacific, but that did not stop him from invoking a Jungian theory of mana in *Hero with a Thousand Faces*, one of the main influences on Star Wars:

> Mythological figures ... are ... controlled and intended statements of certain spiritual principles, which have remained as constant throughout the course of human history as the form and nervous structure of the human physique itself ... The universal doctrine teaches that all the visible structures of the world ... are the effects of a ubiquitous power out of which they rise, which supports and fills them during the period of their manifestation, and back into which they must ultimately dissolve. This is the power known to science as energy, to the Melanesians as mana, to the Sioux Indians as wakonda, the Hindus as Śakti, and the Christians as the power of God. Its manifestation in the psyche is termed, by the psychoanalysts, libido. And its manifestation in the cosmos is the structure and flux of the universe itself. (Campbell 1972: 221)

The authors of early role-playing games, then, read accounts of mana radically divorced from the Pacific. Books like Campbell's were secondary sources based on secondary sources. Even Eliade's material was decades out of date in the 1960s. The image was of mana being a 'Melanesian' primitive idea from the lowest rung of the evolutionary ladder, rather than a 'Polynesian' idea from a 'complex chiefdom'.

The anthropology of the 1960s also downplayed the importance of the Pacific. At this point, Margaret Mead was a conservative columnist for *Red Book*. Marvin Harris's popular work would not truly take hold until the mid-1970s, with *Cows, Pigs, Wars, and Witches* (1974). The key figures during this period were the 'interpretive anthropologists' Clifford Geertz and Victor Turner, whose work was much more accessible to undergraduates than the Lévi-Straussian structuralism that made such waves among intellectual elites. Geertz' Indonesia was the closest to the Pacific that widely read work of this period got. Nor did anthropologists connect with history of religion. Leach's dismissive 1966 review of Eliade in the *New York Review of Books* is typical of the anthropological take on Eliade (Leach 1966).

Mana moves into science fiction and fantasy

The exception was the literature on millennial movements, which was widely read by people interested in radical change, or in radically changing themselves. Norman Cantor's *Pursuit of the Millennium* appeared in 1957, the same year as Peter Worsley's *The Trumpet Shall Sound*. Peter Lawrence's *Road Belong Cargo* appeared in 1964, and John Loftland's *Doomsday Cult* in 1966. It was this literature that ended up prompting one of the key promoters of mana in the 1960s, the science fiction author Larry Niven. During his years as an undergraduate at Washburn University, Niven read *The Trumpet Shall Sound* (Worsley 1968) and in an interview with Golub said that he learned of the concept of mana from that book (Skype interview with Niven, 5 June 2013).

Niven went on to become one of the best-known science fiction writers of his generation. It was his early work that involved mana. He wrote a Nebula Award-winning story entitled 'Not Long before the End' (Niven 1969), which was later expanded (1972). Niven then wrote a novella set in the same imagined universe (1978). In Niven's degradationist vision, mana is a nonrenewable magic energy that permeates the world but is slowly exhausted over time as people use it. In the distant past, powerful Wizards live out the end of their days as their magical potency slowly diminishes thanks to overuse. This idea of a time of ancestral prosperity and power really is similar to what you might find on the North Coast of New Guinea. Niven explains its nature and operation for the benefit of an unfamiliar audience:

> *Mana* can be used for good or evil; it can be drained, or transferred from one object to another, or from one man to another. Some men seem to carry *mana* with them. You can find concentrations in oddly shaped stones, or in objects of reverence or in meteoroids. (Niven 1972: 29)

Niven was not the first author to import mana into a fantasy setting. Niven began writing about magic as mana at a time when the medieval fantasy genre had reached an unprecedented level of popularity. Following the monumental sales of inexpensive paperback editions of J.R.R. Tolkien's *Lord of the Rings* in the mid-1960s, publishers heavily promoted the works of classic fantasy authors like Robert E. Howard (of 'Conan' fame), L. Sprague de Camp, Jack Vance, Fritz Leiber, Poul Anderson, Roger Zelazny and Michael Moorcock. All of these authors featured magic and spellcasting in their stories, though there was no single vision for how magic works.

Fantasy authors often mined scholarly literature for inspiration, or just for concepts they could pepper their stories with to lend them verisimilitude. The year before Niven's 'What Good is a Glass Dagger?' Anderson wrote in his novel *Operation Chaos*: 'Although centuries have passed since anyone served those gods, the mana has not wholly vanished from their emblems' (1971: 204), and this was only one of several works of Anderson's that refer to mana between 1969 and 1973. Vance had dropped mana into his fiction as early as 'The Moon Moth' (1961), referring to 'prestige, face, mana, repute, glory'; Zelazny's *Dream Master* (1966) has a character explain, 'We seek after new objects of value in which to invest this—mana, if you like' (Zelazny 1966: 49). Even in an epic science fiction work like Frank Herbert's *Dune Messiah* (1969), we can find Paul Atreides insisting, 'Religious mana was thrust upon me … I did not seek it' (Herbert 1969: 89). While Niven's use in 1969 was thus not the first time that fantasy fiction met mana, the earlier precedents were just name-dropping. Niven, on the other hand, produced a detailed account of mana, one that was specific enough that it could be incorporated into a game.

From fantasy fiction to role-playing games

Fans of fantasy fiction connected with another subculture of the late 1960s: wargamers, players of games that simulate conflict. The most visible facet of this hobby at the time were the board wargames published by the Avalon Hill company, and later Simulation Publications Inc., which let players refight historical battles like *Gettysburg* (1958). There was also a smaller and more artisanal community that staged wargames with military miniatures, following the influential *Little Wars* (1913) by H.G. Wells. Though there had been many prior experiments with fantasy wargaming (Peterson 2012), the first published system of wargame rules for the fantasy setting was Gary Gygax and Jeff Perren's *Chainmail* (1971).

Chainmail offered wargamers a set of rules that allowed them to 'refight the epic struggles related by J.R.R. Tolkien, Robert E. Howard, and other fantasy writers' (*Chainmail* 1971: 33). For example, a September 1973 article by Gygax explains how the *Chainmail* rules could be used to refight the famous Battle of the Five Armies at the conclusion of *The Hobbit* (Gygax 1973). Given the prominence of wizards in Tolkien, especially Gandalf, the *Chainmail* rules have a specific set of provisions for them. Wizards may cast various sorts of spells, including throwing 'fire balls' or 'lightning bolts' in combat, and performing utility functions like creating magical darkness or summoning elementals to fight on their behalf. While the original system was not especially clear on how frequently these abilities could be used, a clarification published within a year divided wizards into 'four classes of persons with magical ability', in descending order of power the Wizard, Sorcerer, Warlock and Magician (Gygax 1972). The fledgling Magician could cast only three spells per game, while the powerful Wizard could cast six. This system simulates fantasy fictions where some spellcasters are more powerful than others, but it more importantly introduces the notion that spellcasters have some reservoir of magical efficacy which is depleted by casting spells, and that more powerful spellcasters have quantifiably larger reservoirs.

Famously, *Chainmail* served as the basis for the game experiments and variations that resulted in *Dungeons & Dragons* (*D&D*) (1974), published by Tactical Studies Rules (TSR). In it, Gygax, with his co-author Dave Arneson, radically expanded the role of wizards—now called 'Magic-users'—drawing heavily on the vision of magic popularised in Vance's *Dying Earth* anthology and its sequels. *D&D* lets Magic-users choose a set of spells 'that can be used (remembered during any single adventure)'. Players must therefore anticipate which spells might be useful in an adventure beforehand, rather than allowing Magic-users to choose on the fly the spells they might cast (*D&D* 1974, vol. 1: 19). This notion that spells must be memorised in advance can be found in for example Vance's *Dying Earth* story 'Turjan of Miir', in which the titular protagonist possesses 'librams setting forth the syllables of a hundred powerful spells, so cogent that Turjan's brain could know but four at a time' (Vance 1950: 24). Vance's account of memorised magic was influential on several other fantasy authors: Moorcock, for example, has his anti-hero Elric 'memorise a spell' in the story the 'Black Sword's Brothers' (1963: 23). As *D&D* Magic-users become more powerful, they can memorise more spells at once, and moreover have access to more powerful spells than starting wizards could hope to memorise.

D&D was however unclear on how frequently memorised spells could be cast. Some early players argued that Magic-users should be able to cast memorised spells as frequently as they wanted, which would make Magic-users disproportionately powerful in the game. In Vance's account, memorised spells could be cast only once, as in his *Dying Earth* story 'Mazirian the Magician' the protagonist finds after casting that 'the mesmeric spell had been expended, and he had none other in his brain' (Vance 1950: 6–7). This was apparently the intention of Gygax and Arneson, but the first printing of *D&D* had numerous errors, omissions and ambiguities, and by the time they clarified their meaning, players had already begun experimenting with alternative ways of restraining magic.

In the spring of 1975, early adopters of *D&D* in the Los Angeles Science Fiction Society advocated for replacing memorisation with a system that would model the energy required to cast spells in order to prevent wizards from incessantly blasting out magics. Ted Johnstone sketched a model in a local fanzine for 'goetic energy' that would be expended by casting but replenished by inactivity:

'Suppose a Magic-User with 14 points of goetic energy used 5 in a major encounter—say he could restore one point in each full turn of rest or two turns of movement (no spell-casting)' (Johnstone 1975). The term 'goetic energy', however, got little traction; in the following issue, the term 'spell points' appears in a response to Johnstone, and this would prove among the most enduring of names for this concept. One of the first variants of *D&D*, the 1975 game *Warlock* (which developed in Los Angeles), dispenses with the idea of memorisation entirely, and instead uses such 'spell points'. Up to 1977, many such early fan systems or competing games had a concept of 'spell points', 'energy points' or 'fatigue'.

Once systems based on spell points as an expendable resource became widely discussed, it might have been inevitable that they would connect with the idea of mana, roughly as Niven describes it in his fantasy fiction. Niven's work was widely read and discussed in the role-playing game (RPG) community, and Niven himself was involved with the Los Angeles Science Fiction Society, as were several other prominent writers. The process by which mana became integrated into role-playing games cannot be reduced to some arboreal first cause, however; it was an inherently rhizomatic process, with many independent points of transmission and sources of influence.

The earliest reference to mana in role-playing game literature comes from Greg Costikyan, a designer based in New York City. His initial write-up is in his fanzine *Fire the Arquebusiers #1*, from November 1975, produced at the height of confusion about the implementation of magic in *Dungeons & Dragons*. Costikyan recalls earlier Niven stories where mana was a finite resource extracted from the land and used to power magical spells, though Costikyan misremembers the name as 'manna' rather than 'mana'. We will find this misspelling is common in the era. Costikyan muses about a role-playing game setting where mana resides in the land, not in characters, and provides a *D&D* system for a 'Warlock's Wheel', an item familiar from Niven's stories, which exists to sap all of the mana from an area in order to prevent magical practice there.

Curiously, although Costikyan played *D&D* with magic based on a spell point system at this time, he did not yet connect this to the idea of mana: he still used the term 'spell points'. This highlights the distinctions between the mana described by Niven and the early proposals for spell points circulating in 1975. Spell points were, for example, renewable with rest, quite unlike Niven's depleting mana. Although Niven occasionally talks about mana accumulating in people, or deriving from certain actions ('there is mana in murder'), Niven's mana is primarily derived from lands, and where lands lack mana, magic simply doesn't work. The fact that mana is localised in the earth in this fashion, and is an irreplaceable commodity that wizards are depleting, surely had metaphorical relevance to the energy crises in the United States throughout the 1970s.

This almost ecological vision of mana obviously is not coextensive with the idea of spell points as described by early *D&D* players. However, by the end of 1978, several systems would adopt the term 'mana' as the basis for these spell point systems. Broadly, there seem to be three schools of thought about mana that evolved relatively independently, all of which yielded spell point systems named for mana in the 1976–78 timeframe: Berkeley mana, New York mana and Rockville mana.

In Berkeley, we see the first significant connection of mana with the concept of spell points in the *D&D* variant rules circulated in February 1976 as the 'Perrin Conventions'. Steve Perrin was part of a role-playing group in Berkeley, California, that had significant overlap with local fantasy fans and participants in the Society for Creative Anachronism (SCA): Perrin had himself been a Seneschal in the SCA. He distributed his house rules, or his 'Conventions', at the first instance of a Bay Area gaming convention called DunDraCon. In Perrin's system, for each Magic-user, one adds their strength, intelligence, and constitution statistics, divides the result by three, and then multiples that total by level to yield a number of 'spell points'. The term 'spell point' is used throughout the six pages of the original 'Perrin Conventions', though one brief aside on the fifth page notes that the spell point system is 'also known as the "manna point system"'. This variation in terminology suggests that Perrin reflects diverse local practices—though he seems to have been the first to write down a system describing mana. Following DunDraCon, Perrin's rules were widely disseminated and discussed in the growing *D&D* community.

By the middle of the year, two further catalysts had stimulated a sudden uptake of interest in mana as spell points. The first was the publication of Niven's story 'The Magic Goes Away' in *Odyssey* magazine in the summer of 1976. With the real world now deep in the throes of the energy crisis, Niven brings the ecological parable of depleting mana to the fore in this story, which won the prestigious Nebula Award that year—it was widely read by fantasy fans, and surely gamers as well. The second was the endorsement by the creators of *D&D* of spell point systems. In 1976, Gygax made a spell point system part of canonical *D&D* by introducing in *Eldritch Wizardry* the concept of 'psionics', a form of magic where spell-like effects cost an amount of 'psionic strength points' to cast or maintain (*Eldritch Wizardry*, n.p.). While *Eldritch Wizardry* makes no mention of mana, the psionics system kindled even more interest in some kind of quantified energy to cast spells; psi points are renewable by refraining from psychic activity, most effectively by sleeping.

At the second incarnation of DunDraCon, the year after the 'Perrin Conventions' were released, David Hargrave first distributed his *Arduin Grimoire* (1977), an extensive book of variant rules for *D&D*. The *Arduin Grimoire* has a detailed theoretical discussion of the nature of magic, which refers to several possible ways to limit magic in a game, including a variant of klutz systems (where spells have a percentage chance of failure) and a system where spells expend 'manna points'—in the text, the spellings 'manna' and 'mana' both appear in different locations. Hargrave was connected with Perrin's Berkeley group, which had clearly been experimenting with systems along these lines for some time, as he refers to how 'some controversy has also revolved around "manna" or "spell" points and their application towards limiting magic use' (*Arduin Grimoire* 1977: 29).

Hargrave treats mana as a quantity of magical energy possessed by Magic-users, which varies with certain core game statistics: intelligence and level. A starting Magic-user of average intelligence might have only three or four mana points to start with, whereas a mid-level Magic-user of high intelligence would have 50 or more. Throughout Hargrave's descriptions of spells, he lists a 'Mana Cost' for each one: simple spells cost only a single mana point to cast, and few cost more than 10, though he imagines as well some epic works of magic that might cost 35, or even 100 mana points. A Magic-user's mana is renewable with 12 hours of rest. *Arduin* was widely read by role-playing game fans at the time; it received considerable attention in important fanzines like *Alarums & Excursions* (Gold). Hargrave's usage of mana surely inspired many of the systems that would appear the following year.

Early in 1978, another Berkeley resident, Isaac Bonewits, published *Authentic Thaumaturgy*, a booklet that attempted to show how 'real' magic might be incorporated into a role-playing game. Bonewits was a scholar of magical traditions who moved in the same circles as Hargrave and was very active in the SCA. *Authentic Thaumaturgy* notes that Hargrave worked closely with Bonewits in the development of the book; Bonewits first gave a seminar on how to use 'real' magic with *D&D* at DunDraCon II, just as the *Arduin Grimoire* came out. Bonewits provides a detailed, effectively canonical description of mana as it was conceived in Berkeley at the time. *Authentic Thaumaturgy* does make oblique (though scornful) reference to Niven's mana, but as a scholar of magical traditions Bonewits was directly familiar with Eliade and other authors who wrote about mana.

Bonewits approaches mana by attempting to explain 'the methods of raising mana used by real world magicians' (*Authentic Thaumaturgy* 1978: 14). First, he castigates those who conflate 'mana' with 'manna', properly identifying the latter as 'an edible substance', whereas he identifies the former as 'a Polynesian word for magical and spiritual energy' (ibid.). Sanctioned methods for generating mana include singing or chanting, dancing or meditating, though all of these methods take considerable time to accrue mana. Bonewits is careful to relate these practices to existing game descriptions from the *Arduin Grimoire* and a recent game called *Chivalry & Sorcery* (1977), a competitor to *D&D*. He also notes that 'certain beverages and herbal potions can produce enormous amounts of mana and/or open up the mage to large inflows of power' (ibid.: 15) surely the first reference in game literature to the idea of a 'mana potion'. Bonewits counsels us, however, that raising mana so quickly is very dangerous, and can lead to insanity and even demonic possession. *Authentic Thaumaturgy* provides a separate table on 'tapping' mana from various sources, ranging from 'the ether' to a 'magical familiar' or 'magical device', and then 'willing' or 'forced' persons, and finally deities (ibid.: 94). Careful formulas allow gamers to calculate the exact results of tapping mana in this fashion.

Authentic Thaumaturgy was produced by a company called the Chaosium as a generic supplement applicable to any role-playing game. By 1978, several companies had produced fantasy role-playing games to compete with *D&D*, and the Chaosium itself joined the market that year with its game *Runequest*, by 'Steve Perrin & Friends' as the original cover says. While *Runequest* uses a spell point system based on a statistic called 'Power' or 'POW' for short, the rulebook does allude to mana: for example, the chapter on 'Rune Magic' begins with a description of how 'Mana is to the Spirit plane what matter is to the physical world. Power is the capacity to collect mana. Spells then shape the mana to attain a particular effect' (*Runequest* 1978: 56). Although *Runequest* makes no further mention of mana, its conceptual place in the game shows how pervasive the use of mana had become in the Berkeley circles where Perrin and his 'Conventions' circulated. When Bonewits published a description of how his mana system could be applied to dungeon adventuring in the first issue of the Chaosium's house organ *Different Worlds*, these ideas reached a still wider audience.

Outside of Berkeley, numerous other communities incorporated mana into game products in 1978. For example, Simulation Publications Inc., a board wargaming company, published their title *Swords & Sorcery* in May 1978 as a hybrid of a role-playing game and a wargame. Its designer was Greg Costikyan, mentioned above for his 1975 proposal to incorporate Niven's vision of land-based mana into role-playing games. *Swords & Sorcery* unsurprisingly does include mana (given again as 'manna'), this time as a spell point system for characters; clearly this follows from Costikyan's 1975 usage. Whether or not Costikyan's New York version of mana was influenced by the newfound interest in Berkeley is unclear.

Additionally, a company called Little Soldiers in Rockville, Maryland, published Ed Lipsett's rulebook called *The Book of Shamans* (1978). This was one among several generic accessories for role-playing games that Little Soldiers had published since 1976. Apparently without knowledge of either the Berkeley or New York mana systems, this booklet proposes a shaman character class which has expendable mana points for spell casting. The term 'shaman' does appear in the original *D&D* system, but without any real connection to shamanic traditions; *The Book of Shamans* references 'North American Indian lore' as well as 'Aboriginal Australia' and the 'Siberian tradition'. *The Book of Shamans* stipulates that 'the shaman's brand of magic is based entirely on natural things', and that thus 'all of the listed values for mana point costs assume that the shaman is outdoors'. Significant penalties are incurred if a shaman tries to use magic in an urban setting. Shamans may derive mana from many sources. For example, if a shaman defeats 'a large, dangerous mammal', he may take its claw as a reserve of five mana points. Mana may also be drawn from locations in the world, 'usually places of great beauty and loneliness'. Shamans may sacrifice limbs for mana (an eye yields 20 points). A final resort for a shaman to gain power is 'to sleep with a woman without her or anyone else knowing about it' (Lipsett 1978: 56–57). From its included bibliography, Rockville mana purportedly draws directly on Eliade's 'Shamanism' and other sources (Budge, Campbell and Frazer, among others) for its account. Although this system was not immediately influential, it shows how paths of influence potentially independent of Niven may have further popularised the idea of mana in role-playing games.

The idea of mana quickly spread beyond these early adaptations, inaugurating a tradition of mana usage in games. At the very end of 1978, Jeffrey C. Dillon published a new role-playing system called *High Fantasy*. The system for Wizards in *High Fantasy* shows the further spread of the concept of mana in the game industry of the day. In it, 'a wizard casting a spell acts as a conduit for aether energy. The amount of aether a wizard can conduct is a direct function of the wizard's skill and is expressed as manna' (*High Fantasy* 1978: 9). A 'first plane' spell costs only a single 'manna' to cast, where a 'second plane' spell costs two. Wizards automatically regain one 'manna' every 24 hours, regardless of whether they cast or rest in that period. Starting wizards have a maximum capacity of three 'manna' points; while the most powerful command 25. Ultimately, this system likely follows the *Arduin Grimoire*, and derives its misspelling of 'manna' from that book's internal inconsistency.

While all of these systems show mana as synonymous with the pre-existing concept of spell points, there were short-lived experiments that tried to fit mana into role-playing games in other ways. For example, in 1977, Steve Marsh began publishing a variant system through the magazine *Alarums & Excursions* which proposed the concept of 'mana levels'. It was not, however, a spell point system: even normal melee fighters have a 'mana level' that determines their relative efficacy compared to others, and various circumstances made this mana level rise or fall.

By the end of the 1970s, however, numerous role-playing games embraced the concept of mana as a system of spell points. Later editions of *Runequest*, for example, award a larger role to mana. Mana figured as well into many later systems like the *Generic Universal Role-Playing System* (GURPS) published by Steve Jackson. It is difficult to trace direct lines of influence after 1978 because the concept of mana had become so diffuse and pervasive.

From tabletop to computer

Role-playing games made the jump to computers very quickly, thanks to the substantial overlap in the community of computer enthusiasts with fans of games, science fiction and fantasy. Before the personal microcomputer revolution began in the late 1970s, computer games were largely a diversion of college students who had access to university systems and, in some cases, early networks. Those college students were also the core constituency that played role-playing games. The first role-playing games to appear on computers were thus hobbyist products, non-commercial, and often viewed by university authorities as an abuse of computing resources.

The first recorded example of a computer role-playing game was implemented on the PLATO (Programmed Logic for Automated Teaching Operations) network system based at the University of Illinois at Urbana-Champaign, although the surviving account of this game comes from another university on the PLATO network, Cornell. A description by Cornell student Philip Cohen from August 1975 announces that 'D&D can now be played by computer' (Cohen 1975: 4). This early implementation of role-playing via computer did not have any concept of a character class: every character could wield weapons and cast spells. The spell system was extremely simple. Starting characters could only cast one magic spell per trip, but as they advanced in level, they could gain the ability to cast more spells. Already, computer games had embraced the notion that wizards held a reserve of magic power that was expended by casting spells. Only 16 spells were available in the game, and Cohen notes that due to the amateur hobbyist implementation, six of the spells were 'not yet operational' (ibid.).

When the personal microcomputer revolution began in late 1977 with the release of the inexpensive Commodore PET, Tandy TRS-80, and the Apple II, these naturally became a new vector for commercial games to reach the public, along with the Atari Video Computer

System (VCS) console released the same year (Barton 2008). Hobbyists became very interested in the potential for bringing role-playing games to these platforms. This was abetted by the fact that so many of the early adopters and designers of computers were based in the San Francisco Bay Area, which also harboured a vibrant role-playing game community. We can see for example in the November 1978 issue of *People's Computers*, an early microcomputer hobbyist magazine, an article by Steve Perrin about *Runequest*, which promises that 'in this and future issues … we will publish excerpts from *Runequest* and begin building computer programs to (1) assist a gamemaster conducting a game of *Runequest* or (2) implement a simple form of *Runequest* as a computer game' (Perrin 1978: 13). Similarly, Chaosium's *Different Worlds* ran notices in *People's Computers* (and its successor, *Recreational Computing)*, as the overlap in the interested communities was substantial.

By 1979, Gary Gygax hinted in an interview with *White Dwarf* magazine that 'computerized forms' (Livingstone 1979: 24) of *D&D* would be forthcoming as computer products. The earliest commercial microcomputer role-playing games, like the *Temple of Apshai!* (1979) had extremely rudimentary systems, which might not implement character classes or spellcasting in any form. Richard Garriott's *Akalabeth* (1980) allows a choice of playing a mage or a fighter; the uses of the game's crucial 'magic amulet' are however not limited by any constraints in the spellcasting ability of characters.

The early 1980s brought with them a crop of more sophisticated games, such as Garriott's follow-up *Ultima* (1980) and Sir-Tech's *Wizardry* (1981). *Wizardry* followed the precedent of *D&D* in requiring spell memorisation. The *Ultima* series trialed various means of implementing magic, but the most influential was the spell point system of *Ultima III* (1983), especially as the game's Japanese translation was widely imitated in Japanese console role-playing games, including *Dragon Warrior* (1986) and *Final Fantasy* (1987). *Ultima III* referred to its spell points as 'Magic Point' levels, often abbreviated as 'MP', and most Japanese imitators retained the Roman characters 'MP' for their user interface rather than choosing some more localised term.

Much as was the case with role-playing games in the 1970s, this concept of 'magic points', like 'spell points', lingered for some time before it became connected with the idea of mana. Classic titles like

Bard's Tale (1985) and the first *Might & Magic* both utilised 'spell points'; *Phantasie* (1985) had 'magic points' and the first *Legend of Zelda* (1986) simply had 'magic'. The prevalence of the abbreviation 'MP', however, potentially made it easy for 'mana points' to become an alternative to 'magic points' in documentation.

In 1987, the first major personal computer title to incorporate spell point systems as mana appeared: the influential game *Dungeon Master*, by FTL Games, originally for the Atari ST system (although it was quickly ported to the Amiga, Super Nintendo, PC, Apple and numerous other platforms). The *Dungeon Maste*r user interface shows three bar graphs, coloured differently for each character (or 'champion'): health, stamina and Mana. As the manual states, 'The Mana graph will drop as the champion uses up magical energy to cast spells'. Because 'beginning magic users can hold only limited quantities of Mana', it will not be possible for these starting characters to cast spells that require more 'syllables' to cast (*Dungeon Master* 1987: 8). As characters increase in level, their maximum mana increases as well, as we saw in earlier pen-and-paper systems like the 'Perrin Conventions', *Arduin Grimoire* or *High Fantasy*. Mana, along with health and stamina, can be restored rapidly by sleeping. *Dungeon Master* helpfully provides a lengthy description of the theoretical underpinnings of 'Magick', and how Mana relates to them. It is perhaps especially noteworthy that this description explicitly states that mana is restored 'by drawing new Mana from the world around you', which perhaps deliberately echoes the land-based mana described by Niven's fantasy fiction (see also Morgain's chapter on New Age mana, this volume).

Mana on the table

Although many new wargames and role-playing games appeared on computer platforms in the 1980s, innovation on the tabletop did not grind to a halt. In the early 1990s, an important new genre of games emerged: the collectable trading-card game. The first and most influential of these titles was *Magic: The Gathering* (1993), designed by Richard Garfield and published by Wizards of the Coast.

Magic in its classic incarnation is a battle game, played with cards, that simulates a magical conflict between two wizards. Wizards may summon creatures to attack one another, cast a variety of damaging spells, heal themselves of damage sustained, or leverage various artefacts, enchantments and counterspells to assist them in battle. All of these actions are powered by mana. As the original rulebook states, 'The upper right hand corner of each spell card shows the cost of casting the spell. This cost is in mana.' Following Niven's vision of land-based mana exactly, mana is something 'which you get from your lands, and occasionally from other sources' (*Magic* 1993: 10). In the course of the game, players have the opportunity each turn to lay down a single land card, and that card can then be 'tapped' for mana. Mana comes in coloured varieties; for example, plains yield white mana while swamps bestow black mana. Creatures and spells usually require a particular flavour of mana to cast; healing spells, for example, often require white mana.

During the course of a casting a spell, a player may 'tap' multiple lands in this fashion. The mana tapped from lands is not however depleted forever; lands become untapped at the beginning of a player's turn, and may be reused in this fashion each turn for casting new spells. But the debt that this owes to Niven's vision of mana is confirmed by the presence in the earliest edition of *Magic* of a card called 'Nevinyrral's Disk' ('Larry Niven' spelled backwards), an artefact which, like Niven's 'Warlock's Wheel', will deprive magical artefacts, creatures and enchantments of power, and thus destroy them. That said, in a 2013 interview with Jon Peterson, Garfield confirmed that when he designed Magic he was well versed in the mana systems developed for role-playing games, including the *Arduin Grimoire*, so influence no doubt came from several sources (30 October 2013, Seattle).

From its humble origins in 1993, *Magic: The Gathering* quickly became immensely popular and influential. Within a year, virtually any new tabletop or computer game that embraced the concept of mana did so in full awareness of the precedent set by *Magic*.

Warcraft and mana

Magic proved immensely popular, and video game designers played it alongside everyone else. That included the people at Blizzard Games (Craddock 2015), originally located in Irvine, California, who played *Magic* to take a break from designing video games, as did the folks at their sister company, Blizzard North, which was based in the Bay Area.

It was a world tightly knit with the tabletop gaming community; one of Blizzard North's artists, Michio Okamura, had even previously illustrated volumes of the *Arduin Grimoire*.

Blizzard made history in 1994 with the release of the computer game *Warcraft: Orcs & Humans*. This first *Warcraft*—*Warcraft I* as it is now known—was innovative because it was a ground-breaking 'real time strategy' or 'RTS' game. Most older computer strategy games were turn-based, like chess: you moved all of your units, pressed the 'end turn' button, then the computer moved all of its units, then you moved your units, and so on. *Warcraft* took advantage of the computing power of the new PCs and ran in 'real time'—you gave your armies orders and they carried them out right before your eyes, simultaneous with the actions your opponent, which might be a computer or a human. The game had a different rhythm than the jittery, gun-heavy slaughterfests played today; a slow and mounting sense that things were building up. The sense of build-up was increased by the fact that you were literally building up: in *Warcraft* you commanded an economy as well as an army. You started with just a few peons and then slowly built farms, barracks, lumber mills and castles. You had to keep the resources flowing to keep your soldiers pushing the front forward.

The first *Warcraft* included various types of spellcasters, including the Conjurer. In the *Warcraft* user interface, the Conjuror has a bar for 'Magic' and a bar for 'HP' (short for 'hit points', a synonym for health derived from *Dungeons & Dragons*). The green Magic bar models a spell point system, as the Conjurer may cast various spells, each of which costs a quantity of these Magic points. What kind of magical energy was it? This was not initially fleshed out; a single employee had responsibility for creating the fantasy setting of *Warcraft*, and apparently there was little need to detail the workings of magic at first.

Warcraft II: Tides of Darkness, released in 1995, deepened the level of fantastic simulation. *Warcraft II* includes a similar user interface showing the health and magic for units, though this time the 'Magic' bar is blue, rather than green like the health bar. We can for the first time find in the manual for *Warcraft II* hints that this Magic bar should be understood as a quantity of mana. For example, the description of the *Warcraft II* mage spell 'Lightning' reads in part: 'Being the simplest of nature's forces to command, Lightning requires but a fraction of the caster's mana to employ' (*Warcraft II* 1995). The designers of this game must have chosen the term 'mana' because they thought it would be familiar to players—thanks to *Magic* and earlier fantasy systems, it was already in the air.

In 1996, Blizzard North produced the first version of its isomorphic dungeon crawler, *Diablo*. At this point, Blizzard made mana an explicit component of the user interface. The player has two orbs on their display: an 'Orb of Health' and an 'Orb of Mana'. Each is rendered like a globe containing a liquid: red liquid for health and blue liquid for mana. Mana is expended by casting spells, and slowly regenerates over time, although the *Diablo* manual also notes that 'Special mana potions are able to restore the hero's spellcasting abilities by refreshing the body and clearing the mind of the imbiber' (p. 29). Mana was now part of Blizzard's lexicon.

After *Diablo*, Blizzard produced several other games that continued this characterisation of mana, most notably the third installment of the *Warcraft* fantasy wargame series, and then its monumentally successful *WoW* massively multiplayer online role-playing game. *WoW* has brought the concept of mana to more than 10 million players, and is almost certainly the dominant context in which mana is encountered in world culture today.

Conclusion

As we have seen, mana had a long road to *WoW*: beginning from its origins in the Pacific, it travelled to the European world of letters and its quasi-anthropological disciplines, and then spread to the United States in the years after World War II. In this conclusion, we would like to step back from the particulars of this historical narrative and compare anthropologists, quasi-anthropologists and gamers. In discussing the culture of the Pacific Islands, anthropologists often see themselves engaged in dialogue with Pacific Islanders. But as our history reveals, other communities are just as important—and often even more influential—in the dissemination of Pacific Islands' culture to global audiences. Anthropologists interested in the Pacific, then, should recognise and attend to this more complicated dialogue of voices. Anthropologists must also recognise their own placement in a globalised world of cultural production, one in which 'their' concepts have circulated widely. Just as anthropologists seek to contextualise and historicise Pacific Islander experiences, they must also contextualise and historicise their own subject positions, not merely as agents working in the wake of colonialism, but as participants in this wider global conversation. Otherwise we risk producing a dialogue which is ultimately very parochial and inward looking.

The gamers of the late twentieth century inherited a number of religious concepts from academics, novelists, and filmmakers. The history of mana serves as a case study of the ways in which games transformed these ideas. For mana, that process begins with field reporters, who study cultures like that of the Pacific Islanders to capture the utterances and practices of believers. Academics then grapple with the meaning of these activities and ideas, draw cross-cultural comparisons, and provide accounts for their peers and the general public. These may in turn be commandeered by purveyors of popular fiction, who alter and extend these accounts to serve their own narratives; even theories that have become unfashionable in academic circles may prove inspirational to these authors.

Games added a new and most demanding phase to the process. Once gamers embrace a concept like mana, they must eliminate ambiguities and reduce the idea to a formal construct which can be quantified and systemised. The requirements of gamers differ in this fundamental way from that of novelists or anthropologists, who can embrace ambiguity and uncertainty about the nature of mana. Games must be fair, predictable and capable of simulation, which necessitates the concretisation of a concept like mana into something suitable for the ecosystem of a fantastic game world. The resulting game system has nothing of the subtlety and uncertainty of field reports, and a tenuous relationship with its source at best. It would be interesting to compare how the demands of simulation quantify and regiment theories of mana to the ways in which bureaucracies quantify and regiment local and multivalent patterns of kinship and ethnicity in order to govern (Scott 1998; Mullaney 2011). Theoretically speaking, the topic most directly comparable to the history of mana may be the history of ethnogenesis.

It does however render mana a consensual and measurable property of the world gamers' experience when they play in environments like the *WoW*. Mana potions of various strengths sell for stable prices in that world, and as its virtual currency exchanges with real world money, the mana of *WoW* trades as do 'real' commodities. While it is tempting for anthropologists to approach this group of gamers who now speak of 'mana' like it is an ostensibly real substance (within the magic circle of gaming (Huizinga 1971)) in a manner reminiscent of Pacific Islanders, this historical account cautions academics to understand their own role in this transubstantiation of mana, and not to approach contemporary adherents to mana without considering the historical circumstances that redefined it. As games have plundered history and fiction for gods and monsters, scriptures and folklore, academics in many disciplines should be similarly mindful of their part in this process of assimilation.

A second conclusion to be drawn from this chapter is that the study of popular culture requires the same sort of care, erudition and attention to detail that anthropologists may more commonly associate with old-fashioned, museum-based studies of diffusion. As historians and sociologists have long pointed out, a cultural studies approach to this material (which is often stimulating but not particularly rigorous) is not the only, or best, way to examine these phenomena. Indeed, just as anthropologists have learned that Pacific Islanders are experts about themselves, we have seen that fan communities, intellectuals, and independent scholars produce accounts of popular culture that are more rigorous, detailed and elaborated than those produced by university academics.

Third, we emphasise the importance of creating these histories of popular culture. Simply because some of the information used to produce these histories is available online does not mean that synthetic histories will be written—nor does it mean that the information will always remain online. And finally, scattered Internet sources must be supplemented with archival and oral historical research. The need for the latter form of research is particularly pressing now, since many of the original generation of game designers and writers are growing old.

References

Books, journal articles and chapters

Abbott, Andrew. 2011. Library research infrastructure for humanistic and social scientific scholarship in the twentieth century. In *Social Knowledge in the Making*, ed. Charles Camic, Neil Gross and Michèle Lamont, pp. 43–88. Chicago: University of Chicago Press.

Abbott, Andrew Delano. 2014. *Digital Paper: A Manual for Research and Writing with Library and Internet Materials*. Chicago: University of Chicago Press.

Anderson, Poul. 1971. *Operation Chaos*. New York: Doubleday.

Bair, Deirdre. 2003. *Jung: A Biography*. Boston: Little, Brown and Co.

Barton, Matt. 2008. *Dungeons & Desktops: The History of Computer Role-Playing Games*. Wellesley, MA: A.K. Peters.

Blizzard Entertainment. 2008. World of Warcraft® reaches new milestone: 10 million subscribers. Paris. Online: eu.blizzard.com/en-gb/company/press/pressreleases.html?id=10014593 (accessed 22 October 2015).

Bonewits, P.E.I. (Isaac). 1978. *Authentic Thaumaturgy*. Albany, CA: Chaosium.

Bonewits, P.E.I. (Isaac) and Larry Press. 1979. The quest for the Sacred Melita. In *Different Worlds 1*. Albany, CA: Chaosium.

Burleson, Blake Wiley. 2005. *Jung in Africa*. New York: Continuum.

Camic, Charles, Neil Gross and Michèle Lamont (eds). 2011. *Social Knowledge in the Making*, Chicago: University of Chicago Press.

Campbell, Joseph. 1972. *The Hero with a Thousand Faces*. Princeton, NJ: Princeton University Press.

Cantor, Norman. 1957. *Pursuit of the Millennium*. Fairlawn, N.J.: Essential Books.

Capell, Arthur. 1938. The word 'mana': A linguistic study. *Oceania* 9(1): 89–96.

Central Intelligence Agency of the United State of America. 2016. *CIA World Factbook*. Online: www.cia.gov/library/publications/resources/the-world-factbook/ (accessed 17 January 2016).

Codrington, R.H. 1891. *The Melanesians: Studies in their Anthropology and Folk-lore*. Oxford: Clarendon Press.

Cohen, Philip. 1975. Letter to Empire dated 23 August 1975. *Empire* 21:4. New York.

Costikyan, Greg. 1975. Untitled article. In *Fire the Arquebusiers! 1*. New York.

Craddock, David L. 2015. *Stay Awhile and Listen: How Two Blizzards Unleashed Diablo and Forged A Video-Game Empire*. Amazon Digital Services.

Dahl, Kenneth M., Nick Smith, Shih Yin, Dave Clark, and Robert Cowan. 1975. Warlock: How to Play D and D without playing D and D. In *Spartan Simulation Gaming Journal* #9. Pasadena, CA.

de Vries, Jan. 1977. *Perspectives in the History of Religions*, trans. Kees W. Bolle. Berkeley, CA: University of California Press.

Douglas, Claire. 1997. The historical context of analytical psychology. In *The Cambridge Companion to Jung*, ed. Polly Young-Eisendrath and Terrence Dawson, pp. 19–38. Cambridge: Cambridge University Press.

Eliade, Mircea. 1949a. *Le Mythe De L'éternel Retour: Archétypes Et Répétition*. Paris: Gallimard.

——. 1949b. *Traité d'Histoire des Religions*. Paris: Payot.

——. 1958. *Patterns in Comparative Religion*. New York: Sheed and Ward.

——. 1961. History of religions and a new humanism. *History of Religions* 1(1): 1–8.

——. 1967. *From Primitives to Zen: A Thematic Sourcebook of the History of Religions*. New York: Harper & Row.

Fournier, Marcel. 2006. *Marcel Mauss: A Biography*. Princeton, NJ: Princeton University Press.

Gold, Lee (ed.). 1975. *Alarums & Excursions*. Los Angeles, CA: Amateur Press Association.

Golub, Alex. 2014. The history of mana: How an Austronesian concept became a video game mechanic. *The Appendix* 2(2): 27–37.

Gygax, Gary. 1972. Chainmail additions. *International Wargamer* 5(1) (January): 12–14.

——. 1973. The battle of the five armies. In *Panzerfaust 60*. Evanston, IN: Panzerfaust Publications.

Harris, Marvin. 1974. *Cows, Pigs, Wars & Witches: The Riddles of Culture*. New York: Random House.

——. 1991 [1977]. *Cannibals and Kings: The Origins of Cultures*. New York: Vintage Books.

Herbert, Frank, 1969. *Dune Messiah*. New York: Putnam.

Heyerdahl, Thor. 1950. *Kon-Tiki: Across the Pacific by Raft*. Chicago: Rand McNally.

Hixson, Lindsay, Bradford B. Hepler and Myoung Ouk Kim, 2012. *The Native Hawaiian and Other Pacific Islander Population: 2010*. Online: www.census.gov/prod/cen2010/briefs/c2010br-12.pdf (accessed 18 January 2016).

Hogbin, H. Ian. 1936. Mana. *Oceania* 6(3): 241–74.

Huizinga, Johan. 1971 [1938]. *Homo Ludens*. New York: Beacon Press.

Imada, Adria. 2012. *Aloha America: Hula Circuits through the U.S. Empire*. Durham, NC: Duke University Press.

Johnstone, Ted. 1975. B-Roll Negative v.II #117. *APA-L 521*, May.

Jung, Carl Gustav. 1958. *Psyche and Symbol: Selections from the Writing of C.G. Jung*. Garden City, NY: Doubleday.

——. 1959. *Basic Writings of C.G. Jung*. New York: Modern Library.

——. 1960. *The Structure and Dynamics of the Psyche*. Princeton: Princeton University Press.

——. 1971. *The Portable Jung*. New York: Viking Press.

Kirsch, Thomas B. 2000. *The Jungians: A Comparative and Historical Perspective*. London and New York: Routledge.

Kirsten, Sven. 2003. *The Book of Tiki: The Cult of Polynesian Pop in Fifties America*. Köln: Taschen.

Kuklick, Henrika. 1991. *The Savage Within: The Social History of British Anthropology, 1885–1945*. Cambridge: Cambridge University Press.

Lawrence, Peter. 1964. *Road Belong Cargo*. Manchester: Manchester University Press.

Leach, Edward. 1966. Sermons by a man on a ladder. *New York Review of Books*. October.

Lehmann, Friedrich Rudolf. 1922. Mana, der Begriff des 'Ausserordentlich Wirkungsvollen' bei Südenseevölkern. O. Spamer: Leipzig.

Livingstone, Ian. 1979. White Dwarf interviews Gary Gygax. *White Dwarf* 14:23–24.

Lofland, John. 1966. *Doomsday Cult*. Englewood Cliffs, N.J.: Prentice-Hall.

Lovejoy, Arthur. 1906. The fundamental concept of the primitive philosophy. *The Monist* 16(4): 357–82.

Lovensheimer, Jim. 2013. *South Pacific: Paradise Rewritten*. New York: Oxford University Press.

Marett, R.R. 1929 (4th ed.). *The Threshold of Religion*. London: Methuen and Co.

Marsh, Steve. 1977. A page from the Verdigris Testament. In *Alarums & Excursions* 27 (October): n.p.

Masuzawa, Tomoko. 2005. *The Invention of World Religions: Or, How European Universalism was Preserved in the Language of Pluralism*. Chicago: University of Chicago Press.

McGuire, William. 1982. *Bollingen: An Adventure in Collecting the Past*. Princeton, NJ: Princeton University Press.

Melville, Herman. 1846. *Typee: A Peep at Polynesian Life*. New York: Wiley & Putnam.

Menand, Louis. 2010. *The Marketplace of Ideas*. New York: W.W. Norton.

Meylan, Nicholas. 2013. Magie Numérique, Magie Anthropologique: Le Mana dans la Construction de l'Efficacité Rituelle. *Les cahiers du numérique* 9(3):15–40.

Michener, James. 1947. *Tales of the South Pacific*. New York: Macmillan.

Moorcock, Michael. 1963. Black sword's brothers. In *Science Fantasy* (October): 2–45.

Mullaney, Thomas. 2011. *Coming to Terms with the Nation: Ethnic Classification in Modern China*. Berkeley: University of California Press.

Nardi, Bonnie A. 2010. *My Life as a Night Elf Priest: An Anthropological Account of World of Warcraft*. Ann Arbor: University of Michigan Press.

Niven, Larry. 1969. Not long before the end. *The Magazine of Fantasy and Science Fiction* 36(4): 53–62.

——. 1972. What good is a glass dagger? *The Magazine of Fantasy and Science Fiction* 43(3): 6–39.

——. 1976. The magic goes away. *Odyssey Magazine* (Summer): 44–51, 62–80.

——. 1978. *The Magic Goes Away*. New York: Ace Books.

Nongbri, Brent. 2012. *Before Religion: A History of a Modern Concept*. New Haven, CT: Yale University Press.

Otto, Rudolf. 1923. *The Idea of the Holy: An Inquiry into the Non-rational Factor in the Idea of the Divine and Its Relation to the Rational*. London: Oxford University Press.

Perrin, Steve. 1978. Runequest. In *People's Computers* 7(3) (November–December): 13–15.

Peterson, Jon. 2012. *Playing at the World: A History of Simulating Wars, People and Fantastic Adventures, from Chess to Role-playing Games*. San Diego, SC: Unreason Press.

Price, David H. 2004. *Threatening Anthropology: McCarthyism and the FBI's Surveillance of Activist Anthropologists*. Durham, NC: Duke University Press.

Prytz-Johansen, Jørgen. 1954 [2nd ed. 2012]. *The Maori and His Religion in its Non-ritualistic Aspects*. Copenhagen: I Kommission Hos, Ejnar Munksgaard.

Röhr, J. 1919. Das wesen des mana. *Anthropos* 14–15(1–3): 97–124.

Sapir, Edward. 1916. *Time Perspective in Aboriginal American Culture, a Study in Method*. Ottawa: Government Printing Bureau.

——. 1999. Is monotheism Jewish? In *The Collected Works of Edward Sapir, vol. III: Culture*, ed. Reyna Darnell, Judith T. Irvine and Richard Handler, pp. 804–09. Berlin and New York: Mouton de Gruyter.

Schick, Frank. 1958. *The Paperbound Book in America: The History of Paperbacks and Their European Background*. New York: R.R. Bowker.

Scott, James C. 1998. *Seeing Like a State: How Certain Schemes to Improve the Human Condition have Failed*. New Haven CT: Yale University Press.

Shamdasani, Sonu. 2003. *C.G. Jung and the Making of Modern Psychology: The Dream of a Science*. Cambridge: Cambridge University Press.

Skidelsky, Edward. 2008. *Ernst Cassirer: The Last Philosopher of Culture*. Princeton, NJ: Princeton University Press.

Söderblom, Nathan and Rudolf Stübe. 1916. *Das Werden Des Gottesglaubens: Untersuchungen Über Die Anfänge Der Religion*. Leipzig: Deutsche Bearbeitung.

Starr, Kevin. 2009. *Golden Dreams: California in an Age of Abundance, 1950–1963*. Oxford: Oxford University Press.

Stocking, George. 1987. *Victorian Anthropology*. New York and London: Free Press and Collier Macmillan.

Stocking, George. W. Jr. 1982. The Santa Fe Style in American anthropology: Regional interest, academic initiative, and philanthropic policy in the first two decades of the Laboratory of Anthropology, Inc. *Journal of the History of the Behavioral Sciences* 18(1): 3–19.

Tolkien, J.R.R. 1997 [1937]. *The Hobbit or There and Back Again*. London: Harper Collins Publishers.

——. 2003 [1954]. *The Lord of the Rings*. Houghton: Mifflin.

Turner, James. 2014. *Philology: The Forgotten Origins of the Modern Humanities*. Princeton: Princeton University Press.

van der Leeuw, Gerardus. 1938. *Religion in Essence and Manifestations: A Study in Phenomenology*. London: G. Allen & Unwin.

Vance, Jack. 1961. The moon moth. In *Galaxy Science Fiction* 19(6) (August): 159–96.

——. 1950. *The Dying Earth*. New York: Hillman Periodicals.

Webb, Eugene. 1981. *Eric Voegelin, Philosopher of History*. Seattle, WA: University of Washington Press.

Wedemeyer, Christian K. and Wendy Doniger (eds). 2010. *Hermeneutics, Politics, and the History of Religions: The Contested Legacies of Joachim Wach and Mircea Eliade*. New York: Oxford University Press.

Worsley, Peter. 1968. *The Trumpet Shall Sound: A Study of 'Cargo' Cults in Melanesia*. New York: Schocken Books.

Zelazny Roger. 1966. *The Dream Master*. New York: Ace Books.

Games (Alphabetical By Title)

Akalabeth. 1980. Designed by Richard Garriott. California Pacific Computer Co.

Arduin Grimoire. 1977. Designed by Dave Hargrave.

Archive Miniatures. 1978. Designed by P.E.I (Isaac) Bonewits. Burlingame, CA.

Bard's Tale (computer). 1985. Designed by Michael Cranford. Interplay.

The Book of Shamans. 1978. Designed by Ed Lipsett. Rockville, MD: Little Soldier. 1978.

Chainmail. 1971 [2nd ed. 1972]. Designed by Gary Gygax and Jeff Perren. Evansville, IN: Guidon Games.

Chivalry & Sorcery. 1977. Designed by Edward E. Simbialist and Wilf K. Backhaus. Roslyn, NY: Fantasy Games Unlimited.

Diablo (computer). 1996. Blizzard Entertainment.

Dragon Warrior (computer). 1986. Designed by Chunsoft. Enix.

Dungeon Master (computer). 1987. FTL games.

Dungeons & Dragons. 1974. Designed by Gary Gygax and Dave Arneson. Lake Geneva, WI: Tactical Studies Rules, three vols.

Eldritch Wizardry. 1976. Designed by Gary Gygax and Brian Blume. Lake Geneva, WI: Tactical Studies Rules.

Final Fantasy (computer). Designed by Hironobu Sakaguchi. Square Enix.

Gettysburg. 1958. Designed by Charles Hill. Avalon, MD: Avalon Hill Games.

High Fantasy. 1978. Designed by Jeffrey C. Dillow. Indianapolis: Fantasy Productions, Inc.

Legend of Zelda (computer). 1986. Nintendo.

Little Wars. December 1912–January 1913. Designed by H.G. Wells. In *Windsor Magazine*.

Magic: The Gathering. 1993. Designed by Richard Garfield. Renton, WA: Wizards of the Coast.

Might & Magic (computer). 1986. Designed by Jon Van Caneghem. New World Computing.

'Perrin Conventions'. 1976. Designed by Steve Perrin. Berkeley.

Phantasie (computer). 1985. Strategic Simulations, Inc.

Runequest. 1978. Designed by Steve Perrin et al. Albany, CA: Chaosium.

Swords & Sorcery. 1978. Designed by Greg Costikyan. New York: Simulation Publications Inc.

Ultima (computer). 1980. Designed by Richard Garriott. California Pacific Computer Company.

Ultima III: Exodus (computer). 1983. Designed by Richard Garriott. Origin Systems.

Warcraft: Orcs & Humans (computer). 1994. Blizzard Entertainment.

Warcraft II: Tides of Darkness (computer). 1995. Blizzard Entertainment.

Wizardry: Proving Grounds of the Mad Overlord (computer). 1981. Designed by Andrew Greenberg and Robert Woodhead. Sir-Tech.

World of Warcraft (computer). 2004. Blizzard Entertainment.

Afterword: Shape-Shifting Mana: Travels in Space and Time

Niko Besnier and Margaret Jolly

There are perhaps few concepts with the geographical ubiquity, historical resilience and shape-shifting capacity of mana. Emanating from Oceania, but resonating far beyond, the word '*mana*' in many local articulations references contextually specific and contested meanings, and assumes very different inflections as it travels across the space and time of the Pacific and our shared planet. The word and the diverse concepts to which it refers exemplify not only the challenges of communication across languages and cultures, but also the politics of such communication, as well as the ethical parameters of our comparisons. This entails confronting not only the conventional genealogies of *mana* in the discipline of anthropology, with its celebrated (yet often forgotten) ancestors, but also the deeper genealogies of the word and concept for Pacific peoples in precolonial practices manifest in localised bodies and voices and in Oceanic circuits of navigation, migration and exchange. *Mana* has moved between local vernaculars and global *lingue franche* in precolonial and colonial times and in our shared present, a space and time which is global in new and distinctive ways. Just as *mana* captured the imagination of anthropologists, literary theorists and scholars of comparative religion in the late nineteenth and early twentieth centuries, it has also fuelled in the late twentieth and early twenty-first centuries the creative rituals of New Age religions and the fantasies of popular culture: science fictions and video and computer games, in which real and virtual worlds collude and collide.

Grounding the anthropological genealogies of a 'floating signifier'

Several chapters in this volume and, most comprehensively, the introduction plot the genealogy of *mana* in anthropology. We will not rehearse the details of these discussions here but rather highlight the contests and ruptures that punctuate the lengthy and tortuous history of western scholarly discussion. Early analyses of the concept can be found in the dictionaries complied by nineteenth-century missionaries that attempted to explain Polynesian languages to English-speaking readerships, such as Lorrin Andrews' of Hawaiian (1836), John Davies' of Tahitian (1991 [1851]) and George Pratt's of Samoan (1862). But it was the celebrated apical ancestor, the Reverend Robert Henry Codrington, first in correspondence with Max Müller, which the latter interpreted in his 1878 lecture (1910 [1878]), and then in Codrington's own *The Melanesians* (1957 [1891]), where he proposed a definition that would become hegemonic: 'what works to effect everything which is beyond the ordinary power of men, outside the common processes of nature' (118–19).

Within both anthropology and comparative religion, theorists such as Émile Durkheim (1965 [1915]), Marcel Mauss (1972 [1950]) and R.R. Marett (1929) first adduced the concept in their universalist and evolutionary theories of religion. It was later redeployed in the more relativist and functionalist approaches of Ian Hogbin (1936) and Raymond Firth (1940). In these early debates, tensions were already evident, not just between universalist and relativist positions, but also between those who, like Müller, evoked a mystical concept, 'a name for a force that transcends all names and exceeds all forces' (Tomlinson and Tengan, this volume), and those who stressed instead the materiality of *mana*'s efficacy in this world, despite its divine associations. There was also a tension between those who emphasised how this extraordinary power could infuse both human and non-human agency (gods, spirits, or even stones) and others who understood it as an ineffable power beyond nature. Most scholars of that era took for granted the universality of distinctions between nature and culture, natural and supernatural, which, although foundational in western philosophies of the period, were largely foreign to Oceanic peoples.

Later, Claude Lévi-Strauss espoused the ubiquity of the nature–culture distinction in his structuralist model, and saw *mana* as universal, permanent and embracing several antinomies: 'force and action; quality and state; substantive, adjective and verb all at once; abstract and concrete; omnipresent and localised' (1987 [1950]: 64). Anxious to domesticate volatile notions to a structuralist order, Lévi-Strauss affirmed that *mana* was the canonical 'floating signifier':[1] a sign that can refer to seemingly incommensurable antinomies, and one that thus falls outside of structures of oppositions, capable of absorbing meanings at will and, like algebraic symbols, liable to 'take on any symbolic content whatever' (Lévi-Strauss 1987 [1950]: 64).

As Matt Tomlinson and Ty P. Kāwika Tengan (this volume) observe, subsequent anthropologists consummately integrated Oceanic ethnographic and linguistic data with larger theoretical concerns but kept returning to older questions. Roger M. Keesing (1984) argued that *mana* had been misapprehended through the conventional metaphors of foreign languages and western philosophies. Valerio Valeri (1985) argued that, in ancient Hawai'i, the *mana* of the gods did not pre-exist but was rather created by human worship. Bradd Shore (1982, 1989) stressed that the generative potency of the gods was sexualised in eastern Polynesia and desexualised in western Polynesia. Basing his argument on historical linguistic comparisons, Robert Blust (2007) suggested that *mana* was first associated with powerful natural forces like thunder and wind but later denoted a detached and invisible supernatural agency. Alan Rumsey (this volume) addresses linguist Juliette Blevins' (2008) analysis of the linguistic history of *mana* and discerns in the loan word *pawa*, used in Tok Pisin and the Papuan language Ku Waru spoken in the Papua New Guinea Highlands, a congruent notion of divine power or efficacy close to *mana*'s classic meanings in anthropology.

We can reflect critically on how *mana* has been conceived in anthropological and linguistic debates by drawing on more recent thinking about language. First, despite the structuralist attention to the distinction between signifier and signified in early debates, much early discussion of the 'meaning' of *mana* was marred by confusion over whether it was about mana (as a concept), *mana*

1 Alan Rumsey (this volume) reminds us that this term as Lévi-Strauss first used it was already mana-like in its fertility.

(as a word in some meta-language, generally conflated with English or French), or *'mana'* (as a word in a specific language).[2] As a result, early researchers attempted to circumscribe *mana* through doubtful comparisons with other words that resembled it, thus juxtaposing the referents of these various words and drawing inferences about their meanings (e.g. Collocott 1921). These exercises in 'word prospecting' (Tomlinson and Bigitibau, this volume) extracted terms from their discursive context and turned the concepts which scholars believed them to express into discrete and stable entities, separate from the social, cultural and political contexts in which they emerged and were transformed. The same kind of confusion between language and concepts was reproduced by Keesing (1984: 138), who recast mana, the concept, as 'canonically a stative verb not a noun', as if cultural categories were units of language.[3] Language pervades contexts in which *mana* operates, but in a very different way from what these earlier thinkers postulated. These considerations highlight the fact that, to understand *mana* and its workings in its various manifestations across time and space, we must shift our focus away from problems of translation and from attempts to 'match' meanings across languages, and instead engage with the social and cultural practices that surround concepts.

Second, the shifting nature of *mana* and related concepts may be better served by moving it from a structuralist frame into a framework of Peircean semiotics (see also Ohnuki-Tierney 1994). In that framework,

2 Although we make these important distinctions here through the use of different fonts and quote marks, these are not made consistently throughout this text and the chapters in this volume, where mana is occasionally italicised regardless of whether it is used to refer to a word or a concept, to a specific language or a meta-language.

3 To be fair to Keesing, his conclusions were less categorical. To quote the rest of the passage in which this occurs:

> things and human enterprises and efforts are mana. Mana is used as a transitive verb as well: ancestors and gods mana-ize people and their efforts. Where mana is used as a noun, it is (usually) not as a substantive but as an abstract verbal noun denoting the state or quality of mana-ness (of a thing or act) or being-mana (of a person). Things that are mana are efficacious, potent, successful, true, fulfilled, realized: they 'work'. Mana-ness is a state of efficacy, success, truth, potency, blessing, luck, realization, an abstract state or quality, not an invisible spiritual substance or medium. (1984: 138)

Moreover, Keesing suggested that the process of nominalisation and substantivisation was minimal in the western Pacific but more developed in the east and especially in eastern Polynesia, where 'a metaphysic of mana' was developed by a hereditary aristocratic class and an associated class of theologians who 'as part of the sacred chief's entourage, celebrating and rationalizing the chief's sanctity, seem to have elaborated the cosmological implications of mana as metaphoric "power"' (1984: 152).

one semiotic category, namely indexicality, has precisely the qualities that Lévi-Strauss was struggling to capture with the label 'floating signifier', namely the ability to attach itself to different kinds of significations according to context and the capacity to *constitute* that context rather than merely *reflecting* it. This perspective allows us to understand not only the transformations that *mana* has undergone across time and space, but also the fact that change is inherent in the concept itself.

Third, following from this, we can help capture the dynamic nature of *mana* through its reconceptualisation as a performative, in other words as a concept whose invocation has the power of changing the way in which the world is constituted. Judith Butler's (1990) reframing of Austinian performativity (Austin 1962) locates the performative power of utterances in their citationality—the accumulation of prior citation of the same utterance that gives effectiveness to each new manifestation, reinforcing its links to the emotions, cosmologies, sensory experiences, metaphors, deportments and material objects that constitute and surround it—but also raises the possibility of disruption, in the same way that 'keywords' are subject to contestation.

Viewed through this lens, we no longer need to agonise about value-laden questions of authenticity and usurpation in the various transformations that we are witnessing, and we can begin to grapple with the fact that words and concepts travel, sometimes in very different contexts from their origin (Rumsey, Golub, Mawyer, Morgain, this volume). Thus, in reflecting with the editors and contributors to this volume on 'mana anew', we see the exercise not so much as a search for definitive definitions or the core truth of concepts but rather, as Rumsey (this volume) persuasively suggests, approaching *mana* as a 'keyword' in Raymond Williams' (1976) sense, namely a word denoting large labile concepts, and subject to intense contestation and immense transformations across diverse contexts of time and space.

Mana's oceanic travels

This volume is not primarily concerned with plotting the genealogies of *mana* as word and concept in scholarly debates, but rather, and more crucially, in tracking its changing meanings and contexts in Oceania and beyond. As Tomlinson and Tengan (this volume) observe, *mana* is articulated across diverse contexts in contemporary Oceania, most prominently in discourses of cultural loss, cultural resistance and cultural renaissance, as well as in Christian spaces. Most chapter authors explore how *mana*, travelling through space and time, has shape-shifted. There were likely important early transformations in passages across the Pacific in the context of ancient navigations, the first settlements of Austronesian-speaking and Lapita-making peoples and later processes in the regional circulation of peoples, materials and ideas. These transformations can be partially reconstructed through the combined techniques of historical linguistics, archaeology and indigenous oral histories. We can also witness transformations using archival research (especially texts in Pacific Islands languages) and through embodied ethnographies. *Mana* has survived tremendous historical upheavals, including colonialism, labour migrations, diasporic dispersals, the rise and fall of polities, the emergence of state structures, as well as the introduction of new cosmologies, moralities and laws. Its meanings have variously fallen into disuse, been co-opted by new religious configurations or amalgamated with other concepts, and, when one least expected it, re-emerged, Phoenix-like, with new cultural and political vigour. It is this power of transformation that the contributors to this volume attend to in different ways, what Alexander Mawyer (this volume) calls the 'ontologically lush and semantically verdant' qualities of *mana*.

The chapters by Noenoe K. Silva, Mawyer and Andy Mills all use archival sources to witness these transformations. Silva analyses nineteenth-century Hawaiian-language texts produced in the context of Christian conversion and constitutional crises. Her earlier work on Hawaiian-language newspapers, first produced by the foreign Congregational mission from 1834 but under Kanaka Ma'oli control from 1861, revealed the broad base of indigenous resistance to colonial influence and claims of sovereignty (Silva 2004). In newspapers of the period, *mana* is almost exclusively associated with the Christian God, but Silva also detects a crucial contrast between a *haole* missionary text, in which God's *mana* is seen as pre-existent and omnipotent, and that of an indigenous student, in which the *mana* of God was instead dependent on humans and other animated creatures and things. The discursive contexts in which *mana* appeared in early documents suggest a gradual transformation. In the first Hawaiian constitution, the term *'olelo* (to say, tell), rather than *mana,* is used to denote *ali'i* (chiefly) power. By 1850, however, *mana* was being used for the power of government.

Thus Silva discerns that the earlier, deeply relational constitution of *mana* gradually gave way to a more codified sense, which suggested a more inherent and genealogical divine power of the *ali'i nui* (high chiefs, royals) like the Kāmehamehas. The power of introduced laws seems to have aided a shift in the relational power skywards away from the earth, perhaps rendering it more transcendent than immanent. Later, in the context of the dispossession of Hawaiian land, the texts of Samuel Kamakau (1869) critiqued western governance, suggesting that the Kāmehamehas were powerful not because of Jehovah's *mana* or introduced law but because they had the power to grant life and refrain from killing in war, thereby pursuing the ethical value of *pono* (harmony). Silva witnesses the celebration of *pono* and *mana* in the contemporary Hawaiian renaissance not as an individuated life energy (as adherents of some New Age religions posit), but as a shared force of the Indigenous collectivity.

Combining archival sources with contemporary ethnography, Mawyer plots the divergent histories of *mana* in French Polynesia, contrasting the Society Islands with Mangareva in the Gambier Islands to warn against the 'intellectual seductions of reductionism' in searching for a 'singular disciplinary meaning'. Again, the Oceanic travels of *mana* defy such a search. Whereas formerly *mana* was rarely attested in historical records or everyday speech in the Society Islands, today it is often used across diverse contexts. In the few extant nineteenth-century Mangarevan texts, *mana* is similarly 'remarkably absent', but its use today is still rare and restricted. In both places, *mana* has been reconfigured under the influence of Catholic and Protestant missionaries, the movement of commodities and the incursions of French written laws and principles of power and land tenure. Mawyer discerns not so much a process of disenchantment, of the divine associations of *mana* being hollowed out, but the differential flow (and blockages) of both the spectral and the secular powers of *mana*. In Tahiti, *mana* proliferated first in the discourses of Evangelical Protestantism and later in the politics of cultural revival, where it is frequently adduced in literature written in both Tahitian and French. In Mangareva, in contrast, *mana* is now so rarely used that it is a *tapu* word. It usually refers to the marvelous works of ancient culture heroes; when it refers to modern concepts, these are only extraordinarily powerful world-changing acts.

With E.E.V. Collocott (1921), Mills suggests that the Tongan words *mana* and *manava* (viscera) were embodied in the lives of pre-Christian Tongans. Although the two terms have distinct etymological roots, Mills speculates that they may have been linked in broader cultural practices, not just as words but in the dispositions of bodies and spaces. He imagines an indigenous physiology linking body parts and emanations with hegemonies of hierarchy based on rank, seniority and gender. The organs exchange with the world—drawing in oxygen, water, food and semen, excreting carbon dioxide, urine, faeces, blood, semen and babies. The pulses of corporeal life would have been signs of vitality in the respiratory, digestive and reproductive cycles. Mills links them to states of *tapu*, forbidden or closed, which he classifies as episodic, relational or regulatory. Episodic *tapu* is that which ensues from contact with a superior's *mana*. Relational *tapu* was intrinsic and enduring in chiefly–commoner relations. Kinship hierarchies reinscribed this distinction since parents, sisters and elder siblings were of higher rank than, respectively, children, brothers and younger siblings. Relational *tapu* changed as people's vitality, agency, sexual potency, courage and authority increased and declined. Gender-specific trajectories were mapped out in puberty rituals for boys and girls, in birth rituals for women and tattooing for men. Regulatory *tapu* was evinced in kava ceremonies and especially in the royal kava ceremony, which corporealised a stable kingship. Mills suggests that the Christianisation of Tonga, which began in the 1820s, eroded the *tapu* system, entailing a profound transformation in the ontological foundations and phenomenological orientations of Tongan society.

Mana in diverse Christian manifestations

The chapters by Thorgeir Kolshus, Jessica Hardin, Aram Oroi, and Matt Tomlinson and Sekove Bigitibau focus an ethnographic attention on recent reconfigurations of *mana* in the context of Christianity. They evince the diversity of denominational experiences and cultural contexts as *mana* shifts its shape in Vanuatu, the Solomon Islands, Samoa and Fiji.

Working on Mota in North Vanuatu, where Codrington spent two years of his life and on which he based his analysis of *mana*, Kolshus stresses the historical context of Bible translation in the Anglican Melanesian Mission and the circulation of Mota converts and British missionaries who knew Māori to the Melanesian Mission School on Norfolk Island, catalysing new contacts between Pacific Islanders. He observes how *mana* has shape-shifted in the context of a pervasive and indigenised Anglican Christianity. It is most clearly manifest in the Mota liturgy; the power of God and the Holy Spirit is its core, which is concentrated in the clergy and celibate priests and transmitted through the transubstantiation of communion to the congregation. But, as Codrington suggested, *mana* is amoral, in the sense that it can be used for positive or destructive ends (see also Taylor 2015, 2016). Although *mana* can be witnessed in the efficacy of penicillin, the abundance of money or the closely guarded secrets of the *tamate* secret society, its predominant use is in contexts reconfigured by Anglican theology. The Anglican priest Walter Lini, the inaugural prime minister of independent Vanuatu, was credited with enormous and dangerous *mana*. In contrast, Mota Islanders who converted to Assemblies of God (AOG) critique the dominance of the Anglican hierarchy and celebrate instead the channelling of *mana* through ordinary persons, as witnessed in individual possession by the Holy Spirit.

Oroi's study of his home island Makira in the Solomons is also focused on Anglican Christianity's pervasive influence. It can be pragmatically channelled when power is needed; it is a 'spiritual switch', like the button on a torch that releases the battery's energies (see also Morgain, this volume, on electrical metaphors). The clergy and catechists can manifest such power, but so can spirits and sorcerers with whom they compete. Oroi compares the approaches of Codrington, Keesing and Firth with insider indigenous theologians like Esau Tuza (1979) and himself, but contrasts the approach of secular sceptics like Keesing with resident missionaries like Codrington and Fox. Western concepts of *mana* as power can neglect its spiritual essence, independent of action but only realised in action.

Jessica Hardin shifts our focus to Samoa and to the relation between *mana* and *pule* (authority) in embodied Christian practice. AOG adherents in Samoa see their church as being filled with the Holy Spirit's *mana*, which engenders love and togetherness, but Christians must pray and fast to bring this *mana* into their lives and into the church. In everyday practice, this entails a very particular form of 'self-making' but, contrary to the view that Pentecostal Christianity is zealously individualist, they 'de-centre individual agency while revealing the divine as the source of efficacious action'. Hardin sees the Samoan social field as biased against untitled authority and individual agency but Pentecostal churches celebrate the individual's personal relation to God in contrast to mainstream churches, where the clergy are the conduit for the Holy Spirit. Performative utterances and embodiments of faith are like a 'spiritual telephone' to God, healing bodies, filling wallets and replenishing food supplies. AOG adherents intercede on behalf of the sick and the suffering, claiming the *pule* (authority) to do so yet simultaneously authoring themselves as abject, without the *mana* of God. Hardin thus adjudges that the tensions between an individualist and relational sense of self are mediated and redressed through such Pentecostal practices.

Matt Tomlinson and Sekove Bigitibau explore the relation in Fiji between *mana* and another concept, that of *sau* (chiefly power). Performative speech acts in contemporary Fiji often make reference to *mana* to effect some desired outcome or make something come true, such as the abundance of food or the continuity of chiefs' power. Yet some Fijians claim that *mana* is a foreign word while vaunting *sau* as indigenous; others distinguish *sau* from *mana*; and still others use them interchangeably. What is certain is that, particularly under the influence of Methodist Bible translations, *mana* has come to be thought of over time as 'spiritual power' and especially, though not exclusively, that of chiefs (Tomlinson 2006).

The strong historical links between the Methodist church and the chiefly hierarchy is mitigated by tensions between the chiefs and church leaders. Especially since Commodore Frank Bainimarama's military coup in 2006, the close relation between mainstream Methodism and the government has broken down, and this has prompted soul-searching among Fijians about the relation between human and divine power. Tomlinson and Bigitibau trace these debates through the theologies of several Fijian theologians: Ilaitia Sevati Tuwere, whose radically inclusive approach sees a new *mana* in Christ amidst the political turmoil of nationalist pro-chiefly forces; Lesila Raitiqa, who sees *mana* grounded in the land as uniformly good and beautiful in contrast to the moral ambiguity of *sau*; Apete Toko, for whom *mana* is grounded in land and people even if ministers are best able to access it; and Lisa Meo, who sees *mana* as the power to bless and *sau* as the power to curse, and the church as having the legitimate right to claim power for the powerless. These theologians valorise tradition and chiefly hierarchy while simultaneously trying to supersede it.

Engendering contemporary *mana* in art and sport

The chapters of Ty P. Kāwika Tengan and Katerina Martina Teaiwa analyse *mana*'s reclamation in contemporary museums and sports fields, highlighting the gendered nature of this reclamation. In Hawai'i, the Bishop Museum in 2010 brought together again for the first time since the nineteenth century three images of the god Kū from the same temple, one from the British Museum, one from the Peabody Museum in Salem, Massachusetts, and one that had been kept in the Bishop Museum. Tengan situates this recuperative event in the context of the perceived emasculation and feminisation of the Hawaiian nation by the combined forces of colonialism, tourism and militarism. It is not only the land and Hawaiian women that are feminised and sexualised, but also the sovereignty movement, which is dominated by women, who thus appear more endowed with the *mana* of leadership than men. Kū is often known reductively as the 'god of war' but his martial essence is but one manifestation of a much broader notion of male generative potency and efficacious creation. Many images of Kū were literally emasculated by Christian missionaries and indigenous converts, as their genitals were cut off and their whole bodies burnt or buried. Contemporary Kanaka Māoli artist Carl Pao has reflected on that emasculation and restored male potency through sculptures with bountiful large penes and penetrative presence (see Jolly 2008a). Working alongside the project director Noelle Kahanu, Tengan witnessed the power that these images exerted on Kanaka Māoli, especially men. But this remasculation is a rather complex, even contradictory, process, as many men revalue the martial manifestations of anti-colonial masculinity in relation to their service in the United States military (Tengan 2008). The exhibit allowed an assertion of Indigenous continuity despite enormous transformations and afforded a context to reflect on how *mana* could reshape the often strained relations between indigenous people, anthropologists and museums.

Katerina Martina Teaiwa's chapter focuses on diasporic Samoans and Tongans in the world of football, especially the National Rugby League in Australia. Mainstream representations of diasporic Pacific Islanders in Australia are dominated by negative images of young men as large, tough and associated with criminal gangs (see Bolitho 2014). But the visibility of Polynesian men in popular culture and especially sport affords a different image. Elite diasporic Polynesian male athletes are not only fetishised and commoditised brown bodies but are also subjects who embody *mana*. Using discourses of new *mana*, they stress that their strength, efficacy and economic success can benefit not only themselves as individuals but also their families, churches, villages and countries of origin (see also Besnier 2012, 2014). They have introduced Christian prayers as part of training and pre-game rituals, and valorise qualities such as humility and respect (compare Rial 2012 on charismatic Brazilian football players). Teaiwa reads the 2010 Body Pacifica initiative at the Casula Powerhouse in Sydney (exhibitions, performances, workshops, digital displays and a hugely popular calendar) as celebrating not just the physiques of the players but also their *mana*. Their giant photos in the first floor of the gallery became 'god-like images' benevolently watching over the crowds thronging below. The particular settler colonial space of Australia with its 'seriously unresolved racial politics' is 'a kind of open field for Islanders to transform and claim in their own way'. One wonders how that field might also be open to the *mana* of Pacific women in Australia.

Mana in New Age religions and video games

The chapters by Rachel Morgain and Alex Golub and Jon Peterson move *mana* into even more globalised spaces as it is appropriated as an energy or a life force possessed by individuals both in New Age religious movements and in the world of science fiction and video and computer games. The spectre of misrecognition and misappropriation haunts both these essays, although the authors approach this problem with notable subtlety.

Morgain argues that New Age understandings of *mana* were fundamentally shaped by early twentieth-century western philosophies, including psychoanalysis. Max Freedom Long's notion of 'three selves' parallels the Freudian distinction between id, ego and superego, and Wilhelm Reich's 'orgone energy', replete with metaphors of electricity, magnetism and flowing water, which is essentially accessed by individuals in processes of self-transformation. Many others subsequently diverted relational Polynesian philosophies into individualist projects to channel cosmic energies designed to transform the self. The appropriation of the Oceanic concept of *mana* in New Age religions has been scathingly criticised by writers like Lisa Kahaleole Hall as 'not Hawaiian' and as the sham practices of 'plastic shamans'. Morgain situates this critique in the broader context of the characterisation of New Age religions as promiscuously appropriating concepts from divergent times and places, but argues that seeing these practitioners as 'fake' is too simplistic. Still, they have surely shifted the shape of *mana* from a force in a relational collective field to a cosmic substance accessed by privileged individuals.

Alex Golub and Jon Peterson observe that those who invoke *mana* most frequently today are not Pacific peoples or anthropologists, but creators and players of video games. In the very popular *World of Warcraft*, played by about 10 million people worldwide, *mana* is a magical energy that druids, mages, paladins, shamans and warlocks can possess in different degrees. Reflecting on the earlier history of *mana*'s travels, Golub and Peterson suggest that it was not just anthropologists who were fixated on the concept but the broader Victorian world of letters and scholars of comparative religion, in an intellectual genealogy that encompasses Müller, Mauss, Georges Dumézil, Mircea Eliade, J.R.R. Tolkien, Ernst Cassirer and Joseph Campbell. The countercultures of the 1960s and 1970s in the United States were profoundly influenced by the widely circulating paperback editions of Eliade and Tolkien. Fantasy fiction influenced science fiction writers, including Larry Niven, who claims that he first read about *mana* in Peter Worsley's *The Trumpet Shall Sound* (1968). The energy crises of the 1970s further produced competing visions of *mana* as a 'non-renewable' or 'renewable magic energy' in different games. Golub and Peterson suggest that anthropologists must reflect on their own subject position in a globalised world of cultural production. Just as they are engaging in dialogues with Pacific Islanders, anthropologists also need to develop the same respectful dialogues with the expert fans and the independent intellectuals of popular global culture. They eschew questions of misappropriation or inauthenticity as the 'Austronesian concept' of *mana* again shifts its shape in the virtual world.

Final words? Silences and substances

Words and utterances can be valuable commodities, but their worth as commodities is dependent on who controls them, who they are about, and who hears or overhears them. But language can also acquire value when it is interwoven with a host of other signs. Can its absence, in silence for example, just as easily be a symptom of *mana*? We are reminded of the *mana* of high chiefs in Tonga and Samoa, as well as many other parts of the Pacific, which resides in their impassive silence, as they let their attendants do the talking (*matāpule* or *tulāfale*, often awkwardly translated as 'talking chiefs'). Here, *mana* emanates from the stillness of high rank (compare Irvine 1990 on Senegal). Similarly, secrecy, concealment, avoidance, or indirection can all potentially act as sign-vehicles of powerful *mana*, as in the Hawaiian recognition of powerful *kaona* (hidden meanings) in the talk of *ali'i nui*.

This recognition helps us understand the transformations that *mana* has undergone in its travels with Christian conversion, catalysed by both European and Oceanic missionaries, and with colonial and indigenous state formation, as well as indigenous resistance and sovereignty. The arrival and subsequent localisation of Christianity are perhaps the quintessential contexts in which to explore the interdigitation of *mana* with changing ideologies of language, the truth, and humans' relationships to it (see also Keane 2006). In many parts of the Pacific, the *mana* of indigenous gods was in fact the focus of enormous anxiety for early missionaries, who, in their zeal to drain the efficacy of the gods, burnt, drowned or buried sacred manifestations in stone, wood or pandanus, even using sacred stones for the foundations of Christian church buildings, acts of incorporation of unequivocal iconic significance. There is no doubt that the passion of this iconoclastic desacralisation is situated in that longer history pitching Protestants against Catholics in the theology of transubstantiation and the Protestant attack on Catholic statues and relics, which, like Oceanic gods, were often seen to move and even to weep. But there is evidence that, while these efforts were largely successful in replacing one cosmology with another, they did not complete annihilate the building blocks of the old cosmologies.

Observing this process, Tomlinson (2006) suggests that the historical and spatial transformations of *mana* have moved on an arc towards its greater substantivisation. He agrees with Keesing (1984) and Paul Geraghty, the doyen of Fijian linguistics, that *mana* is 'canonically a verb in Fiji' but that contemporary speakers frequently use it in its 'nominalized and substantivized form' (2006: 173). In contemporary discourse, the nominal use of *mana* is frequently adduced in discourses of cultural loss and the decline of chiefly power. A crucial key to these transformations is Christian conversion and the translation of the Fijian Bible, where *mana* denoted 'miracles' and was linked to the homophonous 'manna', the divine food that God gave the Israelites. Keesing failed to recognise the crucial significance of Christianity in the shape-shifting of *mana*, writing dismissively instead about Christianity (2006: 177) and passionately celebrating Kwaio 'pagans' in contrast to their Christian kin on Malaita.

But there is another aspect to this story that has perhaps not been sufficiently credited, namely the heavy engagement of indigenous missionaries from the eastern Pacific, particularly Tahitians, Rarotongans, Samoans and Tongans, in converting those further west. Keesing (1984) suggested that, in the Polynesian polities of Hawai'i, Tahiti, the Marquesas and Māori Aotearoa/New Zealand, the formation of an hereditary aristocracy and dedicated theologians had occasioned a greater sense of *mana* as substantivised power, as a property of chiefs and gods. Tomlinson (2006) also suggests that Polynesian influences from Samoa and Tonga in eastern Fiji might have proved important in a more pronounced nominalisation and substantivisation of *mana*.

Much of the history of Christian missions has been unduly fixated on European missionaries and in particular martyrs such as John Williams, while indigenous missionaries have been referred to as 'native teachers', the dismissive term that European missionaries themselves employed in reference to them. But Polynesians often constituted the vanguard of evangelism and were central in the work of translation and conversion, especially in what were seen as the 'dark and difficult' mission fields of the west (Latai 2015, and many others). Witness the Samoans, men and women of the London Missionary Society in what became Papua New Guinea and Vanuatu. So perhaps it was not only the more metaphysical renditions of *mana* by foreign missionaries but also the rather different Polynesian notions of *mana* that promoted an historical transformation in the western Pacific, even if the role of the latter remains largely unremarked.

Finally, we may ask what the relationship was between these new Christian cosmologies and the novel commodities of a globalising culture of capitalism. Christianities and commodities were not just simultaneous arrivals in the Oceanic world but were intimately entangled in dramatic transformations of Oceanic societies, transformations which gradually reshaped prevailing ideas of persons and things. Arguably, exposure to the commodities of global capitalism and to novel languages of property in persons and things might have facilitated a greater sense of *mana* as a substance or even a commodity (Silva, Tengan, Teaiwa, Morgain, Golub and Peterson, this volume). Such transformations connect dynamics in contemporary Oceania with those New Age religions and video games where *mana* becomes not just a powerful commodity but an increasingly individualised divine energy.

References

Andrews, Lorrin. 1836. *A Vocabulary of Words in the Hawaiian Language*. Lahainaluna: Press of the High School.

Austin, J.L. 1962. *How to Do Things with Words: The William James Lectures Delivered at Harvard University in 1955*, ed. J.O. Urmson and Marina Sbisà. Oxford: Clarendon Press.

Besnier, Niko. 2012. The athlete's body and the global condition: Tongan rugby players in Japan. *American Ethnologist* 39(3): 491–510.

——. 2014. Sports, bodies, and futures: An epilogue. In *Contemporary Sporting Formations in Oceania*, ed. Lisa Uperesa and Thomas Mountjoy. Special issue of *The Contemporary Pacific* 26: 435–44.

Blevins, Juliette. 2008. Some comparative notes on proto-Oceanic *mana: Inside and outside the Austronesian family. *Oceanic Linguistics* 47: 253–74.

Blust, Robert. 2007. Proto-Oceanic *mana revisited. *Oceanic Linguistics* 46(2): 404–23.

Bolitho, Sam. 2014. Chris Lilley comedy Jonah from Tonga slammed as 'deeply offensive'. *ABC News* (5 September) Online: www.abc.net.au/news/2014-05-09/an-chris-lilley27s-jonah-from-tonga-criticised/544163 (accessed 8 September 2014).

Butler, Judith. 1990. *Gender Trouble: Feminism and the Subversion of Identity*. London: Routledge.

Codrington, R.H. 1957 [1891]. *The Melanesians: Studies in their Anthropology and Folk-Lore*. New Haven, CT: Human Relations Area Files Press.

Collocott, E.E.V. 1921. The supernatural in Tonga. *American Anthropologist* 23(4): 415–44.

Davies, John. 1991 [1851]. *Tahitian and English Dictionary with Introductory Remarks on the Polynesian Language and a Short Grammar of the Tahitian Dialect: With an Appendix*. Tahiti: Editions Haere Po.

Durkheim, Émile. 1965 [1915]. *The Elementary Forms of the Religious Life*, trans. J.W. Swain. New York: Free Press.

Eliade, Mircea. 1949a. *Le mythe de l'éternel retour: Archétypes et répétition*. Paris: Gallimard.

——. 1949b. *Traité d'histoire des religions*. Paris: Payot.

——. 1958. *Patterns in Comparative Religion,* trans. Rosemary Sheed. New York: Sheed and Ward.

——. 1961. History of religions and a new humanism. *History of Religions* 1(1): 1–8.

——. 1967. *From Primitives to Zen: A Thematic Sourcebook of the History of Religions*. New York: Harper & Row.

Firth, Raymond. 1940. The analysis of 'mana': An empirical approach. *Journal of the Polynesian Society* 49(4): 483–510.

Habel, Norman C. (ed.). 1979. *Powers, Plumes and Piglets: Phenomena of Melanesian Religion*. Bedford Park, SA: Australian Association for the Study of Religions.

Hall, Lisa Kahaleole. 2005. 'Hawaiian at heart' and other fictions. *The Contemporary Pacific* 17(2): 404–13.

Hogbin, H. Ian. 1936. Mana. *Oceania* 6: 241–74.

Howard, Alan and Robert Borofsky (eds). 1989. *Mana* and *Tapu*. In *Developments in Polynesian Ethnology*. Honolulu: University of Hawai'i Press.

Irvine, Judith T. 1990. Registering affect: Heteroglossia in the linguistic expression of emotion. In *Language and the Politics of Emotion*, ed. Catherine A. Lutz and Lila Abu-Lughod, pp. 126–61. Cambridge: Cambridge University Press.

Jolly, Margaret. 2008a. Moving masculinities: Memories and bodies across Oceania. *The Contemporary Pacific* 20(1): 1–24.

—— (ed.). 2008b. *Re-membering Oceanic Masculinities*. Special issue of *The Contemporary Pacific* 20(1).

Kamakau, S.M. 1869. Ka moolelo Hawaii. *Ke Au Okoa* 5/30 (11 November).

Keane, Webb. 2006. *Christian Moderns: Freedom and Fetish in the Mission Encounter*. Berkeley, CA: University of California Press.

Keesing, Roger M. 1984. Rethinking *mana*. *Journal of Anthropological Research* 40(1): 137–56.

Latai, Latu. 2015. Changing covenants in Samoa? From brothers and sisters to husbands and wives? *Oceania* 85(1): 92–104.

Lévi-Strauss, Claude. 1987 [1950]. *Introduction to the Work of Marcel Mauss*, trans. Felicity Baker. London: Routledge & Kegan Paul.

Lutz Catherine A. and Lila Abu-Lughod (eds). 1990. *Language and the Politics of Emotion*. Cambridge: Cambridge University Press.

Magowan, Fiona and Carolyn Schwarz (eds). 2016. *Conflicts and Convergences: Critical Perspectives on Christianity in Australia and the Pacific*. Brill, Leiden.

Marett, R.R. 1929 (4th ed.). *The Threshold of Religion*. London: Methuen and Co.

Mauss, Marcel. 1972 [1950]. *A General Theory of Magic*, trans. Robert Brain. London: Routledge & Kegan Paul.

Müller, F. Max. 1910 [1878]. *Lectures on the Origin and Growth of Religion as Illustrated by the Religions of India: The Hibbert Lectures, Delivered in the Chapter House, Westminster Abbey, in April, May, and June, 1878*. London: Longmans, Green, and Co.

Ohnuki-Tierney, Emiko. 1994. The power of absence: Zero signifiers and their transgressions. *L'Homme* 34(2): 59–76.

Pratt, George. 1862. *A Samoan Dictionary: English and Samoan, and Samoan and English; with a Short Grammar of the Samoan Dialect*. Malua, Samoa: London Missionary Society Press.

Rial, Carmen. 2012. Banal religiosity: Brazilian athletes as new missionaries of the neo-Pentecostal diaspora. *Vibrant* 9: 130–59.

Shore, Bradd. 1982. *Sala'ilua: A Samoan Mystery*. New York: Columbia University Press.

——. 1989. *Mana* and *Tapu*. In *Developments in Polynesian Ethnology*, ed. Alan Howard and Robert Borofsky, pp. 137–73. Honolulu: University of Hawai'i Press.

Silva, Noenoe K. 2004. *Aloha Betrayed: Native Hawaiian Resistance to American Colonialism*. Durham, NC: Duke University Press.

Taylor, John. 2015. Sorcery and the moral economy of agency: An ethnographic account. *Oceania* 85(1): 38–50.

——. 2016. Two baskets worn at once: Christianity, sorcery and sacred power in Vanuatu. In *Conflicts and Convergences: Critical Perspectives on Christianity in Australia and the Pacific*, ed. Fiona Magowan and Carolyn Schwarz, pp. 139–60. Brill, Leiden.

Tengan, Ty P. Kāwika. 2008. *Native Men Remade: Gender and Nation in Contemporary Hawai'i*. Durham, NC: Duke University Press.

Tomlinson, Matt. 2006. Re-theorizing mana: Bible translation and discourse of loss in Fiji. *Oceania* 76: 173–85.

Tuza, Esau. 1979. Spirits and powers in Melanesia. In *Powers, Plumes and Piglets: Phenomena of Melanesian Religion*, ed. Norman C. Habel, pp. 97–108. Bedford Park, SA: Australian Association for the Study of Religions.

Valeri, Valerio. 1985. *Kingship and Sacrifice: Ritual and Society in Ancient Hawaii*, trans. Paula Wissing. Chicago, IL: University of Chicago Press.

Uperesa, Lisa and Thomas Mountjoy (eds). 2014. *Contemporary Sporting Formations in Oceania*. Special issue of *The Contemporary Pacific* 26.

Williams, Raymond. 1976. *Keywords: A Vocabulary of Culture and Society*. London: Croom Helm.

Worsley, Peter. 1968. *The Trumpet Shall Sound: A Study of 'Cargo' Cults in Melanesia*. New York: Schocken Books.

Contributors

Niko Besnier is Professor of Cultural Anthropology at the University of Amsterdam. His current research addresses topics in transnational mobility, gender and sexuality, language and interaction, and economic relations in times of crisis. His most recent books and guest edited issues of journals are *On the Edge of the Global: Modern Anxieties in a Pacific Island Nation* (2011); *Decentering and Recentering Communicative Competence* (co-edited, 2013); *Gender on the Edge: Transgender, Gay, and Other Pacific Islanders* (co-edited, 2014); and *Crisis, Value, and Hope: Rethinking the Economy* (co-edited, 2014). He is editor-in-chief of *American Ethnologist*.

Sekove Bigitibau is Assistant Lecturer in the School of Language, Arts and Media at the University of the South Pacific and was formerly a Senior Administrative Officer in the Institute of Itaukei (Indigenous Fijian) Language and Culture, Suva, Fiji. He received his Master of Social Sciences in Anthropology degree from the University of Waikato in 2007 for his thesis 'The Challenge to Fijian Methodism: The *Vanua*, Identity, Ethnicity and Change'.

Alex Golub is Associate Professor of Anthropology at the University of Hawai'i at Mānoa. His research focuses on the political anthropology of the Porgera gold mine in Papua New Guinea. He has also conducted research on the video game *World of Warcraft*. His works include *Leviathans at the Gold Mine* (2014) and, in 2010, 'Being in the World of Warcraft' (*Anthropological Quarterly* 83: 1).

Jessica Hardin is Assistant Professor of Anthropology at Pacific University. Her research examines the intersections of Christianity, metabolic disorders, and well-being in Samoa. She received her PhD from Brandeis University in 2014 for her dissertation 'Spiritual Etiologies: Metabolic Disorders, Evangelical Christianity, and Well-Being in Samoa', and co-edited the 2013 volume *Reconstructing Obesity: The Meaning of Measures and the Measure of Meanings* (with Megan McCullough). She has published articles in *Critical Public Health* and *Fat Studies*, and has forthcoming articles in *Medical Anthropology* and *Food, Culture, and Society*.

Margaret Jolly (FASSA) is an Australian Research Council Laureate Fellow and Professor in the School of Culture, History and Language in the College of Asia and the Pacific, The Australian National University. She has taught at The Australian National University, Macquarie University, the University of Hawai'i and the University of California, and has been a visiting scholar in Anthropology at Cambridge University and at the Centre de Recherche et Documentation sur l'Océanie (CREDO) in Marseille, and a visiting professor with the Centre National de la Recherche Scientifique in France. She is an historical anthropologist who has written extensively on gender in the Pacific, on exploratory voyages and travel writing, missions and contemporary Christianity, maternity and sexuality, cinema and art. Her books include *Women of the Place:* Kastom*, Colonialism and Gender in Vanuatu* (1994); *Sites of Desire, Economies of Pleasure: Sexualities in Asia and the Pacific* (ed. with Lenore Manderson, 1997); *Maternities and Modernities: Colonial and Postcolonial Experiences in Asia and the Pacific* (ed. with Kalpana Ram, 1998); *Borders of Being: Citizenship, Fertility and Sexuality in Asia and the Pacific* (ed. with Kalpana Ram, 2001); *Oceanic Encounters: Exchange, Desire, Violence* (ed. with Serge Tcherkézoff and Darrell Tryon, 2009); *Engendering Violence in Papua New Guinea* (ed. with Christine Stewart and Carolyn Brewer, 2012); and *Divine Domesticities: Christian Paradoxes in Asia and the Pacific* (ed. with Hyaeweol Choi, 2014).

Thorgeir Kolshus is Associate Professor at the Department of Social Anthropology, University of Oslo, and a columnist in *Aftenposten*, a leading Norwegian newspaper. Since 1996, he has had a multitemporal fieldwork engagement on the island of Mota in northern Vanuatu. Much of his work addresses the relation between religion and power, combining contemporary ethnography with historical sources and archival material. He is currently working on a monograph on the concept of the soul, on Mota and in anthropological history and theory.

Alexander Mawyer is Assistant Professor at the Center for Pacific Islands Studies at the University of Hawai'i at Mānoa. He has conducted fieldwork focused on language at the intersection of culture and history with the Mangarevan community in French Polynesia, and with Chuukese and Mortlockese communities in the Federated States of Micronesia. He served as one of the co-editors of *Varua Tupu: New Writing from French Polynesia* (2006), the first anthology of Ma'ohi literature to appear in English, and in 2014 he co-edited *Senses of Space: Multiple Models of Spatial Cognition in Oceania and Indonesia*, a special issue of *Ethos* (42: 3). Currently he is associate editor for *The Contemporary Pacific*.

Andy Mills is a curator for the Norfolk Museums Service, UK. He was previously Research Associate on the Fijian Art project at the University of East Anglia, Assistant Curator for Oceania Collections at the Horniman Museum in London, and a weapons researcher for the Pitt Rivers Museum, Oxford. By training an anthropologist, archaeologist and cultural historian, he has previously published on Western Polynesian weaponry and wood sculpture, the history of museum collections and both curatorial and literary representations of Polynesian culture.

Rachel Morgain is an Australian Research Council Postdoctoral Fellow in the College of Asia and the Pacific, The Australian National University. Her work focuses on the anthropological study of the dynamics of social life, with a particular interest in the relationship between religious experience and broader social conditions. She has conducted research on neopaganism in North America and evangelical Christianity in Fiji. With Anna-Karina Hermkens and John P. Taylor, she edited *Gender and Person in Oceania*, a special issue of *Oceania* (2015).

Aram Oroi is an ordained priest in the Anglican Church of Melanesia in Solomon Islands, Vanuatu and New Caledonia. At the Bishop Patteson Theological College, Solomon Islands, he is Dean of Studies and Head of the Theology and Ethics Department. He received his doctorate in 2015 for his dissertation 'Reclaiming Mana for the Church: The Identification of Mana and Its Possible Subversive Impact on a Melanesian Community of Faith'.

Carl Franklin Ka'ailā'au Pao (cover art) was born in Honolulu and raised in Kailua, O'ahu, Hawai'i. He currently teaches art at his alma mater Kamehameha Schools in Honolulu. Pao has exhibited his sculptures, paintings, prints, graphic designs and ceramics throughout Hawai'i; in the continental United States in New York, California, Washington, Kansas and Massachusetts; and in the Pacific in Aotearoa, Sāmoa, and New Caledonia. His artwork can be found in both public and private collections throughout Hawai'i as well as internationally. *Ki'i Kupuna: Maka*, which features on the cover of this publication, was purchased by the Hawai'i State Foundation on Culture and the Arts in November 2014.

Jon Peterson is a fellow at Neustar Inc. with a specialisation in security and network routing, and is also a member of the Internet Engineering Task Force (IETF). As an independent scholar, he documents the early history of role-playing games. His history of the conceptual origins of war- and role-playing games, *Playing at the World*, was published in 2012.

Alan Rumsey is Professor of Anthropology in the College of Asia and the Pacific, The Australian National University. His research fields are Highland New Guinea and Aboriginal Australia, with a focus on speech genres and relations among language, culture and intersubjectivity. His recent publications include 'Language and Human Sociality', in *The Cambridge Handbook of Linguistic Anthropology*, ed. N.J. Enfield, P. Kockelman and J. Sidnell (2014); and 'Bilingual Language Learning and the Translation of Worlds in the New Guinea Highlands and Beyond', *HAU*: *Journal of Ethnographic Theory* 4: 119–140 (2014).

Noenoe K. Silva (Kanaka Hawai'i) is Professor of Indigenous and Hawaiian Politics and Hawaiian Language at the University of Hawai'i at Mānoa. She has conducted extensive research on indigenous Hawaiian language, history and politics. Her book *Aloha Betrayed: Native Hawaiian Resistance to American Colonialism* (2004) was honoured as 'one of the most influential books in Native American and Indigenous Studies of the first decade of the twenty-first century' by the Native American and Indigenous Studies Association. Her second book, *Towards Native Hawaiian Intellectual History*, is forthcoming from Duke University Press.

Katerina Martina Teaiwa is Pacific Studies Convener and Head of the Department of Gender, Media and Cultural Studies at The Australian National University. She is author of *Consuming Ocean Island: Stories of People and Phosphate from Banaba* (2015), and a research fellow in the Framing the Global project at the Center for the Study of Global Change, Indiana University.

Ty P. Kāwika Tengan is Associate Professor of Anthropology and Ethnic Studies at the University of Hawai'i at Mānoa. His research interests include Indigenous theory and methodology, cultural politics in Hawai'i and the Pacific, colonialism, nationalism, and gender and masculinities. He is author of *Native Men Remade: Gender and Nation in Contemporary Hawai'i* (2008). He is also co-editor, with Tēvita O. Ka'ili and Rochelle Tuitagava'a Fonotī, of the first collaborative publication of Indigenous anthropologists in Oceania (in *Pacific Studies*), and with Paul Lyons of a collection on Native Pacific currents in American Studies (in *American Quarterly*).

Matt Tomlinson is an Australian Research Council Future Fellow in Anthropology in the College of Asia and the Pacific, The Australian National University. He has conducted research in Fiji, New Zealand and Sāmoa on the topics of language, politics, ritual and Christianity. He is author of *In God's Image: The Metaculture of Fijian Christianity* (2009) and *Ritual Textuality: Pattern and Motion in Performance* (2014), and he has co-edited volumes including *The Limits of Meaning: Case Studies in the Anthropology of Christianity* (with Matthew Engelke, 2006) and *Christian Politics in Oceania* (with Debra McDougall, 2013).

www.ingramcontent.com/pod-product-compliance
Lightning Source LLC
Chambersburg PA
CBHW040150270326
41926CB00069B/4575
* 9 7 8 1 7 6 0 4 6 0 0 7 5 *